APR 1 3 2007

TRIVIA LOVERS' LISTS OF NEARLY

EVERYTHING

IN THE UNIVERSE

50,000 + BIG & LITTLE THINGS

ORGANIZED BY TYPE AND KIND

Please address inquiries about electronic licensing of any products for use on a network, in software or on CD-ROM to the Subsidiary Rights Department, Random House Information Group, fax 212–572–6003.

This book is available at special discounts for bulk purchases for sales promotions or premiums. Special editions, including personalized covers, excerpts of existing books, and corporate imprints, can be created in large quantities for special needs. For more information, write to Random House, Inc., Special Markets/Premium Sales, 1745 Broadway, MD 6–2, New York, NY 10019 or e-mail specialmarkets@randomhouse.com.

Visit the Random House Reference Web site: www.randomwords.com

Printed in the United States of America

DESIGN BY ELINA D. NUDELMAN

10 9 8 7 6 5 4 3 2 1

Library of Congress Cataloging in Publication Data is available.

ISBN-10: 0–375–42606-X

ISBN-13: 978–0-375–42606–3

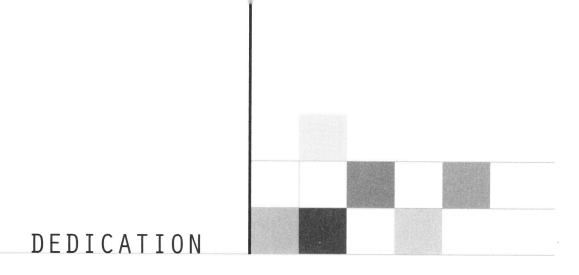

DEDICATION

Some people are born list lovers. Lists catch their eyes, they need to-do lists, they buy books of them, they cut them out of magazines. Others envy the inveterate listmaker, knowing that if they made lists, their lives would be enriched and somewhat more under control. Others still make lists for a few tasks, like buying groceries, but do not realize the benefits of making more lists. List lovers, this book is for you.

I want to thank my husband, Paul Magoulas, who helped me every step of the way and supported this book idea during the fifteen years I tried to sell it!

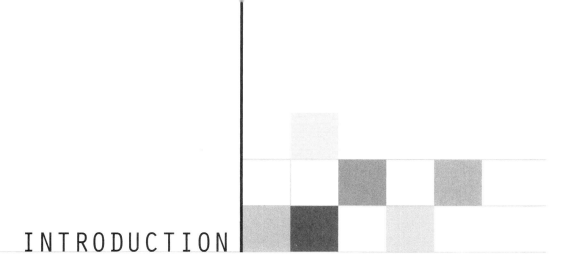

INTRODUCTION

Garrison Keillor was once quoted in the Utne Reader:

Question: What book do you recommend for people who want to be writers?

Keillor's Answer: *Roget's Thesaurus*, the fourth edition (Harper), which has those cool lists of words, like twenty-five types of anchors, a hundred varieties of cheese, forty kinds of saws, on and on. Hammers, mammals, soaps, ships. The Fort Knox of words.

I have written a few thesauruses myself and often the lists in them seem somewhat out of place. They do not contain synonyms, but rather, examples of something. Over time, many of these great lists have been cut out of thesauruses to make space for additional synonyms. I decided to take it upon myself to "save" them from obscurity and collect them in a book. Hence, *Trivia Lovers' Lists!*

Trivia Lovers' Lists is for people looking for ideas, information, or just browsing for fun. *It will expand your world.* It is the ultimate collection, a book full of the "little things in life," encompassing the silly and serious, entertaining and informative, reference and fun. Where else are you going to find lists of pink colors and pigments, citrus fruits, mental states, chicken breeds, types of lighthouses, and kinds of axes? Just think of the reference collection that you would need!

Trivia Lovers' Lists has many uses: generating ideas for something you are writing, creating and solving puzzles, getting ideas for something you want to study or take up as a hobby, finding teaching and research ideas, getting a basic overview of a topic, or finding a useful checklist. You might even use it to organize your work, library, kitchen, music, budget, clothes . . . and your life! This breakdown of our world, this overview of mini-subjects, also serves as a bridge to other reference resources and may ultimately lead you to pursue a subject in depth.

There have been many list books in the past. The *Book of Lists* series contains lists of odd facts and trivia, like "the fifteen best places to live in the United States," "fifteen famous events that happened in a bathtub," "sixteen memorable responses to criticism," and "Allen Ginsberg's eleven greatest blues songs." Many of these are subjective and soon become dated. *Trivia Lovers' Lists* contains more timeless—and useful—lists. Plus, it contains *thousands* as opposed to merely hundreds that are included in each Wallace/Wallechinsky book! The *Book of Lists* series spurred many imitative list books on specific topics, like sports, food, trivia, golf, but nothing particularly comprehensive. Books like *Word Menu* and visual dictionaries, though great for certain purposes, offer limited lists on a few hundred subjects. Though these various books had an appeal, *Trivia Lovers' Lists* is quite different: comprehensive, compulsive, and inspirational.

This book includes both exhaustive and representative lists, arranged alphabetically by subject, and items within each list are alphabetized. By "representative," I mean that a list of black colors and pigments might likely make a mini-book all by itself! In such cases, a comprehensive and representative, but not exhaustive, list is provided.

Hundreds of sources were used to assemble this information: encyclopedias, dictionaries, word books, factfinders, almanacs, books of lists, crossword dictionaries, vocabulary books, record books, thesauruses, textbooks, question-and-answer books, trivia volumes, puzzle books, hints and tips books, and many specialized reference books.

Aborigines

Ainu (Japan)

Aranda (Australia)

Australian

Baiga (Australia)

blackfellow (Australia)

Borinqueño (Puerto Rico)

Ciboney (Cuba)

Dravidian (India)

Igneri (Lesser Antilles)

Jakun (Malay)

Kha (Nepal)

Khmer (Cambodia)

Kodagu (India)

Koko (Australia)

Lucayo (Bahamas)

Miao (China)

Native American

Otomac (Venezuela)

Patagonian (Australia)

Rembaranga (Australia)

Sekhwan (China)

Taino (Greater Antilles, Bahamas)

Tanala (Madagascar)

Tiwi (Australia)

Toda (India, Sri Lanka)

Vedda (Sri Lanka)

Yao (China, Thailand, Laos)

Accelerators

atom smasher

betatron

bevatron

cascade transformer

charge-exchange accelerator

Cockcroft-Walton voltage multiplier

colliding-beam machine or collider

cosmotron

cyclotron

electron accelerator

electron-proton collider

electrostatic generator

induction accelerator

Large Electron-Positron collider or LEP

Large Hadron collider or LHC

linear accelerator or linac

microwave linear accelerator

particle accelerator

positive-ion accelerator

superconducting supercollider or SSC

synchrocyclotron

synchrotron

tevatron

tokamak

Van de Graaff generator

voltage multiplier

wake-field accelerator

ACCENTS AND DIACRITICAL MARKS

acute accent (´)

breve or caron (˘)

cedilla (¸)

circumflex accent (^ or ˜)

dieresis or umlaut (¨)

grave accent (`)

hacek (Cz) or wedge (ˇ)

krozek (°)

ligature (æ)

macron (¯)

schwa (_)

tilde (~)

ACIDS

acetic

acetylsalicylic acid or aspirin

acrylic

amino

arsenic

ascorbic

battery

bile

boric

butyric

carbolic

carbonic

carboxylic

chloric

chlorous

citric

conjugate

cyanic

deoxyribonucleic

dibasic

essential fatty

fatty

fluoric

folic

formic

free fatty

fumaric

gallic

hydrobromic

hydrochloric

hydrocyanic

hydrofluoric

hydroiodic

iodic

lactic

lauric

Lewis

linoleic

maleic

metenoic

micotinic

mineral

monobasic

nitric

nitrohydrochloric

nucleic

organic

oxalic

palmitic

pangamic

para-aminobenzoic

phenol

phosphoric

polyunsaturated fatty

protonic

prussic or
hydrocyanic

ribonucleic

silicic

stearic

strong

sulfuric

tannic

tartaric

trans-fatty

tribasic

uric

vitriol

weak

Addresses and Salutations

Dear

Gentlemen

Gentlewomen

Honorable

Madam

May it please your
Majesty or Royal
Highness

Most Reverend Sir

My dear

My Lady

My Lord

Reverend

Reverend Sir

Right Reverend Sir

Sir

Venerable Sir

Your Eminence

Your Excellency

Your Grace

Your Ladyship

Your Lordship

Your Majesty

Your Royal Highness

Adherents

addict

adept

advocate

apostle

camp follower

cohort

devotee

disciple

follower

henchman or
henchwoman

idealist

ideologue

observer

optimist

partisan

party man or party
woman

pessimist

practicer

satellite

sectary

sectator

sider

supporter

votary

ADHESIVES

acrylic resin

adhesive

adhesive tape

art paste

astringent

binder

birdlime

caulking

cement

compo

court plaster

cresote

daubing

decorative color glue

double-sided tape

drafting tape

duct tape

electrical tape

epoxy

gaffer's tape

gesso

glitter glue

glue

glue marker

glue stick

gluten

glycerin

grout

gum

gummed paper tape

gutta-percha

gypsum

isinglass

joint compound

Krazy Glue

library paste

lime

linseed oil

lute

masking tape

mastic

mortar

mucilage

mud

oakum

parget

paste

pitch

plaster of Paris

pointing

portland cement

putty

rabbit-skin glue

resin

rubber cement

sealant

sealing wax

sizing or size

solder

Spackle

spackling compound

spray adhesive

stucco

Superglue

tape

tar

tarmac

transparent tape

travertine

Velcro

viscin

viscum

wallpaper paste

wax

white paste

wood glue

ADVERTISING METHODS

banner advertising

billboard

blimp

blow-in card

broadcast

broadsheet

brochure

business card

business-to-business

car card

cinema

classified advertising

commercial

digital signage

direct mail

direct response

display advertising

electronic mail

food and beverage container

free sample

fringe media

graffito

handout or fly sheet

hot-air balloon

industrial advertising

information advertising

Internet

interstitial

junk mail

leaflet

magazine

mailer

marketing campaign

mass transit

newsletter

newspaper

opt-in mailing

package advertising

parking meter

playbill

plugola

point-of-purchase

pop-up ad

poster

print

public service announcement

public-relations campaign

radio

rich-media ad

sale promotion

sandwich board

skywriting

sponsorship

stuffer

supermarket cart

television

trade advertising

trailer

window card

window display

yellow pages

Aerials and Antennas

antenna array

artificial antenna

automobile antenna

beam antenna

bowtie antenna

cage antenna

coil antenna

colinear beam antenna

condenser antenna

dipole

direction finder

directional antenna

directive antenna

dish

doublet

eight-ball antenna

end-fire array

FM antenna

frame aerial

long-wire antenna

loop antenna

mast

mobile antenna

monopole

multiband antenna

nondirectional antenna

omnidirectional antenna

open aerial

parabolic antenna

pencil-beam antenna

printed antenna

pylon antenna

rabbit ears

radar antenna

receiving antenna

reflector

resonance wave coil

rhombic antenna

rotary-beam antenna

shortwave antenna

signal squirter

telescope antenna

tuned antenna

turnstile

universal antenna

vertical radiator antenna

wave antenna

whip antenna

yagi

African Peoples

Afars	Efik	Kikuyu	Pokot
Afrikaners	Ejagham	Kongo	Pondo
Agikuyu	Elmolo	Kuba	Pygmies
Akamba	Ewe	Lobedu	Rendille
Akan	Fang	Lozi	Rif
Ameru	Fante	Luba	Samburu
Amhara	Fulani	Lunda	San
Ashanti	Gabra	Luo	Shona
Azande	Galla	Makonde	Somali
Bantu	Ganda	Malinke	Songhay
Baqqarah	Gbaya	Mandingo	Soninke
Barotse	Hausa	Masai	Sotho
Basotho	Herero	Mbundu	Sukuma
Bemba	Hottentot	Mbuti	Swazi
Booran	Hutu and Tutsi	Merina	Teuso
Bushmen	Igbo	Mijikenda	Tubu
Chewa	Ik	Mossi	Turkana
Chokwe	Issas	Ndebele	Wolof
Dinka	Kabyle	Nguni	Xhosa
Dogon	Khoekhoe	Nyoro	Yoruba
Edo	Khoisan	Oromo	Zulu

Ages and Eras of History

Age of Anxiety	Age of Enlightenment	Age of Man	Ages of Humankind
Age of Aquarius		Age of Reason	Air Age

American Revolution
Ancien Régime
Atomic Age
Automobile Age
Belle Epoque
Bronze Age
Christian Era or Common Era
Classical Age
Cold War
Computer Age
Copper Age
Crusades
Dark Ages
Depression Era
Early Middle Ages
Electronic Age
Elizabethan Age
Eolithic Age
Era of Good Feeling
Fin de siècle
Flapper Era
Gay Nineties
Gilded Age
Golden Age
Ice Age
Industrial Revolution
Iron Age
Jacksonian Age
Jacobean Age
Jazz Age
Jet Age
Mauve Decade
Middle Ages
Modern Age
Naughty Nineties
Postmodern Era or Postmodernism
Prehistoric Age
Prohibition Era
Reconstruction Era
Reformation
Renaissance
Roaring Twenties
Roman Empire
Silver Age
Space Age
Steel Age
Stone Age
Technological Age
Victorian Age

AIR

ammonia
argon
carbon dioxide
carbon monoxide
helium
hydrogen
iodine
krypton
methane
neon
nitrogen
nitrogen dioxide
nitrous oxide
oxygen
ozone
silicon
sulfur dioxide
xenon

AIR OR ATMOSPHERIC SCIENCES

acronomy
aerial photography
aeroballistics
aerocartography
aerodontia
aerodynamics
aerogeography
aerogeology
aerography
aerology
aeromechanics
aerometry
aeronautical engineering
aeronautical meteorology
aeronomy
aerophotography
aerophysics

aeroscopy
aerospace research
aerostatics
aerostation
aerotechnics
aerothermodynamics
aircraft design
aircraft hydraulics

aviation medicine
aviation technology
avionics
biometeorology
climatology
hydrometeorology
hydrostatics
hygrometry

jet engineering
kinematics
kinetics
koniology
meteorology
micrometry
photometry
pneumatics

psychrometry
rocket engineering
rocketry
supersonic aerodynamics
supersonics
weather forecasting

AIR POLLUTION TYPES

ash
carbon monoxide
CH_4
CO_2
dust
gases from combustion

gases from organic decomposition
grit
H_2S
HF
liquid droplets and acid deposition
noise

NO_x (nitrogen oxides)
ozone
PAN_8
sea-salt particles
smoke
smoke and ash

SO_2 (sulfur oxides)
soot
tarmac and rubber particles
volcanic dust
volcanic gases and water vapor

AIRCRAFT ENGINES

aeromotor
arc-jet
athodyd
axial-flow turbojet
axial-type
cam
compound
compression-ignition

diesel
double-row radial
fan-jet
gas jet
gas turbine jet
hyper engine
impulse duct
in-line

intermittent duct
internal combustion
inverted
jet
pancake
piston
propeller-drive gas
pulse jet

radial
ramjet
reaction
reciprocating
resonance duct
resonance jet
rocket motor
rotary

scramjet

supercharged

trimotor

true-jet

turbine

turbojet

turbo-propeller jet

turbo-ram jet

turboshaft

twin

vertical

V-type

W-type

Wankel

X-type

AIRCRAFT TYPES

aerodyne

aerostat

air cushion vehicle or ACV

air taxi

Airbus

airliner

airplane

airship

amphibian

anti-submarine

autogrio

balloon

battleplane

biplane

blimp

bogey

bomber

business jet

canard

cargo

carrier fighter

chopper

coleopter

combat plane

convertiplane

copter

crop duster

cyclogiro

delta-wing

dirigible

dive bomber

double-prop

drone

duster-sprayer

fighter

fighter-bomber

floatplane

flying boat

freighter

glider

gyrocopter

gyrodyne

gyroplane

hang glider

heavier-than-air craft

helibus

helicopter

helicopter gunship

helium balloon

high-altitude reconnaissance plane

hot-air balloon

hovercraft

hydroplane

interceptor

jet bomber

jet fighter

jet plane

jetliner

jumbo jet

jump jet

kamikaze

kite

lifting body

lighter-than-air craft

MiG

monoplane

multi-engine

multiplane

multirole combat airplane or MRCA

night fighter

ornithopter

orthopter

parachute

parafoil

paraglider

patrol

propeller

pursuit plane

pusher

radial engine

ramjet

reconnaissance and rescue

rotaplane

rotorcraft

sailplane

seaplane

short takeoff and landing or STOL

single-engine

ski-plane

spotter

spy plane

stealth bomber

stealth fighter

suicide plane

supersonic transport or SST

swept-wing

swing-wing

tandem airplane

tanker

taxiplane

test

tilt-rotor

torpedo bomber

trainer

transport

tri-motor

triphibian

triplane

troop carrier

turbofan

turbojet

turboprop

twin-engine

twin-prop

ultralight

vertical takeoff and landing or VTOL

warplane

waterplane

Zeppelin

AIRPLANE TAIL SHAPES

fin-mounted tail unit

fuselage-mounted tail unit

H-tail unit

triple tail unit

T-tail unit

twin tail unit

V-butterfly tail unit

V-tail unit

Y-tail unit

AIRPLANE WING SHAPES

complex delta wing

flying wing

highly swept wing

moderately swept wing

oblique wing

rectangular straight wing

rounded or elliptical straight wing

simple delta wing

slightly swept wing

swept-back wing

tapered straight wing

variable geometry wing or variable swing wing

variable incidence wing

ALCOHOLIC BEVERAGE TYPES

ale

beer or brew

cider

cocktail or mixed drink

cordial or liqueur

spirit or liquor

wine

ALCOHOLIC MIXED DRINKS AND COCKTAILS

Adam and Eve

after-dinner cocktail

Alabama slammer

Alaska cocktail

alexander

Allegheny

American beauty cocktail

Americana

angel's kiss

apricot cooler

B & B

B-52

Bacardi cocktail

Bahama mama

banana daiquiri

banshee

Barbie's special cocktail

Basin street

bay breeze

beachcomber

bee stinger

beer buster

Bellini

Belmont cocktail

Bermuda Rose

Betsy Ross

between-the-sheets

bijou cocktail

black Maria

Black Russian

black velvet

bloody Caesar

Bloody Mary

blue canary

blue Hawaiian

blue lagoon

blue margarita

blue whale

bocce ball

Bombay cocktail

bosom caresser

Boston cocktail

Boston cooler

bourbon and water

bourbon on the rocks

brandy alexander

brandy cassis

brandy fizz

brandy highball

brandy smash

brandy swizzle

brantini

Brighton punch

Bronx cocktail

buck's fizz

bull and bear

bull's eye

bull's milk

bullshot

buttered rum

caipirinha

Cape Cod

caudle

cement mixer

champagne cocktail

champagne cooler

Chapel Hill

cherry blossom

cherry fizz

Chicago cocktail

chi-chi

clamato cocktail

club cocktail

cobbler

coffee grasshopper

coffee old-fashioned

cooler

Cooperstown cocktail

cosmopolitan

Cuba libre

daiquiri

Daisy Dueller

damn-the-weather cocktail

depth charge

desert sunrise

dingo

dirty banana

dixie julep

dream cocktail

dry martini

eggnog

English highball

fancy gin

Fifth Avenue

firefly

fizz

flip

flying Scotchman

foxy lady

frappe

French connection

French martini

frozen daiquiri

frozen margarita

fuzzy navel

gentleman's cocktail

Georgia mint julep

Georgia peach

Gibson

gimlet

gin and bitters

gin and sin

gin and tonic

gin cooler

gin fizz

gin highball

gin rickey

gin sling

gin sour

gin swizzle

gluhwein

godfather

godmother

golden Cadillac

grasshopper

green dragon

greyhound

grog

Harvard cocktail

Harvard cooler

Harvey Wallbanger

highball

hole-in-one

Hollywood

Honolulu cocktail

hot buttered rum

hot toddy

hurricane

income tax cocktail

Indian Summer

Irish coffee

Irish whiskey

Jack Rose

jack-in-the-box

Jersey lightning

jocose julep

journalist cocktail

kamikaze

Kentucky blizzard

Kentucky cocktail

King Alphonse

Kir

Kir Royale

kiss on the lips

lady finger

liberty cocktail

London cocktail

Long Island iced tea

Louisville cooler

Louisville lady

lover's kiss

madras

mai-tai

Manhattan

margarita

martini

Mary Pickford cocktail

melon ball

melon cooler

merry widow

Metropolitan cocktail

Mexican coffee

midnight cocktail

mimosa

mind eraser

mint julep

Mississippi mud

mojito

morning cocktail

Moscow mule

mudslide

Narragansett

New York cocktail

night cap

nightmare

nineteenth hole

nutcracker

nutty professor

old-fashioned

orange blossom

orgeat

Park Avenue

passion mimosa

peach sangaree

peppermint pattie

Peter Pan cocktail

Pimm's cup

Piña colada

pink lady

pink pussy cat

pink squirrel

planter's punch

polo cocktail

posset

pousse cafa

prairie oyster

presbyterian

Princeton cocktail

punch

Ramos gin fizz

red death

rickey

Rob Roy
rum and coke
rum cooler
rum eggnog
rum old-fashioned
rum runner
rum sour
rusty nail
salty dog
San Juan cooler
sangria
Scarlett O'Hara
Scotch and Soda
scotch highball
scotch on the rocks
scotch sour
screwdriver
seabreeze

Seven and Seven
sex on the beach
shandy
shrub
sidecar cocktail
Singapore sling
slam dunk
sloe gin fizz
smash
snake bite
snowball
society cocktail
sombrero
soother cocktail
southern lady
southern peach
spritzer
stinger

strawberry daiquiri
strawberry margarita
syllabub
tequila sunrise
Thanksgiving special
thoroughbred cooler
to the moon
toasted almond
toddy
Tom and Jerry
Tom Collins
tropical special
Union Jack cocktail
velvet hammer
virgin Mary
vodka and tonic
vodka cooler
vodka gimlet

vodka martini
vodka on the rocks
Wassail
whiskey highball
whiskey sour
white lady
White Russian
white satin
white spider
widow's kiss
wild thing
wine cooler
wu-wu
Yale cocktail
zombie

ALCOHOLIC SPIRITS, CORDIALS, LIQUORS, LIQUEURS

abisante
absinthe
advocaat
alcool blanc
almondrado
amaretto
amer picon

American whiskey
Angostura bitters
anise
anisette
apple brandy
applejack
apricot brandy

apry
aquavit
Armagnac
arrack
Asiago
B and B
bathtub gin

Benedictine
benedictine café
bitters
blended whiskey
bourbon
brandy
calvados

13

Canadian whiskey

cassis

chartreuse

cheri-suisse

cherry marnier

cherry rocher

choclair

chococo

chocolate liqueur

cocoribe

coffee liqueur

coffee sambuca

cognac

Cointreau

cordial Médoc

corn liquor

corn whiskey

Courvoisier

crème d'amande

crème de abricots

crème de bananas

crème de cacao

crème de cassis

crème de cerise

crème de fraise

crème de framboise

crème de menthe

crème de moka

crème de noyaux

crème de rose

crème de violette

curaçao

Drambuie

Dutch gin

eau de vie

framboise

Frangelico

Galliano

geneva

gin

glayva

Goldschalger

grain alcohol

Grand Marnier

grappa

grog

Irish Mist

Irish whiskey

Jamaica gin

Jamaica rum

Kahlúa

Kir

kirsch (wasser)

kummel

Lillet

mai-tai

malt liquor

malt whiskey

mandarine Napoleon

maraschino

marc

mash

mescal

Metaxa

Midori

mocha liqueur

moonshine

negra

okolehao

orange café

ouzo

parfait d'amour

pasha

pastis

pear brandy

peppermint
schnapps

Pernod

plum brandy

poire William

prunella

pulque

raki

ratafia

rock and rye

roiano

ron coco

rum

rye

sambuca

schnapps

sciarada

Scotch whiskey

single-malt Scotch

slivovitz

sloe gin

Southern Comfort

Strega

tequila

Tia Maria

triple sec

tuaca

vodka

whiskey

Wild Turkey

Yukon Jack

ALGAE

acrasiomycete
ameba
blue-green algae
brown algae
carrageen
cellular slime mold
chlorophyte
chrysophyte
chytrid
ciliate
conferva
cryptomonad
diatom
dinoflagellate
dulse
euglena

euglenophyte
flagellate
focus
fucoid
fucus
golden algae
golden-brown algae
green algae
gulfweed
Heterotroph
Iceland moss
Irish moss
kelp
lichen
myxomycete
nostoc

olive-brown seaweed
oomycete
opalinid
phaeophyte
Photosynthetic Autotroph
phytoplankton
plankton
plasmodial slime mold
pond scum
protista
protozoan
pseudopod
pyrrophyte
red algae
reindeer moss

rhodophyte
rockweed
sargasso scum
sea lettuce
sea moss
sea wrack
seaweed
slime mold
spirogyra
sporozoan
stonewort
thallophyte
water mold
wrack
yellow-green algae

ALKALIS

A basic substance with a pH of greater than seven.

barium
beryllium
calcium
cesium

copper
francium
iron
lithium

magnesium
nonacid
potassium
radium

rubidium
sodium
strontium

ALLERGIES

asthma

atopic allergy

blood serum allergy

bronchial asthma

chemical allergy

cosmetic allergy

drug allergy

dust allergy

dye allergy

favism

food allergy

hay fever

hives hypersensitivity reaction

immediate allergy

insect debris allergy

insect venom allergy

lint allergy

Loeffler's syndrome

mold spore allergy

photoallergy

pollen allergy

pollinosis

Type I allergic reaction

Type II allergic reaction

Type III allergic reaction

Type IV allergic reaction

ALLOYS

An alloy is a substance made up of one or more metals.

admiralty metal

air-hardened steel

alloy iron

alloy steel

alnico

aluminum brass

aluminum bronze

amalgam

Babbitt

bell metal

beryllium bronze

bidri

billon

brass

britannia metal

bronze

bush metal

Carboloy

carbon steel

case-hardened steel

cast iron

chromium steel

cinder pig

coin nickel

constantan

Damascus steel

electrum

elinvar

eureka

galvanized iron

graphite steel

green gold

gunmetal

ingot iron

invar

kamacite

magnox

manganese bronze

misch metal

mosaic gold

nickel brass

nickel bronze

nickel silver

nitinol

ormolu

permalloy

perminvar

pewter

phosphor bronze

pig iron

pinchbeck

pink gold

platinoid

red gold

shakudo

silicon steel

silver solder

solder

speculum metal

spiegeleisen

stainless steel

steel

sterling silver

terne

tin

tin bronze

tombac

white gold

white metal

wrought iron

yellow brass

yellow gold

yellow metal

zircaloy

ALPHABETS AND WRITING SYSTEMS

American Sign Language

Anatolian alphabets

Arabic

Aramaic

Armenian

Avestan

boustrophedon

Braille

Coptic

cuneiform

cursive

Cyrillic

demotics

Devanagari

Dongba

Etruscan

finger spelling

futhark

Georgian

Glagolitic

Gothic

Greek alphabet

hanja

Hankul

Hanzi

Hebraic alphabet

hieratics

hieroglyphics

hiragana

ideography

Indus or Harappa script

International Phonetic Alphabet or IPA

Jurchen

kana

kanji

katakana

Kitan

Kufic

Latin alphabet

Linear A

Linear B

manual alphabet

Mayan

Meroitic

mixed alphabet

Morse alphabet

ogham

Old Elamite

Old Italic

Phoenician alphabet

phonetic alphabet

pictography

Pinyin

Proto-Elamite

Psalter

romaji

Roman alphabet

Rongorongo

runic script

Samaritan

Semitic scripts

shorthand

sign language

syllabary

Syriac

Tangut

Ugaritic

Vietnamese

Wade-Giles

Yi

ALTERNATIVE MEDICINE TYPES

acupuncture

Alexander technique

anthroposophical medicine

applied kinesiology

aromatherapy

Ayurveda

bioelectromagnetic-based therapies

biofeedback

biofield therapies

biologically based therapies

chiropractic medicine

color therapy

energy therapies

faith healing

folk medicine

herbal medicine

homeopathy

hydrotherapy

hypnotism

iridology

magnet therapy

manipulative therapies

massage

meditationmegavitamin therapy

mind-body interventions

music therapy

naturopathy

new age healing

osteopathy

prayer

qigong

reflexology

Reiki

Rolfing

shiatsu

therapeutic touch

AMINO ACIDS

arginine

asparagine

aspartic acid

citrulline

cysteine

cystine

glutamic acid

glutamine

glycine

histidine

isoleucine

leucine

lysine

methionine

ornithine

phenylalanine

proline

sarcosine

serine

threonine

tryptophan

tyrosine

valine

AMPHIBIANS

alpine salamander

anuran

axolotl

blindworm

bullfrog

caecilian

cane toad

cave salamander

clawed frog

congo eel

congo snake

crested newt

cricket frog

edible frog

eft

fire-bellied toad

fire salamander

flying frog

frog

giant salamander

goliath frog

grass frog

green frog

hairy frog

hellbender

hop toad

horned frog

horned toad

hyla

leopard frog

lungless salamander

marine toad

marsh frog

midwife toad

mole salamander

mudpuppy

narrow-mouthed toad

natterjack

newt

olm

palmate newt

paradoxical frog

peeper

pickerel frog

platanna

poison-arrow frog

red-eyed tree frog

salamander

siren

smooth newt

spadefoot toad

spring frog

spring peeper

Suriname toad

tiger salamander

toad

tree frog

urodele

waterdog wood frog

Xenopus

AMUSEMENT PLACES, TYPES OF

amusement park

aquarium

arcade

automobile racetrack

band hall or orchestra hall

baseball park

basketball court

beach

bicycle path

billiard parlor or pool parlor

botanical garden

bowling alley

bullfighting arena

casino

club

dance hall

dog racetrack

fairgrounds

fishing body of water

football field

gambling place

golf course

gymnasium

horse racetrack

horseriding farm

ice rink

movie theater

museum

nature center

park

planetarium

playground

playhouse

polo field

rodeo grounds

roller-skating rink

ski area

soccer field

stadium

swimming hole

swimming pool

tennis court

theater

toboggan run

velodrome

water park

zoo

ANALGESICS

A substance that, when ingested, helps alleviate pain.

acetaminophen

acetanilide

acetophenetidin

acetylsalicylic acid or aspirin

amidone

aminopyrine

antipyrine

buffered aspirin

carbamazepine

codeine

cyclazocine

etorphine

fentanyl

heroin

ibuprofen

indomethacin

levorphanol

meperidine

methadone

morphine

nalbuphine

naproxen

nonopioid

nonsteroidal anti-inflammatory drug or NSAID

opioid

oxycodone

oxyphenbutazone

pentazocine

pethidine

phenacetin

phencyclidine

phenylbutazone

propoxyphene

pyrazolone

salicylic acid

sodium salicylate

sulindac

trichloroethylene

ANCHOR TYPES

beam anchor or wall anchor

bower anchor

center anchor

cone anchor

CQR plow anchor

Danforth anchor

dinghy anchor

double-fluked anchor

drag anchor

drift anchor

drogue

floating anchor

fluke

foul anchor

grapnel

grapple

ice anchor

kedge

killick

mooring anchor

mushroom anchor

parachute drogue

plow anchor

port anchor

projectile anchor

sacred anchor

sand anchor

screw anchor

sea anchor

shank

sheet anchor or waist anchor

starboard anchor

stem anchor

stern anchor

stock

stocked anchor

stockless anchor

stream anchor

yachtman's anchor

Angles

acute angle

alternate angle

base angle

central angle

corresponding angle

dihedral angle

face angle

interior angle

oblique angle

obtuse angle

reentering angle

reflex angle

right angle

round angle

salient angle

solid angle

spherical angle

straight angle

supplementary angle

vertical angle

Animal Collective Names

(alligator) congregation or pod

(angel fish) host

(antelopes) herd or troop

(ants) army or colony or swarm

(apes) shrewdness

(asses) herd or drove or pace

(baboons) congress or troop

(badgers) cete or colony

(bass) fleet or shoal

(bat) colony

(bears) sleuth or sloth

(beavers) colony

(bees) colony or grist or hive or hum or swarm

(birds) congregation or dissimulation or flight or flock or volery

(bison) herd or troop

(bloodhounds) sute

(boars) herd or singular or sounder

(bovines) herd

(buffalo) herd

(butterflies) rabble or swarm

(camels) caravan or herd or flock

(caterpillars) army

(cats and dogs) rain

(cats) clowder or cluster or clutter

(cats or wild) dout

(cattle) drove or herd

(cheetahs) coalition

(chickens) brood or clutch or flock or peep

(clams) bed

(colts) rag or rake

(coots) covert or raft

(cows) flink or herd

(coyotes) pack or rout

(cranes) herd or sedge or siege

(crickets) orchestra

(crows) clan or murder

(deers) herd or leash

(dogs) kennel or pack

(dolphins) pod or school

(donkeys) herd or drove

(doves) dole or dule or flight or prettying

(ducks) brace or clatch or clutch or dopping or dropping or flight or flock or flush or gaggle or leash or paddling or raft or team

(eagles) convocation

(eels) knot or swarm

(eggs) clutch

(elephants) herd or host or parade

(elks) gang or herd

(falcons) cast

(ferrets) business or cast

(finches) charm or flight

(fishes) draught or run or school or shoal

(flamingoes) flurry or skein

(flies) business or cloud or swarm

(foxes) leash or skulk

(frogs) army or knot or colony

(geese) flock or gaggle or skein or wedge

(gerbils) horde

(giraffes) corps or herd or troop

(gnats) cloud or horde or swarm

(goats) flock or herd or tribe or trip

(goldfinches) charm or chattering

(goldfish) troubling

(gorillas) band

(grasshoppers) cloud or cluster

(greyhounds) brace or leash or pack

(grouses) covey or pack

(guinea fowls) confusion

(guinea pigs) group

(gulls) colony

(hamsters) horde

(hares) down or husk or leap or trace or trip

(hawks) cast or kettle

(hedgehogs) array or prickle

(hens) brood or flock

(herons) scattering or siege

(hippopotami) herd or huddle or school

(hogs) drift or herd

(horses) harras or herd or pair or stable or stud or team

(hounds) brace or cry or mute or pack or stable

(hummingbirds) hover

(hyenas) clan

(insects) flight or swarm

(jack rabbits) husk

(jays) band or party

(jellyfish) brood or smack

(kangaroos) herd or mob or troop

(kittens) brood or kindle or litter

(lapwings) deceit

(larks) ascension or chattering or exaltation

(leopards) leap

(lice) flock

(lions) flock or pride or sault or troop

(llamas) herd

(locusts) cloud or host or plague

(magpies) tidings

(mallards) flock or flush or sord

(mares) stud

(martens) richness

(mice) nest

(minnows) shoal or swarm

(moles) company or labor or movement

(monkeys) tribe or troop

(mosquitoes) swarm

(mules) barren or pack or rake or span

(mussels) bed

(nightingales) match or watch

(ostrich) flock or troop

(otters) bevy or family

(owls) parliament or stare or wisdom

(oxen) drove or herd or team or yoke

(oysters) bed

(parrots) company or flock

(partridges) covey

(peacocks) muster or ostentation or pride

(penguins) colony or rookery

(pheasants) bouquet or covey or nest or nye or nide or ostentation or pride

(pigeons) flight or flock

(piglets) farrow

(pigs) drove or litter or herd or sounder

(plovers) congregation or flight or wing

(polar bears) aurora

(ponies) herd or string

(porpoises) gam or pod or school

(prairie dogs) coterie or town

(quails) bevy or covey

(rabbits) colony or nest or trace or warren

(raccoons) nursery

(racehorses) field

(rats) colony or horde or mischief

(ravens) conspiracy or unkindness

(reindeers) herd

(rhinoceroses) crash

(roach) shoal

(sardines) family

(seals) pod or herd or school or trip or harem or rookery or spring

(sharks) school or shiver

(sheep) drove or flock or herd or trip

(skunks) stench or surfeit

(slugs) cornucopia

(smelt) quantity

(snakes) bed or den or pit or slither

(snipe) whisper or wisp

(sparrows) host or quarrel

(spiders) cluster or clutter

(squirrels) dray or drey

(starlings) chattering or crowd or murmuration

(storks) herd or mustering

(swallows) flight

(swans) ballet or bank or bevy or game or herd or wedge or whiteness

(swine) doyet or drift or drove or dryft or sounder

(teal) bunch or raft or spring

(tigers) ambush or hide or streak

(toads) knot

(trout) hover

(turkeys) dule or rafter

(turtledoves) pitying

(turtles) bale or bevy or dole

(unicorns) blessing

(vipers) den or nest

(walrus) herd or pod

(wasps) nest or pail or pladge

(waterfowl) plump

(weasels) gam or pack or pod or sneak

(whales) colony or gam or herd or pod or school or shoal or surfers

(wild animals) pack

(wolves) pack or rout

(woodchucks) fall

(woodpeckers) descent

(worms) wriggle

(yaks) herd

(zebras) herd or stripe

Animal Hides, Leathers, Pelts, and Skins

alligator	badger	beaver	box calf
antelope	bearskin	black marten	broadtail

buckskin

buff

buffalo

cabretta

calf leather

calfskin

capeskin

cattlehide

chamois

cheverel

chevrette

chinchilla

coltskin

cony

coonskin

cordovan

corrected grain

cowhide

crocodile

crushed leather

deerskin

doeskin

dogskin

Dongola kid

enameled leather

ermine

fair leather

fleece

fox

frosted mink

fur

glacé kid

glove leather

goatskin

golden sable

grain leather

hairsheep

horsehide

japanned leather

kangaroo

kidskin

krimmer

lambskin

leopard

Levantor Levant morocco

lizard skin

maribou

marmot

marten

miniver

mink

mocha

moleskin

morocco

muskrat

napa nubuck

nutria

otter

oxhide

patent leather

pebble leather

pelt

pigskin

pig suede

puma

rabbit

raccoon

ranch mink

rawhide

red fox

roan

Russian leather

sable

saddle

saffian

sealskin

shagreen

sharkskin

shearling

sheepskin

silver fox

skiver

skunk

snakeskin

shoe leather

stirrup leather

suede

swakara

tawed leather

vair

washleather

white fox

white leather wild mink

ANIMAL KINGDOM

arthropods or Arthropoda

chordates or Chordata

comb jellies or Ctenophora

corals and jellyfish or Cnidaria

echinoderms or Echinodermata

flatworms and flukes or Platyhelminthes

horsehair worms or Nematomorpha

lampshells or Brachiopoda

mollusks or Mollusca

moss animals or Bryozoa

rotifers or Rotifera

roundworms or Nematoda

segmented worms or Annelida

spiny-headed worms or Acanthocephala

sponges or Porifera

velvet worms or Onychophora

water bears or Tardigrada

ANIMAL OILS AND FATS

adipose tissue

beef tallow

blubber

bone oil

bottlenose oil

butter

butterfat

chicken fat

cod-liver oil

fish oil

ghee

goose grease

halibut-liver oil

hog lard

lanolin

lard

lard oil

lipid

lipoma

margarine

neat's-foot oil

oleo

oleomargarine

oleo oil

porpoise oil

salmon oil

sardine oil

seal oil

shark oil

shortening

sperm oil

suet

tallow

tallow oil

tuna oil

whale oil

wool grease

wool oil

ANIMAL YOUNG

(alligator) hatchling

(antelope) calf or kid

(ape) baby

(armadillo) pup

(ass) foal or hinny

(badger) kit or cub

(bat) pup

(bear) cub or whelp

(beaver) kit or kitten or pup

(bee) larva

(bird) fledgling or hatchling or nestling

(bison or buffalo) calf

(boar) farrow or piglet or shoat

(bovine) calf

(butterfly) caterpillar or chrysalis or larva or pupa

(camel) calf

(cat) kit or kitten or kitty

(cattle) calf or yearling

(cheetah) cub

(chicken) chick or poult or pullet or cockerel

(clam) larva

(cow) calf or heifer

(coyote) pup or whelp

(crow) chick

(deer) fawn

(dog) pup or puppy or whelp

(dolphin) calf or pup

(donkey) colt or foal

(duck) duckling

(eagle) eaglet or fledgling

(eel) elver

(elephant) calf

(elk) calf

(falcon) cast or chick

(ferret) kit

(fish) fingerling or fry

(fly) maggot

(fox) cub or kit or pup or whelp

(frog) froglet or polliwog or tadpole

(gerbil) pup

(giraffe) calf or cub or whelp

(gnat) bloodworm

(goat) kid

(goose) gosling

(gorilla) infant

(grouse) cheeper or poult

(guinea pig) pup

(hamster) pup

(hare) leveret

(hawk) eyas

(hen) chick or pullet

(hippopotamus) calf

(horse) colt or filly or foal or yearling

(hyena) cub

(insect) nymph or pupa

(jellyfish) ephyna

(kangaroo) joey

(koala) joey

(lion) cub or whelp

(llama) cria

(mole) pup

(monkey) baby or infant

(moose) cub or calf

(mosquito) nymph or tumbler or wriggler

(opossum) joey

(otter) pup or whelp

(owl) owlet

(ox) calf or stot

(oyster) spat

(panda) cub

(partridge) cheeper

(penguin) chick

(pig) piglet or shoat or farrow or suckling

(pigeon) squab or squeaker

(prairie dog) pup

(quail) cheeper or chick

(rabbit) bunny or kit or kitten or leveret

(racoon) cub

(rat) kitten or pinkie or pup

(reindeer) fawn

(rhinoceros) calf

(rooster) cockerel

(salmon) parr or smolt

(sea lion) pup

(seal) calf or pup

(shark) cub or pup

(sheep) lamb or lambkin or cosset or hog or yearling

(skunk) kit

(spider) spiderling

(squirrel) kit or kitten or pup

(swan) cygnet or flapper

(swine) piglet or shoat or farrow

(tiger) cub or whelp

(turkey) poult or chick

(walrus) cub or pup

(whale) calf

(wolf) cub or whelp

(yak) calf

(zebra) colt or foal

ANIMALS, DUAL-SEX

Atlantic slipper shell

barnacle

bryozoans

cleaner fish

cottony-cushion scale insect

earthworm

European flat oyster

flukes

land snail

liver fluke

parasitic wasp

sea bass

sea hare

sea squirt

shipworm

slug

spoonworm

ANIMALS, MARINE

barracuda

cetacean

conch

crab

crustacean

dolphin

dugong

elephant seal

fish

fur seal

harbor seal

jellyfish

lobster

manatee

mussel

octopus

otter

oyster

phocid

pinniped

porpoise

sand dollar

sea calf

sea cow

sea dog

sea elephant

sea horse

seal

sea lion

sea urchin

shark

shellfish

shrimp

sirenian

sponge

squid

starfish

walrus

whale

ANNIVERSARIES AND HOLIDAYS

Admission Day

Advent

Alaska Day

All Saints' Day or Allhallows

All Souls' Day

American Indian Day

Annunciation

Anzac Day

April Fools' Day

Arab League Day

Arbor Day

Armed Forces Day

Armistice Day

Ascension Thursday or Holy Thursday

Ash Wednesday

Assumption

Australia Day

autumnal equinox

Bairam

Baisakhi

Bastille Day

Bodhi Day

Bon

Boxing Day

Buddha's birthday

Canada Day

Candlemas

Carnival

Chinese New Year

Christmas

Christmas Eve

Chusuk

Cinco de Mayo

Citizenship Day

Columbus Day

Commonwealth Day

Confederate Memorial Day

Confucius's birthday

Constitution Day

Corpus Christi

Dasara

Day of the Dead or Dia de los Muertos

Decoration Day

Dhammacakka

Discovery Day

Diwali

Dominion Day

Double Ten

Durga Puja or Navratri

Dusshera

Earth Day

Easter

Easter Monday

Eid

Eid ul-Adha

Eid ul-Fitr

Election Day

Emancipation Day

Emperor's birthday

Empire Day

Epiphany or Little Christmas or Three Kings' Day

Father's Day

feast day

Flag Day

Fourth of July or Independence Day

Good Friday

Grandparents' Day

Groundhog Day

Guru Gobind Singh's Birthday

Guru Nanak's Birthday

Guy Fawkes Day

Halloween

Hanukkah

High Holy Day

Holi

Holi Mohalla

Holy Innocents' Day

Human Rights Day

'Id al-Adha

Ides of March

Immaculate Conception

Inauguration Day

Independence Day

Islamic New Year's Day

Janmashtami

Karwa Chauth

Kenyatta Day

Kuhio Day

Kwanzaa

Labor Day

Lag b'Omer

Lailat ul-Bara'h

Lailat ul-Isra wal Mi'raj

Lailat ul-Qadr

Lammas

Lantern Festival

Lincoln's birthday

Lunar New Year

Mahashivaratri

Mardi Gras

Martin Luther King Jr. Day

Martinmas

Martyrdom of Guru Arjan

Martyrdom of Guru Tegh Bahadur

Maundy Thursday

May Day

Memorial Day

Mexican Independence Day

Michaelmas

Midsummer Day

Moharram

Mother's Day

Muhammad's birthday

Muhrarran

Nag Panchami

National Day

National Unity Day

Navaratri

New Year's Day

New Year's Eve

Octoberfest
Omisoka
Pagan Sabbats
Palm Sunday
Pan American Day
Passover Pentecost
Posadas
President's Day
Purim
Queen's birthday
Queensland Day
Raksha Bandhan

Ramadan
Rama Naumi
Reformation Sunday
Remembrance Day
Republic Day
Rosh Hashanah
Sadie Hawkins Day
Saint Patrick's Day
Saint Valentine's Day
Santa Lucia Day
Shavuoth
Shrovetide

Shrove Tuesday or
Fat Tuesday
Spring Bank Holiday
Sukkoth
summer solstice
Tet
Thanksgiving
Trinity Sunday
Twelfth Night
United Nations Day
V-E Day
vernal equinox
Vesak

Veterans' Day
Victoria Day
V-J Day
Walpurgis
Washington's
birthday
Whitsunday
Whitsuntide
winter solstice
World Health Day
Yom Kippur

ANTHROPOLOGY BRANCHES

anthropogeography
anthropography
anthropological
linguistics
anthropology
anthropometry
applied anthropology
archaeology
biological
anthropology
business
anthropology
comparative
ethnology

cultural anthropology
dendrochronology
economic
anthropology
epigraphy
ethnoarchaeology
ethnobiology
ethnobotany
ethnography
ethnohistory
ethnolinguistics
ethnology
ethnomethodology

ethnomusicology
ethnopsychology
ethnoscience
genetics and growth
studies
historic archaeology
human evolution
linguistic
anthropology
ontogeny
paleoanthropology
paleontology

philosophical
anthropology
physical
anthropology
praxeology
prehistoric
archaeology
primatology
protohistoric
archaeology
social anthropology
somatology
structural
anthropology

APES AND MONKEYS

anthrapoid ape

ape

baboon

Barbary ape

Bengal monkey

bonnet monkey

bush baby

capuchin

chacma

chimpanzee

colobus

drill

entellus

gelada

gibbon

gorilla

great ape

grivet

guenon

guereza

hamadryas

hanuman

hoolock

howler monkey

king monkey

langur

lar gibbon

leaf monkey

lemur

lion-tailed monkey

loris

macaque

mandrill

marmoset

mountain gorilla

New World monkey

night monkey

Old World monkey

orangutan

owl monkey

pongid

proboscis monkey

rhesus

saki

samango

siamang

sloth monkey

spider monkey

squirrel monkey

talapoin

tamarin

tarsier

titi

uakari

vervet

wanderoo

woolly monkey

woolly spider
monkey

APOSTLES OF JESUS

Andrew

Bartholomew or
Nathanael

James the Greater

James the Less

John

Judas Iscariot (after
his traitordom,
filled by Matthias)

Matthew

Peter

Philip

Simon the Zealot or
Simon the Canaanite

Thaddeus or Jude

Thomas

Appetizers and Hors d'Oeuvres

antipasto
artichoke hearts
blini
brandied fruits
breads
carrots
caviar
celery
cheese
cheese ball
cheese puffs
chicken wings
chips
chutney
cocktail hot dogs
cocktail sausages
cold canapés
corn relish
crabmeat

crackers
cranberry sauce
cucumber
deviled ham
dips
egg rolls
eggs
finger sandwiches
fish balls
fritters
fruit
fruit cup
gherkins
gravad lax
guacamole
ham
hot canapés
humus
kabobs

lobster
meatballs
melon
mini quiches
mushrooms
nuts
olives
onion relish
onions
party mix
pate pâté
pepper relish
pickles
pimentos
pizza bites
popcorn
potato chips
pretzels
prosciutto

radishes
roast beef
rumaki
salad
salmon
sardines
shrimp cocktail
slaw
spanakopitas
steak bites
stuffed mushrooms
stuffed tomatoes
Swedish meatballs
trail mix
turkey
turnovers

Apple Varieties

Adanac
Akane
Albany Beauty

American Mother
Anna
Arctic

Arkansas Black
Aurora
Bailey Sweet

Baldwin
Belle De Boskoop
Belmac

Belmont

Ben Davis

Blue Permain

Braeburn

Bramley

Buckingham

Collins

Cortland

Cox's Orange Pippin

Criterion

Delicious

Discovery

Dorset Golden

Earliblaze

Early Harvest

Ein Shemer

Empire

English Sweet

FortuneFreedom

Freyburg

Fuji

Gala

Gideon

Golden Delicious

Golden Harvest

Golden Supreme

Granny Smith

Gravenstein

Green Sweet

Grimes Golden

Honey Crisp

Hubbardston

Ingram

Irish Peach

Jersey Black

Jerseymac

Jonared

Jonathan

Kidds Orange Red

Lady Sweet

Liberty

Lobo

Lodi

Longfield

Macoun

McIntosh

McMahon

Missouri

Monroe

Mutsu

Newton Pippin

Northern Spy

Oldenburg

Ortley

Permain

Pink Lady

Pippin

Porter

Prima

Priscilla

Rambo

Red Astrachan

Red Delicious

Redfree

Red Rome

Rhode Island Greening

Ribston Pippin

Roman Stem

Rome

Rome Beauty

Roxbury Russet

Russet

Saint Lawrence

Sir Prize

Snowapple

Spartan

Spigold

Starkrimson

Starr

Stayman

Twenty Ounce

Tydeman's Late Orange

Tydeman's Red

Virginia Beauty

Wealthy

Williams

Winesap

Winter Banana

Worcester Pearmain

Yellow Newton

Yellow Transparent

York Imperial

Apricot Varieties

Acme or Chinese or Shense

Alexander or Russian No. 2

bergeron

Blenheim or Shipley's

blushed apricot

Breda or Ananas or DeHollande

Chinese apricot

clingstone

Cluster

compressed apricot

conical apricot

crimson apricot

dessert apricot

early apricot

Early Golden or Dubois

freestone

Goldbar

Goldcot

Goldstrike

Harglow

Harris Hardy

Hemskirke

jumbocot

kitchen apricot

large apricot

Large Early or Gros Precoce

market apricot

medium apricot

Moorpark

Newcastle Early

oblate apricot

oblong apricot

orange apricot

orange de Provence

Orange or Early Orange

Peach or Royal Peach

Perfection

red apricot

Rival

rouge du Roussillon

round apricot

Royal Russian

semiclingstone

Sheridan

small apricot

St. Ambroise

Surprize

Tilton

Tomcot

very large

Wenatchee-Moorpark

white apricot

yellow apricot

Arachnids

baboon spider

beetle mite

bird-eating spider

black widow

button spider

camel spider

cardinal spider

chigger

cogweb spider

crab spider

daddy-long-legs

diadem spider

false scorpion

funnel-web spider

garden spider

harvestman

harvest mite

house spider

hunting spider

huntsman spider

itch mite

jockey spider

jumping spider

katipo

mite

money spider

mygalomorph

orb weaver

orb-web spider

raft spider

redback

red spider mite

retiary spider

scorpion

scorpion spider

sheep tick

solifuge

spider

spider mite

sun spider

tarantula

tick

trapdoor spider

varroa

violin spider

water scorpion

water spider

whip scorpion

white-tailed spider

wind scorpion

wolf spider

wood tick

zebra spider

ARCH TYPES

acute or pointed

arch of discharge

basket handle

blind

catenary

cinquefoil

concentric

corbelled

cycloidal

depressed three-centered

double

drop

elliptical

equilateral

equilateral pointed

equilibrium

equipollent

extrados

fixed

flat

Florentine

foiled

four-centered or Tudor

horseshoe

hyperbolical

inflected or inverted or reversed

interlaced

Janus

lancet

miter or pediment

Moorish

multifoiled Norman

obtuse

ogee or keel

parabolic

pointed

pointed horseshoe

pointed Saracenic

pointed segmental

pointed trefoil

pointed trifoliated

primitive

pseudo four-centered

pseudo three-centered

quatrefoiled

rampant

Roman

Romanesque

rood

rough

round

round trefoil

round trifoliated

rowlock

Saracenic

Saxon

segmental

segmental-pointed

semicircular

semicircular stilted

shouldered

soffited

splayed

stilted

three-centered or basket handle

trefoil

triangular

trussed

Tudor

Venetian

ARCHAEOLOGY

Assyriology

computational archaeology

Egyptology

epigraphy

fossilology historic archaeology

human paleontology

industrial archaeology

micropaleontology

Middle-Eastern archaeology

palaeography

palaeosophy

palaeotypography palaetiology

paleethnology

paleoanthropography

paleoanthropology

paleobiography

paleobiology

paleobotany

paleochorology

paleoclimatology

paleocosmology

paleodendrology

paleoecology

paleoeremology

paleoethnography

paleoethnology

paleogeography

paleoglaciology

paleography

paleoherpetology

paleohistology

paleohydrography

paleolatry

paleolimnology

paleolithy

paleology

paleomammology

paleometeorology

paleontography

paleontology

paleoornithology

paleopathology

paleophysiography

paleophysiology

paleophytology

paleopotamology

paleopsychology

paleornithology

paleozoology

prehistoric anthropology

prehistoric archaeology

prehistory

protoanthropology

protohistory

reconstruction archaeology

Sumerology

underwater archaeology or marine archaeology

ARCHITECTURAL DECORATIONS, DEVICES, ELEMENTS, FEATURES, AND ORNAMENTATIONS

abacus

abutment

acanthus

accolade

acroterium

alcove

alette

anchor

ancon

angle-tie

annulet

anta

antefix

anthemion

apophyge

appentice

apron

apse

arabesque

arcade

arcature

arch

architrave

archivolt

astragal

atlas or atlantes

attic

baguette balconet

balcony

baldachin

ballflower

baluster

balustrade

band

banderole

bandlet

bargeboard

bartizen

basement

bas relief

bastion

battlement

bay leaf garland

bead and reel

beading beak

beakhead

beam

belfrey

bellflower

bezant

billet

blind arcade

blindstory

bolection

boss

bracket

buttress

calotte

cantilever

capital

capstone

cartouche

caryatid

cavetto

ceiling

cella

chamfer

chaplet

chevron

Christian door

cinquefoil

clerestory

cloister

closet

coffer

colonette

colonnade

column

conch

congé or congee

console

coping

corbel

cordon

cornerstone

cornice

corona

cove

crenelation

cresting

crocket

crown

cupola

cusp

cyma

cyma recta

cyma reversa

cymatium

dado

dentil

diamond fret

diaper

die

ditriglyph

dogtooth

dome

door

dormer window

drip

dripstone

dromos

drop

Dutch door

eaves

echinus

ectype

egg and dart

embrasure

entablature

epistyle

escallop

extrados

facet

fanlight

fantail

fanwork

fascade

fascia

fenestella

fenestra

festoon or swag

fillet

finial

fleche

fleur-de-lis

floor

flute flying buttress

foil

foliation

French door

fret

frieze

frontispiece

gable

gableboard

gadroon

gargoyle

garland

gazebo

gorgerin

groin

guilloche

gutta

half round

head

head molding

headpiece

headwork

helix

herms

hood mold

hypophyge

hypostyle

imbrication

impost

inbrex

intrados

jalousie

jamb

joist

keel

key banding

keystone

label

lantern

leaf

lierne

lierne rib

lintel

list

listel

loggia

louver

lozenge

lunette

medallion

metope

modillion

module

molding mullion

mutule

nave

nebulé

necking neckmold

niche

ogee

ogive

overhang

ovolo

pace

paneling

parapet

parquetry

patera

patio

patio door

pavilion

peardrop

pearl molding

pediment

pendant

pergola

peristyle

perron

pier

pilaster

pillar

pocket door

podium

polychromy

poppyhead

porch

portcullis

portico

propylaeum

prostyle

pulvinate frieze

putto

pylon

quadriga

quarter round

quatrefoil

quirk

quoin

rafter

reed

reeding

reglet

regula

relief

repoussé

respond

reveal

rib

rinceau

roof

rosette

rotunda

rustic work

scallop

scotia

scroll

scrollhead

scrolling

scrollwork

shafting

shingle

skylight

sliding door

spandrel

spire

splay

springer

squinch

staircase

steeple

stria

strigil

string

stucco

table

taenia

tailpiece

talon

talon molding

tambour or drum

telamon

terminal thumb

topping

torus or tore

tower

tracery

transom

trefoil

triglyph

trumeau

truss

turret

tympanum vault

vaulting boss

verge

vestibule

vignette

Vitruvian scroll

volute

voussoir

wall

wave molding

window

wreath

zigzag

ARCHITECTURAL ORDERS, CLASSICAL

Composite

Corinthian

Doric

Doric Roman

Ionic

Tuscan

ARCHITECTURAL SPECIALTIES

church architecture or religious architecture or ecclesiastical architecture

civic architecture

civil architecture

college architecture

commercial architecture

computer architecture

domestic architecture

governmental architecture

industrial architecture

institutional architecture

interior design

landscape architecture

library architecture

military architecture   naval architecture   recreational architecture

museum architecture

ARCHITECTURAL STYLES AND TYPES

absolute

academic

action

additive

American colonial

American Georgian

Anglo-Saxon

Art Deco

Art Nouveau

arts and crafts

Babylonian

baroque

Bauhaus

Beaux Arts

brutalism

Byzantine

Cape Cod

Carolingian

Chicago School

Chinese

churrigueresque

cinquecento

Cistercian

classical

Classical Revival

colonial

Colonial Revival

conceptual

Deconstructionism

Decorated Style

de Stijl

directed

Doric

duck

early American

early Christian

Early English

early Gothic

early Renaissance

earthwork

eclectic

ecological

Edwardian Style

Egyptian

Elizabethan

Empire Style

endless

English

English Decorated Gothic

English Georgian

English Renaissance

Federal Style

flamboyant Gothic

formalist

Francois Premier

free classic

French

French Colonial Style

French Renaissance

functionalism

Georgian

German

German Renaissance

gingerbread

Gothic

Great West Road

Greco-Roman

Greek

Greek Revival

hard

high Gothic

high Renaissance

hi-tech

Incan

indeterminate

Indian

International GothicIslamic

Italian

Italianate

Italian Gothic

Italian Mannerism

Italian Renaissance

Jacobean

Japanese

Jesuit

kinetic

Louis XIV

Louis XV

39

Mannerism

Mayan

Medieval

Mesopotamian

Mestizo

Minoan

mission

Moderne

Moorish

neoclassical

neo-Gothic

new brutalism

New England colonial

Norman

organicist

Palladian

Pennsylvania Dutch

perpendicular or rectilinear

Persian

pneumatic

postmodernism

Prairie

Queen Anne Style

Regency

Renaissance

rococo

Roman

Romanesque

Romanesque Revival

Romantic

saltbox

Shingle

Southern Colonial

Spanish

Stuart

tensile

territorial style

transitional

Tudor

Turkish

Tuscan

Utopian

vernacular

Victorian

Victorian Gothic

ARMED FORCES OF THE UNITED STATES

Air Force

Army

Coast Guard

Marines

National Guard

Navy

ARMOR

aegis

ailette

armlet

armor

backplate

bard

basinet

beaver

brassard

breastplate

brigandine

buckler

bulletproof vest

burganet

byrnie

cabasset

camail

casque

casquetel

chain mail

chamfron

coat of mail

coif

corselet

cubitiere

cuirass

cuisse

épaulière

face guard

fauld

footpiece

gas mask

gauntlet

gorget

greave

habergeon

hauberk

headpiece

heaume

helm

helmet

jamb

jambeau

kneepiece

knee plate

lame

lorica

mail

morion

nasal

nosepiece

pallette

paoudron

pavise

placate

plastron

plate

poleyn

rerebrace

rondel

sallet

shield

shoulder piece

skirt of tasses

solleret

surcoat

taces

tasset

tuille

vambrace

visor

ART GROUPS, MOVEMENTS, SCHOOLS, AND STYLES

abstract art

abstract expressionism

action art

action painting

aestheticism

American scene painting

Anglo-Saxon art

art deco

Art Nouveau

Arts and Crafts movement

Ashcan school or the Eight

avant-garde

Barbizon school

baroque

Bauhaus

Biedermeier

body art

Bohemian art

Bolognese

British

Byzantine art

Carolingian art

Celtic art

classical abstraction

classicism

Cobra

Cologne school

conceptual art

concrete art

constructivism

cubism

Dada

de Stijl

Der Blaue Reiter

Die Brücke

divisionism

Dutch

early Christian art

earth art

eclectic

environment art

expressionism

fauvism or Les Fauves

figurative art

Flemish

Florentine school

folk art

Fontainebleau

French

funk art

futurism

genre painting

geometric art

Glasgow

Gothic art

graffiti art

Harlem Renaissance

Hellenistic art

Honfleur

Hudson River

impressionism

International Gothic or International style

Italian

Jugendstil

junk art

kinetic art

L'Age d'or

land art

letrist

Lombard

Madinensor

Madrid

Mannerist

medieval art

metaphysical art

Milanese

minimal art

Modenese

modernism

Momentum

'N'

narrative art

naturalism

Neapolitan

neoclassicism

neoexpressionism

neoimpressionism

Neonism

New Objectivity

New York school

nonrepresentational art

op art

Origine

Paduan

Parisian

perceptual abstraction

performance art

Phases

photorealism

plein-air

pointillism

pop art

postimpressionism

postmodernism

pre-Columbian

prehistoric art

Pre-Raphaelite

primitivism

Raphaelite

realism

Reflex

Renaissance art

representational art

Restany

Rocky Mountain

rococo art

Roman art

romanticism

School of Paris

Scottish Colorists

Sienese

social realism

Spur

superrealism

Suprematism

surrealism

symbolism

tachisme

tenebrists

The Ten

Tuscan

Umbrian

Unit One

Venetian

vorticism

Wanderers

Washington

ART MEDIA AND TECHNIQUES

a trois crayons

abbozzo

abstract art

abstract expressionism

academic

acanthus

achromatic colors

acrylics action painting

advancing and retreating colors

airbrushing

alla prima

alligatoring

amphora

anamorphosis

anthemion

applique

aquarelle

aquatint

arabesque

art nouveau

art rupestre

assemblage

asymmetry

aureole

automatism

avant-garde

bas-relief

batik

biomorphic form

bisque firing

bleed

blending

blister

bloom

blush

bottega

brass rubbing

brown coat

buckeye

cabinet picture

cachet

calendering

calligraphy

caricature

cartooning

ceramics

chalking

charcoal drawing

chasing

checking

chiaroscuro

chromatic colors

chromaticity

chrysography

cinquefoil

cissing

classical

classicism

cleavage

cloisonnism

collage

collotype

color print

color wash

commercial art

concours

conté

crackle

crawl

crayon

cribbled

cubism

Dada

decoupage

deep relief

diorama

distemper

divisionism

double image

dragging stroke

drawing

drollery

dry-brush

drypoint

ebauche

eclecticism

ecorche

electroplate

emboss

en camaieu

enameling

encaustic

engineering drawing

engraving

epigone

etching

exploded view

expressionism

fauvism

fecit

festoon

figurine

filigree

fine art

finger painting

foil

foreshortening

foxing

fresco

frilling

frottage

fugitive colors

gallery tone

garzone

geometric abstraction

gilding

glost fire

glyptic art

goffer

gouache

graphic arts

grisaille

grotesque

guilloche

hatching

hue

icon

idiom

illumination

impasto

impressionism

inlay

inpainting

intaglio

intarsia

intonaco

kickwheel

kinetic art

kitsch

lacuna

landscape

line drawing

lino cut

lithochromy

lithography

lost wax

magic realism

marbling

marouflage

marquetry

matte

mechanical drawing

melt-and-color

metalwork

mezzo fresco

mezzotint

miniature painting

mixed media

mobile

moire effect

monochrome

montage

mosaic

motif

mural painting

neoclassical art

nonobjective art

nouveau

objective art

oil painting

op art

optical mixing

overpainting

painting

palmette

pastels

pastiche

pate-sur-pate

pencil drawing

perspective

petite nature

photography

photogravure

photomontage

photoprint

plastering

pochade

pointillism

polychrome

pop art

portrait

postiche

pouncing

pricking

primitive

profil perdu

psychedelic art

pyrography

realism

relief

relief rubbing

repoussé

retouching

rococo

rubbing

sand painting

scale drawing

scrambled colors

screen printing

scrimshaw

scroll

sculpture

scumble

secco

serigraph

sfumato

sgraffito

shading

silhouette

silk painting

silk screen

silverpoint

sketching

smooch

soft ground etching

sotto in su

spatula painting

splatter painting

spray-can painting

squaring

stained glass

stenciling

still life

stipple

surrealism

tachism

tapestry

tattooing

technical drawing

tempera

tenebrism

thumbnail sketch

tondo

tone

topographic landscape

trompe l'oeil

underpainting

veduta

vignette

vorticism

wash brush

wash drawing

watercolor weaving

wedging

wood carving

woodcut

wood engraving

zincography

Art Styles and Movements: Late 20th–Early 21st Century

Abstract Expressionism

Abstract Illusionism

Art Brut

Bauhaus School

Body Art

Color Field painting

Conceptual art

Constructivism

Cubism

Dada or Dadaism

Der Blaue Reiter or The Blue Rider

Die Brücke or The Bridge

Earthworks

Expressionism

Fauvism

Futurism

Installation art

Kinetic art

Minimalism

Modern art

Naïve art

Neurotic realism

New York School

Op art

Pop art

School of Paris

Secession

Suprematism

Surrealism

Art Styles and Movements: Christianity and Medieval Times

Byzantine art

Carolingian art

Early Christian art

Gothic art

International style

Islamic art

Migration period

Ottonian art

Romanesque art

Art Styles and Movements: Classical and Egyptian

Ancient Greek art   Egyptian art   Hellenistic art   Roman art

Art Styles and Movements: Late 18th–Early 19th Century

Neo-classicism or Neoclassicism   Pre-Raphaelite Brotherhood   Realism

Rococo art   Romanticism

Art Styles and Movements: Late 19th–Early 20th Century

Arts and Crafts movement   Impressionism   Post-Impressionism

Pointillism   Symbolism

Art Styles and Movements: [Asia and the Pacific]

African art	Assyrian art	Buddhist art	Ch'ing dynasty art
African tribal art	Aztec art	cave art	Cycladic art
Ancient Egyptian art	Babylonian art	Chinese art	floating world
Asian art	Benin bronzes	Chinese calligraphy	Fujiwara style

46

Gandharan art

Han dynasty art

Heian style

Indian art

Indus Valley art

Islamic art

Japanese scroll
painting

Japanese woodblocks

Melanesian art

Mesoamerican art

Mesopotamian art

Middle Eastern art

Ming dynasty art

Minoan art

Mogul art

Mycenean art

New Kingdom art

Oceanic art

Old Kingdom art

Ottoman art

Paleolithic art

Pre-Columbian art

prehistoric art

rock painting

Song dynasty art

Sumerian art

sumi-e

Tamily art

Tang dynasty art

Tultec art

Ukiyo-e

Yuan dynasty art

ART STYLES AND MOVEMENTS: PALEOLITHIC AND PRIMITIVE

Period I
(32,000–25,000
years ago)

Period II
(25,000–19,000
years ago)

Period III
(19,000–15,000
years ago)

Period IV
(15,000–10,000
years ago)

Prehistoric cave art
(including Paleolithic)

ART STYLES AND MOVEMENTS: RENAISSANCE TO MIDDLE 18TH CENTURY

Baroque art

Italian Early
Renaissance

Italian High
Renaissance

Italian Proto-
Renaissance

Mannerism

Northern Europe
Renaissance

Renaissance

Renascences

Rococo art

ART STYLES AND MOVEMENTS: WESTERN ART

abstract art

abstract expression

academic art

action painting

Aegean art

aestheticism

Alexandrian school

Anglo-Saxon art

Archaic art

Art Deco

Art Nouveau

Arts and Crafts Movement

Ashcan school

baroque

Bauhaus

Biedermeier

body art

Bohemian art

Bolognese school

Burgundian school

Byzantine art

Carolingian art

Celtic art

Classical Greek art

classicism

Cologne school

conceptual art

constructivism

Coptic art

cubism

Dada

Danube school

de Stijl

Dutch genre painting

Early Christian art

Early Renaissance art

earth art

eclecticism

environmental art

Etruscan art

expressionism

Fauvism

figurative art

Florentine school

folk art

futurism

Germanic art

Gothic art

Grand Manner

Greco-Roman art

Hadrianic art

Hague school

Harlem Renaissance

Hellenistic art

High Renaissance art

impressionism

junk art

magic realism

medieval art

minimal art

naïve art

naturalism

neoclassicism

neoexpressionism

neoimpressionism

New York school

nonrepresentational art

performance art

photorealism

pointillism

Pompeian art

pop art

postimpressionism

postmodernism

Pre-Raphaelite

primitive art

purism

realism

Renaissance

rococo art

Roman school

romanesque art

romanticism

school of Paris

spatialism

surrealism

Symbolism

Tuscan school

Venetian school

ART TOOLS AND MATERIALS

acetone

acrylic brush

acrylic colors

airbrush

alabaster

angular liner

architect's rendering brush

armature

badger blender

bamboo pen

banding wheel

bat

batten board

bisque

blender brush

bright

bristle brush

bulletin cutter

burnisher

camel hair brush

camera lucida

canvas

cardboard

ceramic glaze

charcoal

charcoal paper

chassis

chisel brush

clay

compass

conté crayon

crayon

dagger striper

decorating wheel

drawing board

drawing paper

easel

ellipse guide

enamel

eraser

fan brush

filbert brush

fitch brush

fixative

flag

fluorescent paint

French curve

glue

highliner

kiln

lay figure

lettering brush

light box

loop tools

mahlstick

marker

masking tape

mop

mordant

needle tools

newsprint

oil colors

paint

painting knives

palette

palette knife

panel

pantograph

paper cutter

papier-mâché

pastel

pate

pen

pen points

pencil

plaster

polymer medium

potter's wheel

pounce

protractor

rigger

ruler

scissors

scraper

single-stroke brush

slide projector

spatula

sponge

spotting brush

stenciling brush

striper

stump

taboret

tagboard

tempera

tessera

turning tools

wash brush

watercolor paper

watercolors

X-acto knife

49

ARTHROPODS

Chelicerata (arachnid, mite, scorpion, spider, tick)

Crustacea (crustacean, marine arthropod)

Trilobita (trilobite)

Uniramia (centipede, insect, millipede, myriapod)

ARTIFACT TYPES IN ARCHAEOLOGY

adhesive

amber

antler

basketry

bone artifact

bottle

button

ceramics

charcoal

chipped-stone tool

coal

coin

copper

document

dye

enamel

fiber or thread

figurine

flaked-stone tool

glass

glaze

gold

ground-stone tool

historical artifact

horn

iron

ivory

knapped stone tool

lead

lithic or stone tool

mercury

metal

nail

paint

perishable artifact

pigment

pipe

plaster

projectile point

shell artifact

silver

steel

wood

ASIAN PEOPLES

Ainu

Andamanese

Bashkir

Bengalis

Burmese

Chinese

Chukchi

Cossacks

Dards

Georgians

Hui

Kaffirs

Karen

Khmer

Maratha Mon

Munda

Pashtuns

Samoyed

Sherpas

Sinhalese

Tai

Talaing

Tamils

Tatars

Turkmen

ASTEROIDS OR MINOR PLANETS

Achilles	Davida	Hygeia	1991BA
Adonis	Eros	Icarus	Nysa
Amor	Eugenia	Ida	Otawara
Anne Frank	Eunomia	Interamnia	Pallas
Apollo	Euphrosyne	Iris	Phaeton
Astraea	Europa	Itokawa	Pholus
Aten	Gaspra	Juno	Rodari
Braille	Geographos	Kleopatra	Shipka
Castalia	Hebe	Mathilde	Siwa
Ceres	Hektor	McAuliffe	Toutatis
Chiron	Hidalgo	Mimistrobell	Vesta

ATHLETIC EVENTS

1,500-meter race	5,000-meter race	heptathlon	pole vault
10,000-meter race	50 km walk	high jump	relay race
100-meter race	800-meter race	hurdling	shotput
100-meter relay	biathlon	javelin	sprint
110-meter hurdles	cabertossing	long-distance race	steeplechase
20 km walk	cross-country running	long jump	tetrathlon
200-meter race	decathlon	marathon	triathlon
3,000-meter steeplechase	discus	middle-distance race	triple jump
400-meter race	fell running	modern pentathlon	tug of war
400-meter hurdles	half-marathon	mountain running	walking event
400-meter relay	hammer throw	one-mile race	

ATMOSPHERE, COMPONENTS OF

boundary layer

chemosphere

D layer or region

E layer or Kennelly-Heaviside layer

exosphere

F layer or Appleton layer

F1 layer or F1 region

F2 layer or F2 region

inner Van Allen belt

ionosphere

isothermal region

lower atmosphere

magnetosphere

mesosphere

outer atmosphere

outer Van Allen belt

ozone layer

stratopause

stratosphere

stratospheric sulfate layer or Junge aerosol layer

sulfate layer

substratosphere

thermosphere

tropopause

troposphere

upper atmosphere

Van Allen belt

ATOMIC UNITS AND CONSTANTS

atom

atomic mass

atomic mass constant

atomic number

atomic weight

Avogadro number

Bohr constant or Bohr radius

Boltzmann constant

crystal-lattice constant

Dulong's constant

electron charge

electron mass

elementary quantum of action

Fermi coupling constant

fine-structure constant

gram atom

gram-atomic weight

magnetic quantum number

magneton

mass number

Petit's constant

Planck's constant

proton mass

quantum

quantum number

Rydberg number

speed of light

valence

valence number

ATOMS

acceptor atom

adatom

anion

antiatom

asymmetric carbon atom

Bohr atom

branched chain

cation

diradical discrete atom

excited atom

exotic atom

free radical

hot atom

impurity atom

isobar

isotere

isotopic isobar

labeled atom

monad

neutral atom

normal atom

nuclear isomer

nuclide

radiation atom

recoil atom

straight chain

stripped atom

AUSTRALIAN STATES AND TERRITORIES

Australian Capital Territory

New South Wales

Northern Territory

Queensland

South Australia

Tasmania

Victoria

Western Australia

AUTOMOBILE BODY TYPES

compact

convertible

coupé

fastback

four-door sedan

hatchback

kit car

limousine

microcar

minivan

pickup truck

roadster

sedan

sports car

sports utility vehicle

station wagon

stretch limousine

two-door sedan

AUTOMOBILE ENGINES

air-cooled engine

compression engine

compression-ignition engine

diesel engine

four-stroke cycle engine

fuel injection engine

hemi

internal-combustion engine

power stroke engine

PRV engine

reciprocating engine

rotary engine

slant six engine

spark ignition engine

supercharger

turbocharger

two-stroke cycle engine

V-6

V-8

V-type engine

Wankel engine

water-cooled engine

AUTOMOBILE TYPES

ambulance

armored car

brougham

bubble car

cabriolet

club coupe

compact car

convertible

coupe

dragster

dune buggy

electric car

estate car

fastback

four-door

gran turismo or GT

grand touring car

hardtop

hatchback

hearse

hot rod

hybrid car

hydrogen car

jeep

limousine

lowrider

luxury

microcar

mid-size

mini-bus

minicar

muscle car

passenger car

race car

ragtop

roadster

runabout

saloon

sedan

sedan landaulet

sedan limousine

smart car

sports car

sport utility vehicle

squad car

station wagon

stock car

stretch limousine

subcompact

tourer

touring car

town car

two-door

two-seater

woodie

AUTOMOBILES NAMED AFTER PEOPLE

Alfa-Romeo

Aston Martin

Bugatti

Chevrolet

Chrylser

Citröen

Daimler

Ferrari

Hillman

Honda

Lancia

Maserati

Mercedes

Opel

Peugot

Porsche

Rolls-Royce

Skoda

Toyota

Vanwall

AVIATION BEACONS

airport beacon

anchor light

approach light

blinker light

boundary light

ceiling light or projector

course light

fixed light

flare path

flashing light

high-intensity runway approach light

identification light

land-direction light

landing light

landmark beacon

Lindbergh light

marker navaid

navigation light

non-directional beacon

obstruction light

position light

racon

runway light

sequence flasher

VOR

AWARDS FOR ARTS

Academy Awards or Oscars

Academy of Country Music Awards

American Academy of Arts and Letters Awards

American Institute of Architects Gold Medal

American Music Awards

Berlin International Film Festival

Cannes Film Festival Awards

Director's Guild of America Awards

Emmy Awards

Golden Globe Awards

Grammy Awards

Hasty Pudding Theatricals

Kennedy Center Honors

Miss America

Miss Universe

MTV Video Music Awards

National Medal of Arts

People's Choice Awards

Pritzker Architecture Prize

Pulitzer Prize in Music

Rock and Roll Hall of Fame

Sundance Film Festival Awards

Tony Awards or Antoinette Perry Awards

Toronto International Film Festival

AWARDS FOR SCIENCE AND TECHNOLOGY

Alfred B. Nobel Prize in Chemistry

Alfred B. Nobel Prize in Economic Science

Alfred B. Nobel Prize in Physics

Alfred B. Nobel Prize in Physiology or Medicine

55

Fields Medal	National Inventor of the Year Award	National Medal of Science	Templeton Prize

Awards for Sports

Basketball Hall of Fame

Calder Memorial Trophy (rookie of year in professional hockey)

College Football Coach of the Year

Conn Smythe Trophy (MVP in professional hockey playoffs)

Cy Young Award (American League, National League)

Eclipse Award for Horse of the Year

Frank J. Selke Trophy (defensive forward in professional hockey)

Harness Horse of the Year

Hart Memorial Trophy (MVP in professional hockey)

Heisman Trophy

James E. Sullivan Memorial Trophy (amateur athlete)

James Norris Memorial Trophy (defenseman in professional hockey)

John R. Wooden Award

Lady Byng Memorial Trophy (most gentlemanly player in professional hockey)

Manager of the Year (American League, National League)

Most Valuable Player (American League, National League)

National Baseball Hall of Fame

National Hockey Hall of Fame

NBA Coach of the Year

NBA Defensive Player of the Year

NBA Finals Most Valuable Player

NBA Most Valuable Player

NBA Rookie of the Year

NBA Sixth Man Award

NFL Defensive Player of the Year

NFL Most Valuable Player

NFL Rookie of the Year

Outland Award (college interior lineman)

Pro Football Hall of Fame

Professional Bowlers Association Hall of Fame

Rawlings Gold Glove Award (American League, National League)

Rookie of the Year (American League, National League)

Super Bowl Most Valuable Player

Vezina Trophy (goalie in professional hockey)

Wade Trophy (women's college basketball)

WNBA Finals Most Valuable Player

WNBA Most Valuable Player

WNBA Rookie of the Year

World Series Most Valuable Player

AWARDS FOR WRITING

Academy of American Poets Awards

Alfred B. Nobel Prize in Literature

American Academy of Arts and Letters

Bollingen Prize in Poetry

Booker Prize

Cervantes Prize or Premio Cervantes for Hispanic Literature

Coretta Scott King Award

Edgar Awards

George Foster Peabody Awards

Golden Kite Awards

Hugo Awards

Jerusalem Prize

Le Prix Goncourt

Lincoln Prize

Man Booker Prize for Fiction

National Book Award (Children's Literature, Fiction, Nonfiction, Poetry)

National Book Critics Circle Awards

National Journalism Awards

National Magazine Awards

Nebula Awards

Newbery Award

Orange Prize

PEN/Faulkner Award

Pulitzer Prize in Journalism

Pulitzer Prize in Letters (American Poetry, Biography or Autobiography, Drama, Fiction, General Nonfiction, US History)

Reuben Award

T.S. Eliot Prize

Whitbread Book Awards

AWNING TYPES

aluminum

baldachin

bamboo

blind

canopy

canvas

carport

cotton

fiberglass

marquee

metal

opaque

patio

roll-up

shade

slat

store

striped duck

sunblind

sunshade

translucent

transparent

velarium

vinyl

window

AXES

battle-ax

broadax

common ax

Dayton ax

double-bitted ax

fireman's ax

halberd

hand ax hatchet

Lochaber ax

poleax or poleaxe

tomahawk

western ax

BACTERIA

Bacteria (the plural of bacterium, from Greek *baktrion* 'staff, stick') is any of a group of microscopic organisms that are prokaryotic—that lack a membrane-bound nucleus and organelles. They are unicellular (one-celled) and may have spherical (coccus), rodlike (bacillus), or curved (vibrio, spirillum, or spirochete) bodies.

actinomycete

aerobacter

agrobacterium

Archaebacteria

bacilli

bacillus

bacteria

bacteriophage

blue-green algae

chlorobacteria

cocci

coccus

cyanobacteria

diplobacteria

diplococcus

endospore-forming bacteria

enteric bacteria

enterobacteria

eubacteria

flesh-eating bacteria

gliding bacteria

gram-negative bacteria

gram-positive bacteria

green nonsulfur bacteria

green sulfur bacteria

halobacteria

halophiles

lactic acid bacteria

lactobacillus

methanobacteria

methanogens

micrococcus

Monera

mycobacteria

mycoplasma

myxobacteria

nanobacteria

nitric bacteria

nitrobacter

nitrobacteria

nitrosobacteria

nitrosomonas

nitrous bacteria

photobacteria

phototrophic bacteria

pseudomonad

purple bacteria

purple nonsulfur bacteria

purple sulfur bacteria

rickettsia

salmonella

slime bacteria

spherobacteria

spirilla

spirillum

spirobacteria

spirochete

streptococcus

streptomyces

thermoacidophiles

thiobacillus

trichobacteria

true bacteria

vibrio

vibrion

vibros

xanthomonas

BAGS

backpack

bag

bedroll

bindle

bundle

caddie bag

diplomatic pouch

evening bag

golf bag

gunny sack

handbag

kit bag

mail pouch

moneybag

net

nose bag

packsack

pocketbook

poke

pouch

reticule

sack

saddlebag

satchel

schoolbag

sleeping bag

vanity bag

wineskin

BALKAN STATES

The Balkans, also called Balkan Peninsula, are defined as the easternmost of Europe's three great southern peninsulas, sometimes including northern Greece and the European part of Turkey. The word Balkan is Turkish and means "mountain," and the peninsula is dominated by this type of landform, especially in the west.

Albania

Bosnia and Herzegovina

Bulgaria

Croatia

Macedonia

Moldova

Romania

Serbia and Montenegro

Slovenia

Yugoslavia

BALLET STEPS, POSITIONS, MOVES

adagio

allegro

allonge

arabesque

assemble

assoluta

attitude

attitude a terre

attitude grecque

baisse

balancé

ballon

balloné

ballotté

battement

battement frappé

battement tendu

batterie

beat

bourrée

brisé

brisé volé

cabriole

cambre

Cecchetti method

chainé

changement de pieds

chassé

ciseaux

closed position

coda

colle

combination

contretemps

coryphee

count

coupe

coupee

couru

croise

dégagé

demi plié

demi pointe

développé

divertissement

écarté

échappé

efface

elevation

emboites

en arriere

en dehors

en face

en l'air

en pointe

en seconde

enchaînement

enlevement

entr'acte

entrechat

epaulement

extension

failli

faire les tiroirs

ferme

fifth position

figure

first position

fish dive

fondu

fouetté

fourth position

frappé

gargouillade

glissade

glissé

grand battement

grand batterie

grand jeté

grand pas de basque

grand pas de deux

grand plié

jeté

labanotation

le grand defile

open position

par terre

partnering

pas

pas couru

pas de basque

pas de bourrée

pas de chat

pas de cheval

pas de ciseaux

pas de course

pas de deux

pas de quatre

pas de trois

pas marche

pas seul

passe

penche

petit battement

petit batterie

petit jeté

petit tours

piqué

pirouette

pistolet

placement

plié

pointe work

port de bras

pose

pose tours

promenade

regisseur

relevé

repetiteur

retiré

reverence

revoltade

rolling

rond de jambe en l'air

royale

saut de basque

saut de chat

sauté

second position

sickle foot

sissonne

soubresant

soubresaut

sous-sous

soutenu

stulchak

sur le coup de pied

taquete

temps

temps de fleche

temps de pointe

temps levé

temps lie

tendu

tendus battements

third position

tour

tour a la seconde

tour en l'air

tour jeté

turnout

variation

vole

BALLOONS

air balloon

angioplasty balloon

barrage balloon

blimp

ceiling balloon

detachable balloon

dirigible

fire balloon

frame balloon

free balloon

gastric balloon

horizontal sounding balloon

hot-air balloon

intra-aortic balloon

kite balloon

montgolfier

observation balloon

origin balloon

passive balloon

pilot balloon

radiosonde balloon

rocket balloon

sausage balloon

skyhook balloon

sounding balloon

speech balloon

stratosphere balloon

trial balloon

transport balloon

water balloon

weather balloon

Balls; Sports

air ball	croquet ball	handball	soccer ball
baseball	cue ball	lacrosse ball	softball
basketball	eight ball	Nerf ball	tennis ball
beach ball	field hockey ball	pinball	tetherball
billiard ball	float ball	Ping-Pong ball	volleyball
bocci ball	football	polo ball	whiffle ball
bowling ball	golf ball	rubber ball	
cricket ball	gutter ball	rugby ball	

Balsam Varieties

Balsam (from Latin) is an aromatic and usually oily and resinous substance flowing from various plants, especially any of several resinous substances containing benzoic or cinnamic acid and used in medicine.

balm of Gilead	Canada balsam	Holland balsam	tolu balsam
balsam of sulfur	copaiba	orange balsam	Turlington's balsam
balsam poplar	friar's balsam	Peru balsam	
Brazilian balsam	garden balsam	silver balsam	

Band Types

big band	dance band	marching band	rhythm band
boy band	ensemble	orchestra	rock band
brass band	girl band	pep band	string quartet
chamber orchestra	jazz band	philharmonic	symphony
concert band	jug band	quartet	

Bank Types

- branch bank
- central bank
- commercial bank
- credit bank
- drive-through bank
- Federal Reserve bank
- foreign bank
- home-loan bank
- investment bank
- merchant bank
- national bank
- piggy bank
- reserve bank
- savings bank
- state bank
- thrift bank
- trust company

Bas-Relief and Frieze Types

Relief sculpture is a complex art form that combines many features of the two-dimensional pictorial arts and the three-dimensional sculptural arts. The term frieze refers to any long, narrow, horizontal panel or band used for decorative purposes, for example, on pottery, on the walls of a room, or on the exterior walls of buildings. Friezes are usually on the exterior of a building and are often sculpted in bas-relief. Relief is from Italian *rilievo* 'raised or embossed work' and frieze also came through Italian *fregio* 'border, fringe, ornament' (ultimately from Latin).

- alto-relievo
- bas-relief
- brick relief
- Composite frieze
- Corinthian frieze
- Doric frieze
- egg and dart
- glide reflection frieze
- grand relief
- half relief
- high relief
- horizontal reflection frieze
- horizontal/vertical reflection frieze
- incised relief
- intaglio
- Ionic frieze
- low relief
- mezzo-relievo
- middle relief
- repoussé
- rotation through 180 degrees frieze
- rotation/vertical reflection frieze
- sunken relief
- translation frieze
- Tuscan frieze
- vertical reflection frieze

BASEBALL EQUIPMENT

bar mask

base

baseball

baseball hat

bat

batting cage

batting glove

batting helmet

batting tee

birdcage mask

catcher's mask

catcher's mitt

catcher's throat protector

chest protector

cleats

doughnut first base glove

pine-tar rag

pitching machine

pitching rubber

rosin bag

shin guards

umpire brush

umpire indicator

BASEBALL PITCHES

back door

beanball

bender

breaking ball

brush-off

Captain Hook

change-up circle change

crossfire pitch

curve ball

cut fastball

dime

duster

eefus ball

Eephus pitch

fadeaway

fast ball

floater

Folly floater

forkball

four-seam fastball

gopher ball

intentional walk

knuckleball

knucklecurve

LaLob

off-speed pitch

palmball

palmchange

passed ball

pitchout

reverse curve

roundhouse curve

sailing fastball

screwball

sinker

slider

slow ball

spitball

split-finger fastball

splitter

submarine

two-seam fastball

Uncle Charlie

wild pitch

windmill pitch

BASEBALL POSITIONS

catcher	first base	right field	third base
center field	left field	second base	
designated hitter	pitcher	shortstop	

BASINS AND TUBS

barber's basin	cirque	laver	terrine
bathtub	cistern	punch bowl	trough
bidet	finger bowl	salad bowl	tub
birdbath	gravy boat	sauce boat	tureen
bowl	hip bath	sink	vat
catch basin	Jacuzzi	sitz bath	washbasin
cereal bowl	lavatory	stoup	washtub

BASKETBALL DEFENSIVE STRATEGIES

box-and-chaser	double team	matchup defense	slough
box-and-one defense	full-court press	multiple defense	stack defense
collapsing defense	half-court press	pressure defense	zone defense
combination defense	lane press	sagging defense	
diamond-and-one	man-to-man defense	set pattern	

BASKETBALL FOULS

blocking	false double foul	intentional foul	team foul
charging	false multiple foul	multiple foul	technical foul
dead ball foul	flagrant foul	offensive foul	tripping
disqualifying foul	force-out	personal foul	two-shot foul
double foul	hacking	player control foul	
elbowing	holding	pushing off	

BASKETBALL OFFENSIVE STRATEGIES

backdoor play	four-corner offense	low post	run and gun offense
ball-control offense	gap offense	motion offense	running offense
clear-out one side	give-and-go offense	one-on-one	set offense
criss-cross offense	half-court offense	pick-and-roll	shuffle offense
delay offense	high post	post up	stack offense
double post	high post zone offense	press offense	stall offense
fast-break offense		pressure offense	triangle offense
flip-flop offense	high-low zone offense	rotation offense	zone offense

BASKETBALL SHOTS

airball	bunny	dunk or slam dunk	hook shot
bank shot	charity toss	fadeaway jumper	jump shot
bonus free throw	cripple	finger-roll	lay-in
brick	double pump shot	free throw	lay-up

one-and-one
one-hand shot
open shot
outside shot
penalty free throw
perimeter shot

pivot shot
pump shot
push shot
reverse dunk
reverse layup
running jump shot

scoop shot
set shot
sky hook
slam dunk
stuff shot
swish

three-point field goal
tip-in
turnaround jump shot
two-hand shot

BASKETS

Basketry is the art and craft of making interwoven objects, usually containers, from flexible vegetable fibers, such as twigs, grasses, osiers, bamboo, and rushes, or from plastic or other synthetic materials.

bassinet
breadbasket
buck basket
bushel basket
clothesbasket
clothes hamper
corbeil
corf
creel
cresset

crib
dosser
flasket
flower basket
frail
fruit basket
grocery basket
hamper
market basket
May basket

mocock
pack basket
pannier picnic basket
punnet
reed basket
rush basket
scuttle
sewing basket
skep
splint basket

stave basket
trug
tub basket
wash basket
wastebasket
wicker basket
wire basket
wooden basket
workbasket

BASKIN-ROBBINS
31 ORIGINAL FLAVORS

Banana Nut Fudge
Black Walnut

Burgundy Cherry
Butter Pecan

Butterscotch Ribbon
Chocolate

Chocolate Almond
Chocolate Chip

Chocolate Fudge

Chocolate Ribbon

Coffee

Coffee Candy

Date Nut

Egg Nog

French Vanilla

Green Mint

Lemon Crisp

Lemon Custard

Lemon Sherbet

Maple Walnut

Orange Sherbet

Peach

Peppermint Fudge

Peppermint Stick

Pineapple Sherbet

Pistachio Nut

Raspberry Sherbet

Rocky Road

Strawberry

Vanilla

Vanilla Burnt Almond

BATS

A bat is any member of the order Chiroptera, the only mammals to have evolved true flight. About 900 species are currently recognized, belonging to some 174 genera, the most common of which are listed below.

anvil bat

Barbastelbig brown bat

big-eared bat

bloodsucking bat

blossom bat

brown bat

brown horseshoe bat

bull bat

bulldog bat

butterfly bat

cave bat

cinnamon bat

disk-wing bat

epauletted fruit bat

false bat

false vampire bat

fisherman bat

flower bat

flying fox

forest bat

fox bat

free-tailed bat

frosted bat

fruit bat

funnel-eared bat

ghost bat

golden bat

golden horseshoe bat

hairless bat

hammer-headed bat

harpy bat

hoary bat

hog-nosed bat

hollow-faced bat

horseshoe bat

large brown bat

leaf-nosed bat

leather-winged bat

little bat

little brown bat

long-eared bat

long-legged bat

mastiff bat

monk bat

mouse-eared bat

mouse-tailed bat

moustached bat

myotis

naked bat

noctule

orange bat

painted bat

particolored bat

pipistrelle

pocketed bat

red bat

roussette

sac-winged bat

sea bat

serotine bat

sheath-tailed bat

short-tailed bat

silver-haired bat

slit-faced bat

smoky bat

soricine bat

spearnose bat

specter bat

spotted bat

sucker-footed bat

tomb bat

Trident bat

tube-nosed bat

vampire bat

whiskered bat

white bat

wrinkle-lipped bat

yellow bat

yellow-winged bat

BATTERIES

A battery

AA battery

AAA battery

acid cell

accumulator

air cell

alkaline battery

alkaline cell

atomic battery

B battery

C battery

car battery

cell battery

D battery

dry battery

dry cell

edison battery

electronic battery

filament battery

floating battery

fuel cell

galvanic battery

lead-acid battery

Leyden battery

Leyden jar

lithium ion battery

mercury cell

nickel-cadmium battery

nickel-iron battery

nine-volt battery

primary battery

primary cell

rechargeable battery

secondary battery

secondary cell

solar battery

solar cell

storage battery

storage cell

thermoelectric battery

voltaic battery

voltaic cell

voltaic pile

water battery

wet cell

BAYS AND GULFS

A bay is defined as an indentation of the sea into the land, and this indentation has a wide opening. A gulf is a portion of the sea partially enclosed by a more or less extensive sweep of the coast and it often takes its name from the adjoining land. The

69

word gulf ultimately derives from a Latin word meaning, 'hollow of the waves, depth of the sea.'

Baffin Bay	Bay of Whales	Gulf of Carpentaria	Gulf of Suez
Bay of Bengal	Botany Bay	Gulf of Corinth	Gulf of Thailand
Bay of Biscay	Great Australian Bight	Gulf of Guinea	Gulf of Tonkin
Bay of Campeche	Gulf of Aden	Gulf of Lions	Gulf of Venezuela
Bay of Fundy	Gulf of Alaska	Gulf of Mexico	Gulf of Venice
Bay of Naples	Gulf of Aqaba	Gulf of Oman	Hudson Bay
Bay of Ob	Gulf of Bothnia	Gulf of Panama	Montego Bay
Bay of Quinte	Gulf of California	Gulf of Siam	Persian Gulf
Bay of Skiall		Gulf of St. Lawrence	Table Bay

BEACHES

apposition beach	bayside beach	mid-bay bar beach	strand
barrier beach	boulder beach	pocket beach	tombolo beach
bayhead bar beach	concave beach	raised beach	
bayhead beach	convex beach	spit beach	
baymouth bar beach	lakeshore	straight beach	

BEACONS AND SIGNAL LIGHTS

Beacons and signal lights provide the means for safe transport for boats, trains, buses, and cars.

airway beacon	Bengal light	flasher	indicator light
balefire	blinker	fog light	intermittent light
beacon fire	fanal	fusee	lighthouse
beacon light	flare	green light	lightship

magnesium flare	rocket	signal lamp	turn signal
non-directional light	running light	signal lantern	Very flare
occulting light	sea light	signal light	ward hill
pharos	seamark	signal rocket	watch fire
pilot lamp	sidelight	skyrocket	weather signal
projector	signal beacon	stoplight	
red light	signal flare	traffic signal	

BEAMS

In engineering, a beam is often a solid piece of timber, as in a house, a plow, a loom, or a balance. In modern building construction, a beam is a horizontal member spanning an opening and carrying a load that may be a brick or stone wall above the opening, in which case the beam is often called a lintel. Beams may be of wood, steel, or other metals, reinforced or prestressed concrete, plastics, and even brickwork with steel rods in the bond between bricks.

angle rafter	hammer beam	ridge strut	summertree
balk	H beam	scantling	T beam
batten	hip rafter	sheetrock	tie
boom	I beam	sill	tie beam
box girder	joint	sleeper	transom
breastsummer	lattice girder	spreader	transverse
corbel	lintel	sprit	trave
crossbeam	overhang	stringpiece	traverse
crosstie	plate girder	strut	truss
door beam	prestressed	stud	truss beam
footing beam	rafter	studding	universal
girder	ridgepole	summer	

Beans, Pulses, and Peas

adzuki bean
baked bean
black bean
black-eyed bean
black-eyed pea
borlotti bean
broad bean
bush bean
butter bean
cannellini bean
Carolina bean
chickpea
civit bean
cowpea
cranberry bean
dal

English pea fava bean
field bean
field pea
flageolet
French bean
garbanzo bean
garden pea
green bean
haricot bean
horsebean
jack bean
kidney bean
lentil
lima bean
mangetout
marrowfat pea

Mexican jumping bean
moth bean
mung bean
navy bean
partridge pea
pea bean
petit pois
pink bean
pinto bean
pod pea
pole bean
puy lentil
red bean
runner bean
scarlet runner

Scotch bean
shell bean
snap bean
snow pea
soybean
split pea
string bean
stringless bean
sugar bean
sugar pea
sugar snap pea
tick bean
wax bean
Windsor bean
yellow wax bean

Bears

American black bear
Asian black bear
black bear
brown bear
cave bear

cinnamon bear
giant panda
grizzly bear
Himalayan black bear
honey bear

Kodiak bear
musquaw
polar bear
red panda
sloth bear

spectacled bear
sun bear

Beauty Product Types

aftershave	conditioner	false nails	razor
antiperspirant	cosmetics	fragrance	rinse
astringent	cotton swab	hair dryer	rollers
atomizer	curler	hair net	rouge
balm	curling iron	hair spray	safety razor
balsam	dental floss	highlighter	shampoo
bath oil	dentifrice	lip gloss	shaver
bath salts	deodorant	lipstick	sunscreen
blusher	depilatory	makeup	swabs
bobby pin	eau de Cologne	mascara	talcum powder
bracer	eau de parfum	moisturizer	tissue
brush	electric razor	mousse	toilet paper
bubble bath	emery board	mouthwash	toiletries
clippers	eye shadow	nail polish	toilet water
cold cream	eyebrow pencil	orange stick	toothbrush
cologne	eyelash curler	perfume	toothpaste
coloring	eyeliner	polish remover	tooth powder
comb	face powder	powder	tweezers
compact	false eyelashes	powder puff	

Bed Types

angel bed	bunk bed	cot	divan
bassinet	camp bed	cradle	double bed
bedstead	canopy	crib	double bunk
berth	Colonial bed	daybed	feather bed

foldaway bed
folding bed
four-poster bed
French bed
full-size bed
futon
half-tester
hammock

Hollywood bed
hospital bed
king-size bed
Murphy bed
pallet
palliasse
plank bed
poster bed

queen-size bed
rollaway
single bed
sleeper
sleigh bed
sofa bed
spring bed
studio couch

tent bed
trestle bed
truckle bed
trundle bed
twin bed
waterbed or water bed

BEEF CUTS

arm pot roast
back ribs
blade rib roast
blade roast
boneless neck
boneless rump roast
bottom round roast
brisket
chateaubriand
chuck
chuck arm roast
chuck shoulder pot roast
chuck steak
club steak
crosscut shank
cross rib roast

cross ribs
Delmonico steak
eye of the round
filet mignon
flank
flank steak
flat bone top sirloin
flatiron steak
foreshank
ground beef
hamburger
hanger steak
heel pot roast
hindshank
hip sirloin
London broil

market steak
minute steak
New York strip steak
noisette
Porterhouse ribs
Porterhouse steak
ribeye roast
ribeye steak
rib roast
ribs
rib steak
round
round bone top sirloin
round steak
round tip roast
round tip steak

rump roast
shank
shell steak
short loin
short plate
short ribs
sirloin or sirloin steak
sirloin strip steak
skirt steak
strip steak
T-bone steak
tenderloin
tenderloin roast
top blade steak
top loin steak

Beers

abbey ale

ale

altbier

amber ale

American lager

barley wine

Berliner weisse

Biere de Garde

bitter

bitter stout

bittersweet

blink beer

bock beer

Boston lager

brown ale

bruised beer

California Common
beer

caramel malt

cask-conditioned ale

chicha

choctaw beer

cold filtered beer

copper ale

craft-brewed beer

cream ale

crystal malt

dark beer

diat pils

doppelbock

dort

dortmunder

double cream sprout

draft beer

draught beer

dry beer

dunkel beer

dunkel weissbier

eisbock

faro

festbier

fire-brewed beer

framboise

fruit beer

German lager

golden ale

gueuze

hefe weizen

home brew

ice beer

India pale ale

Irish stout

kellerbier

kolsch

krausen

kriek

kristall weizen

kruidenbier

Kulmbacher beer

kumiss

kvass

lager

lambic beer

light beer

loster bier

maibock

malt liquor

marzen

mead

melomel

microbrew beer

mild beer

Munchener

Munich beer

near beer

needled beer

nonalcoholic beer

nut brown ale

oatmeal stout

obergarig

old ale

organic beer

oscura

pale ale

Pilsner

poker beer

porter

rauchbier

saison

schenk beer

schwarzbier

Scotch ale

small beer

specialty malt

spruce beer

starkbier

steam beer

stock beer

stout

summer ale

Trappist

tripel beer

ur-bock

Vienna beer

weiss beer

weizenbier   wheat beer   winter beer   zwickelbier

Weizenbock   white beer   witbier

BELLS

air bell   cowbell   jingle bell   shop bell

alarm bell   curfew bell   Liberty Bell   signal bell

anchor bell   dinner bell   minute bell   sleigh bell

angelus bell   division bell   news bell   tap bell

Big Ben   doorbell   night bell   telephone bell

bourdon   engine bell   pancake bell   tocsin

breakfast bell   fire bell   passing bell   vesper bell

call bell   fog bell   Sanctus bell   warning bell

chiming bell   gong bell   school bell   watch bell

church bell   handbell   shark bell   wind-bell

clinkum bell   harness bell   sheep bell

computer bell   hour bell   ship's bell

BEVERAGE TYPES

ade   black tea   cappuccino   coffee

alcoholic beverage bouillon   chicory   cola

ambrosia   brew   chocolate milk   cordial

apple juice   buttermilk   cider   cranberry juice

barley water   café au lait   club soda   cream soda

beef tea   café filter   cocktail   dairy drink

beer   café noir   cocoa   Darjeeling tea

birch beer   caffe latte   coconut milk   decaf

Earl Grey tea
egg cream
eggnog
espresso
float
frappé
fruit juice
ginger ale
ginger beer
ginseng tea
grapefruit juice
grape juice
green tea
herb tea
hot chocolate
ice cream soda
iced coffee

iced tea
ice water
infusion
juice
kava
kefir
koumiss
lemonade
limeade
liquor
malted milk
milk
milk shake
mineral water
mixed drink
mixer
mocha

mulled cider
nectar
orangeade
orange juice
orange pekoe tea
pearl milk tea
phosphate
pineapple juice
punch
root beer
root beer float
sarsaparilla
seltzer
shrub
soda or soda pop
soda water
soft drink

soybean milk
spice tea
spirits
sports drink
syllabub
tea
tisane
tomato juice
tonic water
Turkish coffee
vegetable juice
water
whiskey
wine
wine cooler

BIBLE BOOKS

OLD TESTAMENT
Amos
Chronicles 1
Chronicles 2
Daniel
Deuteronomy
Ecclesiastes
Esther

Exodus
Ezekiel
Ezra
Genesis
Habakkuk
Haggai
Hosea
Isaiah

Jeremiah
Job
Joel
Jonah
Joshua
Judges
Kings 1
Kings 2

Lamentations
Leviticus
Malachi
Micah
Nahum
Nehemiah
Numbers
Obadiah

Proverbs

Psalms

Ruth

Samuel 1

Samuel 2

Song of Songs or
Song of Solomon

Zechariah

Zephaniah

NEW TESTAMENT

Acts of the Apostles

Additions to the
Book of Daniel

Additions to the
Book of Esther

Baruch

Book of
Ecclesiasticus by
Sirach

Book of Judith

Book of Revelation
or The Apocalypse

Book of Tobit or
Book of Tobias

Books of Esdras

Books of the
Maccabees

Colossians

Corinthians 1

Corinthians 2

Ephesians

Galatians

James

John

John 1

John 2

John 3

Jude

Letter of Jeremiah

Letter to the
Hebrews

Luke

Mark

Matthew

Peter 1

Peter 2

Philemon

Philippians

Romans

Thessalonians 1

Thessalonians 2

Timothy 1

Timothy 2

Titus

Wisdom of Solomon

BIBLIOGRAPHY TYPES

analytic bibliography

annotated
bibliography

annual bibliography

author bibliography

bibliography of
bibliographies

biobibliography

cartobibliography

critical bibliography

cumulative
bibliography

current bibliography

descriptive
bibliography

historical
bibliography

local bibliography

national bibliography

period bibliography

research bibliography

retrospective
bibliography

selective bibliography

serial bibliography

statistical
bibliography

subject bibliography

textual bibliography

trade bibliography

BICYCLE TYPES

BMX bicycle

comfort bike

cruiser

dirt bike

electric bicycle

exercise bicycle

freestyle bike high-riser

hybrid bicycle

jumping bike

low-rider

monkey bike

motor bicycle

mountain bike

ordinary

pedal bicycle

penny-farthing

push bike

quadricycle

racing bicycle

recumbent bicycle

road bicycle

sidewalk bicycle

stationary bicycle

tandem bicycle

ten-speed

three-wheeler

touring bicycle

trail bike

tricycle

two-wheeler

unicycle

velocipede

water cycle

BILL OF RIGHTS

The Bill of Rights is the first 10 amendments to the United States Constitution. This list of amendments was adopted as a single unit on December 15, 1791. It constitutes a collection of mutually reinforcing guarantees of individual rights and of limitations on federal and state governments.

All powers not delegated to the federal government are reserved to the states, or to the people.

Freedom of speech, press, assembly, and religion.

No arrest without a grand jury indictment; no double jeopardy; no taking of life, liberty or property without due process of law or of private property for public use without just compensation.

No excessive bail or fines or cruel or unusual punishment.

No requirement to quarter troops in peacetime.

No unreasonable searches and seizures.

Right to a public and speedy trial; right to counsel.

Right to a trial by jury.

The right to bear arms.

The rights of the people are not to be understood as limited to those enumerated.

BILLIARDS SHOTS

anchor shot
bank shot
break
bricole
carambole
carom

combination shot
draw shot
follow shot
gather shot
jump shot
massé shot

natural
nip draw
off-the-rail shot
rail shot
safety
scratch

spread
stab
straight shot

BIOLOGY BRANCHES

aerobiology
agrobiology
anatomy
aquatic biology
aquatic microbiology
autoecology
bacteriology
biobehavioral science
biochemical genetics
biochemistry
biodynamics
bioecology
biogeography
biometrics
bionics
biophysics
bioremediation

biostatistics
biotechnology
biothermodynamics
botany
cell biology
cell physiology
chronobiology
cryobiochemistry
cryobiology
cytogenetics
cytology
cytotaxonomy
ecology
electro-biology
electrophysiology
embryology
enzymology

ethnobiology
eugenics
evolution
exobiology genetics
genomics
gnotobiosis
histology
human ecology
hydrobiology
hydrology
limnology
mammalogy
marine biology
mathematical biology
medicine
microbiology
molecular biology

morphology
natural classification
natural history
neurobiology
neurochemistry
neuroendocrinology
neurogenetics
neuroscience
organology
ornithology
paleontology
palynology
parasitology
photobiology
phylogenetic classification
physiology

population biology   radiobiology   taxonomy   zoology

population genetics   sociobiology   teratology

primatology   somatology   virology

psychobiology   synecology   zoogeography

BIRD FEATHER TYPES

contour feather   down feather or   primary feather or   wing feather
                       plumule   flight feather
covert feather or
roost feather   filoplume   tail feather

BIRD FEET TYPES

lobate-toed foot   perching bird foot   taloned foot   webbed foot

BIRD ORDERS

Anseriformes
(ducks)

Apodiformes
(hummingbirds,
swifts)

Apterygiformes
(kiwis)

Caprimulgiformes
(nightjars)

Casuariiformes
(cassowaries)

Charadriiformes
(gulls, plovers, terns,
waders)

Ciconiiformes
(herons, storks)

Coliiformes
(mousebirds)

Columbiformes
(pigeons)

Coraciiformes
(hoopoes, hornbills,
kingfishers, touans)

Cuculiformes
(cuckoos)

Falconiformes
(eagles, hawks,
vultures)

Galliformes (game
birds)

Gaviiformes (divers)

Gruiformes (cranes,
rails)

Passeriformes
(perching birds,
sparrows, thrushes)

Pelecaniformes
(cormorants,
gannets, pelicans)

Piciformes
(woodpeckers)

Podicipediformes
(grebes)

Proceillariiformes
(albatross, petrels)

Psittaciformes
(cockatoos, parrots)

Pteroclidiformes
(sand grouse)

Rheiformes (rheas)

Strigiformes (owls)

Struthioniformes (ostriches)

Trogoniformes (trogons

Spheniciformes (penguins)

BIRDS

albatross	bunting	cowbird	gnatcatcher
American eagle	butcherbird	crake	goldfinch
Audubon's warbler	buzzard	crane	gooey bird
auk	California condor	crow	goose
avocet	Canada goose	cuckoo	goshawk
bald eagle	canary	curlew	grackle
Baltimore oriole	cardinal	dipper	grebe
bank swallow	carrier pigeon	diver	greenfinch
barn owl	cassowary	dodo	grey heron
barn swallow	catbird	dove	grouse
bee-eater	chaffinch	duck	guinea fowl
bird of paradise	chewink	dunlin	gull
bittern	chickadee	eagle	harrier
blackbird	chicken	egret	hawk
blackcap	chicken hawk	emu	hawk owl
bluebill	chimney swift	falcon	heron
bluebird	cliff swallow	finch	homing pigeon
blue jay	cockatiel	flamingo	honeycreeper
bobolink	cockatoo	flycatcher	hoot owl
bowerbird	condor	frigate bird	hornbill
brown thrasher	coot	frogmouth	horned owl
bufflehead	corbie	fulmar	house finch
bullfinch	cormorant	gannet	hummingbird

ibis	mourning dove	pochard	skua
jackdaw	mud hen	prairie chicken	snipe
jaeger	myna	puffin	snowbird
jay	nighthawk	purple martin	snow bunting
kestrel	nightingale	quail	snow goose
king eider	notornis	raptor	songbird
kingfisher	nutcracker	ratite	song thrush
kite	oriole	raven	sparrow
kiwi	osprey	razorbill	spoonbill
kookaburra	ostrich	redbird	starling
lapwing	ouzel	redpoll	stork
lark	owl	redwing	sunbird
linnet	oystercatcher	reedbird	surfbird
loon	parakeet	rhea	swallow
lory	parrot	ring-necked duck	swan
lovebird	partridge	roadrunner	takahe
macaw	passenger pigeon	robin	tern
magpie	peacock	rook	thrasher
mallard	peafowl	sandpiper	thrush
manakin	pelican	sapsucker	tit
mandarin duck	penguin	scissortail	titmouse
man-o-war bird	petrel	screech owl	toucan
martin	pewit	seabird	towhee
mavis	pheasant	sea gull	turkey
meadowlark	pigeon	secretary bird	turkey buzzard
merlin	pigeon hawk	shag	turkey vulture
mockingbird	pintail	shama	turtledove
moorhen	pipit	shelduck	vulture
moundbird	plover	shrike	wader

wagtail	weaverbird	woodcreeper	yellow finch
warble	whippoorwill	wood owl	yellowhammer
waterfowl	whitethroat	woodpecker	
water hen	wigeon	wren	
waxbill	woodcock	yellowbird	

BIRDS THAT CANNOT FLY

cassowary	emu	moa	rail
cormorant	great auk	nandu	rhea
dinornis	kakapo	ostrich	
dodo	kiwi	penguin	

BIRDS, CAGED

avadavat	cockatiel	jako	parakeet
budgerigar	cockatoo	Java sparrow	parrot
cageling	estrildine finch	lovebird	thrush
canary	finch	macaw	waxbill
cardueline finch	grassfinch	myna	
chaffinch	hill mynah	nightingale	

BIRDS, EXTINCT

Ornithologists estimate that there have been 150,000 avian species since birds first appeared millions of years ago. If that figure is close to being correct, then almost 94 percent of those species have gone extinct over time.

archaeopteryx	great auk	jibi	solitaire
dodo	huia	moa	
elephant bird	ichthyornis	passenger pigeon	

BIRDS, GAME

In gastronomy, game birds are wild birds suitable for food.

black-bellied plover	fighting cock	peafowl	stone curlew
black duck	francolin	pheasant	thrush
black grouse	golden pheasant	pigeon	turkey
bobwhite	goose	plover	waterfowl
bustard	grouse	ptarmigan	wild duck
capercaillie	guinea fowl	quail	wildfowl
chukar	hazel grouse	rail	wild turkey
coot	hazel hen	red grouse	willow grouse
crested guinea fowl	lark	ring-necked pheasant	wing game
curassow	moorfowl	ruffed grouse	woodcock
dove	mud hen	sage grouse	woodgrouse
duck	partridge	snipe	

BIRDS, LAND AND SONG

American eagle	Baltimore oriole	bee-eater	Blackburnian warbler
ani	bank swallow	bellbird	blackcap
antbird	barbet	bird of paradise	bluebill
Audubon's warbler	barn owl	black grouse	bluebird
bald eagle	barn swallow	blackbird	blue jay

bobolink

bobwhite quail

bowerbird

broadbill

brown thrasher

brown thrush

brush turkey

budgerigar

bulbul

bullfinch

bunting

bush tit

bush wren

bustard

butcherbird

button quail

buzzard

California condor

canary

capercallie

caracara

cardinal

cassowary

catbird

cattle egret

cedar bird

cedar waxwing

chaffinch

chat

chewink

chickadee

chicken

chicken hawk

chiffchaff

chimney swift

chipping sparrow

cliff swallow

cockatiel

cockatoo

cock-of-the-rock

condor

corbie

cotinga

cowbird

crane

creeper

crossbill

crow

cuckoo

culver

curassow

dipper

dodo

dove

drongo

eagle

egret

emu

English sparrow

erne

falcon

finch

flicker

flycatcher

francolin

frogmouth

gnatcatcher

goatsucker

golden eagle

goldfinch

goshawk

grackle

grosbeak

grouse

guacharo

guan

guinea fowl

gyrfacon

harpy eagle

harrier

hawk

hawk owl

hemipode

hermit thrush

hoatzin

hobby

honey guide

honeycreeper

hoopoe

hoot owl

hornbill

horned owl

horned screamer

house finch

house martin

hummingbird

indigo bunting

ivory-billed
woodpecker

jacamar

jackdaw

jay

junco

jungle fowl

kea

kestrel

killdeer

kingbird

kinglet

kite

kiwi

kookaburra

lammergeier

lanner

lapwing

lark

laughing jackass

linnet

lorikeet

lorry

lovebird

lyrebird

macaw

magpie

mallee fowl

manakin

marabou

martin

mavis

meadowlark

megapode

merle

merlin

mistle thrush

moa

mockingbird

motmot

moundbird

mound builder

mourning dove

myna or mynah

nighthawk

nightingale

nightjar

notornis

nutcracker

nuthatch

oilbird

oriole

ortolan

ostrich

ouzel

ovenbird

owl

oxpecker

parakeet

parrot

partridge

passenger pigeon

peacock

peafowl

peregrine falcon

pewee

pheasant

phoebe

pigeon

pigeon hawk

pipit

pitta

plover

potoo

prairie chicken

ptarmigan

purple finch

purple martin

quail

quelea

quetzal

raptor

raven

redbird

red grouse

red-headed
woodpecker

redpoll

redstart

redwing

red-winged blackbird

reedbird

reed bunting

rhea

ringdove

ring-necked pheasant

ring ouzel

roadrunner

robin

rock dove

roller

rook

rosella

ruffed grouse

sage grouse

sage hen

sapsucker

scarlet tanager

scissortail

screamer

screech owl

scrub fowl

secretary bird

seriema

shama

shrike

siskin

snipe

snowbird

snow bunting

solitaire

song sparrow

song thrush

sparrow

sparrow hawk

starling

stork

suboscine

sunbird

sun bittern

swallow

swift

swiftlet

tanager

tercel

thrasher

thrush

tinamou

tit

titlark

titmouse

tody

toucan

touraco

towhee

tragopan

tree swallow

trogon

troupial

trumpeter

turkey

turkey buzzard

turkey vulture

turtledove

tyrant flycatcher

veery

vesper sparrow

vireo

vulture

wagtail

warbler

water ouzel

water thrush

waxbill

waxwing

weaver

wheatear

whippoorwill

whistler

white-eye

whydah

woodcock

woodcreeper

wood owl

woodpecker

wood pigeon

wood warbler

wren

wren-tit

wryneck

yellowbird

yellow finch

yellowhammer

yellow-rumped warbler

yellowthroat

zebra finch

BIRDS, PREDATORY

accipiter

American eagle

bald eagle

barn owl

bird of jove

bird of minerva

bird of night

buzzard

California condor

caracara

chicken hawk

condor

eagle

erne

falcon

fish hawk

golden eagle

goshawk

gyrfalcon

harpy eagle

harrier

hawk

hawk owl

hobby

hoot owl

horned owl

jaeger

kestrel

kite

lammergeier

lanner

merlin

osprey

owl

peregrine falcon

pigeon hawk

raptor

screech owl

sea eagle

secretary bird

shrike

skua

sparrow hawk

tercel

turkey buzzard

turkey vulture

vulture

wood owl

Birds, Sea

albatross

anhinga

auk

auklet

avocet

barnacle goose

belted kingfisher

bittern

bluebill

booby

brant

bufflehead

Canada goose

canvasback duck

coot

cormorant

corn crake

crake

crane

curlew

dabbling duck

dabchick darter

diver

dovekie

duck

dunlin

egret

eider

erne

fish hawk

flamingo

frigate bird

fulmar

gallinule

gannet

garganey

godwit

goldeneye

gooney bird

goose

graylag

grebe

greenshank

guillemot

gull

halycon

hammerhead

heron

honker

ibis

jacana

jaeger

killdeer

kingfisher

kittiwake

knot

lily-trotter

limpkin

loon

mallard

mandarin duck

man-o-war bird

marabou

merganser

mew

moorhen

murre

mute swan

muttonbird

nene

night heron

notornis

osprey

ostercatcher

pelican

penguin

petrel

pewit

pharlarope

pintail

plover

pochard

puffin

rail

razorbill

redhead

redshank

ring-necked duck

ring ouzel

ruddy duck

sacred ibis

sanderling

sandpiper

scaup

scoter

sea duck

sea eagle

seafowl

sea gull

sea hen

sea raven

shearwater

sheldrake

shoebill

shoveler

skimmer

skua

snipe

snow goose

spoonbill

stilt

stint

stone curlew

stork

stormy petrel

surfbird

swan

swan goose

takae

teal

tern

tropic bird

turnstone

water hen

waterfowl

whimbrel

whooper swan

widgeon

willet

wood duck

yellowlegs

BIRTHDAY FLOWERS AND BIRTHSTONES

January: carnation, snowdrop; garnet

February: violet, primrose; amethyst

March: jonquil, violet; jasper, bloodstone, aquamarine

April: daisy, sweet pea; sapphire, diamond

May: hawthorn, lily of the valley; agate, emerald

June: rose, honeysuckle; emerald, pearl, moonstone, alexandrite

July: larkspur, water lily; onyx, ruby

August: gladiolus, poppy; carnelian, sardonyx, peridot

September: morning glory, aster; chrysolite, sapphire

October: calendula, cosmos; aquamarine, opal, tourmaline

November: chrysanthemum; topaz

December: narcissus, holly, poinsettia; ruby, turquoise, zircon

BLACK COLOR VARIETIES

aniline black

arsenic black

black

blue-black

Brunswick black

carbon black

charcoal black

chrome black

coal black

corbeau

direct black

drop black

ebony

ink black

ivory black

japan

jet

jet black

lampblack

night black

nigrosine

pitch-black

Prussian black

pure black

raven black

sable

slate black

sloe black

soot black

subfusc

sulfur black

BLACKBERRY VARIETIES

Agawam

Allen

amber

Apache

Arapaho

black

Black Butte

Black Satin

Boyne

Briton

Brunton

conical

Chester

Chickasaw

Choctaw

Cox

Crandall

Dallas

Early Harvest

Eldorado

Erie

Evergreen

Heritage

Hull

Iceberg

Illini Hardy

Killarney

Kiowa

Kittatinny

Latham

Lawton

Logan

Mammoth

Mercereau

Minnewaska

Navaho

oval

Perron Noir

purple

Rathbun

red

Reveille

round

Shawnee

Snyder

Stone

Taylor

thornless

thorny

Triple Crown

Triumph

Wachusett

Ward

white

Wilson

yellow

BLANKETS

Afghan

baby

bed

blanket stitch

camping

carriage

cat

crib

dog

doll

electric

featherstitch

horse

hospital

Hudson's Bay

lap robe

mackinaw

manta

military

quarter

receiving   sarape   stable   thermal

saddle   security   steamship

BLOOD CELL TYPES

Blood cell formation is a continuous process by which the cellular constituents of blood are replenished as needed. Blood cells do not originate in the bloodstream itself but in specific blood-forming organs, including bone marrow, lymphatic tissues, tissues of the spleen, liver, lymph nodes, and other organs.

acanthocyte   killer cell   microcyte   reticulocyte

acidophil   leucocyte or white   microphage   sickle cell

basophil   blood cell   monocyte   siderocyte

corpuscle   lymphocyte   myelocyte   spherocyte

eosinophil   macrocyte   neutrophil   target cell

erythrocyte or red   macrophage   plasma cell   thrombocyte or

blood cell   megaloblast   platelet   blood platelet

granulocyte   megalocyte

BLOOD TYPES

A-   AB+   O-   Rh-positive

A+   B-   O+

AB-   B+   Rh-negative

BLUE COLOR VARIETIES

air force blue   aquamarine   azulene   azurite blue

aniline blue   azo blue   azure   baby blue beryl

bice

blue

blueberry

bluebonnet

blue-gray

blue-green

blue turquoise

blue-violet

bright blue

Brunswick blue

cadet blue

calamine blue

cerulean

Chinese blue

cobalt blue

Copenhagen blue

cornflower

cyan

dark blue

daylight blue

deep blue

delft blue

denim blue

Dresden blue

electric blue

Empire blue

flag blue

French blue

gentian blue

gray-blue

greenish blue

Havana lake

Helvetia blue

huckleberry

hyacinth

hydrangea

ice blue

indigo

isamine blue

jouvence

kingfisher-blue

lacmoid

lapis lazuli

lavender blue

light blue

lucerne

lupine

madder blue

marine blue

midnight blue

milori blue

Napoleon blue

navy blue or navy

pale blue

peacock blue

perse

Persian blue

powder blue

Prussian blue

purple-blue

reddish blue

robin's-egg blue

royal blue

sapphire blue

Saxe blue

sea blue

sky blue

slate blue

smalt

smoke blue

steel blue

teal blue

turquoise

ultramarine

Venetian blue

violet-blue

water blue

Wedgwood blue

wisteria blue

woad

zaffer

BODY SYSTEMS

circulatory

digestive

endocrine

excretory

integumentary (skin)

lymphatic

musculoskeletal

nervous

reproductive

respiratory

urinary

BODY TYPES

ectomorph   endomorph   mesomorph

BOMB TYPES

aerial bomb

antiballistic missile

antimissile missile

antipersonnel bomb

antisubmarine bomb

ashcan

atomic bomb

azon bomb ballistic
missile

blockbuster

buzz bomb

cherry bomb

citybuster

claymore mine

cluster

cluster bomb

concussion bomb

conventional bomb

delayed-action bomb

demolition bomb

depth charge

dynamite

dynamite bomb

explosive

fireball

fire bomb

firecracker

fission bomb

fougasse

fragmentation bomb

fuel-air explosive

fusion bomb

gas bomb

grenade

hand grenade

hydrobomb

hydrogen bomb

incendiary bomb

intercontinental
ballistic missile

MIRV

missile

Molotov cocktail

napalm

neutron bomb

nitroglycerin

nuclear bomb

nuke

Patriot

petard

pineapple

pipe bomb

plastic explosive

plutonium bomb

robot bomb

rocket

rocket bomb

satchel charge

Scud

Sidewinder

smart bomb

smoke bomb

stink bomb

surface-to-air missile

tear-gas bomb

thermonuclear bomb

time bomb

TNT

torpedo

TOW

V-1 rocket

V-2 rocket

warhead

BOND TYPES

In finance, a bond is a loan contract issued by a local, state, and national government or by a private corporation specifying an obligation to return borrowed funds. The borrower promises to pay interest on the debt when due at a stipulated percentage of the face value (apparent worth as opposed to real worth) and to redeem the face value of the bond at maturity in legal tender.

adjustment bond

admiralty bond

annuity bond

appreciation bond

assented bond

asset-backed bond

assumed bond

average bond

baby bond

bail bond

bearer bond

bearer certificate

bid bond

blanket bond

bond anticipation note

callable bond

collateral trust bond

commercial blanket bond

completion bond

consolidated stock

continued bond

contract bond

convertible bond

convertible debenture

corporate bond

coupon bond

court bond

currency bond

current income bond

debenture bond

deep-discount bond

defense bond

deferred bond

definitive bond

depository bond

discount bond

discovery bond

endorsed bond

equipment bond

equipment note

equipment trust

equipment trust bond

equipment trust certificate

extended bond

Fannie Mae bond

farm loan bond

Federal Agency bond

FICO bond

fiduciary bond

first mortgage bond or first

foreign bond

forfeiture bond

franchise bond

Freddie Mac bond

general mortgage bond

general obligation bond

gilt-edged bond

Ginnie Mae bond

gold bond

government bond

guaranteed bond

high-grade bond

highway bond

high-yield bond or junk bond

income bond

indenture

individual bond

installment bond

interchangeable bond

interim bond

joint bond

Liberty bond

license bond

long-term bond

lottery bond

mortgage-backed bond

municipal bond

negotiable bond

noncallable bond

nonnegotiable bond

optional bond

par bond

participating bond

performance bond

perpetual bond

premium bond

purchase money bond

redeemable bond

refunding bond

registered bond

registered certificate

revenue bond

savings bond

second mortgage bond

secured bond

serial bond

Series EE bond

Series HH bond

short-term bond

sinking-fund bond

small bond

state bond

subordinated bond

surety bond

tax anticipation note

tax-exempt bond

tax-free bond

treasury bill

treasury bond

treasury note

trust indenture

trustee mortgage bond

turnpike bond

unsecured bond

utility bond

voting bond

war bond

Z-bond

zero coupon bond

BONES, HUMAN

acetabelum

aitchbone

alveolar arch

anvil or incus

astragalus or anklebone or talus

basioccipital bone

calcaneus or heel bone

calf bone

cannon bone

carpal bones or wrist bones

chinbone

clavicle or collarbone

coccyx or tailbone

costa

cranial bones

cranium

cuboid bone

edgebone

ethmoid bone

femur or thighbone

fibula

floating rib

frontal bone

funny bone

gladiolus

hallux or big toe

haunch bone

humerus

hyoid or lingual bone

ilium

incisive bone

inferior maxillary

innominate bone or hipbone

interparietal bone

ischium

lacrimal bone

lunate bone or semilunar bone

malleus or hammer

mandible and maxilla or jawbone

manubrium

mastoid bone

maxillary

metacarpal bones

metatarsal bones

nasal bone

navicular bone or scaphoid bone

occipital bone

palate bone

palatine bone

parietal bone

patella or kneecap or whirl bone or kneepad

pectoral girdle

pelvis

periotic bone

petrosal bone or petrous bone

phalanx or phalanges

pisiform

pterygoid bone

pubis or pubic bone

rachidial

radius

rib

sacrum

scapula or shoulder blade

sesamoid bones

shinbone or tibia

shoulder blade scapula

skull

sphenoid bone

spinal column or backbone or spine or vertebral column

stapes or stirrup bone

sternum or breastbone

styloid process

tarsus bones

temporal bone

tibia or shinbone

trapezium

trapezoid

ulna

vertebra

vomer

zygomatic bone or cheekbone

Book Types

almagest

almanac

annals

anthology

armorial

atlas

bestiary

bible

bilingual dictionary

biographical dictionary

breviary

cambist

catalog

catechism

chapbook

children's book

children's dictionary

classic

coffee-table book

college dictionary

coloring book

commonplace book

concordance

cookbook

dictionary

directory

encyclopedia

etymological dictionary

festschrift

field guide

foreign-language dictionary

formulary

gazetteer

guidebook

handbook

herbal

hornbook

how-to-book

idioms dictionary

incunabulum

index

lectionary

lexicon

manual

missal

monograph

omnibus

pharmacopoeia/ dispensatory

picture book

primer

psalter

reference book

reprint

rhyming dictionary

schoolbook

storybook

telephone book

text book

thesaurus

trade book

trilogy

unabridged dictionary

usage dictionary

vade mecum

variorum

BOTANY BRANCHES

agriculture

agrobiology

agronomy

agrostology

algology

applied botany

aquiculture

bacteriology

botanical histochemistry

bryology

carpology

dendrology

descriptive botany

desmidiology

economic botany

ethnobotany

evolution

floriculture

floristics

forestry

fungology

genetics

geobotany

gnotobiology

hepaticology

histology

horticulture

hydrophytology

hydroponics

mycology

olericulture

orchidology

paleobotany

palynology

phycology

physiology

phytobiology

phytochemistry

phytoecology

phytography

phytology

phytosociology

plant anatomy

plant biochemistry

plant breeding

plant cytology

plant ecology

plant geography

plant morphology

plant pathology

plant physiology

plant taxonomy

pomology

pteridology

research botany

seed biology

silviculture

taxonomy

BOTTLES

amphora

beaker

calabash

canteen

carafe

carboy

caster

cooler

cruet

cruse

decanter

demijohn

ewer

fifth

flacon

flagon

flask
flasket
ginger jar
gourd
hip flask
hot-water bottle
jar

jeroboam
jug
keg
krater
lota
magnum
olla

phial
pocket flask
potiche
rehoboam
schooner
squeeze bottle
stoup

tankard
thermos
vacuum bottle
vial
vinaigrette

BOWLING SCORES

5–7 split
7–10 split
8–10 split
baby split or Murphy
baby split with company
bed posts
big ears
bucket

Christmas tree
Cincinnati
dime store
double pinochle
double wood or tandem
fence
fit-in split
fit split

Golden Gate
Greek church
kresge
left fence
light seven
lily
mother-in-law
poison ivy

railroad
right fence
sour apple
strike split
three quarter bucket
washout
Woolworth

BOXES AND CASES

ammunition box
attaché case
ballot box
bandolier
billfold
bin

boot
bread box
briefcase
caisson
card case
carton

casculum
casket
cedar chest
chest
cigarette case
cist

clamshell
coffer
coffin
compact
crate
dispatch box

ditty box
drawer
envelope
etui
footlocker
glasses case
hatbox
hope chest
humidor

hutch
laptop case
locker
mailbox
matchbox
money box
nesting box
package
packet

packing case
parcel
pillbox
portfolio
safe-deposit box
sarcophagus
shadow box
snuffbox
strongbox

suitcase
tea chest
till
tinderbox
trunk
vanity case
wallet

BOXING PUNCHES

backhand
backstroke
body blow
bolo punch
chop
combination
corkscrew punch
counter-punch
cross
flanker

follow-up
haymaker
hook
jab
kidney punch
knockdown punch
knockout punch
ko punch
left
left hook

Long Melford
mishit
one-two one-two punch
rabbit punch
right hook
right round-arm blow
roundhouse
short-arm blow
sideswipe

sidewinder
sucker punch
solar-plexus punch
straight punch
straight right hand punch
Sunday punch
swing
swipe
uppercut

BOXING WEIGHTS

bantamweight
cruiserweight
featherweight

flyweight
heavyweight
junior bantamweight

junior featherweight
junior flyweight
junior lightweight

junior middleweight
junior welterweight
light flyweight

light heavyweight

light middleweight

lightweight

light welterweight

middleweight

strawweight

super featherweight

super heavyweight

super middleweight

super welterweight

welterweight

Boy Scout Merit Badges

American business

American cultures

American heritage

American labor

Animal science

Archaeology

Archery

Architecture

Art

Astronomy

Athletics

Atomic energy

Auto mechanics

Aviation

Backpacking

Basketry

Bird study

Bugling

Camping

Canoeing

Chemistry

Cinematography

Citizenship in the community

Citizenship in the nation

Citizenship in the world

Climbing

Coin collecting

Collections

Communications

Computers

Cooking

Crime prevention

Cycling

Dentistry

Disabilities awareness

Dog care

Drafting

Electricity

Electronics

Emergency preparedness

Energy

Engineering

Entrepreneurship

Environmental science

Family life

Farm mechanics

Fingerprinting

Fire safety

First aid

Fish and wildlife management

Fishing

Fly fishing

Forestry

Gardening

Genealogy

Geology

Golf

Graphic arts

Hiking

Home repairs

Horsemanship

Indian lore

Insect study

Journalism

Landscape architecture

Law

Leatherwork

Lifesaving

Mammal study

Medicine

Metalwork

Model design and building

Motorboating

Music

Nature

Oceanography

Orienteering

Painting

Personal fitness

Personal management

Pets

Photography

Pioneering

Plant science

Plumbing

Pottery

Public health

Public speaking

Pulp and paper

Radio

Railroading

Reading

Reptile and amphibian study

Rifle shooting

Rowing

Safety

Salesmanship

Scholarship

Sculpture

Shotgun shooting

Skating

Small-boat sailing

Snow sports

Soil and water conservation

Space exploration

Sports

Stamp collecting

Surveying

Swimming

Textile

Theater

Traffic safety

Truck transportation

Veterinary medicine

Waterskiing

Weather

Whitewater

Wilderness survival

Wood carving

Woodwork

BRACKETS

ancon bracket

angle bracket

angle iron bracket

brace bracket

cantilever bracket

cheek bracket

console bracket

corbel bracket

curly bracket or brace

curtain bracket

gusset bracket

modillion bracket

peg-board bracket

plant-hanging bracket

rail bracket

round bracket or parenthesis

shade bracket

shelf bracket

shoulder bracket

spring-loaded folding bracket

square bracket or crochet

strut bracket

thumbscrew bracket

truss bracket

BRAIN PARTS AND REGIONS

amygdala

appestat

association area

basal ganglia

brain stem

Broca's area

caudate nucleus

central sulcus

cerebellum

cerebral aqueduct

cerebral cortex

cerebral hemisphere

cerebrum

choroid plexus

cingulum

claustrum

commissure

cornu

corpus callosum

corpus striatum

crus cerebri

culmen

Deiters' nucleus

diencephalon

ependyma

flocculus

forebrain

fornix

frontal lobe

globus pallidus

gray matter

gyrus

hindbrain

hippocampus

hypercolumn

hypothalamus

infundibulum

insula

lateral ventricle

left brain

limbic system

lobe

medulla oblongata

meninges

mesencephalon

midbrain

motor cortex

neencephalon

occipital lobe

optic chiasma

optic cup

palaeencephalon

parietal lobe

pineal body

pituitary gland

pons

pons Varolii

prosencephalon

putamen

rhombencephalon

right brain

satiety center

speech center

splenium

sulcus

Sylvian fissure

telencephalon

temporal lobe

thalamus

third ventricle

vasomotor center

ventricle

vermis

white matter

BRAND NAMES THAT HAVE BECOME WORDS

aspirin

band-aid

corn flakes

cube steak

dry ice

escalator

excelsior

gramophone

granola

gunk

heroin

hoover

kerosene

lanolin

linoleum

mimeograph

moxie

nylon

raisin bran

shredded wheat

simonize

spam

teflon

thermos

trampoline

yo-yo

zipper

Brass Varieties

alpha
beta
brazen yellow
calamine
cartridge
common

coppered
deep-yellow
English
green
horse
low

naval
orange
orichalc
ormolu
pale-yellow
prince's metal

red
red-yellow
violet
white

Breads

altar bread
anadama
bagel
baguette
banana bread
bannock
batter bread
bialy
black bread
bleeding bread
Boston brown bread
brioche
brown bread
bun
caraway seed bread
challah
chapatti

ciabatta
cinnamon bread
corn bread
corn pone
cottage loaf
crackling bread
crescent roll
croissant
crouton
crumpet
dark bread
dinner roll
egg bread
English muffin
enriched bread
finger roll
flatbread

foccaccia
French bread
garlic bread
graham bread
grissini
holiday bread
hush puppy
Irish soda bread
Italian bread
Jewish rye
Kaiser roll
landbroed
lavash
matzo
melba toast
monkey bread
muffin

non-wheat bread
non-yeast bread
nut bread
oatcake
oatmeal bread
oil-rich bread
onion roll
Parker House roll
pita
plain white roll
popover
poppy-seed plait
Portuguese
potato bread
pretzel
pulled bread
pumpernickel bread

raisin bread

roll or small bread

rusk

Russian rye

rye bread

salt-rising bread

scone

semolina

seven-grain

sourdough bread

stollen

sweet bread

tea bread

tortilla

unleavened bread

vasilopita

Vienna bread

wafer bread

white bread

whole meal bread

whole wheat bread

zwieback

BRICKS, STONES, AND TILES

acoustical tile

adobe

asbestos tile

ashlar

asphalt

asphalt shingle

asphalt tile

azulejo

blacktop

bluestone

brickface

brownstone

capstone

castiron

cast stone

ceiling tile

cement

ceramic

ceramic tile

cinderblock

clay brick

cobble

cobblestone

common brick

concrete

copestone

cork tile

cullet

curbing

curbstone

cut stone

damask

face brick

ferroconcrete

firebrick

flag

flagstone

freestone

glass brick

glass tile

limestone

macadam

marble

marl

masonry

masonry veneer

pantile

prestressed concrete

quarry tile

red brick

reinforced concrete

roof tile

rough-cut stone

rubble

rubblework

shake

slate

steel plate

terra cotta

tessera

BRIDGE BIDS

approach bid

artificial bid

asking bid

bidding convention

borderline bid

business double

control bid

cue-bid

demand bid

double

forcing bid

forcing pass

free bid

grand slam

insufficient bid

jump bid

jump shift

natural bid

no-trump bid

one-over-one

opening bid

original bid

overbid

pass

preemptive bid

preference bid

psychic bid

rebid

redouble

renege

response

reverse bid

sacrifice bid

score bid

second bid

shift bid

shut-out bid

sign-off

skip bid

slam bid

suit bid

takeout bid

takeout double

two-bid

underbid

weak-two bid

BRIDGE HANDS

balanced hand

closed hand

doubleton

exposed hand

goulash hand

helping hand

long suit

long trump

major tenace

minor tenace

no-trumper

offensive strength

perfect tenace

piano hand

pianola hand

short suit

side strength

singleton

split hand

tenace

two-suiter

unbalanced hand

void

yarborough

BRIDGES

aqueduct

arch bridge

Bailey bridge

bascule bridge

beam bridge

bridle-chord bridge

cable-stay bridge

caisson

cantilever bridge

catenary bridge

chain bridge

clapper bridge

deck arch bridge

double-leaf bascule bridge

drawbridge

fixed bridge

floating bridge

gangplank

girder bridge

half-through arch bridge

humpback bridge

lift bridge

multiple-span beam bridge

portal bridge

single-leaf bascule bridge

single-span beam bridge

skew brings

suspension bridge

swing bridge

through arch bridge

transporter bridge

vertical-lift bridge

BRONZE VARIETIES

alpha bronze

aluminum bronze

antimonial bronze

antique bronze

bell bronze

beryllium bronze

coinage bronze

commercial bronze

gilt bronze

leaded bronze

manganese bronze

naval bronze

nickel bronze

phosphor bronze

silicon bronze

statuary bronze

steel bronze tobin bronze

tungsten bronze

white bronze

BROWN COLOR VARIETIES

acorn

alesan

amber

anthracene

antique bronze

antique brown

antique drab

auburn

autumn leaf

baize

bay

beaver

beige

biscuit

Bismarck brown

bistre

bone brown

Bordeaux

brick

brindle

bronze

brown

brown madder

brunet

brunette

buff

burgundy

burnt almond

burnt ocher

burnt sienna

burnt umber

butternut

café au lait

café noir

camel

caramel

Castilian brown	Havana brown	nutmeg	seal
chestnut	hazel	nutria	sedge
chocolate	henna	oatmeal	sepia
cinnamon	Italian earth	ocher	sienna
cocoa	Italian ocher	olive brown	sorrel
coconut	ivory brown	orange-brown	suntan
coffee	khaki	otter brown	tan
Cologne brown	leather	oxblood	tanaura
copper	liege	pale brown	taupe
cordovan	light brown	peat-brown	tawny
dark brown	light red-brown	peppercorn	terra cotta
dead leaf	liver brown	piccolpasso	terra sienna
doeskin	madder brown	pongee	terra umbra
drab	mahogany	putty	Titian
Dresden brown	manganese brown	raffia	toast
dun	manila	raw sienna	topaz
earth	maple sugar	raw umber	tortoiseshell
ecru	Mars brown	reddish-brown	umber
fallow	mineral brown	roan	Vandyke brown
fawn	mink	russet	walnut
foliage brown	mocha	rust	yellow-brown
fox	nougat	sand	
ginger	nut	sandalwood	

BRUSHES

acrylic brush	bamboo brush	bottle brush	bristle brush
air brush	body brush	bright brush	calligraphic brush

camel hair brush	funny brush	paintbrush	spotter
ceramic brush	gilder's tip brush	pan blender brush	steel brush
clothes brush	hairbrush or hair brush	paste brush	stencil brush
duster		pastel brush	striping brush
dusting brush	hake	sabeline brush	suede brush
easel brush	hard brush	sable brush	Sumi brush
fan brush	hat brush	script brush	toothbrush
faux finishing brush	lettering brush	scrub brush	utility brush
filbert brush	metallic brush	shader	varnish brush
fitch brush	nailbrush	shaving brush	wash brush
flat brush	numbered brush	shoe brush	watercolor brush
foam brush	ox hair brush	soft brush	wire brush

BUDDHA'S EIGHTFOLD PATH

The Eightfold Path teaches that the way Buddhists lead their lives should be correct in eight important aspects. Those who follow the noble Eightfold Path are freed from the suffering that is an essential part of human existence and are led ultimately to nirvana, or enlightenment.

Right action (not harming, not stealing, not overindulging)

Right effort (attempting to do meritorious things)

Right livelihood (earning a living by not harming others)

Right speech (not lying, criticizing, hurting with words)

Right concentration (meditation and avoidance of excess)

Right intentions (kindness and compassion)

Right mindfulness (being aware and alert)

Right understanding (seeing the world as it really is)

BUDDHA'S FOUR NOBLE TRUTHS

The Buddha taught the Four Noble Truths, which explain the Buddhist attitude toward suffering and how happiness and fulfillment can be achieved. The Truths say that suffering is always present in the world; that the human search for pleasure is the source of suffering; that it is possible to be free from these desires; and that the way is through the Eightfold Path. These four truths are universally recognized by Buddhist schools.

Life is full of suffering.	Suffering is caused by attachment, greed, or desire.	Suffering will end when we see the impermanence of everything.	There is a path to peace and contentment, the Eightfold Path.

BUDDHISM TYPES

Hinayana	Nikaya or Conservative	Soto	Vipassana or Insight Meditation
Jodo Shinshu	Nyigma-pa	Tantrism	Won
Kegon	Pure Land	Tendai	Yogacara
Lamaism	Rinzai	Theravada	Zen
Mahayana	Shingon	Tibetan Buddhism	
Nichiren		Vajrayana	

BUDGET TYPES

administrative	city	household	revenue estimate
allotment	equipment	long-term	short-term
annual	family	monitoring	state
appropriation	federal	operating	town
balanced	fixed	organization	
business	flexible	personal	
capital	governmental grant	project	

Building and Construction Types

adobe	carriage house	hermitage	maisonette
A-frame	castle	high-rise	mall
alcazar	chalet	hippodrome	manor
amphitheater	chateau	hogan	manse
apartment	church	homestead	mansion
arena	condominium	hostel	market
auditorium	conservatory	hotel	mobile home
aviary	coop	house	mosque
balok	cottage	houseboat	motel
barn	country house	hovel	mud hut
barracks	crib	hut	Nissen hut
basilica	dacha	hutch	obelisk
bathhouse	dormitory	igloo	outbuilding
bi-level	duplex	inn	outhouse
blockhouse	earth lodge	izba	pagoda
boardinghouse	farmhouse	jacal	palace
booth	flat	kennel	palazzo
bower	flatlet	kiosk	parsonage
bungalow	frame house	lake dwelling	pavilion
cabana	garage	lean-to	pen
cabin	gazebo	lighthouse	pension
campanile	grange	lodge	penthouse
Cape Cod cottage	greenhouse	loft	pied-a-terre
caravan	hall	log cabin	pile dwelling
caravansary	hangar	longhouse	posada

111

prefab
priory
pueblo
pyramid
Quonset hut
ranch house
rectory
resort
rest home
rialto
roadhouse
rotunda
saltbox
shack

shanty
shebang
shed
shop
skyscraper
split-level
stable
stadium
stall
stand
studio apartment
studio flat
stupa
supermarket

synagogue
tabernacle
tavern
temple
tenement
tent
tepee
terminal
terraced house
theater or theatre
tholos
town house
tract home
trailer

tree house
triplex
tupik
vicarage
villa
warehouse
washhouse
wickiup
wigwam
woodshed
yurt
ziggurat

BULLETS AND SHOT

ammunition
ball
bar shot
baton round
bird shot
buckshot
bullet
canister shot
cannon ball

case shot
chain shot
crossbar shot
duck shot
dumdum bullet
dust shot
expanding bullet
explosive bullet
grapeshot or grape

high-explosive shell
lead shot
manstopping bullet
pellet
plastic bullet
rifle ball
round shot
rubber bullet
shell

shrapnel
slug
small shot
soft-nosed bullet
split shot
swan shot
tracer bullet
wadcutter

BURIAL TYPES

barrow
beehive tomb
box grave
burial chamber
burial mound
catacombs
charnel house

cist
cist grave
cromlech
crypt
dolmen
grave
mastaba

mausoleum
mummy chamber
ossuary
passage grave
pit
pyramid
reliquary

sepulcher
shaft grave
shrine
stupa
tomb
tumulus
vault

BUTTERFLIES

admiral
Adonis blue
alpine
anglewing
arctoc
argis
azure
birdwing
blue butterfly
brown butterfly
buckeye
cabbage
cleopatra

comma
copper
danaid
dog face
dryad
emperor
fritillary
hairstreak
Hesperiidae
leaf butterfly
Lepidoptera
lycaenid
Lycaenidae

Megathymidae
Microlepidoptera
milkweed butterfly
monarch
nymph
nymphalid
Nymphalidae
owl butterfly
painted lady
papilionid
Papilionidae
peacock butterfly
pierid

Pieridae
plain tiger
red admiral
ringlet
satyrid
satyrid skipper
sulfur butterfly
swallowtail
tortoiseshell
vanessid
white
zebra

Cabbage Family

bok choy

broccoli

Brussels sprouts

Calabrese broccoli

cauliflower

celery cabbage

Chinese cabbage

chou

collard

green cabbage

head cabbage

Italian kale

kale

kohlrabi

Maori cabbage

meadow cabbage

Napa cabbage

pak choi

pickling cabbage

red cabbage

Savoy cabbage

sea cabbage

spring cabbage

sprouting broccoli

thousand-headed kale

white cabbage

wild cabbage

winter cabbage

Calculators

abacus

adding machine

arithmograph

arithmometer

calculating machine

cash register

compass

computer

counter

difference engine

electromechanical calculator

hand-held calculator

isograph

mechanical calculator

Napier's bones or rods

number-cruncher

online calculator

pocket calculator

programmable calculator

quipu

rule

scientific calculator

slide rule or sliding scale

suan pan

tabulator

tally or tally stick

totalizator

Turing machine

CALENDARS

Abyssinian

Aztec

Babylonian

Buddhist

Chinese

church or ecclesiastical

Egyptian

Episcopalian liturgical

French Revolutionary

Greek

Greek Orthodox

Gregorian

Hebrew

Hindu

Inca

Indian

Islamic

Jewish

Julian

lunar

lunisolar

Mayan

Mexican

Newgate

Orthodox Christian

perpetual

Roman

Roman Catholic

Runic

Sikhist or Sikh

solar

Western

CALISTHENIC EXERCISES

aerobics

chin-up

high jump

hop and balance

in-place running

jump and stretch

jumping jack

leg lift

push-up

rope skipping

shuffle

side bend

sit-up and leg stretch

sit-up or crunch

squat thrust

stepping

trunk twist

CALLIGRAPHY SCRIPTS

Batarde

Carolingian

Copperplate

Foundational

Gothic

Half Uncials

Italic

Roman capitals

Uncials

Versals

CAMERA LENSES

achromatic lens
adjustable-focus lens
anamorphic lens
anastigmatic lens
aplanatic lens
apochromatic lens
autofocus lens

close-up lens
convertible lens
fisheye lens
fixed-focus lens
long-focus lens
macro lens
manual-focus lens

normal lens
objective lens
portrait lens
process lens
semi-fisheye lens
shift/perspective-control lens

standard lens
stereo camera
telephoto lens
wide-angle lens
zoom lens

CAMERAS

35 mm camera
advanced photo system or APS
aerial-reconnaissance camera
animation camera
autofocus camera
bellows camera
box camera
camcorder
camera lucida
camera obscura
compact camera

digital camera
disc camera
disposable camera
electronic camera
fixed-focus camera
flash camera
folding camera
infrared camera
instant camera
lens-shutter camera
miniature camera
minicam

motion-picture camera
nannycam
panoramic camera
pinhole camera
point-and-shoot camera
Polaroid
portrait camera
rangefinder camera
reflex camera
single-lens reflex camera

single-use camera
stand camera
stereocamera
still camera
stop action
studio camera
surveillance camera
television camera
twin-lens reflex camera
underwater camera
video camera
view camera

CAMOUFLAGE CREATURES

Arctic fox

assassin bug

chameleon

copperband butterfly fish

crane-fly

cuttlefish

elephant hawk moth

fluke

giraffe

horned toad

king page butterfly

lapwing

leaf insect

nudibranches

octopus

polar bear

praying mantis

rock ptarmigan

snowshoe hare

stick insect

tiger

trapdoor spider

CANADIAN FOOTBALL POSITIONS

center

defensive back

defensive end (2)

free safety

fullback

left cornerback

left guard

left inside linebacker

left outside linebacker

left tackle

noseguard

quarterback

right cornerback

right guard

right inside linebacker

right outside linebacker

right tackle

slotback

split end

strong safety

tailback or running back

tight end

wide receiver

CANADIAN PROVINCES AND TERRITORIES

Alberta

British Columbia

Manitoba

New Brunswick

Newfoundland and Labrador

Northwest Territories

Nova Scotia

Nunavut

Ontario

Prince Edward Island

Quebec

Saskatchewan

Yukon Territory

CANDIES, CONFECTIONS, AND SWEETS

bark
boiled sweet
bonbon
brittle
bubble gum
butterscotch
candied fruit
candy bar
candy cane
candy corn
caramel
chewing gum
chocolate
chocolate bar
chocolate drop
comfit

cotton candy
crystallized fruit
divinity
dragee
fondant
frangipane
fudge
ganache
glacé
gobstopper
gum
gumdrop
halvah
hard candy
horehound
jawbreaker

jellybean
jimmies
jujube
kiss
lemon drop
licorice
Life Saver
lollipop
M&M
marchpane
marshmallow
marzipan
mint
nonpareil
nougat
pastille

peanut brittle
peanut butter cup
penuche
peppermint
praline
red hot
rock candy
saltwater taffy
sugarplum
taffy
toffee
truffle
Turkish delight
turtle
tutti-frutti

CANONICAL HOURS

Eight daily prayer events developed and recognized by the Christian church.

compline
lauds

matins
none

prime
sext

terce
vespers

CAPITAL STYLES

baroque

Byzantine

composite

Corinthian

cushion-cap

Doric

Gothic

Greek

Greek Corinthian

Greek Ionic

Ionic

Moorish

post-Renaissance

Renaissance

Roman Corinthian

Roman Doric

Romanesque

Roman Ionic

Tuscan

CARBOHYDRATES

aldose

altrose

amino sugar

anhydrous sugar

arbinose

bamboo sugar

barley sugar

beet sugar

British gum

brown sugar

cane sugar

castor sugar

cellobiose

cellulose

clinical dextrain

compound sugar

confectioners' sugar

corn sugar

date sugar

demerara sugar

deoxyribose

dextran

dextrin

dextro-glucose

dextrose

disaccharide

erythrose

fructose

fruit sugar

fucose

furanose

galactose

glucagon

glucose

glycogen

granulated sugar

grape sugar

gulose

hexose sugar

idose

inulin

lactose

levulose

lyxose

maltose

malt sugar

mannose

maple sugar

melibiose

milk sugar

molasses

monosaccharide

nipa sugar

palm sugar

pentosan

pentose sugar

potato sugar

powdered sugar

raffinose

raw sugar

refined sugar

rhamnose

ribose

saccharide

simple sugar

sorbose

spun sugar

starch

sucrose

superfine sugar

tabasheer

table sugar

tagatose   tree sugar   turbinado sugar   wood sugar

talose   trelialose   vanilla sugar   xylose

tree molasses   trisaccharide   white sugar

CARD SUITS

clubs   diamonds   hearts   spades

CARDINAL VIRTUES

fortitude   justice   prudence   temperance

CARNIVOROUS PLANTS

bladderwort   hooded pitcher   pitcher plant   Venus flytrap

butterwort   huntsman's horn   sundew   waterwheel plant

cobra lily   pink fan   sweet trumpet

CARPETS AND RUGS

area rug	Brussels carpet	handwoven	ingrain
Astroturf	camel's hair rug	Heriz	kaross
Aubusson	Caucasian rug	hooked	kilim
Axminster	chenille	imperial Brussels	Kirman
bearskin rug	dhurrie	Indian rug	Kurdistan
Belouch	drugget	Indo-Heriz	mat
body Brussels	flat-woven	indoor-outdoor carpeting	mohair
Bokhara	flokati		moquette
broadloom	flossa	Indo-Tabriz	nap

Navaho rug
numdah
nylon carpeting
Oriental rug
Persian carpet
Persian rug
puma rug

rag
runner
rya
Savonnerie
Saxony carpet
scatter rug
shag

sheepskin
steamer rug
Tabriz
tapestry Brussels
tapestry rug
throw rug
Tientsin

Turkish
Turkoman
twist
Venetian
wall-to-wall carpet
Wilton

CARRIAGES AND CARTS

araba
barouche
berlin
brake
break
breaking cart
Britzska
brougham
buckboard
buggy
bullock cart
cab
cabriolet
caisson
calash
calèche
Cape cart
caravan
carriole

carryall
chaise
charabanc
chariot
charrette
clarence
coach
coach-and-four
Conestoga wagon
coupé
covered wagon
curricle
dearborn
dogcart
drag
dray
droshky
ekka
equipage

fiacre
fly
four-in-hand coach
gambo
gharry
gig
Gladstone
glass coach
growler
hack
hackney
handcart
hansom
hay cart
haywain
herdic
jaunting car
jinker
jinrikisha

kibitka
kittereen
landau
limber
mail cart
mud wagon
one-horse carriage
oxcart
phaeton
post chaise
prairie schooner
random
ratha
rickshaw
rig
road cart
rockaway
runabout
sidecar

sociable

spider phaeton

spring wagon

stagecoach

stanhope

sulky

surrey

tallyho coach

tandem

tarantass

tilbury

tonga

trailer

tram

trap

trishaw

troika

trolley

tumbrel

unicorn

Victoria

vis-à-vis

voiturette

wagon

wagonette

wain

whim

CASKS

anker

barrel

barrico

breaker

butt

cade

dolium

drum

firkin

harness

hogshead

keg

kilderkin

octave

pipe

powder

puncheon

quarter

rundlet

scuttlebutt

tierce

tumbling barrel

tun

vat

water butt

CASTLES AND PALACES

aftercastle

alcazar

casbah

castelet

castlet

chateau

chatelet

fortification

fortress

fortress castle

mansion

mote castle

motte-and-bailey castle

palace castle

sand castle

schloss

seraglio

water castle

CATS, DOMESTIC

Abyssinian cat

American Bobtail

American Curl

American shorthair

American Wirehair

Angora cat

Australian Mist cat

Balinese

Bengal cat

bicolor cat

Birman cat

blue-point Siamese

Bombay cat

British shorthair

Burmese cat

calico

California spangled

chartreuse cat

Chartreux

Chinese

chocolate-point Siamese

colorpoint shorthair

Cornish Rex

Devon Rex

domestic shorthair cat

Egyptian cat or Egyptian Mau

European Burmese

exotic shorthair

Havana Brown

Himalayan

Japanese Bobtail

Javanese

Kashmir

Korat

LaPerm cat

longhair cat

Maine coon

Malayan cat

Maltese cat

Manx

marmalade cat

Munchkin cat

Nebelung cat

Norwegian Forest cat

Ocicat

Oriental cat

Oriental Shorthair cat

Persian cat

RagaMuffin

Ragdoll

rex

Russian blue

Russian shorthair

Scottish fold

seal-point Siamese

Selkirk Rex

shorthair cat

Siamese cat

Siberian cat

Singapura

Somali cat

Sphynx

tabby

tiger cat

Tonkinese cat

tortoiseshell cat

Turkish Angora

Turkish cat

Turkish Van cat

York Chocolate cat

CATS, WILD

African lynx

African wild cat

black-footed cat

bobcat

Caffre cat

caracal

catamountain

chaus

cheetah

Chinese desert cat

civet

clouded leopard

colocolo

cougar

Egyptian wildcat

European wild cat

eyra

fishing cat

flat-headed cat

golden cat

jaguar

jaguarundi

leopard

leopard cat

liger

lion

lynx

manul margay

mountain cat

mountain lion

musion

ocelot

ounce

pampas cat

panther

puma

ring-tailed cat
sand cat
serval

snow leopard
tiger
tiger cat

tigon
wagati
wildcat

CATTLE BREEDS

Aberdeen Angus
Africander
Alderney
Andalusian
Ankole
Ayrshire
Barotse
Beefalo
Belted Galloway
Black Angus
Boran
Brahman
Brown Swiss

Cattalo
Charbray
Charolais
Dairy Shorthorn
Devon
Dexter
Durham
Dutch Belted
Egyptian
Fjäll
French Canadian
Fribourg
Fulani

Galloway
Guernsey
Guzerat
Hariana
Hereford
Holstein
Icelandic
Jersey
Lincoln Red
Longhorn
Milking Shorthorn
Norwegian Red
Park Cattle

Polled Hereford
Red Dane
Red Poll
Red Sindhi
Santa Gertrudis
Shetland
Shorthorn
Sindhi
Sussex
Texas Longhorn
Welsh or Welsh
Black
West Highland

CATTLE, WILD

African buffalo
American bison
anoa
Asiatic buffalo
auroch

banteng
bison
Brahmin
buffalo
cape buffalo

European bison
gaur
gayal
Indian bison
kouprey

lowland anoa
mountain anoa
musk ox
ox
sapi-utan

seladang   tsine   wild ox

takin   urus   yak

tamarau   water buffalo   zebu

CAVE AND GROTTO TYPES

boulder cave or talus cave

breathing cave

canyon

catacomb

cavern

chemically formed cave

crevice cave

dissolutional cave

eolian cave

erosion cave

fissure cave

glacier cave

glaciere

gypsum cave

ice cave

lava cave

lava tube cave

limestone cave

master cave

mechanically formed cave

rock shelter

sandstone cave

sea cave

sink

sinkhole

solution cave or karst cave

souterrain

suffosional cave

talus cave or boulder cave

tectonic cave

CELL TYPES

absorption cell

A cell

alpha cell

antigen-presenting cell

antipodal cell

basal cell

B cell

beta cell

blood cell

chief cell

connective tissue cell

cytotoxic T cell

dendritic cell

egg cell

epithelial cell

eukaryotic cell

generative cell

germ cell

glial cell

helper cell or helper T cell

liver cell

mast cell

memory cell

mother cell

mycoplasma

oxyntic cell

parietal cell

plasma cell

primary cell

prokaryotic cell

red blood cell

Schwann cell

secondary cell

sex cell

sperm cell

stem cell

suppressor cell or suppressor T cell

T cell

white blood cell

CEMENT VARIETIES

alumina

anchoring

asbestos

asphalt

beeswax

board

contact

dental

diamond

ferro-cement or iron cement

flashing cement

hydraulic

Keene's

masonry cement

Parian

plastic cement

portland cement

pozzolana

PVC cement

Roman

roofing

rubber

rust

silicious

slag

solvent cement

waterproof

CERAMICS

agateware

Albion ware

Allervale pottery

Arita ware

Arretine ware or terra sigillata

basalt

Belleek ware

Berlin ware

bisque

Bizen ware

blackware

blue and white ware

bone china

Canton ware

Castleford ware

Castor ware

cast ware

champlevé

Chelsea porcelain

china or chinaware

Ch'ing porcelain

clayware

cloisonné Coalport

cottage china

crackleware

creamware

crockery

crouch ware

Crown Derby ware

Dedham pottery

delft

Derby porcelain

Doulton ware

Dresden china or Meissen porcelain

earthenware

eggshell porcelain

enamel or enamelware

faience

glassware

glazed ware

gombroon

hard-paste porcelain

Hirado ware

Hizen porcelain

hotel china

Imari ware

industrial ceramics

ironstone

istoriato ware

Jackfield ware

jasper ware

Kakiemon

Karatsu ware

Kinkozan ware

lambrequin

Leeds pottery

Limoges

Lowestoft ware

lusterware

majolica

mezza-majolica

Minton ware

Nabeshima ware

Nanking ware

Old Worcester ware

ovenware

Palissy ware

Parian ware

Pennsylvania Dutch ware

porcelain

porcelain enamel

queensware

redware

refractory ware

Rockingham ware

Royal Copenhagen porcelain

Royal Doulton porcelain

Royal Worcester porcelain

salt-glazed ware

Samian ware

sanda ware

sanitary ware

Satsuma ware

semiporcelain

Seto ware

Sèvres

slipware

soft-paste porcelain

Spode

spongeware

Staffordshire

stoneware

Sung ware

T'ang ware

terra cotta

Tiffany glass

ting ware

Toft ware

tulip ware

Wedgwood

whiteware

willowware

Worcester ware

yellowware

yi-hsing ware

CERAMICS SUPPLIES

armature

bat

batten

bead tree

brush

caliper

clay

clay paddle

clay recycling barrel

cone

decorating wheel

drape mold

elephant ear sponge

extruder

firebrick

glaze

grog

hardwood tool

heat-resistant glove

kiln

kiln furniture

kiln screen

kiln wash

loop tool

open storage

plaster of Paris

potter's rib

prop

pug mill

pyrometer

rolling pin

scale

scraper

sink

slab roller

spray booth

spray bottle

star stilt

turntable

wheel

CEREAL CROPS, GRAINS, AND GRASSES

African millet	Indian corn	pearl millet	sorghum
barley	maize	ragi	teff grass
buckwheat	millet	rice	wheat
corakan corn	oats	rye	wild rice
finger millet	oryza	secale	zea mays

CETACEANS, DOLPHINS, AND WHALES

Amazon dolphin	bowhead whale	minke whale	sei whale
baleen whale	cachalot	Mysticeti	sperm whale
beaked whale	calf	narwhal	spinner dolphin
beluga	dusky dolphin	Odontoceti	sulfur-bottom whale
blackfish	finback	orca	toothed whale
black whale	fin whale	pilot whale	tucuxi
blue whale	grampus	porpoise	whalebone whale
bottlenose dolphin	gray whale	right whale	white-sided dolphin
bottlenose whale	humpback whale	river dolphin	white whale
bouto	killer whale	rorqual	zeuglodon

CHAIRS, COUCHES, AND SOFAS

Adirondack chair	banquette	Barcelona chair	bar stool
armchair	barber chair	barrel chair	basket chair

bath chair

bench

bentwood chair

box seat

Brewster chair

bucket seat

butterfly chair

camp chair

cane chair

captain's chair

Carver chair

cathedra

chaise

chaise longue

channel back chair

chesterfield

Chippendale chair

club chair

collapsible chair

comb back chair

confidente

contour chair

couch

courting chair

curule chair

Dante chair

davenport

daybed

deck chair

Derbyshire chair

desk chair

dining chair

director's chair

divan

dos-a-dos

duchesse

Eames chair

easy chair

ergonomic chair

faldstool

fanback chair

farthingale chair

fauteuil

folding chair

footstool

Glastonbury chair

highchair or high chair

inglenook

ladderback chair

lawn chair

lounge chair

love seat

meridienne

milking stool

Morris chair

ottoman

overstuffed chair

page chair

panel-back chair

parlor chair

pew

platform rocker

porch swing

porter chair

potty-chair

pouffe

prayer chair

prie-dieu

Queen Anne chair

recliner

rocking chair

rout seat

Savonarola chair

scissors chair

seat

sectional

settee

settle

Shaker chair

Sheraton chair

side chair

sleeper

sling chair

slipper chair

sociable

sofa

sofa bed

spindle-back chair

squab

stall

stool

straight-backed chair

studio couch

swing

swivel chair

tablet chair

tabouret

tête-à-tête

throne

triclinium

tub chair

tuxedo sofa

upright chair

wagon seat

wheelback chair

wheelchair

wicker chair

Windsor chair

wing chair

Yorkshire chair

CHARACTERISTICS OF LIFE

excretion/metabolism

growth

movement

nutrition

reproduction

respiration

response to stimuli

CHARMS, GOOD LUCK

amulet

ankh

birthstone

cross

crucifix

fetish

four-leaf clover

horseshoe

juju

love charm

lucky bean

lucky charm

mandala

mascot

medallion

pentacle

periapt

philter

rabbit's foot

scarab

shamrock

talisman

tiki

totem

CHEESE

American

angelot

appetitost

asiago

baker's cheese

Banon

Bavarian blue cheese

Beaufort

Bel paese

Bleu de Bresse

blue cheese

Blue Cheshire

Blue Vinny or Dorset

bondon cheese

boule

Boursin

brick cheese

brie

brynza

Caciovallo

Caerphilly

Camembert

Cantal

Charolais

cheddar

Cheshire cheese

chevre

Chevret

clabber cheese

colby cheese

cook cheese

cottage cheese

cream cheese

cup cheese

Danish blue

Derby

Devon

Dolcelatte

Dunlop

Dutch cheese

Edam

Edelpilzkase

Emmenthaler

Epoisses

farmer cheese
Feta
Fontina
fromage
full-cream cheese
gammelost cheese
gervais
Gjetost
Gloucester
goat cheese
Gorgonzola
Gouda
green cheese
Gruyere
hand cheese
Havarti
hoop cheese
Jack cheese
Jarlsberg
kebbuck
Kumminost

Lancashire
Leicester
Leiden
Liederkranz
Limburger
Liptauer
Livarot
loaf cheese
longhorn cheese
Maroilles
mascarpone
Mimolette
Monterey Jack
Montrachet
mozzarella
muenster
Neufchatel
New England Sage
Pannerone
Parmesan
Parmigiano Reggiano

pasta filata cheese
Pecorino
pimento cheese
pineapple cheese
Pont l'Eveque
Port Salut
pot cheese
pressed cheese
process cheese
provolone
Quargel
queso blanco
raclette
rat cheese
red Windsor
ricotta
Romano
Roquefort
sage cheese
Samsoe
sapsago

Scamorza
Shropshire
smoked cheese
sour milk cheese
St. Marcellin
St. Nectaire
Stilton
store cheese
string cheese
Swiss
Teleme
Tillamook
Tilsiter
Tome au raisin
Trappist cheese
Vacherin
washed-curd cheese
White Wensleydale
York

CHEMICAL ADDITIVE TYPES

acid flavoring
acidity regulator
acidulant
anticaking agent
antioxidant

artificial coloring
artificial flavoring
artificial sweetener
bleaching agent
buffer

chelating agent
clarifying agent
clouding agent
color stabilizer
coloring

discoloration inhibitor
emulsifier
enhancer
firming agent

flavor

flavor enhancer

foam stabilizer

gelling agent

leavening agent

moisture maintainer

nutrient

preservative

stabilizer

stimulant

tartness agent

thickening agent

whipping agent

whitening agent

CHEMICAL COMPOUND TYPES

acetal

acetate

acid

acid anhydride

alcohol

aldehyde

aldohexose

aldol

aldose

alkaloid

alkane

alkene

alkyne

aluminate

amide

amine

amino acid

azide

azine

azo compound

base

bicarbonate

borane

borate

boride

bromide

carbide

carbohydrate

carbonate

carboxylic acid

chlorate

chloride

chlorite

chlorofluorocarbon

chromate

cyanide

detergent

diol

enzyme

epoxide

ester

ether

fluoride

fluorocarbon

halide

hexose

hydrocarbon

hydroxide

iodide

ketone

ketose

lactate

lactone

nitrate

nitride

nitrite

nitro compound

oxide

paraffin

peptide

permanganate

peroxide

petrochemical

phenol

phosphate

polymer

protein

saccharide

salt

silane

silicate

silicide

silicone

soap

stearate

suboxide

sugar

sulphate

sulphide

sulphite

sulphonamide

superoxide

tartrate

terpene

thiosulphate

triol

zeolite

zincate

CHEMICAL ELEMENT GROUPS

actinide series

alkali earth metals or sodium family

alkaline earth metals or calcium family

coinage metals

halogen family

inert gases or noble gases

lanthanide series

metalloids or semimetals

non-metals

other metals or poor metals

platinum-group metals

representative metals

transfermium

transition metals

transuranium elements

typical metals

CHEMICAL ELEMENTS

actinium or Ac

aluminum or Al

americium or Am

antimony or Sb

argon or Ar

arsenic or As

astatine or At

barium or Ba

berkelium or Bk

beryllium or Be

bismuth or Bi

bohrium or Bh

boron or B

bromine or Br

cadmium or Cd

calcium or Ca

californium or Cf

carbon or C

cerium or Ce

cesium or Cs

chlorine or Cl

chromium or Cr

cobalt or Co

copper or Cu

curium or Cm

darmstadtium or Ds

dubnium or Db

dysprosium or Dy

einsteinium or Es

erbium or Er

europium or Eu

fermium or Fm

fluorine or F

francium or Fr

gadolinium or Gd

gallium or Ga

germanium or Ge

gold or Au

hafnium or Hf

hassium or Hs

helium or He

holmium or Ho

hydrogen or H

indium or In

iodine or I

iridium or Ir

iron or Fe

krypton or Kr

lanthanum or La

lawrencium or Lr

lead or Pb

lithium or Li

lutetium or Lu

magnesium or Mg

manganese or Mn

meitnerium or Mt

mendelevium or Md

mercury or Hg

molybdenum or Mo

neodymium or Nd

neon or Ne

neptunium or Np

nickel or Ni

niobium or Nb

nitrogen or N

nobelium or No

osmium or Os

oxygen or O

palladium or Pd

phosphorus or P

platinum or Pt

plutonium or Pu

polonium or Po

potassium or K

praseodymium or Pr

promethium or Pm

protactinium or Pa

radium or Ra

radon or Rn

rhenium or Re

rhodium or Rh

rubidium or Rb

ruthenium or Ru

rutherfordium Rf

samarium or Sm

scandium or Sc

seaborgium or Sg

selenium or Se

silicon or Si

silver or Ag

sodium or Na

strontium or Sr

sulfur or S

tantalum or Ta

technetium or Tc

tellurium or Te

terbium or Tb

thallium or Tl

thorium or Th

thulium or Tm

tin or Sn

titanium or Ti

tungsten or W

ununbium or Uub

ununhexium or Uuh

ununoctium or Uuo

ununpentium or Uup

ununquaternium or Uuq

ununseptium or Uus

ununtrium or Uut

unununium or Uuu

uranium or U

vanadium or V

xenon or Xe

ytterbium or Yb

yttrium or Y

zinc or Zn

zirconium or Zr

CHEMICAL ELEMENTS, ANCIENT

antimony

carbon

copper

gold

iron

lead

mercury

silver

sulfur

tin

CHEMICAL ELEMENTS, ARTIFICIAL

americium

astatine

berkelium

californium

curium

einsteinium

fermium

lawrencium

mendelevium

neptunium

nobelium

plutonium

promethium

technetium

unnilennium

unnilhexium

unniloctium

unnilpentium

unnilquadium

unnilseptium

CHEMICAL ELEMENTS, SINGLE-SYMBOL

boron (B)

carbon (C)

fluorine (F)

hydrogen (H)

iodine (I)

nitrogen (N)

oxygen (O)

phosphorus (P)

potassium (K)

sulfur (S)

tungsten (W)

uranium (U)

vanadium (V)

yttrium (Y)

CHEMICAL PROCESSES

acetification

acidification

alkalization

anion exchange

aromatization

carbonation

catalysis

chain reaction

chlorination

combustion

condensation

copolymerization

cyclization

decay

electrolysis

electrophilic reaction

endothermic reaction

exothermic reaction

fermentation

geometric isomerization

heterolysis

heterolytic fission

homolysis

homolytic fission

homopolymerization

hydration

hydrogenation

hydrolysis

hydroxylation

ionization

isomerization

isotope effect

metabolism

metamerization

neutralization

nitration

nitrification

nucleophilic reaction

optical isomerization

oxidation

oxidization

phosphatization

photochemical reaction

photosynthesis

polymerization

position isomerization

pyrolysis

radiochemical reaction

reduction

reversible reaction

ring opening

saturization

sulfation

sulfatization

sulfonation

synthesis

tautoisomerization

CHEMICALS

acetic acid

acetone

acetylene

alcohol

alum

alumina baking soda or sodium bicarbonate

baryta

borax

boric acid

calcium oxide

carbon tetrachloride

chloroform or trichloroethane

corundum or sodium cyanide or potassium cyanide

dinitrogen monoxide

ether

ethyl alcohol

firedamp

folic acid

formaldehyde

formic acid

glycerine

gypsum

hydrochloric acid

lead oxide

lithium oxide

magnesia

magnesium sulphate

massicot

methane

nitric oxide

phenol

phosphoric acid

plaster of Paris

potassium hydroxide

potassium nitrate

potash

sodium chloride

silica

slaked lime sodium carbonate

sodium hydroxide

strontia

sucrose

vitriol

xylene zirconium oxide

CHEMISTRY BRANCHES

actinochemistry

agricultural chemistry

alchemy or alchemistry

analytical chemistry

applied chemistry

astrochemistry

atomic chemistry

biochemistry

biogeochemistry

business chemistry

capillary chemistry

catalysis

chemistry

chemical dynamics

chemical engineering

chemical physics

chemicobiology

chemicoengineering

chemophysiology

chemurgy

colloid chemistry

colorimetry

combinatorial chemistry

computational chemistry

cosmochemistry

crystallography

cytochemistry

electrochemistry

engineering chemistry

femtochemistry

galactochemistry

galvanochemistry

geochemistry

histochemistry

hydrochemistry

iatrochemistry

immunochemistry

industrial chemistry

inorganic chemistry

lithochemistry

macrochemistry

magnetochemistry

metachemistry

metallurgy

microchemistry

mineralogical chemistry

natural product chemistry

neurochemistry

nuclear chemistry

organic chemistry

pathological chemistry

petrochemistry

pharmaceutical chemistry

phonochemistry

photochemistry

physical chemistry

physiological chemistry

phytochemistry

piezochemistry

pneumatochemistry

polymer chemistry

psychobiochemistry

pure chemistry

qualitative analysis

quantitative analysis

quantum chemistry

radiochemistry

reaction kinetics

Reppe chemistry

soil chemistry

sonochemistry

spectrochemistry

stereochemistry

structural chemistry

surface chemistry

synthetic chemistry

technochemistry

theoretical chemistry

thermochemistry

topochemistry

ultramicrochemistry

zoochemistry

zymurgy

zyochemistry

Chemistry Lab Equipment

aerator

agitator

alembic

alkalimeter

aludel

aspirator

atmometer

atomizer

balance

beaker

Beckmann thermometer

bell jar

blender

blowpipe

boiling tube

Buckner funnel

Bunsen burner

burette

calorimeter

capillary tube

centrifuge

clamp

condenser

conical flask

crucible

de-aerator

deflagrating spoon

dessicator

Dewar flask

dialyzer

diatometer

disperser

distillation equipment

dropper

drum

dryer

Erlenmeyer flask

evaporating dish

evaporator

feeder

fermentation tube

filter

filter flask

filter funnel

filter paper

filter pump

flask

Florence flask

fluted funnel

fume cupboard

funnel

funnel tube

gas bottle or gas jar

gauge

Geissler tube

graduated cylinder

grinder

hopper

hotplate

kettle

Kipp's apparatus

Kjehdahl flask

laboratory still

Liebig condenser

manometer

measures

measuring cylinder

Meker burner

melting-point apparatar

mixer

mortar

muttle furnace

nitrometer

oven

oxygen generator

pail

pestle

pinchcock

pipette

platinum wire

pneumatic trough

precipitate bottle

propeller

pump

pyncnometer

pyrometer

reactor

reagant bottle

receiver

reflux condenser

roller mill

round-bottomed flask

scale

scoop

screen

separating funnel

shaker

sieve

sink

sintered-glass crucible

siphon

spatula

stand

still

stirrer

tank

thermometer

trough

tubing

U-tube

vacuum still

vial

volumetric flask

washing bottle

watchglass

weighing bottle

work table

CHERRY VARIETIES

Amarelle

American

Angouleme

Archduke

Australian

Baldwin

Barbados

Bessarabian

Bigaroon

bigarreau

Bing

bitter

black

blackheart

Carnation

Centennial

Cerise

Chapman

Choisy

chokecherry

Cleveland

Coe

Cornelian

Downer

Duke

Dyehouse

Eagle

Early Basle or Ceret

Early Burlat

Early Purple

Early Rivers

Elkhorn

Elton	Ida	Lutovka	Queensland cherry
English cherry	Japanese	marasca	red
Eugenie	Kearton	maraschino	Reverchon
European bird	Kermes	May-duke	Sand
Florida cherry	Kermesite	Mazzard	Surinam cherry
Gean	King	Merry	Whiteheart
ground	Knight	Montmorency	wild
Heart	Large Montmorency	morello	William
Hedelfingen Giant	Late Duke	Nanking	winter
Hortense	Late Kentish	Napoleon	
Hoskins	Lithauer	native	

CHESS PIECES OR CHESSMEN

bishop	knight or horse	queen
king	pawn	rook or castle

CHICKEN BREEDS

American game fowl	Brahma	Dominique	Langshan
Ancobar	Buckeye	Dorking	Leghorn
Ancona	Buttercup	Faverolle	lesser prairie chicken
Andalusian	Campine	Frizzle	Mille Fleur
Araucana	Cochin	Hamburg	Minorca
Australorp	Cornish	Holland	New Hampshire red
Bantam	Crevecoeur	Houdan	Orpington
Barred Plymouth Rock	Delaware	Ixworth	Plymouth Rock
	Dominick	Jersey black giant	Rhode Island red

139

Rhode Island white   Spanish   Turken   Wyandotte

Rock   Sultan   Welsumer

Rock Cornish   Sumatra   whitebelly

Silkie   Sussex   white Leghorn

CHILE PEPPERS

Aji	El Paso	Manzano	Puya
Anaheim	Espanola	Mirasol	Red Savina Habanero
Ancho	Fresno	Mulato	Rocotillo
Bahamian	Guajillo	Negro	Sandia
Banana Bell	Guindilla	New Mexico	Santa Fe Grande
Bird's Eye capsaican	Habanero	Nora	Santaka
Carolina Cayenne	Haimen	Numex Big Jim	Scotch Bonnet
Cascabel	Hidalgo	Pasilla	Serrano
cayenne	Hontaka	Peperoncino	Shipkas
Cherry	Hot Wax	Pepperoncini	Super Chile
Chiltecpin	Jalapeno	Pequin	Tabasco
Chipotle	Jaloro	Pimiento	Tabiche
Choricero	Jamaican Hot	Piquin	Thai
Coronado	Kumataka	Poblano	Togarashi
De Arbol	Malagueta	Pulla	Yatsafusa

CHINESE CALENDAR ANIMALS

dog	monkey	rabbit or hare	sheep or goat
dragon	ox or buffalo	rat	snake
horse	pig or boar	rooster	tiger

CHISEL VARIETIES

beveled-edge firmer chisel

blacksmiths' cold chisel

bradawl

celt

chisel

cold chisel

diamond-nose chisel

firmer chisel

floor chisel

gad

gouge

jackhammer

machine-mortising chisel

plumbers' chisel

ripping chisel

round-nose chisel

slicker chisel

CHRISTIAN HOLY DAYS, FESTIVALS, FASTS, AND SEASONS

Advent

All Saint's Day, Hallowmas, Allhallowmas

All Soul's Day

Annunciation or Lady Day

Ascension or Holy Thursday or Maundy Thursday

Ash Wednesday

Assumption of Blessed Virgin Mary

Candlemas or Presentation Christmas

Circumcision or Holy Name Day

Corpus Christi

Easter

Easter Eve or Holy Saturday

Eastertide

Ember days

Epiphany or Twelfth Day or Three Kings' Day

Fat Tuesday or Mardi Gras or Shrove Tuesday or Pancake Tuesday or Carnival

First Sunday of Advent

Good Friday

Holy Week or Passion Week

Immaculate Conception

Lammas or Feast of St. Peter's Chains

Lent

Martinmas

Michaelmas

Nativity of the Virgin

Palm Sunday

Passion Week or Holy Week

Pentecost or Whitsunday

Quadragesima

Saturday of Lazarus

Saturday of Souls

Second Saturday of Souls

Septuagesima

Shrove Monday

Shrove Sunday

Solemnity of Mary

St. Joseph's Day

St. Patrick's Day

Sunday of Orthodoxy

Third Saturday of Souls

Transfiguration

Trinity Sunday

Trinitytide or Pentecost season

Triodion

Whitmonday

Whit-Tuesday

Whitweek

CHRISTIAN MOVEMENTS AND HERESIES

Abelianism

Adoptionism

Ambrosianism

Antinomianism

Antipaedobaptism

Apollinarianism

Arianism

Arminianism

Augustinianism

Barclayism

Basilidianism

Biblicism

Brownism

Caesaro-papism

Calvinism

Catharism

Charismatic Movement

Chiliasm

Cursillo

Docetism

Donatism

Ebionitism

Ecumenical Movement

Evangelicalism

Fundamentalism

Gallicanism

Gnosticism

Hussitism

Iconoclasm

Jansenism

Latitudianarianism

Liberation Theology

Liturgical Movement

Lollardy

Lullism

Mandeism

Manichaeism

Marcionism

Millenarianism

Monarchianism

Monophysitism

Monothelitism

Montanism

Moral Majority

Moral Rearmament

Mormonism

Nestorianism

Nonconformism

Oxford Group

Oxford Movement

Patripassianism

Paulicianism

Pelagianism

Pentecostalism

Pietism

Protestantism

Psilanthopism

Puritanism

Sabellianism

Socianism

Tractarianism

Trinitarianism

Ultramontanism

CHURCH WINDOW TYPES

cusp

cusping

dagger

foil

lancet

light

mouchette

mullion

multifoil

plate tracery

quatrefoil

shaft

tracery

transom

trefoil

wheel window or Catherine wheel

CINEMA GENRES

3-D

A movie or A picture

action

action adventure

animated or animation

art film

B movie or B picture

biographical

blaxploitation

blue movie

buddy picture

cartoon

chick flick

chiller

cinema *vèrité*

comedy

costume film

cowboy picture

crash and burn film

date movie

detective picture

disaster picture

documentary

epic

experimental film

exploitation film

family

fantasy

film noir

gangster film

hard-core

home movie

horror

horse opera

independent film

industrial film

law-and-order film

melodrama

musical

newsreel

new wave

nouvelle vague

oater

period piece

pornographic film

prequel

remark

romance

romantic comedy

scary movie

science fiction

screwball comedy

sequel

serial

sexploitation

shocker

shoot' em-up

short subject

silent film

skin flick

slapstick comedy

slasher movie

snuff film

soft-core

space adventure

spaghetti western

stag movie

student film

talkie

tearjerker

teen picture

television movie

thriller

travelogue

underground movie

western

whodunit

CIRCULATORY SYSTEM COMPONENTS

anterior tibial artery

anterior tibial vein

aorta

basilic vein

brachial artery

cephalic vein

exterior jugular vein

external carotid artery

femoral artery
femoral vein
great saphenous vein
heart
iliac artery
iliac vein

inferior vena cava
interior jugular vein
internal carotid artery
posterior tibial vein
pulmonary artery

pulmonary vein
radial artery
renal artery
renal vein
small saphenous vein
subclavian artery

subclavian vein
superior vena cava
ulnar artery

CLAY VARIETIES

acid
astringent
ball
bleaching
blue
blue mud
bond

brick
ceramic
china
deep-sea
fire
flint
glacial

Japanese acid
kaolin
loam
mudstone
pipe
porcelain
pot

potter's
red
refractory
shale
silty
stoneware

CLERGYPEOPLE

archbishop
archdeacon
archpriest
bishop
brother
canon
cardinal
chancellor
chaplain
cleric

confessor
curate
Dalai Lama
deacon
deaconess
dean
ecclesiastic
elder
eparch
evangelist

exarch
father
friar
imam
metropolitan
minister
monk
monsignor
Mother Superior
nun

ordinand
padre
parson
pastor
pontiff
pope
preacher
prebendary
precentor
prelate

primate   rabbi   rural dean   televangelist
prior   rebbe   sexton   vicar
proctor   rector   suffragan
provost   reverend   swami

CLIMATES AND CLIMATIC ZONES

arctic   humid subtropical   polar   temperate
arid   humid-long summer   polar ice cap   temperate rainy
boreal   humid-short summer   polar tundra   trade-wind littoral
continental   ice cap   semiarid   tropical
continental humid   marine   steppe   tropical rain forest
desert   marine west coast   subarctic   tropical savanna
dry subtropical   Mediterranean   subhumid   tropical wet
equatorial rainforest subtropical   subtropical   tropical wet-dry
highland   monsoon   subtropical humid   tundra

CLOAKS AND OVERGARMENTS

academic gown   birrus   capote   cowl
academic hood   burka   capuchin   doctor's gown
academic robe   burnoose   cardinal   dolman
afghan   bursati   cashmere   domino
ahuula   caftan   cassock   duster
analabos   cap and gown   chasuble   ferraiolone
bachelor's gown   capa   chlamys   frock
bardocucullus   cape   choga   gaberdine
bautta   capelet   coat   galabia

145

haik	mantle	rhason	tabard
hooded cloak	mantua	riding hood	talma
houppelande	master's gown	robe	tilma
huke	military cloak	roquelaure	tippet
Inverness cape	monk's robe	sagum	toga
jacket	opera cloak	scapular	toga virilis
jellaba	overcoat	serape	tunic
judge's robe kaftan	paenula	shador	vestment
kimono	pallium	shawl	wrap
kirtle	paludamentum	shoulderette	wrap-around
manta	pelerine	shuba	wrapover
manteau	pelisse	slop	wrapper
mantelet	peplos	smock	wrap-up
mantelletta	peplum	soutane	
mantellone	plaid	stole	
mantilla	poncho	surcoat	

CLOTHING COLLARS

banded	button-down	cowl hood	funnel
Barrymore	cape	crew	galilla
batwing	chevesaile	dickey	Gladstone
Bermuda	chin	dog's ear	high
bertha	Chinese	Dutch	jabot
bib	choker	Eton	johnny
bishop	clerical	falling band	low
boatneck	collaret	fan	macaroni
Buster Brown	convertible	fanon	Mandarin
butterfly	cowl	fraise	Medici

moat	polo-neck	sailor	tab
mock turtle	Prussian	scarf	Talleyrand
mousquetaire	Puritan	Shakespeare	tulip
Napoleon	Quaker	shawl	turtleneck
Nehru	rabat	shirtwaist	tuxedo
notched	rabatine	spread	Vandyke
Peggy	rebato	standing band	Victorian
petal	regency	stand-up	V-neck
Peter Pan	Robespierre	step	whisk
Pierrot	rolled	stiff	wing
plunging	roll-neck	surplice	
poets'	Roman	swallow-tail	
poke	ruff	sweetheart	

CLOTHING ACCESSORIES, FEATURES, AND PARTS

accessory	bargello	binding	breast
accordian pleat	barrel cuff	bird's-eye	bretelle
acid-washed	barter stitch	bishop sleeve	buckle
A-line	basket weave	blanket stitch	burl
applied casing	batting	bodice	bustle
applique	batwing sleeve	body	bustline
argyle	beadwork	bonded	button
arm	bell-bottom leg	bosom	buttonhole
armhold	belt	box pleat	button stand
backstitch	bertha	brace	cable-stitch
band	beson pocket	braid	caddis
banded	bias	braiding	candlewicking

cap sleeve

casing

catch

caul

chain

chain stitch

check

cinch

cire

clamp

clasp

cleavage

clew

clip

clocks

close stitch

coattail

collar

colorfast

coordinate

cord

cording

couching

crewel embroidery

crimping

crocheting

cross-stitch

crotch

crystal pleat

cuff

custom-tailored

damasse

darn

dart

designer

diaphanous

dolman sleeve

double-knit

double stitch

drawstring

D-ring

drop seat

dropped waist

earflap

ease

elastic

embroidery

empire waist

epaulette

eyelet

facing

fagoting

fastener

featherstitch

fell

felting

fiber

filling

Florentine stitch

flounce

flue

fluting

fly front

frayed

French cuff

French seam

fret

fringe

frog

froufrou

furbelow

galloon

gathering

gauging

gigot sleeve

godet

goffering

gore

gray goods

gros pont

gusset

handtag

harlequin

haute couture

hem

hemline

herringbone

hook

hook and eye

hoop

hound's tooth

inseam

intarsia

interfacing

interlining

inverted pleat

jetted pocket

kick pleat

kimono sleeves

knife pleat

knit

knit and purl

lace

lap

lapel

leg

lifted waist

lining

locker loop

long-waisted

loop

machine-stitch

macramé

magyar sleeve

mannequin

mercerizing

missy	pinstripe	ribbing	shoulder pad
modiste	piping	ribbon	shoulder strap
motley	placket	rickrack	shuttle
nape	plaid	ring	silkscreen printing
neck	plain weave	rope	sizing
neckline	plaiting	ruching	skirt
neutral color	pleat	ruffle	slash pocket
nonwoven fabric	pocket	running stitch	sleeve
notch	pocket flap	runway	slip stitch
nubby	polka dot	saddle shoulder	smocking
off-the-rack	pompom	saddle stitch	soutache
outer garment	pouf	safety pin	spaghetti strap
overcastting	preshrunk	saillette	spangles
overlock seam	prewashed	sartorial	standaway
overskirt	primary color	satin weave	stay
padding	print	Savile Row cut	stitching
pagoda sleeve	pucker	scalloped edge	stonewashed
passementerie	purl	seam	strap
patch pocket	quilling	seat	strapless
pattern	quill work	seconds	string
peekaboo	quilting	selvage	stripes
peg	rag trade	sennit	stud
peg leg	raglan sleeve	sequin	sunray pleat
peplum	raveled	set-in sleeve	suspenders
permanent press	readymade	shirring	swatch
petit point	ready-to-wear	shirt front	tack
pile	resist dye	shirttail	tail
pin	revers	short-waisted	tails
pincushion	reversible	shoulder	tambour

tanning
tape
tassel
tatting
template
tent stitch
thread
tie
tie-dyeing
tinsel
toggle
topstitch
torsade
train

tram
tuck
tuft
turn-up
twill
twine
two-ply
undergarment
underlining
understitching
unisize
unixex apparel
Velcro
vent

vulcanization
waist
waistband
waistline
wale
warp
warp knit
watch pocket
waterproof
water-repellent
water-resistant
Watteau back
wearing ease
weave

weaving
webbing
weft
welting
welt pocket
whipstitch
wool
worsted
wristband
yoke
zipper

CLOTHING, 16TH–19TH CENTURIES

Adelaide boots
aigrette
albert overcoat
ankle jacks
Apollo knot
apron
Artois buckles
bagwig
banyan
bases
basque

batwing
bavolet
beaver
bedgown
Benjamin
Benoiton chains
beret
bertha
biggin
billiment
blackwork

bloomers
boa
bob wig
bodice
bodyes
bolero
bollinger
bombast
bonnet
boot hose
bowler

braces
breastplate
breeches
Brunswick
buffon
buffskin
burnouse
bustle
cadogan
calash
canions

capote

caraco

carcenet

cardigan

cardinal

catagan

caul

chatelaine

chemise

chemise robe

chemisette

chesterfield

chin-clout

chopines

clocks

cod-piece

commode

copotain

cornet

cornette

corset

cossacks

cravat

crinoline

cummerbund

damask

deerstalker cap

Dolly Varden dress

doublet

duster

Dutch breeches

echelles

English hood

ermine

fantail hat

farthingale

fly cap

follow-me-lads

fontange

French cloak

French hood

frock coat

frogging

gaberdine

gaiters

galligaskins

Garibaldi shirt

garter

gauntlets

gibus

girdle

gorget

great coat

Grecian bend

guards

head-rail

Hessians

highlows

hoop

hose

Inverness

jacket bodice

jerkin

kerchief

kirtle

knickerbockers

lappet

loose gown

mackintosh

major wig

mandilion

mantle

mantua

Mary Stuart hood

Milan bonnet

milkmaid hat

mob cap

modesty piece

morning gown

muckminder

muff

mules

nightcap

nightgown

night rail

open robe

paletot

panes

pantaloons

pantofles

pauldrons

peascod

pelerine

pelisse

Persian vest

petenlair

petticoat

petticoat breeches

piccadilly

pinner

plumpers

points

poke bonnet

polonaise

porkpie hat

princess dress

puffs

pumps

rail

rationals

rebato

rerebrace

reticule

riding habit

riding habit skirt

rollups

ruching
ruff
rump
russet
sable
sack
sailor suit
shag
shawl
shift
shoe rose
skeleton suit

slashing
slops
smock
snoskyn
spangles
Spanish breeches
Spanish cloak
Spanish farthingale
spats
Spencer
startups
Steinkerk

stomacher
sugarloaf hat
surtout
tam-o'-shanter
tea gown
three storeys and a basement
tippet
top coat
top hat
tricorne
trilby

trunk hose
trunk sleeve
tucker
ugly
ulster
vambrace
velvet
Venetians
waistcoat
whangee
wideawake
wings

CLOTHING, ANCIENT GREEK AND ROMAN

abolla
ampyx
baltaeus
birrus
calceus
cestus
chiton
chitoniscus
chlamys
clavus

crepida
cucullus
cuirass
diplax
Greek fillet
himation
laena
loincloth
paenula
palla

paludamentum
petasos
pilleus
pilos
sagum
sakkos
sandals
splendone
stephane
stola

toga
toga candida
toga cinctus Gabinus
toga picta
toga praetexta
toga pulla
toga pura
tribon
tunica
tunica palmata

CLOTHING, LITURGICAL

alb
almuce
amice
apron
bands
biretta
black gown
buskins
calotte
cap
capuche
cardinal's hat
cassock
chasuble
chimere
cincture
cingulum

clerical collar
cope
cotta
cowl
crucifix
cuculla
dalmatic
ephod
fanon
frock
Geneva bands
Geneva gown
habit
hood
infula
kippa
lappet

maniple
mantle
miter
mozzetta
orosier
orphrey
pallium
pectoral
rabat
reversed collar
rochet
Roman collar
rosary
sanctuary slippers
scapular
shovel hat
simar

skullcap
soutaine
stole
subcingulum
superhumeral
surplice
tallith
tippet
tunic
tunicle
vestment
wimple
yarmulke
zucchetto

CLOTHING, MEDIEVAL

aglets
agrafe
anelace
baguette
bainbergs
balandrana

baldric
barmecloth
bascinet
beaver
belays
bliant

bouchette
bourdon
brassards
rayette
buskins
bycocket

camail
capa
cappa clausa
cappa nigra
capuchon
caputium

153

casque	dorelet	hatere	plate
cassock	doublet	hauberk	points
cendal	dunster	helm	ponge
chain mail	enbraude	heuke	poulaines
chapel de fer	epaulieres	hure	ray
chausses	ermine	jambarts	rerebrace
cingulum	fitchets	kennel	roskyn
cockers	fret	kersche	sabbatons
coif	frontlet	kirtle	sable
coif-de-mailles	frounce	latchet	samite
colobium	fustian	lettice	sequanie
cote	gambeson	liripipe	slops
cote-hardie	gardcorp	mahoitres	standard of mail
coudieres	gauntlet	mantle	surcoat
cowl	gazzatum	mentonieres	taces
cracowes	genuilliers	misericord	tilting helm
crespine	gipon	nifles	tippet
cuirass	gipser	nouch	tunic
cuir-bouilli	girdle	pauldrons	vair
cuissards	gite	pelicon	vambraces
dagges	gorget	petticoat	visor
damask	greaves	pilch	volupere
diaper	grise	pilion	wimple

CLOUD FORMATIONS AND TYPES

altocumulus	billowing	cirrus	cumulocirrus
altostratus	cirrocumulus	cloud street	cumulonimbus
anvil cloud	cirrostratus	contrails	cumulostratus

cumulus
funnel cloud
halo
incus
lenticular cloud
mammatocumulus

mare's tails
nebula
nimbostratus
nimbus
noctilucent cloud
rack

rain cloud
scud
storm cloud
stratocirrus
stratocumulus
stratus

thundercloud
virga
woolpack
wrack

CLOWN TYPES

antic
Auguste
bagpudding
Boetian
buffoon
carter
character
chawbacon

circus
clubhutchen
European whiteface
or Pierott
fool
grotesque whiteface
hobo or tramp
Joey

merry-andrew
mountebank
mudhead
pantomime
parade
pickle-herring
pleasant
rube

sliving
straight whiteface
talking
traditional
tummler
whiteface

CLUE ROOMS, SUSPECTS, AND WEAPONS

ballroom
billiard room
conservatory
dining room
hall
kitchen

library
lounge
study
Colonel Mustard
Miss Scarlet
Mr. Green

Mrs. Peacock
Mrs. White
Professor Plum
candlestick
knife
lead pipe

revolver
rope
wrench

COALS

anthracite barley
bituminous coal
black
blind
block
bone
broken
buckwheat
bunker
candle

cannel
cherry
chestnut
cobble
coking
dry
earth
egg
flaxseed
fluid

gas
glance
grate
lignite
lump
mineral
mustard-seed
nut
paper
pea

peat
pit
pitch
rice
river
sea
smithing
steam stove
subbituminous
wood

COAST TYPES

artificial coast
barrier beach
bayhead beach
concordant coastline

depositional
shoreline
discordant coastline
drowned coast
emergent coastline

erosional shoreline
fjord coastline
highland coast
lowland coast

mangrove shoreline
strand-plain coast
submergent coastline
tombolo

COATS AND JACKETS

achkan
anorak
balmacaan

battle jacket
bed jacket
bellboy jacket

benjamin
bietle
blanket-coat

blazer
blouse
body-coat

bolero

bomber jacket

box coat

bridge coat

buffcoat

Burberry

bush jacket

business suit

camelhair coat

cape

capote

capuchin

car coat

cardigan

cassock

chaqueta

chesterfield

claw-hammer coat

cloth coat

coach coat

coatee

coolie jacket

covert coat

crispin

cutaway coat

denim jacket

dinner jacket

dolman

donkey jacket

double coat

double-breasted jacket

doublet

down jacket

dreadnought

dress coat

dressing jacket

duffle coat

duster

Eton jacket

fearnought

fingertip coat

fitted coat

flack jacket

fleece jacket

frock fur coat

fur-lined coat

fur-trimmed coat

greatcoat

hacking jacket

happi coat

housecoat

Inverness

jerkin

jumper

leather coat

Lindbergh jacket

loden coat

London Fog™

long coat

lounging jacket

lumberjack jacket

macfarlane

mackinaw

mackintosh

mandarin coat

Mao jacket

maxicoat

mess jacket

midicoat

mink coat

monkey jacket

morning coat

Nehru jacket

Newmarket

Norfolk jacket

oilskin

overcoat

paletot

parka

peacoat

petersham

pilot jacket

pinchback

Prince Albert

raglan

raincoat

redingote

reefer reversible coat

sable coat

sack safari jacket

sanbenito

shawl

sheepskin coat

shell jacket

shirt jacket

shooting jacket

single-breasted jacket

ski jacket

sleeve waistcoat

slicker

slip-on

smoking jacket

sou'wester

spencer

spiketail

sport coat

sports jacket

suit coat

surcoat or surcot

surtout

swagger coat

swallow-tailed coat
sweater coat
swing coat
tabard
tail coat or tails

teddybear coat
topcoat
topper
trench coat
tuxedo jacket

ulster
watch coat
waterproof
Windbreaker
winter coat

woolly
wrap-around

COUNTRIES WITH LONGEST COASTLINES

Australia
Canada

China
Indonesia

Japan
Norway

Russia
United States

COUNTRIES WITH SHORTEST COASTLINES

Belgium
Bosnia
Iraq

Jordan
Monaco
Nauru

Slovenia
Togo
Zaire

COFFEE DRINK TYPES

automatic drip
café au lait
café noir
caffeinated
cappuccino

decaffeinated drip coffee
espresso
filter coffee
French drip
Greek coffee

iced
instant coffee
Irish coffee
latté
mocha
mochaccino

Neapolitan
percolated
pressed soluble
Turkish coffee
urn
vacuum-made

COFFEE OR COFFEE BEAN VARIETIES

African

American

arabica

blended

Blue Mountain

Brazilian

Caribbean

Chagga

continental roast

dark roast

decaffeinated

espresso

estate

exotic

flavored

French roast

grand crus

Green Mountain

ground

Hawaiian

Indonesian

Italian roast

Java

Kenyan

Kona

Liberica Mysore

organic

robusta

Santos

South American

Viennese

COLLEGE AND UNIVERSITY TYPES

A and M

accredited

art school

arts college

Bible college

B school

business school

cluster college

community college

cow college

distance learning university

divinity school

free university

graduate school

Ivy League university

junior college

laboratory school

land-grant college

law school

medical school

military college

multiversity

normal school

professional school

research institute

seminary

senior college

state college

teachers college

theological seminary

training college

university college

war college

yeshiva

COMETS

elliptical orbit

exotic ice

fireball

gegenschein

hyperbolic comet

ion tail

long-period comet

Oort cloud

periodic

short-period comet

zodiacal light

COMPUTER HARDWARE

accumulator

acoustic coupler

arithmetic/logic unit

buffer

card

carriage

cathode-ray tube

CD drive

central processing unit

code-decoder

console

converter

digitizer

disk drive

display

dot-matrix printer

drive

DVD drive

emulator

Ethernet card

expansion slot

external slot

file server

firewall

floppy disk drive

front-end processor

gateway

graphics tablet

hard drive

input/output device

I/O port

impact printer

ink-jet printer

keyboard

laptop computer

laser printer

letter-quality printer

line printer

logic board

magnetic disk

mainframe

microcomputer

microprocessor

minicomputer

modem

module

monitor

motherboard

near-letter-quality printer

notebook computer

optical scanner

palmtop

parallel port

parallel printer

personal computer

port

read/write head

router

scanner

screen

serial port

serial printer

server

smart terminal

supercomputer

supermini

surge protector

thermal printer

thimble printer

video card

workstation

COMPUTER SCIENCE BRANCHES

artificial intelligence or AI

automata theory

combinatorial processes

compiler design

computer applications

computer architecture

computer graphics

computer systems

computer-aided design

computer-aided learning

computer-aided manufacturing

computer-aided molecular design

computer-aided testing

computer-based learning

computer-integrated manufacture

computer-managed instruction

cybernetics

data entry

data processing

desktop publishing

electronic data processing

industrial data processing

information retrieval

information storage and retrieval

information technology

language processing

logical design

machine organization

management information system

natural language processing

neural networks

nonnumerical applications

numerical analysis

numerical applications

office automation

operating systems

optimization

programming

programming languages

robotics

simulation

software engineering

switching theory

symbol manipulation

systems analysis

theory of computation

theory of formal languages

utility programs

COMPUTER SOFTWARE

adware

anti-virus

applet

application

archiving

assembly language

authoring system

automatic data processing

background program

benchmark program

bridgeware

browser

bundled software

censorware

compiler

compression

courseware

database

database management system

debugger

defragmenter

demonstration

diagnostic

disk operating system

driver

educational software

emulation or emulator

engine

executable code

expert system

file management system

firewall

firmware

freeware

front end

graphical user interface

graphics program

groupware

high-level language

interpreter

low-level language

machine language

middleware

object code

operating system

personal productivity

portal

presentation software

productivity software

public-domain software

relational database

search engine

shareware

spreadsheet

structured language

system software

text editor

user interface

vaporware

ware

word processing

CONCLUSIONS AND COMPLIMENTARY CLOSES

affectionately

always

best wishes

cheers

cordially

cordially yours

ever

ever yours

faithfully

faithfully yours

fondly

lovingly

most sincerely

namaste

regards

respectfully

respectfully yours

sincerely

sincerely yours

with all good wishes

with all my love

with love

with peace

yours affectionately

yours faithfully

yours most sincerely

yours respectfully

yours sincerely

yours truly

CONDIMENTS

aioli

anchovy

angostura bitters

aspic

barbecue sauce

Bearnaise sauce

black pepper

bread and butter pickle

butter

caper

catsup or ketchup

cheese

cheese dip

chili sauce

chocolate

chutney

clam dip

cornichon

cranberry sauce

cream cheese

dill pickle

dip

dressing

duck sauce

gherkin

guacamole

herb

hoisin sauce

honey

horseradish

hot pepper

jalapeño pepper

jam

jelly

ketchup

leek

lemon

lemon curd

lemon peel

lime

maple syrup

marinade

marmalade

mayonnaise

mint sauce

mustard

onion

pepper

pepper sauce

picante sauce

pickle

pimento

preserves

radish

relish

remoulade

salad dressing

salsa

salt

sashimi

sauce

seasoning

shallot

sour cream

soy sauce

spice

steak sauce

stuffing

sugar

sweet pickle

Tabasco

taco sauce

tahini

tartar sauce

vinegar

Worcestershire sauce

zest

CONJUNCTIONS

according as

afore

after

against

albeit

also

although

an

and

as

as far as

as how

as if

as long as

as soon as

as though

as well as

because

before

being

both

but

'cause

considering

directly

either

ere

ergo

except

excepting

for

for and

forasmuch as

fore

gin

how

howbeit

however

if

immediately

inasmuch as	other than	tho	whereinto
in case	otherwise	though	whereof
in order that	plus	till	whereon
insofar as	provided	unless	whereso
insomuch as	providing	unlike	wheresoever
instantly	rather than	until	wherethrough
lest	save	well	whereto
let alone	saving	what	whereunder
like	seeing	when	whereunto
much as	since	whence	whereupon
much less	so	whenever	wherever
nay	so long as	whensoever	wherewith
neither	so sobeit	where	whether
never mind	so that	whereabout	while
nor	still	whereabouts	whiles
notwithstanding	still less	whereas	whilst
now	supposing	whereat	whither
once	syne	whereby	why
once that	than	wherefore	without
only	that	wherefrom	yet
or	then	wherein	

CONSTELLATIONS

Andromeda or the Chained Lady

Antlia or the Air Pump

Apus or the Bird of Paradise

Aquarius or the Water Bearer

Aquila or the Eagle

Ara or the Altar

Aries or the Ram

Auriga or the Charioteer

Boötes or the Herdsman

Caelum or Caela Sculptoris or the

Sculptor's Tool or Chisel

Camelopardalis or the Giraffe

Cancer or the Crab

Canes Venatici or the Hunting Dogs

Canis Major or the Larger Dog or Orion's Hound

Canis Minor or the Lesser Dog

Capricorn or the Goat

Carina or the Keel

Cassiopeia or the Lady in the Chair

Centaurus or the Centaur

Cepheus or the Monarch

Cetus or the Whale

Chamaeleon or the Chameleon

Circinus or the Compasses

Columba or Noah's Dove

Coma Berenices or Berenice's Hair

Corona Australis or the Southern Crown

Corona Borealis or the Northern Crown

Corvus or the Crow

Crater or the Cup or the Goblet

Crux or the Southern Cross

Cygnus or the Swan

Delphinus or the Dolphin

Dorado or Swordfish or the Goldfish

Draco or the Dragon

Equuleus or the Little Horse

Eridanus or the River

Fornax or the Furnace

Gemini or the Twins

Grus or the Crane

Hercules

Horologium or the Clock Hydra or the Sea Serpent

Hydrus or the Water Snake

Indus or the Indian

Lacerta or the Lizard

Leo Minor or the Lesser Lion

Leo or the Lion

Lepus or the Hare

Libra or the Balance

Lupus or the Wolf

Lynx or the Lynx

Lyra or the Lyre

Mensa or the Table

Microscopium or the Microscope

Monoceros or the Unicorn

Musca or the Fly

Norma or the Rule

Octans or the Octant

Ophiuchus or the Serpent Bearer

Orion or the Hunter

Pavo or the Peacock

Pegasus or the Winged Horse

Perseus or the Hero

Phoenix or the Phoenix

Pictor or the Painter

Pisces or the Fishes

Piscis Australis or the Southern Fish

Puppis or the Stern

Pyxis or the Mariner's Compass

Reticulum or the Net Sagitta or the Arrow

Sagittarius or the Archer

Scorpius or the Scorpion

Sculptor or the Sculptor

Scutum or the Shield

Serpens or the Serpent

Sextans or the Sextant

Taurus or the Bull

Telescopium or the Telescope

Triangulum Australe or the Southern Triangle

Triangulum or the Triangle

Tucana or the Toucan

Ursa Major or the Big Dipper

Ursa Minor or the Little Dipper

Vela or the Sails

Virgo or the Virgin

Volans or Piscis Volans or the Flying Fish

Vulpecula or the Little Fox

CONTINENTS

Africa

Asia

Europe

South America

Antarctica

Australia

North America

CONTRACEPTIVES

birth control pill or oral contraceptive

cervical cap

coil

coitus interruptus

condom

contraceptive jelly

diaphragm

douche

female condom

female sterilization

intrauterine device or IUD

morning-after pill

mucus method

rhythm method

skin implant

spermicidal cream or jelly

spermicide

sponge

sympto-thermal method

vasectomy

withdrawal

CONTRACTIONS

aren't

can't

couldn't

could've

didn't

doesn't

don't

hadn't

hasn't

haven't

he'd

he'll

here's

he's

I'd

I'll

I'm

isn't

it'll

it's

I've

let's

mightn't

might've

mustn't

oughtn't

shan't

she'd

she'll

she's

shouldn't

should've

that's

there's

they'd

they'll

they're

they've

wasn't

we'd

we'll

we're

weren't

we've

what's   wouldn't   you'll
who's   would've   you're
won't   you'd   you've

COOKERS

autoclave   Crockpot   grill   rotisserie
baker   deep fat fryer   haybox   samovar
barbecue   double boiler   hibachi   slow cooker
boiler   Dutch oven   hotplate   smoker
brazier   electric cooker   infrared broiler   solar box cooker
broiler   electric frying pan   infrared cooker   steamer
camp stove   electric roaster   microwave oven   stove
chafer   electric toaster   oven   toaster
chafing dish   field range   percolator   toaster oven
coffee maker   fireless cooker   pressure cooker   waffle iron
convection oven   fry-cooker   pressure saucepan   waterless cooker
cook stove   galley stove   range
cooktop   gas grill   rice cooker
corn popper   griddle   roaster

COOKIE TYPES

animal cracker   chocolate chip   gingersnap   macaroon
bar   cookie   graham cracker   oatcake
biscuit   fig bar   hardtack   oatmeal cookie
brandy snap   florentine   hermit   oatmeal-raisin cookie
brownie   fortune cookie   jumble   palm leaf
butter   garibaldi   ladyfinger   panettone
                    gingerbread man

peanut butter cookie   pretzel   shortbread   tollhouse

petit beurre   ratafia   sugar cookie   wafer

COOKING METHODS

bake	deep-fry	pickle	slow-cook
barbecue	devil	poach	smoke
baste	fire	pre-cook	spit-roast
blanch	fricassee	pressure-cook	steam
boil	fry	reduce	stew
braise	griddle	reheat	stir-fry
brew	grill	roast	tandoori
brown	heat	sauté	tenderize
caramelize	marinate	scallop	thicken
charbroil	oven-roast	scramble	toast
coddle	pan-broil	sear	
cure	pan-fry	shirr	
curry	parboil	simmer	

COOKING OILS AND FATS

almond oil	coconut oil	grapeseed oil	partially hydrogenated vegetable oil
avocado oil	corn oil	hazelnut oil	
bacon fat	cottonseed oil	lard	peanut oil
butter	drippings	margarine	poppyseed oil
canola	extra virgin olive oil	oleomargarine	pumpkin oil
chicken fat	ghee	olive oil	rapeseed
cocoa butter	goose grease	palm oil	rendered chicken fat

rice bran oil

safflower oil

schmaltz

sesame oil

shortening

solid vegetable
shortening

soya oil

soybean oil

suet

sunflower oil

vegetable oil

virgin olive oil

walnut oil

wheat germ oil

COOKS AND SERVERS, TYPES OF

baker

barkeeper

barmaid

barman

bartender

busboy

carhop

caterer

chef

chef de cuisine

chief cook

confectioner

cook

dishwasher

headwaiter

host

hostess

innkeeper

kitchen mail

maitre d'hotel pastry
chef

pastry cook

prep cook

publican

restaurateur

scullery maid

server

short-order cook

soda jerk

sommelier

sous-chef

steward

waiter

waitperson

waitress

waitron

wine steward

COOLING SYSTEMS

air conditioning

air cooling

cool cells

coolant system

drip system

evaporative cooling

fan

fogging system

liquid cooling

misting system

refrigerated cooling

thermal cool storage

water cooler

CORN VARIETIES

baby

dent

edible

field

flint

flour

grain maize

green

hulled

Indian

maize

popcorn

soft

squaw

sugar

sweet

white

Yankee

yellow

COTTON VARIETIES

absorbent

American

duck

Egyptian

French

island or upland

muslin

Nankeen

pearl

percale

Peruvian

pima

sea or sea island

sewing

COUNTRIES WITH COMPULSORY VOTING

Argentina

Australia

Austria

Belgium

Bolivia

Brazil

Chile

Congo

Costa Rica

Cyprus

Dominican Republic

Ecuador

Egypt

El Salvador

Fiji

Greece

Honduras

Lebanon

Libya

Liechtenstein

Luxembourg

Madagascar

Mexico

Nauru

Panama

Paraguay

Philippines

Singapore

Thailand

Turkey

Uruguay

Venezuela

COURT AND LEGAL BODY TYPES

adjective law

administrative law

admiralty law

appellate court

bar association

canon law

case law

circuit court

city magistrate's court

civil law

commercial law

common law

constabulary

constitutional law

county court

county grand jury

county supreme court

court of appeals

court of chancery

court of claims

court of common pleas

court of customs appeals

court of inquiry

court of law

court of record

court of sessions

criminal court

criminal law

customs court

district court

divorce court

federal court

felony court

grand jury

Hammurabi Code

Inns of Court

international law

Justinian Code

juvenile court

kangaroo court

legal aid

maritime law

military law

moderator

moot court

municipal court

Napoleonic code

night court

patent law

police court

probate court

procedural law

Roman law

small-claims court

special court

state appellate court of appeal

state circuit court of appeal

state supreme court

superior court

Supreme Court

surrogate's court

tax court

tort law

traffic court

trial court

tribunal

United States armed forces court

United States District Court

United States Supreme Court

CRAFT TYPES

amber craft

appliqué

basketry

batik

beadwork

block printing

boneworking

bookbinding

bookcraft

burlap crafting

cabinetmaking

calligraphy

candlemaking

caning

carving

casting

ceramics

chenille work

cloisonné

copper enameling

coralworking

crewelwork

crocheting

cut-paper collage

damascening

deadworking

decalcomania

dechirage

découpage

discharge printing

doll making

dyeing

egg decorating

embossing

embroidery

enameling

engraving

etching

etui

fabric making

fabric painting

featherwork

felt crafting

fiber arts

flower making

fraktur

frottage

gem cutting

glass etching

glass painting

glassblowing

handicraft

ikat

ikebana

inlay

intaglio

ivoryworking

jetworking

jewelry making

jewelsmithing

kitemaking

knitting

lacemaking

lacquerwork

lapidary

leathercrafting

lithography

macramé

marbling

maskmaking

metalworking

mizuhiki

mobile making

mosaic

needlecraft

needlepoint

niello

origami

papercraft

paper flower making

papermaking

paper sculpture

papier-mâché

patchwork

pebble-and-stone polishing

perfumery

plaiting or braiding

plastic work

pokerwork

poonah work

potato printing

pottery

printmaking

puppetry

pyrography

quillwork

quilting

raffia

repoussage

resist printing

rubbing

rug hooking

rugmaking

rushwork

scrapcraft

scrimshaw

seed collage

serigraphy

sewing

shell carving

shellwork

silhouetting

silkscreen

spinning

stained glass work

stenciling

stitchery

stonework

straw working

string pictures

textiles

theorem painting

tie-dyeing

tincrafting

toymaking

trapunto

tritik

watermark design

weaving

whittling

wickerworking

wood carving

wood engraving

woodworking

yarn making

CRAYOLA™ CRAYONS

apricot

aquamarine

bittersweet

black

blue

blue gray

blue green

blue violet

brick red

brown

burnt orange

burnt sienna

cadet blue

carnation pink

copper

cornflower

flesh or peach

forest green

gold

goldenrod

gray

green

green blue

green yellow

Indian red or chestnut

lavender

lemon yellow

magenta

mahogany

maize

maroon

melon

mulberry

navy blue

olive green

orange

orange red

orange yellow

orchid

periwinkle

pine green

plum

Prussian blue or midnight blue

raw sienna

raw umber

red

red orange

red violet

salmon

sea green

sepia

silver

sky blue

spring green

tan

thistle

turquoise blue

violet blue

violet or purple

violet red

white

yellow

yellow green

yellow orange

CRAYON TYPES

anti-roll

chalk

chunk

conté

extra-large

fabric

gem tones

giant or hexagon

glitter

multicultural skin tones

neon

non-toxic

pastel

plastic marker

retractable

scented

sparkle

square

standard

unwrapped

washable

wax

window

wrapped

CREATURES WITH BIOLUMINESCENCE

anglerfish

bathysphere fish

coral shrimp

dinoflagellates

elaterid beetle

firefly

fire worm

glowworm

hatchetfish

Indo-Pacific fish

lantern fish

luminous bacteria

luminous fish

luminous fungi

luminous jellyfish

luminous mollusks

luminous planktonic organisms

luminous shrimp

luminous squid

protozoa

sea anemone

squid

CREATURES THAT ARE MONOGAMOUS

albatross

anglerfish

badger

beaver

budgerigar

crane

dik-dik

dove

fox

gibbon

goose

gorilla

hooded seal

jackdaw

lovebird

mongoose

Montague's harrier

orangutan

parrot

penguin

pigeon

stork

swan

termite

vulture

wolf

CRICKET POSITIONS

bowler

cover-point

deep fine leg

first slip

gully

mid-off

mid-on

second slip

square leg

third man

wicketkeeper

CRIME TYPES

abduction

accessory after the fact

accessory before the fact

accessory during the fact

aggravated assault

arson

assault

automobile theft

battery

blackmail

breach of contract

breaking and entering

bribery

burglary

capital crime

check forgery

child abuse

child molestation

civil offense

coercion

collusion

concealment

conspiracy

contempt of court

contributory negligence

counterfeiting

defamation

disorderly conduct

drug trafficking

embezzlement

espionage

extortion

false pretense

felony

forgery

fraud

graft

grand larceny

harassment

homicide

illegal gambling

involuntary manslaughter

jury tampering

kidnapping

larceny

malicious mischief

malpractice

manslaughter

misdemeanor

moral turpitude

murder

negligence

obstruction of justice

peculation

perjury

petty larceny

pickpocketing

racial harassment

racketeering

rape

reckless endangerment

resisting arrest

robbery

sabotage

sexual abuse

sexual assault

sexual harassment

shoplifting

skip bail

slander

smuggling

sodomy

statutory rape

subornation

treason

trespass

undue influence

vagrancy

vandalism

voluntary manslaughter

war crime

white collar crime

CROSSES

anchor

ankh

Avelian

botonnée

calvary

cardinal's

Celtic

chi-rho

Constantinian

crosslet

fitchée

fleury

formée

fourchée

graded

Greek

Latin

Lorraine

Maltese

Moline

orthodox

papal

patriarchal

pommée

potent

quadrate

rood or holy rood

Russian

St. Andrew's

St. Anthony's

St. Peter's

swastika or fylfot or gammadion

Y cross

CRUSTACEANS

aesop prawn

amphipod

barnacle

bass yabby

beach flea

branchiopod

branchipus

brine shrimp

copepod

crab

crawdad

crawfish

crayfish

cumacean

daphnia

decapod

decorator crab

fairy shrimp

fiddler crab

fish louse

freshwater flea

ghost shrimp

glass crab

gribble

hairy crab

hermit crab

horseshoe crab

isopod

king crab

krill

lobster

locust lobster

mantas shrimp

mantis crab

mussel shrimp

opossum shrimp

ostracod

pea crab

pebble crab

pod shrimp

porcupine crab

prawn

sailor shrimp

sand borer

sand hopper

sand skater

scorpion lobster

sea centipede

sea flea

sea slater

shellfish

shore crab

shrimp

skeleton louse

skeleton shrimp

soft-shell crab

sow bug

Spanish lobster

spider crab

spiny lobster

sponge crab

sponge shrimp

stenetrium

stomatopod

tadpole shrimp

tropical prawn

water flea

weed shrimp

well shrimp

whale louse

wood lice

CUPBOARDS AND CABINETS

airing cupboard

almirah

armoire

aumbry

Biedermeier cabinet

bookcase

bookshelf

breakfront

broom closet

buffet

bunker

bureau

caddy

canterbury

cassone

cellaret

chest

chest of drawers

chiffonier

chifforobe

china cabinet

closet

clothes chest

cocktail cabinet

coffer

commode

console

corner cupboard

court cupboard

crate

credenza

display case

dresser

dry sink

escritoire

étagère

filing cabinet

hamper

highboy

Hoosier cabinet

hope chest

hutch

icebox

kitchen cabinet

larder

liquor cabinet

locker

lowboy

mantel

meat safe

medicine cabinet

pantry

playpen

poudreuse

press

rack

safe

sea chest

secrétaire

shelf

shelves

sideboard

storage unit

strongbox

tabernacle

tallboy

tea caddy

tea wagon

trunk

under-stairs cupboard

vanity

vitrine

wall unit

wardrobe

Welsh dresser

wet bar

whatnot

wine rack

Yorkshire dresser

CUPS AND DRINKING VESSELS

beaker
beer glass
beer mug
blackjack
bottle
bowl
brandy snifter
cannikin
chalice
coffee cup
coffee mug

demitasse
flagon
flask
glass
goblet
highball glass
jigger
jorum
jug
juice glass
liqueur glass

loving cup
mug
noggin
pannikin
pony
rhyton
rummer
schooner
seidel
shot glas
snifter

stein
stoup
tankard
teacup
tumbler
water glass
wine glass
yard of ale

CURRANT VARIETIES

black
buffalo
cherry
clove
fetid

flowering
garden
golden
Indian
Missouri

mountain
native
red
red and white
skunk

spice
white
wild
winter

CURRIES

Balti
Bhuna
Birjani
Ceylon
Dhansak

Dopiaza
Gobi Masala
Jalfrezi
Karahi
Kashmir

Korma
Madras
masala
Pasanda
Phal

Rhogan Josh
Thal
Tikka Masala
Vindaloo

Curtains and Draperies

arras
bamboo shade
blind
café curtain
contour curtain
draw curtain
drop curtain
fire curtain

fire screen
jalousie
panel
partition
priscilla curtains
purdah
rollup shade
Roman shade

safety curtain
screen
shade
shoji screen
shower curtain
shutter
swag
tapestry

theater curtain
tieback curtain
valance
veil
venetian blind
window shade

Curves

arc
Archimedean spiral
bell curve
brachistochrone
cardioid
catenary
characteristic curve
circle
cissoid
closed
conchoid

crescent
cycloid
ellipse
epicycloid
equiangular spiral
evolute
French curve
Gaussian curve
helix
hyperbola
hypocycloid

involute
Jordan curve
lemniscate
logarithmic spiral
logistic curve
normal curve
oval
parabola
polar curve
sigmoid curve
simple closed

simple
sine curve
sinusoid
skew
solidus
spiral
spline
transition curve
trochoid

CUTLERY, FLATWARE, AND SILVERWARE

after-dinner coffee spoon

Asian-style cleaver

bird's-beak paring knife

bone cleaver

boning knife

bouillon spoon

bread knife

butter knife

butter spreader

carving fork

carving knife

cheese knife

chocolate spoon

chopsticks

citrus spoon

cleaver

cocktail fork

coffee spoon

cook's knife

cutlery

demitasse spoon

dessert fork

dessert knife

dessert spoon

dinner fork

dinner knife

electric knife

filleting knife

fish fork

fish knife

five o'clock spoon

flatware

fondue fork

fork

fruit fork

fruit knife

grapefruit knife

grapefruit spoon

ham knife

ice cream spoon

iced-beverage spoon

kitchen knife

knife

lobster fork

luncheon fork

luncheon knife

offset knife

oyster fork

oyster knife

paring knife

pastry fork

place spoon

runcible spoon

salad fork

salt spoon

sandwich knife

Santoku knife

seafood fork

serrated knife

serving spoon

sheep's-foot paring knife

silverware

slicer

slicer with granton edge

soup spoon

spoon

steak knife

sundae spoon

tablespoon

teaspoon

utility knife

vegetable knife

CYCLE TYPES

all terrain vehicle/ATV

bicycle

bicycle-built-for-two

bike

BMX bike

chopper

dandy

dirt bike

hog

hybrid bike

minibike

monkey bike

monocycle

moped

motorbike

motorcycle

motor scooter

mountain bike

off-road bike

ordinary

pedicab

quadricycle

racing bike

scooter

sidewalk bike

tandem

ten-speed

touring bike

trail bike

tricycle

trike

trishaw

unicycle

velocipede

DAIRY PRODUCTS

bonnyclabber	curds	heavy cream	oleo
butter	dairy food	ice cream	sour cream
cheese	eggs	kefir	sweet butter
clabber	frozen yogurt	leben	whey
cream	goat's milk	light cream	whipping cream
crème fraiche	half-and-half	milk	yogurt

DANCE TYPES

aerobic dancing	barn dancing	ceremonial dancing	comedy ballet
agricultural dancing	basket dancing	character dancing	country dancing
animal dance	belly dancing	choral dancing	court dancing
ballet	boogie-woogie	circle dancing	dirty dancing
ballroom dancing	break dancing	classical ballet	disco dancing
bamboo dance	candle dancing	clog dancing	eagle dancing

exotic dancing

fan dancing

feather dancing

flamenco

folk dancing

folklorico

garland dancing

go-go dancing

gypsy dancing

handkerchief dancing

interpretive dancing

jazz dancing

jazz tap

jitterbugging

lap dancing

line dancing

macumba

marathon dancing

modern ballet

modern dance

morris dancing

nude dancing

rain dancing

ritual dancing

round dancing

rumba

samba

slam dancing

snake dancing

social dancing

soft-shoe dancing

solo dancing

square dancing

step dancing

striptease

swing dancing

sword dancing

tango

tap dancing

taxi dancing

toe dancing

waltz

war dancing

DEATH CUSTOMS AND RITES

black arm band

black clothing

charitable donation

death notice

doorway crepe

epigraph

epitaph

extreme unction

flowers

funeral

funeral notice

last rites

Mass

Mass card

memorial

mourning

obituary

prayer

religious service

sympathy card

veil

wake

will

DECATHLON

100-meter run

110-meter high hurdles

1500-meter run

400-meter run

discus throw

high jump

javelin throw

long jump

pole vault

shot put

DECKS

after deck

anchor deck

awning deck

boat deck

bridge deck

cargo deck

flight deck

forecastle deck

forward deck

fourth deck or orlop deck

freeboard deck

gun deck

half deck

hurricane deck

landing deck

lower deck

main deck

middle deck

platform deck

poop deck

promenade deck

protective deck

quarterdeck

second deck

shelter deck

spar deck

splinter deck

sun deck

superstructure deck

third deck

turret deck

upper deck

weather deck

DEER AND ANTELOPE

addax

American antelope

axis deer

barasingha

barking

beira

beisa

bezoar antelope

blackbuck

black-tailed deer

blesbok

bongo

bontebok

brocket

brown

bulbaline antelope

burrow

bushbuck

caribou

chamois

chevrotain

Chinese water deer

chital

dibatag

dik-dik

duiker

eland

elk

fallow deer

four-horned antelope

gazelle

gemsbok

gerenuk

gnu

goat antelope

goral

grazing antelope

greater kudu

grysbok

guemal

harnessed antelope

hartebeest

hirola

hog deer

impala

klipspringer

kob

kudu

lechwe

marsh antelope

marsh deer

moose

mountain antelope

mountain goat

mouse deer

mule deer

muntjac

musk deer

musk ox
nilgai
nyala
okapi
oribi
oryx
pampas deer
Pere David's deer
pronghorn antelope
pudu
puku
pygmy antelope
red deer
reedbuck
reindeer
rhebok
roan antelope
roe deer
royal antelope
royal stag
rusa
sable antelope
saiga
sambar
sasin
serow
sika
sitatunga
sorel
spiral-horned antelope
springbok
steenbok
suni
swamp deer
takin
thamin
Tibetan antelope
topi
tsessebi
tufted deer
Virginia deer
wapiti
water antelope
waterbuck
water deer
white-tailed deer
wildebeest

DENTISTRY SPECIALTIES

cosmetic dentistry
dental orthpedics
dental surgery
endodontics
exodontics
family dentistry
general dentistry
gerodontics
implantology
laser dentistry
operative dentistry
oral and maxillofacial pathology
oral and maxillofacial radiology
oral and maxillofacial surgery
oral surgery
orthodontics or orthodontia
pediatric dentistry
pedodontics
periodontics
prosthetic dentistry
radiodontics

DESERT TYPES

coastal
cold or frigid
desert pavement
extraterrestrial
hot
hot and dry
mid-latitude
monsoon
mountain
paleodesert
plateau
polar
rain shadow
rock
sand
semiarid
stony
temperate
trade wind

DESIGN SPECIALTIES

accessory design

appearance design

architectural design

automotive design

book design

clothing design or fashion design

computer-aided design

costume design

ergonomics

environmental design

fashion design

furniture design

garden design

graphic design

industrial design

information design

interior design

jewelry design

landscape architecture

lighting design

package design

pottery design

process design

product design

research design

stage design

systems design

textile design

typographic design

urban design

DESSERTS

ambrette

ambrosia

angel cake

angel food cake

angel pie

apple charlotte

apple cobbler

apple crisp

apple pandowdy

apple pie

baked Alaska

baklava

banana split

bananas foster

Banbury tart

bannock

banoffi pie

Battenberg cake

Bavarian cream

blacking pudding

blancmange

blintze

bombe

Boston cream pie

brandy snap

bread pudding

Brown Betty

brownie

butterscotch

cake

candy

cannoli

cassata

charlotte

charlotte russe

cheesecake

cherries jubilee

chess pie or chess cake

chocolate

chocolate cake

chocolate chip cookie

chocolate mousse

clafouti

cobbler

coffeecake

compote

cookie

cottage pudding

coupe

cream puff

crème Aanglais

crème brûlée

crème caramel

crème Chantilly

crème patissiere

crêpe suzette

crisp

cruller

crumble

cupcake

custard

Danish pastry

death by chocolate

deep-dish pie

dessert cheese

devil's food cake

doughnut or donut

duff

éclair

Edinburgh fog

egg cream

egg custard

Eskimo pie

fig bar

flan

floating island

flummery

frangipane

frappe

frozen custard

frozen dessert

frozen yogurt

fruitcake

fruit cup

fruit pie

frumenty

funnel cake

galatoboureko

gâteau

gelatin

gelato

genoise

gingerbread

gingersnap

granita

halvah

hasty pudding

honey cake

hot cross bun

ice box cake

ice cream

ice cream bar

ice cream cake

ice cream float

ice cream sandwich

ice cream soda

ice cream sundae

Indian pudding

Italian ice

Jell-O

jelly roll

junket

key lime pie

kuchen

ladyfinger

layer cake

lemon meringue pie

loaf cake

macaroon

Madeira cake

madeleine

marble cake

marrons glacées

marshmallow

mela stregata

meringue

milkshake

millefeuille

Mississippi mud pie

mousse

mud pie or
Mississippi mud pie

napoleon

Nesselrode

pandowdy

panettone

parfait

pashka

pastry

patisserie

pavlova

peach Melba

pecan pie

petit four

pie

pineapple upside-
down cake

plum pudding

poached pear

popover

pound cake

profiterole

prune whip

pudding

pumpkin pie

rhubarb crumble

rice pudding

rum baba

Sacher torte

Sally Lunn

savarin

scone

sherbet

shoo-fly pie

shortbread

shortcake

simnel cake

s'mores

snow cone

snow pudding

sorbet

soufflé

spice cake

sponge cake

spumoni

steamed pudding

stolen

strawberry shortcake

streusel

sugar cookie

sugar wafer

sundae

sweet potato pie

sweet roll

syllabub

tapioca

tart

tartlet

tartufo

teacake

tiramisu

Toll House cookie

torte

tortoni

trifle

turnover

upside-down cake

vacherin

wafer

waffle

wedding cake

white cake

yellow cake

zabaglione

zuppa inglese

DEVIL'S DESIGNATIONS

Adversary

Angel of the
bottomless pit

Angel of darkness

Antichrist

Apollyon

Archfiend

Author of Evil

Beelzebub

Belial

Common Enemy

Demon

Deuce

Devil Incarnate

Dickens

Eblis

Evil One

Evil Spirit

Father of Evil

Father of Lies

Fiend

Foul Fiend

Haborym

His Satanic Majesty

Hornie

Lord of the Flies

Lucifer

Mastema

Mephistopheles

Old Bendy

Old Boy

Old Clootie
or Auld Clootie

Old Enemy

Old Gentleman

Old Gooseberry

Old Harry

Old Ned

Old Nick

Old Poker

Old Scratch

Old Serpent

O-Yama

Prince of Darkness

Prince of the Devils

Prince of the
power of the air

Prince of this world

Satan

Shaitan

The Tempter

The Devil

Typhon

Wicked One

DICE POINTS AND ROLLS

blanket roll or soft-pad roll

boxes or hard eight

craps

doublet

drop shot

dump over shot

eight, eighter from Decatur, Ada from Decatur, Ada Ross, Ada Ross the stable hoss

English, ass English, body English, Jonah

even roll

fimps or hard ten

five, fee-bee, fever, phoebe, little Phoebe

four, little Dick Fisher, little Dick, little joe, little joe from Baltimore, little joe from Chicago, little joe from Kokomo

greek shot

little natural or slow crap

nine, carolina, carolina nina, nina from caroliner, nina from carolina

number or point

puppy feet

seven, natural, little natural, pass, craps, skinny Dugan

six, captain hicks, sister hicks, Jimmy Hicks, sixie from dixie, sixty days, sice

ten, big dick, big Joe from Boston, slow crap

three or cock-eyes

twelve, boxcars, high noon, Gary Cooper

two, snake eyes, Dolly Parton

DICTIONARY TYPES

art

bilingual

business

CD-ROM

children's

cliché

collegiate

computing

conceptual

concise

cooking

crossword

desk

dialectal

electronic

encyclopedic

etymological

euphemism

finance

foreign language

general

glossary

historical

idiom

law

learner's or English as a Second Language

lexical database

lexicon

machine-readable

medical

metaphor

monolingual

new words

onomasiological

phrase

pocket

pronunciation

regional

religious

reverse

scholarly

science

semasiological

slang

special subject

spelling

sports

student

synonym

technology

thematic

unabridged

usage

visual or picture

word game

Digestive System Components

alimentary canal

anus

ascending colon

cecum

descending colon

duodenum

esophagus

gall bladder

ileum

jejunum

large intestine or colon

liver

mouth or oral cavity

pancreas

pharynx

rectum

salivary glands

small intestine

stomach

teeth

tongue

transverse colon

sigmoid colon

Dinosaurs

Alamosaurus

Albertosaurus

Allosaurus

Anchiceratops

Anchisaurus

Ankylosaurus

Apatosaurus

Atlantosaurus

Barosaurus

Brachiosaurus

Brontosaurus

Camarasaurus

Camptosaurus

Ceratops

Cetiosaurus

Chasmosaurus

Coelophysis

Coelosaurus

Compsognathus

Corythosaurus

Deinocheirus

Deinonychus

Dilophosaurus

Diplodocus

Dromaeosaurus

Dryosaurus

Edmontosaurus

Fabrosaurus

Gallimimus

Gigantosaurus

Hadrosaurus

Hetero-dontosaurus

Hylaeosaurus

Iguanodon

Kentrosaurus

Leptoceratops

Megalosaurus

Melanorosaurus

Microvenator

Monoclonius

Morosaurus

Orthinomimus

Orthitholestes

Oviraptor

Pachycephal-osaurus

Paleosaurus

Parasaurolophus

Pentaceratops

Plateosaurus

Procompsognathus

Protoceratops

Psittacosaurus

pterodactyl

raptor

Riojasaurus
Saurolophus
Sauropelta
Scelidosaurus
Seismosaurus

Staurikosaurus
Stegosaurus
Styracosaurus
Syntarsus
Tarbosaurus

theropod
Thescelosaurus
Titanosaurus
Torosaurus
Triceratops

Troödon
Tyrannosaurus
Ultrasaurus
Utahraptor
Velociraptor

DISASTER TYPES, NATURAL

avalanche
blizzard
drought
earthquake
ecocatastrophe
epidemic
famine

fire
flash flood
flood
forest fire
hailstorm
heat wave
hurricane

ice age
ice storm
impact event
landslide
mud slide
plague
sinkhole

snowslide
solar flare
supervolcano
tidal wave
tornado
tsunami
volcanic eruption

DISEASE TYPES

acute disease
allergy
atrophy
autoimmune disease
bacterial disease
blood disease
bone disease
brain disease
cancer
cardiovascular disease

circulatory disease
collagen disease
communicable disease
congenital disease
connective-tissue disease
coronary artery disease
deficiency disease
degenerative disease
digestive disease

endemic disease
endocrine disease
environmental disease
epidemic disease
functional disease
fungal disease
gastric disease or stomach disease
gastroenterological disease

gastrointestinal disease
genetic disease
geriatric disease
glandular disease
heart disease
hepatic disease or liver disease
hereditary disease
hypertrophy
iatrogenic disease
idiopathic disease

infectious disease

inflammatory disease

inherited disease

intestinal disease

joint disease

mental disease

muscular disease

neurological disease

noninfectious disease

nutritional disease

occupational disease

ophthalmic disease or eye disease

organic disease

pandemic disease

parasitic disease

pediatric disease or childhood disease

periodontal disease

protozoan disease

psychiatric disease

psychological disease

psychosomatic disease

pulmonary disease

radiation disease

renal disease or kidney disease

respiratory disease

sexually-transmitted disease, STD, venereal disease

skin disease

social disease

tropical disease

urogenital disease

viral disease

wasting disease

worm disease

DISHES, EATING

after-dinner cup and saucer

bowl

breakfast cup and saucer

cereal bowl

coffee cup

cup

demitasse

dessert bowl

dessert plate

dinner plate

dish

eggcup

fruit bowl

luncheon plate

mug

plate

porringer

salad bowl

salad plate

saucer

soup bowl

teacup

DISHES, SERVING

boat

bowl

breadbasket

bread tray

buffet plate

butter dish

cake plate

charger

coffeepot

compote

cookie jar

creamer

cruet

decanter

fish plate

gratin dish

gravy boat

jar

jug

kylix

lazy Susan

noggin

pitcher

platter

punch bowl

ramekin

salad bowl

salt and
pepper shakers

salt cellar

salver

service plate

sugar bowl

teapot

tea service

tray

tureen

DISNEY CHARACTERS, FIRST 100

Abner

Agnes

Ant Ena

Apollo

Aunt Jemima

Baby Weems

Bambi

Bambi's Mother

Bashful

Ben Ali Gator

Ben Buzzard

Big Bad Wolf

Blynken

Br'er Bear

Br'er Fox

Br'er Rabbit

Captain Churchmouse

Captain Doberman

Captain Katt

Casey

Casey, Jr.

Chicken Little

Chip

Christopher Columbus

Clarabelle Cow

Clementine

Cock Robin

Daisy Duck

Dale

Dewey

Doc

Donald Duck

Dopey

Ducky Lucky

Dumbo

Eega Beeva

Einstein

Eli Squinch

Ezra Beetle

Ferdinand the Bull

Figaro

Gepetto

Goosie Gander

Grumpy

Happy

Henny Penny

Hitler

Hortense

Huey

Humpty Dumpty

Ichabod Crane

Jack Horner

Jack Spratt

Jenny Wren

Jiminy Cricket

Johnny Appleseed

King Neptune

Little Hiawatha

Little Minnehaha

Little Toot

Mademoiselle
Upanova

Mammy Two Shoes

Mary, Mary, Quite
Contrary

Max Hare

Mickey Mouse

Minnie Mouse

Monstro

Montmorency Rodent

Mortimer Mouse
(previously Oswald
the Lucky Rabbit)

Mother Goose

Mother Hubbard

Mr. Bluebird

Noah

Nod

Pecos Bill

Pegleg Pete

Phantom Blot

Pied Piper

Pinocchio

Pluto

Reason

Red Riding Hood

Santa Claus

Simple Simon

Sleepy

Sluefoot Sue

Sneezy

Snow White

Stromboll

Sylvester Shyster

Tar Baby

Tetti Tatti

Three Blind
Mouseketeers

Thumper

Thursday

Turkey Lurkey

Ugly Duckling

Widomaker

Wynken

Yensid

DIVES, SWIMMING

armstand

backward or back

belly flop

butterfly

closed pike

feet-first

forward

front

full twist

half gainer

half twist

handstand

header

head-first

inward

jackknife

one-and-
a-half cutaway

open pike

racing

reverse

somersault

straight

swan

tuck

twist

DIVINATION FORMS

aeromancy

alectryomancy

aleuromancy

alphitomancy

anthracomancy

anthropomancy

arithmancy

aspidomancy

astragalomancy

astrodiagnosis

astrology

augury

austromancy

axinomancy

belomancy

bibliomancy

botanomancy

capnomancy

cartomancy

catoptromancy

cephalomancy

ceromancy

chalcomancy

chirognomy

chiromancy

chronomancy

cleromancy

coscinomancy

crystallomancy

cubomancy

dactyliomancy

extispicy

gastromancy

geomancy

gyromancy

halomancy

hieromancy

hippomancy

horoscopy

hydromancy

I Ching

ichthyomancy

idolomancy

lithomancy

logomancy

meteoromancy

myomancy

necromancy

nomancy

numerology

oenomancy

oneiromancy

onomancy

onychomancy

ophiomancy

ornithomancy

osteomancy

Ouija board

palmistry

pedomancy

podomancy

psychomancy

pyromancy

rhabdomancy

scapulimancy

scatomancy

sciomancy

sideromancy

sortilege

spodomancy

sycomancy

tarot cards

tephromancy

theomancy

xylomancy

zoomancy

DOG BREEDS

affenpinscher

Afghan hound

Aidi

Airedale

Akita

Alaskan husky

Alaskan Malamute

Alsatian

American Eskimo dog

American foxhound

American pit bull terrier

American Staffordshire terrier

American toy fox terrier or amertoy or toy terrier

American water spaniel

Australian cattle dog

Australian terrier

Basenji

basset hound

beagle

Bearded Collie

Bedlington terrier

Belgian sheepdog

Bernese mountain dog

Bichon Frise

black Labrador

Blenheim spaniel

bloodhound

border collie

Border terrier

borzoi

Boston terrier

Bouvier des Flandres

boxer

Briard

Brittany spaniel

Brussels griffon

bulldog or bull

bull mastiff

bullterrier

cairn terrier

carriage dog

Chesapeake Bay retriever

Chihuahua

Chinese crested

chow or chow chow

clumber spaniel

Clydesdale terrier

cocker spaniel

collie

coonhound

corgi

Curly-coated Retriever

dachshund

Dalmatian

Dandie Dinmont

deerhound

Doberman pinscher

drahthaar

elkhound

English bulldog

English cocker spaniel

English foxhound

English setter

English shepherd

English springer spaniel

English toy spaniel

Eskimo dog

field spaniel

flat-coated retriever

foxhound

fox terrier

French bulldog

gazelle hound

German shepherd

German short-haired pointer

German wirehaired pointer

giant schnauzer

Goldendoodle

golden retriever

Gordon setter

Great Dane

Great Pyrenees

greyhound

griffon

Groenendael

harrier

hound
husky

Iceland dog

Icelandic sheepdog

Irish setter

Irish terrier

Irish Water Spaniel

Irish wolfhound

Italian greyhound

Jack Russell terrier

Japanese Chin

kangaroo dog

keeshond

kelpie

Kerry Blue Terrier

King Charles spaniel

Komondor

kuvasz

Labradoodle

Labrador retriever

Lakeland terrier

Lhasa apso

malamute

Malinois

Maltese

Manchester terrier

mastiff

Mexican Hairless

miniature pinscher

miniature poodle

miniature schnauzer

Newfoundland

Norfolk spaniel

Norwegian elkhound

Norwich terrier

Old English sheepdog

otterhound

papillon

Pekingese

pit bull terrier

pointer

police dog

Pomeranian

poodle

pug

puli

rat terrier

retriever

Rhodesian ridgeback

Rottweiler

Russian owtchar

Russian wolfhound

Saluki

Samoyed

schipperke

schnauzer

Scottish deerhound

Scottish terrier

Sealyham terrier

setter

Shar-Pei

shepherd dog

Shetland sheepdog

Shih Tzu

Siberian husky

silky terrier

Skye Terrier

spaniel

spitz

springer s paniel

St. Bernard

Staffordshire bull terrier

Sussex spaniel

terrier

Tibetan terrier

Toy Manchester

toy poodle

toy spaniel

toy terrier

Vizsla

water spaniel

Weimaraner

Welsh collie

Welsh corgi

Welsh Springer Spaniel

Welsh Terrier

West Highland white terrier

whippet

wirehaired terrier

wolfhound

yellow Labrador

Yorkshire terrier

DOME TYPES

dagoba

domal

dome or cupola

domical

drum dome

geodesic dome

onion dome

pendentive

sail dome

segmented dome

semi-dome

umbrella or parachute

DOORS, PARTITIONS, AND WALLS

accordion door

accordion partition

archway

back door

barbed wire

bearing wall

board fence

cantilever wall

climbing wall

common wall

contravallation

curtain wall

Cyclone fence

dead wall

dike

dividing wall

doorway

double door

Dutch door

entrance

entryway

espalier

exterior wall

façade

faced wall

fixed door

folding door

folding partition

fortified wall

French door

front door

garden wall

gate

gateway

grille

half door

hatch

hedge

hoarding

interior wall

louver

moon gate

multi-unit wall

non-bearing wall

overhead door

paling

palisade

parapet

partition door

passageway

patio door

perpend wall

picket fence

pocket door

portal

power-assisted door

prehung door

rail fence

railing

rampart

retaining wall

revolving door

ring fence

scaffolding

scarp wall

screen door

shutter

sliding door

sliding folding door

standing wall

stockade

stone wall

storm door

swinging door

transom

trapdoor or trap door

trellis

Trombe wall

vallation

vallum

vault door

Venetian door

weir

zigzag fence

DRAWING MATERIALS

charcoal pencils

colored pencils

Conté crayons

drawing board

drawing mat

erasers

heavy drawing paper

large metal clips

newsprint paper

pastel sticks

pencil sharpener

pencils

pens

photocopy paper

DRAWING TYPES

architectural

brush

caricature

cartographic

cartoon

chalk

charcoal

chiaroscuro

contour

crayon

detail

draft

engineering

free-hand

graph

life

line

mechanical

outline

pastel

perspective

plan

profile

scale

schematic

silhouette

sketch

technical

DRESSES AND SKIRTS

A-line skirt

arisaid

ballet skirt

backwrap

ball gown

basic dress

body dress

bouffant skirt

bridal gown

chemise

cheongsam

chiton

coat dress

cocktail dress

court dress

crinoline

culottes

dinner dress

dirndl

divided skirt

double gown

evening dress

farthingale

formal

frock

full skirt

fustanella

gathered skirt

gown or evening gown

granny dress

grass skirt

gymslip

harem skirt

hobble skirt

hoopskirt

housedress

hula skirt

jumper

kilt

kimono

kirtle

knee-length skirt

lavalava

little black dress

mantua

maternity dress

maxiskirt

microminiskirt

midiskirt

miniskirt

Mother Hubbard

muu-muu

overdress

overskirt

pannier

pantdress

pantskirt

pareu

pasin

peplum

petticoat

pinafore

pleated skirt

princess dress

sack

sari

sarong

saya

sheath

shift

shirt-dress

short gown

skort

slit skirt

sundress

sweater dress

tank dress

T-dress

tea gown

tent dress

tube dress

tunic dress

tutu

underskirt

wraparound

wrap dress

wrap skirt

DRINKS, SOFT

birch beer

bitter lemon

carbonated water

club soda

cola

cream soda

dandelion and burdock

fizzy water

ginger ale

ginger beer

ginger pop

lemonade

limeade

lolly water

mineral water

orangeade

orange soda

phosphate

quinine water

root beer

sarsaparilla

seltzer water

soda

soda water

sports drink

spring water

tonic water

DRIVE-ON-THE-LEFT LOCATIONS

Anguilla

Antigua and Barbuda

Australia

Bahamas

Bangladesh

Barbados

Bermuda

Bhutan

Botswana

British Virgin Islands

Brunei

Cayman Islands

Channel Islands

Cook Islands

Cyprus

Dominica

Falkland Islands

Fiji

Grenada

Guyana

Hong Kong

India

Indonesia

Jamaica

Japan

Kenya

Kiribati

Lesotho

Macau

Malawi

Malaysia

Malta

Mauritania

Mauritius

Montserrat

Mozambique

Namibia

Nepal

New Zealand

Niue

Norfolk Island

Pakistan

Papua New Guinea

Republic of Ireland

Seychelles

Sikkim

Singapore

Solomon Islands

Somalia

South Africa

Sri Lanka

St. Helena

St. Kitts and Nevis

St. Lucia

St. Vincent and
the Grenadines

Surinam or Suriname

Swaziland

Tanzania

Thailand

Tonga

Trinidad and Tobago

Tuvalu

Uganda

United Kingdom

Virgin Islands

Zambia

Zimbabwe

DRUG TYPES

anabolic steroid

analgesic

anesthetic

anti-anxiety drug

antibacterial drug

antibiotic

anticoagulant drug

antidepressant

antidysrhythmic drug

anti-epileptic drug

antifungal drug

antihistamine

anti-inflammatory
analgesic

antimanic

antiparasitic drug

anti-Parkinson drug

antipsychotic drug

antipyretic drug

antiviral drug

contraceptive

cytotoxic drug

depressant

fibrinolytic drug

general
anesthetic

hallucinogen

histamine

hormone drug

local anesthetic

narcotic

opioid analgesic

oxytocin drug

sedative-
hypnotic drug

stimulant

DRUGSTORE OR PHARMACY LIST

acetaminophen

acne medication

adhesive bandages
or Band-Aids™

adhesive tape

after-shave lotion

allergy medications

antacid

anti-diarrheal
medicine

antihistamine

anti-itch medicine

antiperspirant

antiseptic ointment

aspirin

astringent

athletic bandage

baby oil

bath soap

bathroom cups

blush

body lotion

body powder

boric acid

breath mints

bubble bath

burn ointment

calamine lotion

cold cream

cold medication

cologne

concealer

contact lens case

contact lens solution

contraception

corn plaster

corn remover

cosmetic bag

cosmetics

cotton balls

cotton swabs

cough medication

dandruff shampoo

dental floss

denture supplies

deodorant

depilatory cream

diapers

diaper wipes

distilled water

diuretic

electric shaver

enema

Epsom salts

eye drops

eyeglass cleaner

eyeliner

eye shadow

face cream

face powder

face soap

facial hair bleach

fiber supplement

first-aid cream

first-aid kit

foundation makeup

gauze pads

hair accessory

hairbrush

hair coloring

hair comb

hair conditioner

hair curler

hair dryer

hair spray

hand cream

heating pad

hemorrhoid
medication

hydrogen peroxide

ice pack

ipecac syrup

laxative

lip balm

lipstick

makeup brush

manicure supplies

mascara

medicated powder

medicine dropper

medicine spoon

mineral oil

mineral supplement

mirror

mouthwash

muscle-pain ointment

nail clippers

nail file

nail polish remover

nasal decongestant medicine

nasal spray

pain reliever

perfume

petroleum jelly

pregnancy test kit

prescriptive medication

pumice stone

razor

razor blades

reading glasses

rubbing alcohol

salt tablets

sanitary supplies

scissors

scrub brush

shampoo

shaving cream

shaving kit

shower cap

sinus medication

skin wound protectant

sponge

styptic pencil

sunblock

sunscreen

suntan lotion

thermometer

tissues

toilet paper

toothache medication

toothbrush

toothpaste

vaporizing cold medicine

vitamins

zinc oxide ointment

DRUPES

A drupe is a one-seeded indehiscent fruit having a hard bony endocarp, a fleshy inside texture, and a thin outer skin that is flexible (as in the cherry) or dry and almost leathery (as in the almond).

almond

apricot

betel palm

blackberry

cherry

coconut

date

elderberry

mango

mulberry

nectarine

olive

peach

plum

DYES AND PIGMENTS

acid dye

acridine dye

alizarin

alkanet

anil

aniline dye

annatto

anthracene

artificial dye

azo dye

basic dye

biological stain

bister

black iron oxide

boneblack

brazilin

brown ocher

butternut

cadmium yellow

carbon black

carmine

carotene

catechu

Chinese white or zinc white

chrome red

chrome yellow

chromotrope

cinnabar

cobalt blue

cochineal

Congo red

copper sulphate

crocein

cyanine

developing dye

disazo dye

eosin

fast dye

flavin

fluorescein

food color

fuchsine

fustic

garancine

gentian violet

henna

Indian yellow

indigo

induline

jewelers' rouge

kermes

lake

lampblack

litmus

madder

magenta

mauveine

mineral pigment

mordant dye

naphthol

nature dye

nigrosine

orcein

orchil or cudbear

orpiment

phosphine

phthalocyanine

picric acid

Prussian blue

purpurin

red arsenic

reddle

red lead

red ocher

rhodamine

rosanaline

safflower

saffron

sappanwood

Saxon blue

sienna

sumac

tannin

tartrazine

terre-verte

titanium white

trinitroaniline

Turkey red

turmeric

Tyrian purple

ultramarine

umber

vegetable dye

vermilion or mercuric sulfide

viridian

weld or dyer's rocket

white lead

woad

xanthene dye

yellow ocher

zedoary

Earth Sciences

aerology

aeronomy

astrogeology

bathymetry

biogeography

biological oceanography

biostratigraphy

cataclysmic geology

chemical oceanography

chronostratigraphy

climatology

crystallography

economic geology

engineering geology

environmental geology

fossilology

gemology

geobotanical prospecting

geobotany

geochemistry

geochronology

geochronometry

geocosmogony

geodesy

geodynamics

geography

geological cartography

geology

geomagnetism

geomorphology

geophysics

geopolitics

geostatistics

glacial geology

glaciology

gravimetry

historical geology

hydrography

hydrology

igneous petrology

invertebrate paleontology

limnology

lithostratigraphy

magnetostratigraphy

marine geology

medical geology

metamorphic petrology

meteorology

micropaleontology

mineralogy

mining geology

oceanography

oceanology

paleobiogeography

paleobotany

paleoceanography

paleoclimatology

paleogeography

paleogeophysics

paleolimnology

paleomagnetism

paleontology

paleopedology

palynology

pedology or soil science

petrochemistry

petrogenesis

petrography

petroleum geology

petrology or lithology

physical climatology

physical geography

physical geology

physical oceanography

planetology

plate or global tectonics

quaternary geology

radiometric dating

sedimentary petrology

sedimentology

seismography

seismology

stratigraphy

structural geology

submarine geology

tectonic geology or tectonics

tectonophysics

thalassography

topography

urban geology

vertebrate paleontology

volcanology

EBAY PROHIBITED ITEMS

academic software

advertisements

alcohol

animals and wildlife products

artifacts

batteries

beta software

bootleg recordings

cable television descramblers

catalogs (current issues)

catalytic converters and test pipes

contracts

counterfeit currency and stamps

credit cards

downloadable media

drugs and drug paraphernalia

embargoed goods

firearms

fireworks

food

freon and other refrigerants

government IDs and licenses

hazardous materials

human body parts

imported and emission non-compliant vehicles

lock-picking devices

lottery tickets

mailing lists and personal information

mature audience items

mod chips, game enhancers, and boot discs

movie prints

OEM software

offensive material

pesticides

plants and seeds

police-related items

postage meters

prescription drugs and devices

recalled items

slot machines

stocks and securities

stolen property

surveillance equipment

tobacco

travel

URLs

used airbags

weapons and knives

EDIBLE CRUSTACEANS AND GASTROPODS

crab

crayfish

langostino

langouste

langoustine

limpet

periwinkle

prawn

rock lobster

scampi

sea urchin

shrimp

spiny lobster

turban snail

whelk

EDIBLE FLOWERS

allium

angelica

anise hyssop

apple blossom

arugula

banana blossom

basil

bee balm

bergamot

borage

calendula

chamomile

carnation

chevil

chicory

chive

chrysanthemum

citrus blossom

clover

courgette

daisy

dandelion

day lilly

dill

evening primrose

fennel

fuchsia

hibiscus

hollyhock

hyacinth

hyssop

impatiens

lavender

lemon verbena

lilac

linden

marigold

marjoram

mint

mustard

nasturtium

okra

oregano

peach blossom

petunia

primrose

Queen Anne's lace

radish flower

rocket

rose

rosemary

safflower

saffron

sage

savory

snapdragon

squash blossom

sunflower

thyme

tiger lily

tulip petal

viola

violet

yucca petal

EDIBLE MOLLUSKS

abalone

Atlantic oyster

Atlantic sea scallop

basket cockle

bay scallop

blood clam

blue mussel

boring clam

California mussel

clam

cockle

European flat oyster

freshwater clam

geoduck clam

golden neck clam

great scallop

greenlip mussel

hard shell clam or quahog

Hog Island oyster

Japanese sea scallop

Kumamoto oyster

little neck clam

Manila clam

Mediterranean mussel

mussel

New Zealand cockle

New Zealand rock oyster

octopus

Olympia oyster

oyster

pink scallop

pipi clam

razor clam

scallop

soft shell clam

squid

surf clam

EDUCATION INSTITUTIONS

academy

adult school

alternative school

Bible school

boarding school

church school

common school

conservatory

consolidated school

continuation school

convent

country day school

day school

ecole

elementary school

finishing school

free school

grade school

grammar school

gymnasium

Hebrew school

high school

intermediate school

junior high school

kindergarten

language institution

Latin school

Lycée

magnet school

middle school

military academy

Montessori school

night school

nursery school

palestra

parish school

parochial school

preparatory school

preschool

primary school

private school

public school

schoolhouse

schoolroom

secondary school

seminary

senior high school

storefront school

summer school

Sunday school

trade school

training school

ulpan

upper school

vocational school

yeshiva

EGG DISHES

baked

Benedict

boiled

coddled

creamed

curried

deviled

dropped

eggs in
a mold

en cocotte

florentine

fried

fritatta

hard-boiled

huevos
rancheros

neptune

omelette

poached

quiche

Scotch

scrambled

shirred

soft-boiled

soufflé

stuffed

EGG TYPES

bird

brown

candy

caviar

chicken

chocolate

duck

fish

fowl

frog

goose

guinea
fowl

insect

lizard

ostrich

quail

reptile

robin's

sea
urchin

shad roe

shark

swan

toad

turkey

white

ELECTRIC CURRENTS

Electrons pushed through the wires of a circuit form an electric current. The push on the electrons is called electromotive force (e.m.f.).

absorption current
action current
active current
alternating current or AC
conduction current
convection current
delta current
dielectric displacement current
direct current or DC
displacement current
earth current or ground current

eddy current
emission current
exciting current
free alternating current
galvanic current
high-frequency current
induced current
induction current
interrupted current
ionization current
juice

low-frequency current
magnetizing current
multiphase current
oscillating current
periodic current
pulsating direct current
reactive current
reverse current
rotary current
single-phase alternating current

sneak current
stray current
supercurrent
thermionic current
thermoelectric current
three-phase alternating current
transient current
voltaic current
watt current
wattless current or idle current

ELECTRICAL SCIENCES

electrical engineering
electroacoustics
electroballistics
electrobiology
electrochemistry
electrodynamics
electrokinematics
electrokinetics

electromagnetics
electromagnetism
electromechanics
electrometallurgy
electrometry
electronics
electro-optics
electrophotomicro-graphy

electrophysics
electrophysiology
electrostatics
electrotechnology
electrotherapeutics
electro-thermancy
electrothermics
galvanism

hydroelectricity
magnetics
magnetometry
photoelectricity
pyroelectricity
thermionics
thermoelectricity
voltaism

ELECTRONS

An electron is the lightest stable subatomic particle known. It carries a negative charge which is considered the basic charge of electricity. The electron reacts only by the electro-magnetic, weak, and gravitational forces and was the first subatomic particle discovered.

Auger electron

beta particle

bonding electron

bound electron

cathode ray

Compton electron

conduction electron

d-electron

delta ray

electron pair

excess electron

extranuclear electron

f-electron

free electron

K electron

L electron

M electron

N electron

negatron

nuclear electron

orbital electron

p-electron

peripheral electron

photoelectron

pi electron

planetary electron

positive electron

primary electron

recoil electron

secondary electron

s-electron

spinning electron

surface-bound electron

thermoelectron

valence electron

wandering electron

ELEMENTS FOUND IN THE EARTH'S CRUST

aluminum

calcium

iron

magnesium

other elements

oxygen

potassium

silicon

sodium

ELEVATORS AND ESCALATORS

automated guideway transit

conveyor

dumbwaiter

electric elevator

food elevator

freight elevator

grain elevator

heavy-lift elevator

high-speed elevator

hoistaway

hydraulic elevator

lift

low-rise elevator

moving sidewalk

moving staircase

moving stairway

passenger elevator

people mover

pneumatic elevator

rapid-descent
elevator

service elevator

traction elevator

travelator

EMBROIDERY STITCHES

blanket stitch

buttonhole filling

buttonhole
stitch

buttonhole stitch
wheel

cable chain stitch

chain stitch

closed buttonhole
stitch

closed Cretan stitch

closed featherstitch

closed fly stitch

cloud-filling stitch

cross-stitch

darning stitch

double blanket stitch

double cross-stitch

double darning stitch

double featherstitch

double herringbone

featherstitch

fishbone

hemstitch

herringbone

Holbein stitch

interlaced running
stitch

Japanese darning
stitch

knotted blanket
stitch

lazy daisy stitch

long blanket stitch

long-armed
cross-stitch

long-armed
featherstitch

needlepoint

open Cretan stitch

petit point

raised needle
weaving

running stitch

satin stitch

short blanket stitch

split stitch

square chain stitch

tent stitch

threaded chain stitch

threaded
herringbone

tied herringbone

twisted chain
stitch

vandyke

wave stitch

weaving stitch

whipped running
stitch

whipped web

woven web

zigzag chain
stitch

ENCYCLOPEDIA TYPES

art encyclopedia

business
encyclopedia

CD-ROM
encyclopedia

children's
encyclopedia

collegiate
encyclopedia

computing
encyclopedia

concise encyclopedia

cooking
encyclopedia

desk encyclopedia

211

electronic encyclopedia

finance encyclopedia

general encyclopedia

legal encyclopedia

medical encyclopedia

pocket encyclopedia

religious encyclopedia

science encyclopedia

special subject encyclopedia

sports encyclopedia

student encyclopedia

technology encyclopedia

thematic encyclopedia

wine encyclopedia

ENDANGERED SPECIES, CAUSES OF

competition from other species

damming of rivers

disease

drainage and filling of swamps and marshes

habitat destruction

hunting

hybridization with other species and subspecies

introduction of exotic species

leveling of forests for residential and industrial development

limited distribution

oil spills

overexploitation

overharvesting

poisoning

pollution

predation

strip mining

trapping

unregulated killing or illegal killing

water pollution

ENDOCRINE GLANDS

adrenal gland

corpora allata

corpora cardiaca

corpus luteum

hypothalamus

islets of Langerhans

liver

lymph node

ovary

pancreas

parathyroid gland

pineal gland

pituitary gland

testis or testicle

suprarenal gland

thymus

thyroid gland

Energy and Fuel Sources and Types

anthracite

atomic power

benzol

biofuel

biogas

biomass energy

bitumen

butane

chemical energy

coal

coke

diesel

electrical energy

electromagnetic energy

firewood

fission energy

fossil fuel

fusion energy

gas

gas oil

gasohol

gasoline

geothermal energy

heat energy

hydroelectric power

kerosene

kinetic energy

light energy

lignite

liquefied petroleum gas or LPG

mechanical energy

methane

natural gas

nitromethane

nuclear energy

oil

paraffin

peat

petrol

petroleum

photosynthesis

potential energy

producer gas

propane

radiant energy

renewable energy

shale oil

solar energy

sound energy

steam power

synthetic fuel

tidal power

water power

wave power

whale oil

wind power

Engineers

aeronautical engineer

aerospace engineer

agricultural engineer

architectural engineer

army engineer

audio engineer

automotive engineer

ceramic engineer

chemical engineer

civil engineer

combat engineer

communications engineer

computer engineer

construction engineer

earthquake engineer

efficiency engineer

electrical engineer

electronics engineer

field engineer

flight engineer

food technology engineer

geological engineer

highway engineer

hydraulic engineer

illuminating engineer

industrial engineer

irrigation engineer

knowledge engineer

maintenance engineer

marine engineer

materials engineer

mechanical engineer

metallurgical engineer

military engineer

mining engineer

municipal engineer

naval engineer

nuclear engineer

ordnance engineer

petroleum engineer

power engineer

product engineer

radar engineer

radio engineer

railroad engineer

refrigeration engineer

research engineer

rocket engineer

sanitary engineer

social engineer

software engineer

sound engineer

steam engineer

structural engineer

telephone engineer

textile engineer

tool engineer

traffic engineer

transportation engineer

ventilation engineer

water-supply engineer

ENGRAVING TYPES

acid-blast

aquatint

black-line engraving

cerography

chalcography

chalk engraving

chasing

chemigraphy

copperplate engraving

crayon engraving

cribbling or manière criblée

drypoint or draw-point engraving

eccentric engraving

electric engraving

electro-engraving

etching

galvanography

gem engraving

glass-cutting

glyptics or glyptography

graphotype

gypsography

halftone engraving

intaglio

lignography

line cut

line engraving

linocut

lithography

metal cut

metal engraving

mezzotint

photoengraving

photomechanical

plate engraving

pyrography

recess engraving

relief etching

relief method

soft-ground etching

steel engraving

stipple engraving

wood engraving

woodburning or woodcut

xylography

zinc etching

zincography or zinc engraving

ENTERTAINER TYPES

acrobat

actor

actress

aerialist

artist

artiste

auteur

bankable star

bareback rider

busker

clown

comedian

comedienne

comic

conjuror

contortionist

dancer

disc jockey

diva

drag artist

emcee

escape artist

exotic dancer

extra

fire-eater

go-go dancer

harlequin

host

hypnotist

illusionist

impersonator

impressionist

instrumentalist

jester

jongleur

juggler

lap dancer

leading lady

leading man

lion tamer

love interest

magician

master of
ceremonies

merry andrew

method actor

mime artist

mimic

mind reader

minstrel

monologist

mummer

musician

organ grinder

performing
artist

player

puppeteer

raconteur

raconteuse

ringmaster

singer

snake charmer

soloist

song-and-dance act

stand-up comedian

star

starlet

straight man

stripper

strongman

stunt man

stunt woman

superstar

supporting actor

supporting actress

sword-swallower

thespian

tightrope
walker

tragedian

tragedienne

trapeze artist

trouper

tumbler

vaudevillian

ventriloquist

virtuoso

ENVELOPES

#10 business
#6 3/4 personal
#9 reply
airmail
announcement
banker's flap or wallet flap
baronial
booklet

business
catalog
chain
clasp
form
interoffice
letter-sheet
manila

padded
paper
pay
plastic
recycled
registered
remittance
return

self-addressed stamped
stamped
string-and-button
tear-resistant
two-way
unbleached
window

ENVIRONMENTAL SCIENCES

anthropogeography
anthroponomy
autecology
bioecology or bionomics
biogeochemistry
conservation biology
ecology
ecophysiology

environmental archaeology
environmental biology
environmental chemistry
environmental design
environmental economics
environmental engineering

environmental geography
environmental geology
environmental health
environmental horticulture
environmental management
environmental toxicology

euthenics
forestry
human ecology
land management
resource economics
synecology
urban ecology
wildlife management
zoo-ecology

ENZYME TYPES

ATPase

hydrolase

isomerase

kinase

ligase

lipase

lyase

nuclease

oxido-reductase

phosphatase

polymerase

protease

synthase

transferase

EQUESTRIAN OBSTACLES

artificial gate

brush

brush and rail

double

double oxer

fence

gate

jump

liverpool

oxer

parallel oxer

plank

post
and plank

post and rail

rail

spread

treble

triple bar

vertical

wall

wall
and rail

water jump

ERASERS

air

artgum

blackboard

cordless

electric

extra-soft

gum

handheld

ink

kneaded

latex

Magic Rub

pencil

Pink Pearl

plastic

retractable

rubber

soap

whiteboard

vinyl

ESPIONAGE TYPES

acoustic intelligence

acoustical surveillance

biographical intelligence

black border crossing

black infiltration

black list

black propaganda

bugging

civil censorship

cloak-and-dagger

communication deception

counterdeception

counterespionage

counterintelligence

countersabotage

counterspying

countersubversion

covert operations

critical intelligence

cryptanalysis

cryptology

cyberwarfare

dead drop

double agent

encryption

evasion and escape intelligence

foreign instrumentation signals intelligence

gray infiltration

gray propaganda

imagery intelligence

industrial espionage

infiltration

money laundering

political intelligence

psychological consolidation activity

psychological operations

psychological warfare

radar intelligence

radiation intelligence

radio deception

reconnaissance

secret agent

signals intelligence

spying

subversion

target intelligence

tradecraft

Trojan horse

white infiltration

white propaganda

EVIDENCE TYPES

Seemingly insignificant traces or items left at the scene of the crime by the criminal or victim are important clues in police investigations.

admissible

after-discovered

anecdotal

character

circumstantial

clear and convincing

cogent

competent

conclusive

corroborating

counter

cumulative

deathbed

demonstrative

direct

DNA

documentary

empirical

expert

external

extrinsic

eyewitness

fingerprint

footprint

hearsay
inadmissible
incompetent
indirect
insufficient
internal

involuntary or coerced
king's
material
microphonic
moral
oral

presumptive
prima facie
queen's
real
rebuttal
scientific

secondary
self
state's
tainted
voluntary
wiretap

EXOCRINE GLANDS

buccal gland
Cowper's gland
digestive gland
gastric gland
lacrimal gland

Lieberkuhn's gland
liver
mammary gland
nabothian gland
pancreas

parotid gland
preputial gland
prostate gland
salivary gland
sebaceous gland

sublingual gland
submandibular gland
sweat gland
tarsal gland
vestibular gland

EYEGLASSES

aviator
Ben Franklin
bifocals
blinkers
butterfly glasses
cheaters
clip-ons
contact lenses
dark glasses
glasses

goggles
granny glasses
half-glasses
harlequin
horn-rims
Lennon specs
lorgnette
lorgnon
louchette
monocle

opera glasses
owl glasses
peepers
pince-nez
planos
prescription
progressive-lens glasses
quizzing glass
reading glasses
safety glasses

scissors glasses
shades
single-vision glasses
specs
spectacles
sunglasses
tortoiseshell
trifocals
varifocals
wraparound

219

Fabrics and Textiles

aba	barathea	buckram	cashmere
acetate	batik	buckskin	castor
acrylic	batiste	buffalo cloth	challis
African hair	bayadere	bunting	chambray
alamode	Bedford cord	burlap	chamois cloth
Algerian stripe	bengaline	butcher linen	charmeuse
alpaca	bocking	byssus	cheesecloth
Angola cloth	bolting cloth	calamanco	chenille
angora	bombazine	calico	cheviot
armure	boucle	cambric	chiffon
aster cloth	bourette	camel's hair	chinchilla
astrakhan	brilliantine	candlewick	chino
baize	broadcloth	Canton crepe	chintz
balbriggan	brocade	canvas	ciré
baldachin	brocatel	casement cloth	cloque

cloth	eponge	hopsack	maline
cloth of gold	Estron	horsehair	marocain
combing wool	faille	huckaback	marquisette
cord	farmer's satin	Irish linen	marseilles
corduroy	felt	jaconet	mat
cotton	flannel	jacquard	melton
cottonade	flannelette	jardiniere	merino
Courtelle	fleece	jean	mesh
crash	Fortisan	jersey	messaline
crepe de Chine	foulard	jewel cloth	mohair
cretonne	frieze	jute	moire
Crimplene	fustian	Kendal green	moleskin
crinoline	gabardine	kersey	monk's cloth
Dacron	galatea	khaki	moquette
damask	gauze	lace	mousseline
denim	Georgette	lame	muslin
dimity	gingham	lawn	nainsook
doeskin	glass cloth	leatherette	nankeen
Donegal tweed	glove silk	leno	needlecord
douppioni	gossamer	linen	netting
drill	grenadine	linsey-woolsey	ninon
drugget	grogram	lisle	nylon
ducape	grosgrain	lisse	oilcloth
duck	gunny	loden	oilskin
duvetyn	haircloth	Lurex	organdy
duffel	Harris tweed	Lycra	organza
dungaree	herringbone	mackinaw	organzine
ecru	homespun	mackintosh	Orlon
eiderdown	honan	madras	paduasoy

paisley

panne

paramatta

percale

percaline

petersham

Pima

pinwale

pique

plaid

plush

pointelle

polyester

pongee

poplin

prunella

ragg

ratine

raw silk

rayon

rep

russet

sackcloth

sacking

sailcloth

samite

sarcenet

sateen

satin

scrim

seersucker

serge

shag

shalloon

shantung

sharkskin

sheer

Shetland wool

shoddy

shot silk

silesia

silk

spandex

stockinette

suede

surah

swansdown

swanskin

tabaret

tabby

taffeta

tapestry

tattersall

terry cloth

thibet cloth

ticking

tiffany

toile

toweling

tricot

tricotine

tulle

tussah

tweed

twill

velour

velvet

velveteen

Venetian cloth

vicuna

viscose

voile

watered silk

webbing

whipcord

wire cloth

wool

worsted

FARM AND FARMING TYPES

boutique farming

collective farming

commercial farming

contour farming

crop farming

dairy farming

dirt farming

dryland farming

factory farming

fish farming

fruit farming

fur farming

grain farming

grassland farming

hydroponics

intensive farming

livestock farming

mixed farming

organic farming

sharecropping

share farming

single-crop farming

slash-and-burn

strip farming

stubble-mulch
farming

subsistence
farming

tenant farming

tree farming

truck
farming

FARM MACHINERY

aerator	grinder	mowing machine	shredder
baler	grub hook	mulcher	silage cutter
binder	harrow	picker	snap machine
breaker	harvester	planter	sprayer
churn	hay conditioner	plow	spreader
combine	haymaker	pulverizer	stag gang
crop duster	header	pump	swather
cultivator	husker	rake	tedder
cutter	lathe	reaper and binder	threshing machine
digger	lister	scooter	tiller
disk	loader	seeder	tractor
drag	middlebreaker	self-feeder	truck
drill	milking machine	separator	windmill
grain elevator	milling machine	sheller	windrower

FAT TYPES

animal	dietary	low-density lipo-protein or LDL milk	solid
baby	edible		subcutaneous
body	high-density lipoprotein or HDL	monounsaturated	trans
brown		polyunsaturated	triglyceride
cholesterol	hydrogenated	soap	unsaturated

FAULT TYPES

A fault, in geology, is a fracture in the rocks of the earth's crust, where compressionor tension causes the rocks on the opposite sides of the fracture, or fault, to be displaced relative to each other.

cross	horizontal	overthrust	thrust
dip	horst	reverse	transcurrent
distributive	inclined	step	transform
graben	normal	strike	vertical
hinge	oblique	tear	

FERNS

adder's-tongue	bladder fern	Christmas fern	ditch fern
Alice's fern	bogfern	cinnamon fern	elephant ear fern
alpine lady fern	Boston fern	cliff brake	elkhorn fern
alpine woodsia	bottle fern	climbing fern	evergreen wood fern
American ostrich fern	boulder fern	cloak fern	felt fern
American shield fern	bracken	clover fern	female fern
asparagus fern	Braun's holly fern	club moss	finger fern
Australian brake	bristle fern	coffee fern	floating fern
backache brake	brittle fern	cotton fern	flower-cup fern
ball fern	broad beech fern	creek fern	fragile fern
bamboo fern	buckhorn fern	creeping fern	fringed fern
basket fern	buckler fern	curly grass	giant fern
beech fern	bulblet fern	cycad	giant holly fern
bird's nest fern	calamite	dagger fern	golden fern
black tree fern	chain fern	deer fern	grape fern

grass fern

ground fern

hairy lip fern

Hartford fern

hart's tongue

hay-scented fern

holly fern

horsetail

interrupted fern

Japanese climbing fern

king fern

lace fern

lady fern

leather fern

licorice fern

lip fern

lycopod

maidenhair

male fern

marsh fern

Massachusetts fern

meadow fern

moonwort

mosquito fern

mountain fern

New York fern

oak fern

old-man fern

osmunda

ostrich fern

pod fern

polypody

potato fern

prickly shield fern

queen fern

quill fern

rattlesnake fern

regal fern

rock brake

royal fern

saw fern

scale fern

seed fern

sensitive fern

shield fern

shoestring fern

shrubby fern

silver tree fern

silvery spleenwort

snuffbox fern

squirrel's foot fern

staghorn fern

strawberry fern

sweet fern

sword fern

toothed
sword fern

tree fern

tropical fern

true fern

umbrella fern

venus'-hair fern

walking fern

wall fern

water clover

water fern

wood fern

woodsia

FIBERS AND THREADS, NATURAL

alpaca

angora

astrakhan

baize

balbriggan

batiste

brocade

brocatelle

buckram

bunting

burlap

calico

cambric

camel's hair

canvas

cashmere

challis

chambray

cheesecloth

cheviot

chiffon

chinchilla

chino

chintz

corduroy

cotton

crepe

crepe de Chine

crinoline

damask

denim

doeskin

Donegal tweed

drill

duck

duffel

dungaree

faille

felt

flannel

flannelette

flax

fleece

foulard

frieze

fustian

gabardine

gauze

Georgette crepe

gingham

goat's hair

gossamer

grenadine

grosgrain

gunny

Harris tweed

hemp

herringbone

hessian

hopsack

horsehair

huck

jacquard

jersey

jute

kapok

lamé

linen

lisle

loden

mackinaw

mackintosh

madras

marseilles

melton

merino

messaline

mohair

moiré

moleskin

mousseline

muslin

nainsook

nankeen

netting

organdy

organza

panne velvet

percale

piqué

plaid

plush

pongee

poplin

raffia

russet

sackcloth

sacking

sailcloth

sateen

satin

seersucker

serge

shantung

sharkskin

shot silk

silk

sisal

suede

tabaret

tarpaulin

terry

ticking

toile

tricot

tulle

tweed

twill

velour

velvet

velveteen

vicuna

webbing

wool

worsted

FIBERS AND THREADS, SYNTHETIC

acetate

acetate rayon

acrylic

artificial silk

Celanese

Dacron

leatherette

lycra

microfiber

nylon

Orlon

polyacetate

polyamide

polyester

polyvinyl chloride or PVC

rayon

viscose

FIELD EVENTS

Field events—those involving jumping and throwing—are among the oldest athletic events in the world.

discus throw

hammer throw

high jump

javelin throw

long jump

pole vault

shot put

triple jump

FIELD HOCKEY POSITIONS

center forward

center half

goalkeeper

left back

left half

left inner

left wing

right back

right half

right inner

right wing

FIG VARIETIES

Adriatic

Alma

amber

Beall

bellone

Black Ischia

bourjasotte

Bourjassotte Grise

Brown Turkey

Brunswick

buissone

caprifig

Celeste
col de dame
common
Conadria
dark
dauphine violette
Deanna
dessert
dried
Early Violet

Endrich
Excel
Flanders
fresh
Genoa
green
Hardy Chicago
Hunt
Ischia
Kadota

King
Lattarula
light
Marseilles
Mission
Monaco Bianco
Monstrueuse
Negronne
Osborn Prolific
Panachee

purple
red
Reine Blanche
Saint Jean
San Pedro
San Pietro
Smyrna
Tena
white

FIGURES OF SPEECH

adynaton
agnomination
allegory
alliteration
allusion
amplification
anacoluthon
anadiplosis
analogy
anaphora
anapodoton
anastrophe
antanaclasis
anthimeria
antimetabole

antiphrasis
antisthecon
antithesis
antonomasia
aphaersis
apocope
apophasis
aporia
aposiopesis
apostrophe
auxesis
axiom
catachresis
chiasmus
circumlocution

climax
congeries
conversion
correctio
double entendre
ecphonesis
ellipsis
emphasis
enallage
enantiosis
epanalepsis
epanaphora
epanodos
epanorthosis
epenthesis

epidiplosis
epiphora
epistrophe
epizeuxis
eroteme
erotesis
euphemism
exclamation
gemination
gradatio
hendiadys
hypallage
hyperbaton
hyperbole
hypozeugma

hypozeuxis
hysteron proteron
imagery
inversion
irony
isocolon
kenning
litotes
malapropism
meiosis
metalepsis
metaphor
metathesis

metonymy
mixed metaphor
obsecration
occupatio
onomatopoeia
oxymoron
paradiastole
paradox
paragoge
paralepsis
paregmenon
parenthesis
periphrasis

personification
pleonasm
ploce
polyptoton
polysyndeton
preterition
prolepsis
prosopopoeia
prosthesis
regression
repetition
rhetorical question
sarcasm

scesis onamaton
simile
similitude
spoonerism
syllepsis
symploce
syncope
syncrisis
synecdoche
tautology
trope
Wellerism
zeugma

FIRE TYPES

A (wood, paper, cloth, rubber)

B (oil, gas, grease)

C (electrical equipment)

D (heavy metals, sodium, magnesium)

FIREWORKS

aerial parade
banger
Bengali-light
big Bertha
bomb
candlebomb
cannon cracker

cap
Catherine wheel
chaser
cherry bomb
cloudbuster comet
colored fire
cracker

cracker bonbon
dueling dragons
evening party
firecracker
fireflies
fire wheel
fizgig

fizzer
flame
flare
flowerpot
force-and-spark
fountain
gerbe

girandole
ladyfinger
mandarin cracker
maroon
pastille
petard
pharaoh's serpent

pinwheel
rocket
Roman candle
serpent
shot cake
six-inch salute

skyrocket
snake
son of a gun
sparkler
squib
tantrum
throwdown

torpedo
tourbillion
Vesuvius fountain
volcano
wheel
whiz-bang

FIRST AID KIT

absorbent cotton
Ace bandage
acetaminophen
adhesive strip bandages
adhesive tape
antacid
antibiotic ointment
antiseptic soap
aspirin
blanket
burn ointment

cold packs
cotton balls
cotton swabs
first aid manual
fresh razor blade
gauze roll
hydrogen peroxide
measuring spoons
medication alert
mild laxative
mild sedative

motion-sickness medication
needle
paper cups
personal prescriptions
poison-ivy medication
rubbing alcohol
safety pins
salt tablets
scissors

sheet
smelling salts
snakebite kit
splints
sterile gauze pads
sunburn lotion
thread
towels
triangular bandage
tweezers
water purification tablets

FISH, COMMON TYPES OF

albacore
alewife
alligator gar

amberfish
amberjack
American flag fish

anchovy
angelfish
arauana

archerfish
argusfish
balloonfish

bamboo fish

barberfish

barracuda

barred perch

basking shark

bass

batfish

bay shark

bellows fish

belted kingfisher

beluga

betta

blackfish

blackmouth bass

blindfish

blowfish

blue cod

bluefish

boarfish

bonefish

bony fish

bowfin

boxfish

bream

brook trout

buffalo fish

bullhead

butterfish

butterflyfish

candlefish

capelin

cardinalfish

carp

cartilaginous fish

catfish

cavefish

char

chimaera

chub

cichlid

clingfish

clown anemone

clownfish

cod

codfish

cowfish

cutlassfish

damselfish

danios

darter

devilfish

devil ray

discus

doctorfish

dogfish

dollarfish

dolphin

dragonfish

eel

electric eel

electric ray

flatfish

flounder

flying fish

freshwater bass

frogfish

garpike

ghostfish

giant bass

globefish

goatfish

goby

goldfish

gourami

grayling

grouper

gudgeon

guppy

haddock

hagfish

hake

halibut

hammerhead shark

hatchetfish

headstander

herring

hogfish

ide

jawless fish

kelpfish

killifish

kingfish

koi

lake trout

lamprey

lanternfish

largemouth bass

lionfish

loach

lumpfish

mackerel

manta

marlin

minnow

molly

monkfish

mudfish

mudskipper

mullet

needlefish

northern pike

oarfish

oscar

paddlefish

paradise fish

parrotfish

perch

pickerel

pike

pikeperch

pipefish

piranha

platyfish

pollack

pompano

porcupinefish

porgy

primitive fish

puffer

pupfish

rainbow perch

rainbow trout

ray

red snapper

redfin

redfish

sailfish

salmon

salmon trout

sandfish

sardine

sawfish

sea bass

sea horse

seaperch

sea trout

shad

shark

shiner

silver perch

skate

smelt

snapper

snook

sole

spearfish

squawfish

stingray

stonefish

striped bass

sturgeon

sucker

sunfish

surffish

surfperch

swordfish

swordtail

tang

tarpon

tetra

tigerfish

tiger shark

triggerfish

trout

tuna

weakfish

whitefish

white shark

wimplefish

yellowtail

zander

zebrafish

FISH DISHES AND EDIBLE FISH

abalone

anchovy

angelfish

Arbroath smokie

bacalao

bass

blackfish

bloater

bluefish

Bombay duck

bonito

bouillabaisse

butterfish

calamari

catfish

caviar

chowder

clam

cod

codfish

codfish stew

conch

coquilles St. Jacques

coral

coulibiac

crab

crab cakes

crab Imperial

crawdad

crawfish

crayfish

eel

escargot

fillet of sole

finnan haddie

fish and chips

fish cake

fish fritter

fish mousse

fish sticks

flounder

gefilte fish

goujons

gravadlax

gravlax

grunion

haddock

halibut

herring

John Dory

kedgeree

kipper

langoustine

lobster

lobster Thermidor

lotte

lox

mackerel

mahimahi

matelote

milt

monk

mussel

mussels marinière

octopus

orange roughy

oyster

oysters Rockefeller

perch

pompano

prawn

red snapper

rissoles

roe

rollmops

salmon

sand dab

sardine

scallop

scallops bonne
femme

scampi

scrod

scungilli

sea bass

sea urchin

shad

shark

shellfish

shrimp

shrimp
cocktail

skate

smelt

smoked salmon

snail

snapper

softshell crab

sole

sole bonne femme

sole meunière

sprat

squid

steamed fish

striped bass

sturgeon

surimi

swordfish

teal

terrapin

tile

tomalley

trout

tuna

tuna salad

tuna
tetrazzini

turbot

whitefish

yellowtail

FISHING TACKLE
AND EQUIPMENT

angleworm

antenna float

archer tackle

arlesey bomb

artificial bait

artificial fly

backlash

bait

bait-casting rod	creel	fixed-reel seat	jigging lure
baitfish	cut bait	fixed-spool reel	jigging rod
bait kettle	cuttyhunk	float	Jock Scot
balanced tackle	dead bait	floating-diving plug	keeper ring
barb	diamond sinker	fly	keep net
barbless hook	dipsey sinker	fly book	Kendal sneck bent
barrel knot	disgorger	fly box	landing net
barrel swivel	diving plug	fly leader	leader
bass bug	dobber	fly line	ledger
bird's nest	double-taper line	fly reel	ledger line
black gnat	drifter	fly rod	line
blood knot	drift net	gaff	live bait
boat rod	drop net	gang hook	lobster pot
bob	dry fly	gill net	lock-snap swivel
bobber	dusty miller	golden shiner	loop knot
boulter	ferrule	grasshopper	lure
bubble float	fiberglass rod	hackle	mayfly
bucktail	fighting chair	hackle fly	midge
bucktail jig	fish box	hand line	monofilament
cast	fish eyes	harpoon	multiplier
casting rod	fishfinder	hatch boat	muskie rod
chugger	fishhook	hip boots	nail knot
clinch knot	fishline	hook	net
closed-faced reel	fish stringer	ice auger	nymph
cloudbait	fishing line	ice skimmer	palmer
corkball float	fishing pole	ice sounder	pencil float
cork bug	fishing rod	ice spud	phantom
courge	fishing smack	jig	pillars
crawlers	fishing vest	jig and eel	pirn

234

plastic ball float

plastic lure

plug

plummet

plunker

point

popper

popping plug

popping rod

pork rind

pounds test

priest

purse line

purse seine

pyramid sinker

quill

reel

reel crank

revolving-spool reel

rig

rod

rod butt

rod guide

rod rest

rod ring

rod tip

roe

saltwater bait

seaboot

seine

shank

single-action fly reel

sinker

sinking plug

sliding float

sliding-clamp reel seat

snap swivel

spear

spent wing fly

spider fly

spinner

spinning reel

spinning rod

split shot

split-shot sinker

spool

spoon

sproat

stink bait

streamer fly

surf rod

surface disturber

surface plug

swivel

tackle box

tag

tailer

tapered leader

tilt

tip guide

tippet

tip-up

trace

trammel net

trawler

trawl line

trawl net

treblehook

trident

trolling reel

trotline

tube fly

turle knot

ultralight spinning tackle

waders

wading staff

waist boots

wet fly

worm fly

FISHING TYPES

angling

bait casting or spinning

bait fishing

big-game fishing

bottom fishing

bowfishing

coarse fishing

deep-sea fishing

drift fishing

electrofishing

float fishing

fly fishing

freshwater fishing

game fishing

ice fishing

kite fishing

lake fishing

long-lining

margin fishing

match fishing

| nymph fishing | saltwater fishing | sportfishing | stream fishing |
| reef fishing | spin casting | still fishing | trolling |

FIVE KHANDS OF SIKHISM

These are the stages of spiritual progress for a Sikh who is moving from manmukh (self-willed, perverse individual) to gurmukh (pious individual who obeys the Guru).

| Dharam Khand | Karam Khand | Saram Khand |
| Gian Khand | Sach Khand | |

FIVE PILLARS OF FAITH OF ISLAM

There are five duties that every Muslim must obey and these are known as the Five Pillars of Islam. They include sincere declaration of faith that there is no other God but Allah and that Muhammad is his prophet, praying five times a day, giving money to the poor, fasting during Ramadan, and making the pilgrimmage to Mecca.

| Hajj | Sawm | Zakat |
| Salah | Shahadah | |

FIVE-SPICE POWDER

Five-spice powder is a mixture of five spices commonly used in Bengali cookery. Its name is a translation of Hindi *panchphoran*. Five of the following ingredients are combined to make this.

black mustard	cumin	nigella seeds	star anise
cinnamon	fennel	Sichuan pepper	
clove	fenugreek		

FLAG SHAPES

bunting

burgee

descate

double pennant or double triangle

fanion

flag with Schwenkel

gonfalon

lanceolate

oriflamme

pennant

pointed

rectangular

rounded

shield

square

square with Schwenkel

streamer

swallowtail

swallowtail and tongue triangle

triangle with flammules

wind sock

FLOOD TYPES

annual

coastal

flash

glacier outburst

ice jam

lava

river

snow

spring

urban

FLOURS

all-purpose

almond

barley

bleached

bolted

bread

break

buckwheat

bulgur

cake

carob

chickpea

clear

corn

durum

enriched

farina

fortified

gluten

graham

hard wheat

instant

lima bean

non-wheat

nut

oat

organic

pastry

patent

pea

peanut

phosphated

plain

potato

red-dog

refined

rice

rye

self-rising

semolina

soft wheat

soy

unbleached

wheat

wheat germ

white

whole grain

whole wheat

FLOWER FORMS

There are different forms or structures of flower heads that are recognized as a type of classification.

capitulum

composite head or discoid flower head

curled cyme

cyme

helicoid cyme

hollow flower head

panicle

raceme or simple raceme

spadix

spike or racemose spike

umbel or simple umbel

FLOWER TYPES

actinomorphic

annual

artificial

bilabiate

bird-pollinated

bulb

campanulate

carpophore

complete

desert

dialipetalous

dioecious

fall or autumn

floret

funnel-shaped

garden

imperfect

incomplete

insect-pollinated

mammal-pollinated

meadow or field

monoecious

perennial

perfect

pistillate

polypetalous

spring

staminate

summer

sympetalous

tropical

tubular

water-pollinated

wild

wind-pollinated

zygomorphic

FLOWERING PLANTS AND SHRUBS

acacia

acanthus

adobe lily

African daisy

African violet

alpine gold

amaranthus

amaryllis

anemone arbutus

arrowhead

asphodel

aster

autumn crocus

azalea

baby's breath

bachelor's button

balloon flower

begonia

belladonna

billy buttons

bitterroot

bittersweet

black-eyed Susan

blazing star

bleeding heart

bluebell

blue-eyed Mary

bluet

bougainvillea

bridal wreath

broom

brown-eyed Susan

buttercup

cactus

calendula

calla lily

camellia

campanula

candytuft

carnation

cat's-paw

cattail

century plant

chamomile

Chinese lantern

Christmas cactus

Christmas rose

chrysanthemum

cineraria

clematis

clover

cockscomb

columbine

common daisy

coral drops

cornel

cornflower

cosmos

cowbell

cowslip

crocus

cyclamen

daffodil

dahlia

daisy

damask rose

dandelion

day lily

delphinium

dogtooth violet

Dutchman's-breeches

Easter lily

edelweiss

eglantine

elderflower

English daisy

fireweed

flame flower

flax

fleur-de-lis [Fr]

forget-me-not

forsythia

foxglove

foxtail

frangipani

freesia

fuchsia

gardenia

gentian

geranium

German iris

gladiolus

globeflower

goldenrod

groundsel

guelder rose

harebell

hawthorn

heather

hepatica

hibiscus

hollyhock

honeysuckle

horehound

hyacinth

hydrangea

hyssop

impatiens

Indian paintbrush

indigo

iris

jack-in-the-pulpit

japonica

jasmine

jonquil

kingcup

laburnum

lady's-slipper

larkspur

lavender

lemon lily

lilac

lily

lily of the valley

lobelia

lotus

love-lies-bleeding

lupine

magnolia

mallow

marguerite

marigold

marshmallow

marsh marigold

mayflower

meadow saffron

Michaelmas daisy

mignonette

milkwort

mimosa

moccasin flower

mock orange

monkshood

moonflower

morning glory

moss rose

motherwort

mullein

musk rose

myrtle

narcissus

nasturtium

old maid flower

oleander

opium poppy

orchid

oxalis

oxeye daisy

painted daisy

pansy

paper-white narcissus

passionflower

pennyroyal

peony

periwinkle

petunia

phlox

pink

plumbago

poinsettia

polyanthus

poppy

portulaca

pot marigold

primrose

primula

Queen Anne's lace

ragged robin

ragwort

rambler rose

ranunculus

ray flower

resurrection plant

rhododendron

rose

safflower

shooting star

smilax

snapdragon

snowdrop

spiraea

St. John's wort

stock

strawflower

sunflower

sweet alyssum

sweetbrier

sweet pea

sweet william

tea rose

Texas star

thistle

tiger lily

trailing arbutus

trillium

trumpet creeper

tulip

twinflower

umbrella plant

valerian

Venus's flytrap

verbena

veronica

viburnum

viola

violet

wake-robin

wallflower

water hyacinth

water lily

water milfoil

water pimpernel

wax flower

waxplant

white clover

white lily

white zinnia

wild flower

wisteria

wolfsbane

wood anemone

wood hyacinth

wood sorrel

woody nightshade

yarrow

yellow water lily

yucca

zinnia

FOLD TYPES

A fold is a buckled, bent, or contorted rock, an undulation or series of waves in the stratified rocks of the earth's crust. Folds result from complex processes including fracture, sliding, shearing (layers moving laterally), and flowage (movements of ice, rock, etc.).

anticline

asymmetrical

basin

disharmonic

dome

isocline

kink or chevron

monocline

nappe

nonplunging

overfold or plunging

ptygmatic

recumbent

symmetrical

syncline

synclinorium

upright

FOOD AND BEVERAGES NAMED FOR PLACES

american cheese

baked Alaska

bialy

bisque

bologna

Bombay duck

Bordeaux wine

bourbon whiskey

brie cheese

brussels sprouts

Burgundy wine

Camembert cheese

cantaloupe

cayenne pepper

champagne

cheddar cheese

Chianti wine

cognac brandy

colby cheese

currant

Edam cheese

Fig Newton

frankfurter

Gorgonzola cheese

Gouda cheese

Gruyère cheese

hamburger

Hollandaise sauce

jalapeno

java

lima bean

Limburger cheese

Madeira wine

mayonnaise

mocha

Monterey Jack cheese

muenster cheese

Parmesan cheese

pilsner beer

port wine

romaine lettuce

Romano cheese

Roquefort cheese

Scotch whiskey

seltzer water

Stilton cheese

Swiss cheese

Tabasco sauce

tangerine

Thousand Island dressing

Toll House cookie

turkey

Worcestershire sauce

Food Groups

cereal group

fatty and sugary group

fruit and vegetable group

meat or protein group

milk group

Foods for Alertness

apple

broccoli

chicken

fish

grapes

lean beef

lowfat yogurt

nuts

peach

peanuts

pear

poultry

skim milk

tofu

Foods Named for People

beef Stroganoff

beef Wellington

boysenberry

Caesar salad

carpaccio

Chateaubriand

chicken Tetrazzini

Cobb salad

crêpes suzette

Dom Pérignon

Earl Grey tea

eggs Benedict

fettuccine Alfredo

Filbert nut

graham cracker

lobster Newburg

loganberry

Macadamia nut

Melba toast

mirepoix

napoleon

oysters Rockefeller

peach Melba

Praline

Salisbury steak

sandwich

FOODS, APHRODISIAC

almond	chocolate	honey	pine nut
aniseed	clove	licorice	prune
apricot	coriander or cilantro	lobster	raspberry
arugula	cuttlefish	macaroni	snail
asparagus	eel	mustard	spicy food
avocado	fig	nutmeg	spinach
banana	frog's legs	oyster	strawberry
carrot	garlic	parsnip	thyme
caviar	ginger	peach	truffle
celery	ginseng	pineapple	vanilla

FOODS, BLAND

broth	eggs	mild-flavored vegetable juice	potatoes
cake	fruit juice	milk	pudding
cooked cereals	Jell-O	pasta	refined breads
cookie	lean meat	pie	refined cereals
crackers	marshmallows	plain rice	soft banana
decaf coffee			tofu

FOODS, BREAKFAST

bacon	coffee	farina	milk
bagel	croissant	fruit	oatmeal
breakfast burrito	doughnut	grits	pancake
cereal	egg	juice	pastry

roll

sausage

scrapple

streudel

tea

toast

waffle

yogurt

FOODS, SOFT

applesauce

breakfast drink

canned fruit

cooked cereal

cooked fruit

cooked vegetables

cottage cheese

couscous

custard

eggs

ice cream

Jell-O

macaroni
and cheese

mashed
potatoes

meat loaf

milkshake

muffin

pasta

pastry

pudding

smooth peanut
butter

soft bread

soft cheese

soft fruit

soft
vegetables

sorbet

soup

yogurt

FOOTBALL EQUIPMENT

arm pads

athletic cup and
supporter

chin strap

cleats

face mask

flak jacket extension

football

gloves

helmet

hip pads

jaw pads

jersey

kicking tee

kneepads

mouth guard

neck roll

numbers

pads

pants

shirt
or jersey

shoes

shoulder
pads

socks

tact gloves

thigh pads

wireless
communication
system

wrist coach

FOOTBALL FORMATIONS

3–4 defense

4–3 defense

4 3 2 2

4–4 defense

5–2 defense

6–1 defense

6 2 2 1

7 diamond

A formation

balanced line

box defense

dime defense

double coverage

double wing or wingback formation

flexbone or flex defense

flying wedge

huddle

I formation

kickoff

man-to-man defense

multiple offense

nickel defense

Notre Dame box

option

overshift

power I

prevent defense

pro set

punt formation

run-and-shoot offense

shotgun offense

short punt formation

single coverage

single wing or wingback formation

slot

split end

split T

spread formation

straight T

strong side

T formation

tight end

undershift

veer

weak side

wedge

wing back formation

wing T

wishbone formation

wishbone T

zone blocking

zone defense

FOOTBALL OFFICIALS

back judge

chain gang

field judge

head linesman

line judge

referee

side judge

umpire

FOOTBALL PASS PATTERNS

buttonhook

circle

crisscross

crossing pattern

curl

down-and-in

down-and-out

flag pattern

flare or swing pass

flood

fly

hail Mary

245

hitch and go

post pattern

square-in

up the middle

hook and ladder

screen pass

square-out

zig in

hook pattern

sideline pass

streak pattern

zig out

look-in pass

slant-in pattern

turn-in

Z pattern

option pass

spot pass

turn-out

FOOTBALL PENALTIES

10-yard penalty

15-yard penalty

5-yard penalty

clipping

clothesline

crackback block

dead-ball foul

defensive holding

defensive interference

delay of game

double foul

encroachment

excessive timeouts

face mask

fair catch interference

faking a roughing

false start

holding

illegal blocking below the waist

illegal formation

illegal motion

illegal position

illegal procedure

illegal shift

illegal use of hands

ineligible receiver

intentional grounding

interference

kick-catching interference

kicking an opponent

late hit

lining up in the neutral zone

more than 11 players on the field

offensive holding

offensive pass interference

offside

out-of-bounds kickoff

pass interference

personal foul

piling on

roughing the kicker

roughing the passer

running into the kicker

second forward pass

spearing

striking an official

striking an opponent

tackling by the facemask

too many men on the field

tripping

unnecessary roughness

unsportsmanlike conduct

FOOTBALL PLAYS AND CALLS

audible

blitz or red dog

bomb

bootleg

buck lateral

bump and run

check off

conversion

counter
cutback
draw
end around
end run
fair catch
flare pass
flea-flicker
forward pass
goal-line stand
hail Mary
hand-off

inside run
keeper
lateral pass
or lateral
man in motion
mousetrap
naked bootleg
naked reverse
off-tackle slant
onside kick
option
pass

pitch
pitchout
play-action pass
plunge
point after
touchdown
or PAT
power sweep
pump fake
quarterback sneak
quick kick
reverse

rollout
safety blitz
scramble
screen pass
slant
Statue
of Liberty
stunt
sweep
trap
two-point
conversion

FOOTBALL POSITIONS

back
center
defensive back
end
field-goal kicker
free safety
fullback
guard
halfback
inside linebacker
kicker
left cornerback

left defensive end
left defensive tackle
left guard
left halfback
left inside linebacker
left outside
linebacker
left safety
left tackle
linebacker
middle linebacker
nose guard

nose tackle
outside linebacker
punter
quarterback
right cornerback
right defensive end
right defensive
tackle
right guard
right halfback
right inside
linebacker

right outside
linebacker
right safety
right tackle
running back
slotback or flanker
split end
strong safety
tackle
tailback
tight end
wide receiver

FOOTWEAR

ankle boots

baby shoes

ballet shoes

baseball shoes

basketball shoes

bluchers

boots

bowling shoes

buskins

climbing shoes

clogs

combat boots

court shoes

cowboy boots

cross-trainers

deck shoes

elevator shoes

espadrilles

flip-flops

football shoes

galoshes

ghillies

golf shoes

gym shoes

high-tops

hip boots

huaraches

jelly shoes

lace-ups

loafers

Mary Janes

moccasins

mules

open-toed shoes

overshoes

oxfords

penny loafers

platforms

plimsolls

pumps

riding boots

rubber boots

rubbers

running shoes

saddle shoes

sandals

scuffs

sling-backs

slip-ons

slippers

sneakers

snow boots

snowshoes

soccer shoes

sport shoes

stilettos

tap shoes

tennis shoes

thongs

track shoes

trainers

waders

walking shoes

Wellington boots

wing tips

work shoes

zoris

FORCES

air resistance force

applied force

at-a-distance force

centripetal force

compression

contact force

electrical force

electromagnetic force

frictional force

gravitational force

magnetic force

normal force

shear force

spring force

strong force or strong nuclear force

tensional force

torsion

upthrust

weak force or weak nuclear force

FOREST AND WOOD, TYPES OF

ancient forest

bonsai

boreal coniferous forest

boreal forest

broadleaf forest

chaparral

climax forest

cloud forest

coniferous forest

copse

deciduous forest

dry tropical forest

elfin forest

evergreen forest

fog forest

gallery forest

garigue

high forest

indigenous forest

jungle

maquis

Mediterranean scrub

mixed forest

monsoon forest

mountain rain forest

national forest

old-growth forest

orchard

petrified forest

rain forest

scrub

state forest

subtropical forest

taiga

temperate forest

temperate rain forest

thorn forest

timber forest

topiary

tropical deciduous forest

tropical forest

tropical rain forest

urban forest

virgin forest

FORKS

carving fork

cocktail fork

dessert fork

dinner fork

fish fork

fondue fork

fruit fork

lobster fork

luncheon fork

oyster fork

pastry fork

salad fork

seafood fork

toasting fork

FORTUNE-TELLING METHODS

aptitude test

astrology

belomancy

cartomancy

Chinese astrology

chirography

chirology

chiromancy

clairvoyance

crystal ball gazing

divination sticks

dream interpretation

fortune cards

fortune cookie

geloscopy

graphology

gyromancy

I Ching

ichthyomancy

intelligence quotient test

knissomancy

lecanomancy

lithomancy

Magic 8-Ball

mantology

metopomancy

myomancy

necromancy

numerology

ololygmancy

oracle consultation

palmistry

pegomancy

personality test

phrenology

retromancy

runes

séance

soothsaying

stone-casting

Tarot card reading

tea-leaf reading

xenomancy

FOSSIL FUELS

bitumen

coal

natural gas

petroleum

shale oil

FOSSIL TYPES

altered remains

body fossil

cast fossil

compression fossil

coprolite

dinosaur

fossil hominid

fossilized substance

gastrolith

index fossil

invertebrate fossil

mold fossil

mummy

pseudofossil

trace fossil

true form fossil

unaltered remains

vertebrate fossil

FOWL AND POULTRY BREEDS AND TYPES

Ameraucana

Ancona

Andalusian

Araucana

Australorp

Aylesbury duck

Bantam

bobwhite

Brahma

Broad-Breasted turkey

Buckeye

Buttercup

Campine

Chantecler

chicken

Cochin

Cornish

crested
duck

Crevecoeur

Delaware

domestic fowl

Dorking

duck

Faverolle

Frizzle

game fowl

geese
or goose

grouse

guinea fowl

Hamburg

Holland

Houdan

Jersey Giant

Langshan

Leghorn

Malay

Minorca

Muscovy duck

Narragansett
turkey

New Hampshire
Red

Orpington

partridge

peafowl

pheasant

Phoenix

pigeon

Plymouth Rock

Polish

quail

Rhode
Island Red

Rock

Spanish

Sumatra

Sussex

turkey

wild fowl

woodcock

Wyandotte

FOXES

Arctic fox

bat-eared fox

black fox

blue fox

corsac fox

crab-eating
fox

cross fox

dog fox

fennec

gray fox

hoary fox

kit fox

pale fox

prairie fox

red fox

Samson fox

sand fox

silver fox

swift fox

white fox

zorro

FRACTURES

articular fracture

avulsion fracture

comminuted fracture

compound fracture

compression fracture

depressed fracture

greenstick
fracture

impacted fracture

multifragmentary
fracture

multiple fracture

oblique fracture   simple fracture   stress fracture

pathological fracture   spiral fracture

FRISBEE FLIGHT PERIODS

waft or   warp or turn   waste   well or climb
float
                  was or   wax   whelm or
wane   touch   release or hatch
                                   wedge or insertion

FRUIT TYPES

apple	bullace plum	date	juneberry
apple banana	calmyrna	date plum	kiwi
apricot	camu camu	durian	kumquat
apricot plum	canistel	elderberry	lemon
atemoya	cantaloupe	fig	lime
avocado	carambola	gooseberry	longan
banana	cherimoya	granadilla	loganberry
bayberry	cherry	grape	loquat
beach plum	citron	grapefruit	mandarin orange
berry	clementine	greengage	mango
bilberry	coconut	ground cherry	May apple
blackberry	crabapple	guava	maypop
black currant	cranberry	haw	medlar
blood orange	currant	honeydew melon	melon
blueberry	custard apple	huckleberry	mulberry
boysenberry	damson	jackfruit	muskmelon
breadfruit		jujube	

nannyberry

navel orange

nectarine

olive

orange

papaw

papaya

partridgeberry

passion fruit

pawpaw

peach

pear

pepino

Persian melon

persimmon

pineapple

pitaya

plantain

plum

pomegranate

pomelo

prickly pear

prune

quince

quinoa

raisin

rambutan

raspberry

sapodilla

sapote

satsuma

sea grape

soursop

strawberry

tamarillo

tamarind

tangelo

tangerine

tomato

ugli fruit

Valencia orange

watermelon

wild cherry

FRUIT VEGETABLES
OR VEGETABLE FRUITS

aubergine

autumn squash

avocado

bitter melon

cantaloupe

chayote

chili

courgette

cucumber

eggplant

gherkin

green bean

green sweet pepper

hot pepper

marrow

muskmelon

okra

olive

pumpkin

red sweet pepper

seedless cucumber

squash

sweet pepper

tomatillo

tomato

watermelon

wax gourd

yellow sweet pepper

zucchini

FRUITS THAT DO NOT RIPEN AFTER PICKING

blackberry	lemon	pineapple	tangerine
blueberry	lime	plum	watermelon
cherry	litchi	raspberry	
grape	olive	strawberry	
grapefruit	orange	tangelo	

FRUITS THAT RIPEN AFTER PICKING

apple	cherimoya	muskmelon	pear
apricot	fig	papaya	persimmon
avocado	kiwi	passionfruit	sapote
banana	mango	peach	soursop

FRUITS WITH LOW SUGAR CONTENT

apricot	gooseberry	papaya	tangerine
avocado	grapefruit	passionfruit	tomato
blackberry	honeydew melon	peach	watermelon
cantaloupe	lemon	plum	
casaba melon	lime	prickly pear	
cranberry	olive	strawberry	

FRUITS, BERRIES

avignon berry or French berry

avocado

banana

baneberry

Barbados cherry

bearberry

bilberry

blackberry

black raspberry

blueberry

boxberry

boysenberry

buffalo berry

candleberry

cankerberry

caper berry

checkerberry

cloudberry

cranberry

cucumber

currant

date

dewberry

dogberry

elderberry

gooseberry

gourd

grape

heathberry

Himalaya berry

honeyberry

huckleberry

Indian berry

jaundice berry

Jesuit berry

Juneberry

juniper berry

kiwano

kiwi

lemon

lime

limeberry

lingonberry

litchi

loganberry

melon

mulberry

orange

orange berry

partridgeberry

Persian berry

persimmon

rambutan

raspberry

red currant

sala berry

salmonberry

serviceberry

shadberry

shot berry

spiceberry

strawberry

tomato

turkeyberry

watermelon

whortleberry

FRUITS, BRAMBLE

blackberry

boysenberry

cloudberry

loganberry

raspberry

tayberry

wineberry

FRUITS, CITRUS

African cherry orange

bergamot orange

bitter orange or Seville orange

calamondin

citrange

citrangedin

citrangequat

citron

clementine

forbidden fruit

grapefruit

Ichang lemon

king orange

kumquat

lemon

lime

mandarin lime

mandarin orange

naartje

orange

orangelo

ortanique

Otaheite orange

pomelo

rangpur or lemanderin

satsuma

sweet lime

tangelo

tangerine

ugli fruit

FRUITS, POME

This type of fruit has corpels that run up the center, surrounded by edible flesh.

apple

chokeberry

crabapple

hawthorn

Japanese plum

juneberry

loquat

medlar

pear

quince

rose hip

rowan

service tree

FRUITS, STONE

apricot

cherry

date

mango

nectarine

olive

peach

plum

pluot

FRUITS, TROPICAL

akee

Asian pear

avocado

banana

breadfruit

camucamu

carambola

cherimoya

coconut

custard apple

durian

feijoya

fig

guarana

guava

horned melon

Indian fig

jaboticaba

jackfruit

Japanese persimmon

jujube

kiwi

litchi

longan

mamoncillo

mango

mangosteen

papaya

passion fruit

pepino

pineapple

plantain

pomegranate

prickly pear

rambutan

rose apple

salak

sapodilla

soursop

tamarillo

tamarind

FUELS

alcohol

anthracite or hard coal

aviation fuel

bagasse

benzine

bituminous coal or soft coal

blind coal

briquette

broken coal

brown coal

buckwheat coal

buffalo chips

bunker fuel

butane

cannel

carbon

carbureted water gas

charcoal

chestnut coal

coal

coal gas

coke

crude oil

diesel fuel

egg coal

electricity

ethane

ethanol

ethyl gasoline

firewood

flaxseed coal

fuel cell

fuel oil

furnace oil

gas carbon

gasohol

gasoline

glance coal

grate coal

heptane

hexane

high-octane gasoline

hog fuel

isobutane

isooctane

jet fuel

kaoliang

kerosene

leaded gasoline

lignite or brown coal

liquefied petroleum gas

liquid oxygen

lump coal

manufactured gas

methane

methanol

motor fuel

mustard-seed coal

naphtha

natural gas

nuclear power and nuclear energy

nut coal

octane

oil or petroleum

packaged fuel

pea coal

peat or turf

pentane

petroleum coke

premium gasoline

producer gas

propane

propellant

regular gasoline

renewable energy

rocket fuel

sea coal

shale oil

solar power

steamboat coal

stove coal

synfuel

synthol

triptane

unleaded gasoline

water power

white gasoline

wind power

wood

zip fuel

FUNDAMENTAL PHYSICAL CONSTANTS

atomic mass constant

Avogadro constant

Boltzmann constant

electron rest mass

electron specific charge

elementary charge

Faraday constant

gravitational constant

million electron volt unit

molar gas constant

molar volume of ideal gas

neutron rest mass

Planck's constant

proton rest mass

speed of light in vacuo

FUNERAL TYPES AND SERVICES

burial

ceremony

church service

cremation

death march

graveside service

interment

memorial

military

mourning

prearranged

pyre

Requiem Mass

suttee

vigil

wake

Fungi, Mushrooms, and Toadstools

agarics

ambrosia fungus

anther smut

ascomycetes

Ascomycota

aspergillus

basidiomycetes

Basidiomycota

bear's-head

beech fungus

beefsteak fungus

bird's-nest fungus

black bread mold

black mold

blight

blue-green mold

blue mold

boletus

bracket fungus

bread mold

brittlegill

button mushroom

caterpillar fungus

cattail fungus

cellular slime molds

champignon

chanterelle

club fungus

club mold

coffee fungus

coral fungus

crumblecap

cup fungus

dead-man's fingers

deathcap

deuteromycetes

Deuteromycota

devil's-snuffbox

downy mildew

dry rot

dung fungus

ear fungus

earthstar

earth tongue

edible fungus

enoki mushroom

ergot

Eumycota

false mildew

false morel

felt fungus

field mushroom

fire fungus

fish fungus

flask fungus

fly fungus or fly mold

Fungi Imperfecti

gill fungus

gooseberry mildew

green mold

groundwart

hart's truffle

hedgehog fungus

imperfect fungus

Indian paint fungus

inky cap

jelly fungus

lorchel

luminous fungus

magic mushroom

Mastigomycotina

meadow mushroom

micromycete

mildew

milkcap

mold

moniliales

morel

mushroom

mushroom pimple

myxomycetes

Myxomycota

nest fungus

oak fungus

onion smut

oyster cap or oyster mushroom

penicillium

perfect fungus

phycomycetes

pink disease fungus

pink gill

poisonous fungus

pore fungus

powdery mildew

puffball

read bread mold

ringstalk

ringworm fungus

roof mushroom
rust
sac fungus
sacred mushroom
scalecap
sheath mushroom
shelf fungus
shell fungus

shoestring fungus
skin fungus
slime molds
slime mushroom
smoothcap
smut
stinkhorn
straw mushroom

thrush fungus
toadstool
tooth fungus
tricholoma
truffle
verticillium
waxy cap
webcap

white fungus
witches' butter
woodcrust
yeast
yellow spot fungus
zygomycetes
Zygomycota

FURNACE TYPES

air
aludel
annealing
arc
arsem
ash
balling
blast
bustamente
coal-fired
continuous

converting
diaphragm
electric
electric-arc
floor
flowing
forced-air
Franklin
gas
gas-fired
heating

induction
industrial
metallurgical
oil
open-front
open-hearth
pernot
pot
recuperative
reducing
regenerative

reheating
shaft
slag
soldering pot
tank
wall
wedge
wind

FURNITURE FEATURES AND FINISHES

acanthus
ankle

antique
arch

bombe
boulle

cabriole
caning

cartouche

carving

claw

crest

crossband

Danish oil or tung

distressed

dull

fan

feather

festoon

finial

flocking

flower

fluting

fretwork

frieze

gilding

grained

hand-rubbed

high-gloss

inlaid

inlay

knob

lacquer

latex paint

leaf

limed

lozenge

marquetry

mission

natural

oil-based paint

oiled

painted

paneling

pedestal

pendalt

pilaster

plaque

polyurethane

refinished

rosette

sanded

satin

scallop

scroll

sealant

serpentine work

shell

shellac

slat

spiral

stained

stringing

tassel

turnings

underbracings

unfinished

upholstery

varnish

veneer

vermiculated

waxed

FURNITURE FEET

ball

block

bracket

brass

bun

claw

club

dolphin's head

drake

early bracket

Flemish scroll

French bracket

hoof foot

Marlborough

melon

ogee bracket

ogive bracket

pad

paw

pedestal

snake

spade

Spanish foot

Spanish scroll

splayed bracket

stile.

straight bracket

web

FURNITURE LEGS

Adam

American Empire

beaded

cabinet

cabriole

chair

Chippendale

clawfoot

clustered column

colonial

column

Dublin

Duncan Phyfe

Empire

fluted

gate-leg

Heppelwhite

hock

Jacobean

Lawson

lion

Louis Quinze

Louis Seize

mission

modern

octagonal

Paris

pedestal

post

Queen Anne

rope

saber

scroll

Sheraton

spindle

spiral

spool

table

tapered

trumpet

truss

turned

William-and-Mary

FURNITURE STYLES, PERIOD, AND TYPES

Adam

Adapted Colonial

Adirondack

American Chippendale or Pilgrim

American Empire

American Jacobean

American Moderne

American Queen Anne

American Regency or Directory

American Restoration or Pillar and Scroll

Anglo-Dutch

Art Deco

Art Nouveau

Arts and Crafts

Baroque

Bauhaus

Belter

Biedermeier

Block-front

Boston Chippendale

boule or boulework

Byzantine

Chinese Chippendale

Chinoiserie

Chippendale

Colonial or Campaign

Contemporary

Cotswold School

Country Chippendale

Cromwellian or Commonwealth

De Stijl

Desornamentado

Directoire

Duncan Phyfe

Early American

Early Georgian

Eastlake Movement

Egyptian

Elizabethan style

Empire

Federal

Francois Premier

French Provincial

French Renaissance

Georgian furniture

Gothic

Gothic-Renaissance

Greek Revival

Hepplewhite

International or
International Gothic

Italian Renaissance

Jacobean

Japanese

Japonisme

Late Regency

Later Victorian

Louis XIII

Louis XIV

Louis XV

Louis XVI

Mannerist

Mission

Modern

Modernist

Morris style

National
Romanticism

Naturalistic

Neoclassical

Neo-Gothic or
Cathédrale

Neo-Grec

Newport
Chippendale

New York
Chippendale

Palladian

Pennsylvania Dutch

Philadelphia
Chippendale

Pop Art

Queen Anne

Regency

Renaissance furniture

Renaissance Revival

Restoration or
Carolean

Rococo

Rococo Revival or
Louis Philippe or
Louis XV Revival

Romano-Byzantine
or Italo-Byzantine or
Romanesque

Scandinavian Modern

Second Empire

Shaker

Sheraton

Spanish Renaissance

Stuart

Tudor

Turkish

Venetian

Victorian

Viking Revival or
Dragonesque

William and Mary

FURNITURE WOODS

ash

bamboo

basswood

beech

bentwood

birch

cedar

cherry

chestnut

ebony

elm

fruitwood

hardwood

hazelwood

hickory

knotty pine

mahogany

maple

oak

palm

pine

plywood

ponderosa pine

rattan

redwood

rosewood

satinwood

softwood

sugar maple

sweet gum

teak

tulipwood

walnut

white poplar

wicker

willow

yellow poplar

FURS

badger	fox	muskrat	sable
bear	jaguar	nutria	seal
beaver	lamb	ocelot	skunk
cheetah	leopard	opossum	squirrel
chinchilla	lynx	otter	timberwolf
coyote	mink	rabbit	wolverine
ermine	mole	raccoon	
fisher	muskox	ringtail cat	

FUSES

base fuse	delayed-action fuse	plug fuse	slow-blow fuse
capped fuse	detonating fuse	point	s-type fuse
cartridge fuse	electrical fuse	proximity fuse	time fuse
chemical fuse	friction fuse	safety fuse	time-lag fuse
concussion fuse or percussion fuse	impact-action fuse	screw-plug fuse	variable-time fuse

GALAXY SHAPES

Galaxies differ from one another in shape, with variations resulting from the way in which the systems were formed. Depending on the initial conditions in the pregalactic gas some 15,000,000,000 (billion) years ago, galaxies formed either as slowly turning, smoothly structured, round systems of stars and gas or as rapidly rotating pinwheels.

barred spiral	irregular	spiral
elliptical	lenticular	

GAMES, BOARD AND TABLE

acey-deucy	Candyland	Clue	halma
backgammon	checkers	Connect Four	Life
Balderdash	chess	dominoes	ludo
Battleship	Chinese checkers	draughts	mah-jongg
billiards	Chinese chess	fox-and-geese	mancala
bingo	Chutes and Ladders	go	merels

Monopoly

morris

Mousetrap

Operation

Othello

Ouija

Parcheesi

Pictionary

pool

Risk

Scattergories

Scrabble

Scruples

shogi

snakes and ladders

snooker

Sorry

steeplechase

table hockey

table tennis or
Ping-Pong

tiddlywinks

tivoli

trick-track

Trivial Pursuit

Trouble

Uno

Yahtzee

GAMES, CARD

all fours

American whist

auction bridge

authors

baccarat

banker or broker

beggar-my-neighbor

bezique

blackjack or twenty-
one or vingt-et-un

Black Maria

blind poker

boodle

Boston

brag

bridge

California jack

canasta

casino

chemin de fer

Chicago

clubs

concentration

contract bridge

cooncan

crazy eights

cribbage

dig

donkey

draw poker

duplicate bridge

Earl of Coventry

écarté

eights

euchre

fan-tan

faro

fish

five-card stud

five hundred

flinch

frog

gin

gin rummy

go fish

hearts

high-low-jack

I doubt it

keno

knockout

knockout whist

knock poker

knock rummy

loo

lottery

lotto

memory

Michigan

Milles Bornes

monte

nap or napoleon

nine-card brag

old maid

ombre

pairs

patience

penny ante

pinochle

piquet

Pit

pitch

poker

pontoon

Pope Joan

primero

quadrille

quince

racing demon

red dog

rouge et noir

rubber bridge

rummy

Russian brag

Russian whist

Saratoga

seven-card brag

sevens

seven-up

short whist

skat

slapjack

snap

snipsnapsnorum

solitaire

solo

speculation

straight poker

strip poker

stud poker

tarot

thirty-one

three-card brag

three-card monte

war

whist

GAMES, CHILDREN'S AND PARTY

alphabet game

apple bob

beanbag toss

blind man's bluff

button button

buzz

capture the flag

card toss

catch

cat's cradle

charades

Chinese whispers

consequences

cops and robbers

crambo

cup and ball

dodge ball

duck duck goose

egg and spoon race

egg carry race

follow the leader

freeze tag

frog in the middle

geography

ghost

grandmother's footsteps

hangman

hidden treasure

hide-and-seek

hide the thimble

hopscotch

horseshoes

hot or cold

hot potato

I spy

it

jacks

jackstraws

jump rope

kickball

kick the can

king of the castle

leapfrog

London Bridge

mailman

marbles

memory game

Mother, may I?

mumbledypeg

murder in the dark

musical chairs

noughts and crosses

observation

pantomime

paper-clip fishing

paper-plate throw

pass the parcel

pat-a-cake

peekaboo

pick-up sticks

pig in the middle

piñata

pin the tail on the donkey

postman's knock

post office

potato sack race

prisoner's base

red rover

267

relay race

ring-a-ring o'roses

ringtoss

roadside alphabet

rock paper scissors

sack race

sardines

scavenger hunt

Simon says

spin the bottle

statue tag

stoop tag

tag

telephone

three-legged race

tic-tac-toe

tiddlywinks

tig

tug of war

twenty questions

What am I?

wheelbarrow race

Who am I?

GAMES, GAMBLING

all fours

auction bridge

baccarat

bank craps

bezique

bingo

blind hookey

blind poker

brelan

bridge

canasta

casino

chemin de fer

chuck-a-luck or birdcage

contract bridge

crack-loo

craps

crazy eights

cribbage

dice

draw poker

écarté

euchre

fan-tan

faro

fish or go fish

four-card monte

gin

gin rummy

hazard

heads or tails

hearts

high, low, jack, and the game

jai alai

keno

loo

lottery

lotto

lowball poker

Michigan

monte

numbers or policy

odd man wins

old maid

ombre

paddle wheel or raffle wheel

penny ante

picquet

pinball

pinochle

pitch and toss

poker

poker dice

quinze

rondo

rouge et noir

roulette

rum

rummy

seven-up

shell game

slot machine or slot

stud poker

thirty-five

three-card monte

tip-it

trente-et-quarante

twenty-one or blackjack or vingt-et-un

twenty-six

two-up

war

wheel of fortune or big six wheel

whist

Games, Word

acrostic
alphabet game
alternade
anagram
antigram
beheadment
Boggle
charades
charitable word
chronogram
concrete poetry
crossword
cumulative game
curtailment

dictionary game
enigma
grid game
guessing game
homonyms
kangaroo word
letter game
letter rebus
linkade
lipogram
malapropism
metallege
miming
nonpattern word

Outburst
oxymoron
palindrome
pangram
paronomasia
piano word
pun
punning game
rebus
reversal
rhyming game
riddle
Scrabble
semantic poetry

spelling game
spoonerism
stinky pinky
synonyms
Tom Swiftie
tongue-twister
transposition
typewriter word
univocalic
word-building game
word-finding game
wordplay
word search
word square

Garden Types

allotment
alpine garden
antique garden
apiary
arboretum
beer garden
border garden
botanical garden
bottle garden

conservatory
cottage garden
cutting garden
dish garden
dry garden
flower bed
flower garden
formal garden
fragrance garden

French formal
garden
greenhouse
hanging garden
heirloom garden
herbarium
herb garden
home garden
hotbed

hothouse
hydroponics
indoor garden
Italian garden
Japanese garden
kitchen garden
knot garden
market garden
maze garden

nursery

orchard

organic garden

ornamental garden

physic garden

potager

rockery

rock garden

roof garden

rose garden

sunken garden

tea garden

terraced garden

terrarium

truck garden

vegetable garden

victory garden

walled garden

water garden

winter garden

xeriscape

GASES

A gas is any substance without a shape or size—a vapor.

acetylene or ethyne

air gas or producer gas

ammonia

argon

arsine

avgas

biogas

blackdamp

blister gas

blue gas

boron trifluoride

bottled gas

butane

carbon dioxide

carbonic-acid gas

carbon monoxide

carbureted water gas

carbureted-hydrogen gas

chlorine

chlorofluorocarbon

CN gas or chloracetophenon

coal gas

compressed gas

cyanogen

damp

dichloroethyl sulfide

ethane

ether

ethyl chloride

ethylene

ethylene oxide

firedamp

flue gas

fluorine

fluorocarbon

formaldehyde

Freon

greenhouse gas

helium

hydrogen

hydrogen bromide

hydrogen chloride

hydrogen cyanide

hydrogen fluoride

hydrogen iodide

hydrogen sulfide

ideal gas or perfect gas

illuminating gas

inert gas

ketene

krypton

lewisite

liquefied petroleum gas

liquid oxygen

marsh gas or swamp gas

mephitis

methane

mustard gas

natural gas

neon

nerve gas

nitric oxide

nitrogen

nitrogen dioxide

nitrogen mustard

nitrous oxide

noble gas

oil gas

oxygen

ozone

phosgene or
carbonyl chloride

phosphine

Pintsch gas

poison gas

propane

propylene

radon

refrigerator
gas

sewer gas

sneeze gas

sulfur dioxide

sulfur mustard

synthesis gas

tear gas or
lachrymatory gas

vesicatory gas

vinyl chloride

war gas

water gas
or blue gas

xenon

Gem Cuts

American

baguette

brilliant

brilliant full

briolette

cabochon

double brilliant

double rose

emerald

French

Kohinoor

Lisbon

marquise or navette

oval

pear

pendeloque

Portuguese

rectangular cushion

rectangular faceted

rectangular step-cut

regent

rose

round

single

single brilliant

square cushion

square faceted

square
step-cut

star

step or trap or
cushion

Swiss

table

top and back

Gemstones

achroite

agate

alexandrite

amazonite

amber

amethyst

andradite

aquamarine

beryl

black opal

bloodstone

brilliant

cabochon

carbuncle

carnelian

cat's-eye

chalcedony

chevee

chrysoberyl

chrysolite

chrysoprase

citrine

coral

cordierite

demantoid

diamond

emerald

fire opal

garnet

girasol

harlequin opal

heliotrope

hiddenite

hyacinth

hyalithe

jacinth

jade

jargoon

jasper

jet

kunzite

lapis lazuli

moonstone

morganite

onegite

onyx

opal

pearl

peridot

plasma

pyrope

rhodolite

rose quartz

ruby

sapphire

sard

sardonyx

siberite

spinel

sunstone

tanzanite

tiger's eye

topaz

tourmaline

turquoise

unakite

water sapphire

white sapphire

zircon

Geography Branches

cartography

chorography

cultural geography

demography

dialect geography

earth science

economic geography

environmental geography

geodesy

geophysics

geoscopy

human geography

hydrography

hypsography

hysometry

linguistic geography

meteorology

oceanography

oceanology

orography

paleogeography

physical geography

selenography

social geography

soil science

topography

GEOLOGICAL PROCESSES

abrasion
aftershock
antipodes
avalanche
body wave
cataclysm
cementation
chemical reaction
chemical weathering
coalification
columnar jointing
comminution
compaction
compression
concretion
contact metamorphism
continental drift
creep
crystallization
decomposition

deep ocean current
deflation
deposition
diagenesis
diastrophism
disintegration
drift
earthquake
emergent coast
erosion
eruption
eustasy
fault
fold
foliation
foreshock
fracture
freezing
gasification
glaciation

hydrologic cycle
isostasy
landslide
leaching
lithification
meander
metamorphism
microseism
orogeny
permeability
petrification
plate tectonics
plucking
porosity
radioactive decay
recrystallization
regional metamorphism
ring of fire
rock cycle
seafloor spreading

sedimentation
seismic wave
shearing
sheeting
slump
soakage
stack
strain
stratification
stress
subduction
surface wave
tension
thawing
traction
tsunami
upheaval
upthrust
volcano
weathering

GEOLOGICAL TIME PERIODS

Algonkian
Archean
Archeozoic

Cambrian
Carboniferous
Cenozoic

Comanchean
Cretaceous
Devonian

Eocene
Glacial
Hadean or Priscoan

Holocene or Recent Epoch

Jurassic

Lower Cretaceous

Lower Tertiary

Mesoproterozoic

Mesozoic

Miocene

Mississippian

Neogene

Neoproterozoic

Oligocene

Ordovician

Paleocene

Paleogene

Paleoproterozoic

Paleozoic

Pennsylvanian

Permian

Phanerozoic

Pleistocene

Pliocene

Precambrian

Proterozoic

Quaternary

Silurian

Tertiary

Triassic

Upper Cretaceous

Upper Tertiary

GEOLOGY BRANCHES

agricultural geology

archaeological geology

astrogeology

cataclysmic geology

chronostratigraphy

crystallography

dynamic geology

earth science

ecology

economic geology

engineering geology

environmental geology

geobotany

geochemistry

geochronology

geochronometry

geodesy

geodynamics

geognosy

geomorphology

geophysics

geopolitics

glaciology

historical geology

hydrogeology

hydrology

lithology

magnetostratigraphy

marine geology

metallurgy

micro-geology

mineralogy

mining engineering

mining geology

morphology

oceanography

orography

paleogeography

paleontologic geology

paleontology

pedology

petroleum geology

petrology

photogeology

physical geology

physiographic geology

phytogeography

planetology seismology

plate tectonics

soft-rock geology

soil science

stratigraphy

structural geology

tectonics

volcanology

Geometric Figures and Shapes

acute triangle
circle
cone
cube
cuboid
cusp
cylinder
decagon
dodecagon
dodecahedron
equilateral triangle
foursquare
frustrum
gnomon
heptagon
hexagon

hexagram
hexahedron
hypercube
icosahedron
isosceles triangle
nonagon
oblong
obtuse triangle
octagon
octahedron
oxygen
parallelepiped
parallelogram
pentagon
pentahedron
Platonic body

polygon
polyhedron
prism
prismoid
pyramid
quadrangle
quadrant
quadrature
quadrilateral
quindecagon
rectangle
rhombohedron
rhombus
right triangle
scalene
triangle

sphere
square
tetragon
tetragram
tetrahedroid
tetrahedron
trapezium
or trapeze
trapezohedron
trapezoid
triangle
trigon
trihedron
trilateral
truncated
pyramid

Girl Scout Badges/Patches

A Healthier You
Across Generations
Adventure Sports
Aerospace
Architecture
Art in 3-D

Art in the Home
Art to Wear
Becoming a Teen
Being My Best
Books
Business Wise

Camera Shots
Camp Together
Car Care
Careers
Caring for Children
Celebrating People

Ceramics and Clay
"Collecting" Hobbies
Communications
Computer Fun
Consumer Power
Court Sports

Creative Solutions

CyberGirlScout

Dance

Discovering
Technology

"Doing" Hobbies

Do-It-Yourself

Drawing and Painting

Earth Connections

Eco-Action

Environmental
Health

Family Living Skills

Field Sports

Finding Your Way

First Aid

Folk Arts

Food, Fibers, and
Farming

Food Power

Frosty Fun

Fun and Fit

Girl Scouting Around
the World

Girl Scouting in My
Future

Girl Scouting
in the USA

Global Awareness

Globe-Trotting

Healthy
Relationships

High on Life

Highway to Health

Hiker

Horse Fan

Horse Rider

Humans and
Habitats

It's Important to Me

Jeweler

Leadership

Lead-On

Let's Get Cooking

Local Lore

Looking your Best

"Making" Hobbies

Making It Matter

Making Music

Math Whiz

Model Citizen

Money Sense

Ms Fix-It

Music Fan

My Community

My Heritage

Now and Then
Stories

Oil Up

On My Way

Outdoor Cook

Outdoor Creativity

Outdoor Fun

Outdoors in the City

Pet Care

Plants and Animals

Prints and Graphics

Puzzlers

Ready for Tomorrow

Rocks Rock

Safety First

Science Discovery

Science in Action

Science in
Everyday Life

Science Sleuth

Sew Simple

Sky Search

Small Craft

Sports Sampler

Stress Less

Swimming

Textile and Fibers

The Choice
Is Yours

The Cookie
Connection

The World in My
Community

Theater

Toymaker

Traveler

United We Stand

Visual Arts

Walking for Fitness

Water Fun

Water Wonders

Weather Watch

Wildlife

Winter Sports

Women's Stories

World Neighbors

Write All About It

Yarn and Fabric
Arts

Your Outdoor
Surroundings

GLACIER AND ICE CAP TYPES

cirque glacier

cold glacier

continental glacier

drumlin

erratic

esker

firn

floe

hanging glacier

ice cap

icefall

icefield

ice sheet

ice shelf

ice stream or outlet glacier

kame

mountain glacier

neve

nunatak

pack ice

piedmont glacier

snow bridge

surging glacier

temperate glacier

tidewater glacier

valley glacier

warm glacier

GLANDS

adrenal gland

apocrine gland

buccal gland

corpus luteum

Cowper's gland

ductless gland

eccrine gland

endocrine gland

exocrine gland

gastric gland

gonad

holocrine gland

islet of Langerhans

lacrimal gland

lacteal gland

liver

lymph gland

mammary gland

meibomian gland

merocrine gland

ovary

pancreas

parathyroid gland

parotid gland

pineal body

pituitary gland

preputial gland

prostate gland

salivary gland

sebaceous gland

sublingual gland

submandibular gland or submaxillary gland

suprarenal gland

sweat gland

tear gland

testicle or testis

thymus

thyroid gland

GLASS TYPES

actinic glass

agate glass

antimony glass

arsenic glass

art glass

Baccarat glass

basalt glass

Bilbao glass

blown glass

Bohemian glass

bone glass

borax glass

borosilicate glass
bottle glass
Bristol glass
brodeglass
bubble glass
bulletproof glass
cameo glass
camphor glass
canary glass
carnival glass
cased glass
cathedral glass
cellular glass
Chevalier glass
coralene
cranberry glass
crown glass
cryolite glass
crystal
custard glass
cut glass
cylinder glass
daylight glass

drawn glass
engraved glass
etched glass
Fiberglas
figured glass
flashed glass
flat glass
flint glass
float glass
Florentine glass
Fostoria
frosted glass
fused quartz
glass bead
glass brick
glass wool
green glass
ground glass
heat-resistant glass
hobnail glass
ice glass
lace glass
Lalique glass

laminated glass
lead crystal
lead glass
milk glass
mirror
natural glass
obsidian
opal glass
opaline
optical glass
ornamental glass
Orrefors glass
photosensitive glass
plastic glass
plate glass
porcelain glass
pressed glass
prism glass
Pyrex
quartz glass
reinforced glass
rhinestone
rock crystal

ruby glass
safety glass
Sandwich glass
satin glass
sheet glass
show glass
Silex glass
soft glass
stained glass
Steuben glass
Swedish glass
Syracuse
watch glass
tempered glass
uranium glass
uviol glass
Venetian glass
Vitaglass
vitreous silica
Waterford
glass
window glass
wire glass

GLASSES, DRINKING

Alsace glass
baker
beer glass

beer mug
bordeaux glass
brandy snifter

burgundy glass
champagne coupe
champagne flute

champagne saucer
champagne tulip
cocktail glass

cordial glass

deep-saucer
champagne glass

flagon

footed pilsner

goblet

heavy goblet

highball glass

jigger glass

juice glass

liqueur glass

mug

mug stein

old-fashioned glass

Paris goblet

pilsner glass

pony

port glass

punch cup

red-wine glass

rummer

seidel

sherry glass

shot glass

shot snifter

snifter

sour glass

sparkling wine glass

stein

stemware

tankard

toby

tulip goblet

tumbler

water goblet

whiskey sour glass

white-wine glass

wine glass or
wineglass

yard of ale

GOATS

American la Mancha

Anglo-Nubian

Angora

Apulian

Bagot

bezoar

Chamois-Colored

Dutch White

French Alpine

Golden Guernsey

Grisons
Striped

ibex

Kashmiri

markhor

Murcian

Nubian

Rock
Alpine

Saanen

Somali

Soviet Mohair

Spanish ibex

Swiss Alpine

Syrian Mountain

tahr

Telemark

thar

Toggenburg

tur

Valais Blackneck

GOAT-ANTELOPES

Goat-antelopes are ruminant mammals of a group that combines the characteristics of both goats and antelopes.

chamois

chikara

gnu

goral

gray Himalayan

mazame

mountain goat

musk ox

Rocky Mountain goat

saiga

serow

takin

GOD, NAMES FOR

Adonai

Allah

Almighty

Alpha and Omega

Amun

Ancient of Days

Creator

Deity

Divine

El

Elohim

Eternal

Father

Father, Son, and Holy Ghost

First Cause

God Almighty

Godhead

God the Father

God the Son

Holy Ghost

Holy Spirit

Holy Trinity

Immanuel

Jah

Jehovah

King of Glory

King of Kings

Light of the World

Loki

Lord

Lord of Hosts

Lord of Lords

Maker

Our Father

Prime Mover

Redeemer

Sabaoth

Savior

Shaddai

Supreme Being

Trinity

Yahweh

Yahweh Sabaoth

GOLF EQUIPMENT

1 iron or driving iron

2 iron or two iron

3 iron or three iron

4 iron or four iron

5 iron or five iron

6 iron or six iron

7 iron or seven iron

8 iron or eight iron

9 iron or nine iron

baffing spoon

ball or pill

ball washer

blade putter

brassie

bulger

chipping iron club

cleek

club cover

cup

driver

driving iron

driving mashie

driving putter

fairway wood

flagstick

gap wedge

golf bag

golf cart

golf glove

iron

jigger

lob wedge

lofting iron

long iron

mallet

marker

mashie

mashie iron

mashie-niblick

midiron

mid-mashie

niblick

number 1 wood or one wood or driver

number 2 wood or two wood

number 3 wood or three wood

number 4 wood or
four wood

number 5 wood or
five wood

number 6 wood or
six wood

number 7 wood or
seven wood

pitching iron

pitching niblick

pitching wedge

pull cart

putter

rake

running iron

run-up

rutting iron

sand wedge or sand
iron

scorecard shag bag

short iron

spade mashie

spoon

tee blocks or tee
markers

tee or peg

Texas wedge

third wedge

track iron

utility iron

utility wedge

utility wood

wedge

wood

GOLF GRAND SLAM

British Open

Masters

PGA Championship

United States Open

GOLF SHOTS

air shot

airmail

approach put

approach shot

bend one

blast

block

bowker

bunker shot

bunt

chili dip

chip and run or
chip and roll or
bump and run

chip shot

come back shot

control shot

cut shot

draw shot

drive

dubbed shot

duck hook

dunch

explosion shot

fade

fairway wood shot

fan or whiff

flier

flop shot

full shot

gimme

half shot or half
swing

hole in one

hole out

hook

jumper

kill the ball

knockdown

lag

lay up

lob

lofted shot

long iron shot

Mulligan

pitch

pitch and run

pop up

pull

pull hook

punch

push

putt

quail high

quarter shot

recovery shot

run-up

sand shot

sclaff

slice snake

snap hook

tap in

tee shot

toe hook

touch shot

trouble shot

up

water shot

windcheater

wormburner

GOVERNMENT FORMS

absolute monarchy

absolutism

anarchy

aristocracy

autarchy/autarky

authoritarianism

autocracy

autonomy

bureaucracy

caretaker government

coalition government

collectivism

communism

constitutionalism

constitutional monarchy

crown

democracy

despotism

diarchy

dictatorship

duarchy

duumvirate

dyarchy

fascism

federalism

feudalism

gerontocracy

gynarchy

gynecocracy

hagiarchy/hagiocracy

heptarchy

hierocracy

imperialism

isocracy

junta

matriarchy

meritocracy

militarism

mobocracy

monarchy

monocracy

ochlocracy

octarchy

oligarchy

one-man rule

pantisocracy

parliamentary government

patriarchy

pentarchy

pluralism

plutocracy

presidential government

protectorate

provisional government

regency

republic

self-government

self-rule

socialism

state government

statism

stratocracy

synarchy

technocracy

thearchy

theocracy

timocracy

totalitarianism

triarchy

triumvirate

tyranny

GRAINS AND CEREALS, EDIBLE

barley	farina	masa	raisin bran
blue cornmeal	flour	millet	rice
bran	grain	muesli	rice grass
buckwheat	granola	mush	rolled oats
bulgur	grits	oat bran	rye
cereal	groats	oatmeal	semolina
corn	gruel	oats	shredded wheat
cornflakes	hominy	polenta	sorghum
cornmeal	Indian corn	porridge	wheat
couscous	kasha	puffed rice	wheat germ
einkorn	maize	puffed wheat	wild rice

GRANITE VARIETIES

Granite is coarse- or medium-grained intrusive (forced while in a plastic state into cavities or between layers) igneous rock that is rich in quartz and feldspar. It is the most common plutonic rock (formed by solidification of magma deep within the earth and crystalline in structure) of the Earth's crust.

aplite	crushed	hornblende	syenitic
binary	cumulo	paver	veneer
black	curb	pegmatite	
block	gneissoid	porphyritic	
concretionary	graphic	rhyolite	

GRAPE VARIETIES

Alicante Gouschet

Almeria

arroyo grape

Barbera grape

bird grape

blue grape

bullace grape

bush grape

Cabernet Sauvignon grape

canyon grape

Catawba grape

Chardonnay grape

Chenin Blanc

chicken grape or frost grape

Cinsaut grape

Concord grape

Delaware grape

downy grape

everbearing grape

fox grape

Gewurztraminer

Isabella grape

Italia grape

Labrusca grape

Ladyfinger

malvasia

Merlot

mountain grape

Muscadet

muscadine grape

muscat grape

pigeon grape

Pinot Blanc

Pinot grape

Pinot Grigio

Pinot Noir

plum grape

post-oak grape

raisin grape

red grape

Ribier grape

Riesling grape

river grape

sand grape

Sauvignon blanc

Sauvignon grape

seedless grape

Semillon

Shiraz grape

Spanish grape

summer grape

Syrah

Thompson seedless grape

Tokay grape

vinifera grape

wild grape

wine grape

winter grape

Zinfandel

GRAPHIC ARTS

Graphic arts are defined as the visual or technical arts based on the use of line and tone—especially design, drawing, printing—rather than three-dimensional work or the use of color.

aquatint

block print

cerography

chalcography

decalcomania

drawing

drypoint

engraving

etching

glyptography

gold point

graphic design

gravure

hyalography

intaglio

linocut

lithography

mezzotint

monotype

painting

photogravure

printmaking

repoussé

serigraphy

silkscreen

silverpoint

steel engraving

sumi-e

tortillion

wash drawing

website design

woodblock

woodcut

xylography

zincography

GRASSES, PULSES, RUSHES, AND SEDGES

These groups of plants are monocotyledons—flowering plants whose seedlings possess a single cotyledon, or seed leaf. In common with other monocotyledons, grasses, pulses, and sedges have long narrow leaves with parallel veins. They have tiny flowers in clusters or spikes.

grasses

alfalfa

alfilaria

Australian rye grass

Bahia grass

bamboo

barley

barn grass

barnyard grass

beach grass

beard grass

bengal grass

bent

bent grass

Bermuda grass

black bent

blue grama

bluegrass

bluejoint

bog grass

bristle grass

bristly foxtail grass

bromegrass

broomcorn

buckwheat

buffalo grass

bulrush

bunch grass

button grass

canary grass

cane

cat's-tail grass

China grass

chufa

clubrush

cock's-foot cogon

cordgrass

corn

cotton grass

couch grass

crab grass

cutgrass

cutting grass

darnel

deergrass

dogstail

durra

durum wheat

eelgrass

elephant grass

English rye grass

esparto

feather grass

fescue

finger grass

florin

flyaway grass

four-leaved grass

foxtail

frog's-bit

galingale

gama grass or sesame grass

grama

guinea grass

hair grass hassock

hay

herd's grass

horsetail

Indian corn

Italian rye grass

Japanese lawn grass

Job's-tears

kangaroo grass

Kentucky bluegrass

khus-khus

Korean lawn grass

lawn grass

lemon grass

little quaking grass

lovegrass

lyme grass

maize

meadow fescue

meadow foxtail

meadow grass

mesquite grass

millet

myrtle grass

oat

oat grass

orchard grass

paddy

palm-leaved grass

pampas grass

panic grass

papyrus

pearl millet

peppergrass

pin grass

plume grass

pony grass

quack grass

quitch

razor grass

red fescue

redtop

reed

reed grass

reed mace

Rhode Island bent

ribbon grass

rice

rush

rye

ryegrass

scotch grass

scouring rush

scutch

sedge

sesame

sheep's fescue

silk grass

slender foxtail

sorghum

sour grass

spear grass

squirrel-tail grass

squitch

star grass

striped grass

sugarcane

switch grass

sword grass

tear grass

timothy

tufted hair grass

tule

twitch grass

umbrella plant

vernal grass

vetiver

viper's grass

wheat

wild oat

wild rice

wild rye

windlestraw

wire grass

witch grass

wood meadow grass

woodrush

woolly beard grass

worm grass

yellow-eyed grass

zebra grass

zoysia

GRAY COLORS VARIETIES

ash
ash gray
bat
battleship gray
blue-gray
cadet gray
charcoal gray
cinder
cinereous
cloud
crystal gray
dark gray
dove
field gray

flint
French gray
glaucous gray
granite
gray-white
greige
grey
gun metal
iron
lead
light gray
lilac gray
merle
mole gray

moleskin
mouse
mushroom
neutral
nutria
obsidian
olive gray
opal gray
Oxford gray
oyster gray
pale gray
pearl
pearl gray
pelican

plumbago
powder gray
Quaker gray
salt-and-pepper
shell gray
silver
silver-gray
slate gray
smoke gray
steel gray
taupe
zinc gray

GREAT LAKES

Erie
Huron

Michigan
Ontario

Superior

GREEN COLOR VARIETIES

absinthe
apple green
aqua green
aquamarine

avocado
bay
beryl
bice

blue-green
bottle green
brewster
Brunswick green

cadmium green
celadon
chartreuse
chartreuse green

chrome green
chrome oxide green
chrysolite green
citron green
civette green
clair de lune
cobalt green
corbeau
cucumber
cypress
dark green
drake
duck green
eau de nile
Egyptian green
emerald
fir green or fir
flagstone
forest green
gallein
glauconite

glaucous green
grass green
gray-green
green ocher
Guinea green
gunpowder
holly green
Irish green
ivy green
jade
Janus green
jungle green
kelly green
Kendal green
leaf green
leek green
light green
lime
Lincoln green
lizard
loden

lotus
malachite
marine
methyl green
mignonette
mint
moss
myrtle
Niagara green
Nile green
olive
pale green
Paris green
parrot
patina
pea green
pistachio green
Quaker green
reseda
sage green
sap green

sea green
serpentine
shamrock
Spanish green
spruce
teal
terre-verte
tourmaline
turquoise
verdant green
verdet
verdigris
vert
Vienna green
virescent
viridian
Wedgwood green
willow green
yellow-green
yew
zinc

GREETINGS AND FAREWELLS

a bientot
a demain
a toute a l'heure
adieu

adios
ahoy
all hail
aloha

arrivederci
au revoir
Auf Wiedersehen
ave

be good
be seeing you
bless you
bon matin

bon soir

bon voyage

bonjour

bonne nuit

buenas noches

buenas tardes

buenos dias

buon giorno

buona notte

buona sera

bye

bye-bye

catch you later

check

cheerio

cheers

chin-chin

ciao

come again

das vedanya

enjoy

fare thee well

farewell

g'day

glad to see you

God be with you

God bless

Godspeed

good afternoon

good day

good evening

good luck

good morning

good night

good to see you

good-bye

greetings

gute Nacht

guten Abend

guten Morgen

guten Tag

hail

hallo

halloo

happy trails

hasta la vista

hasta luego

hasta mañana

have a good one

have a nice day

hello

hello there

hey

hey-ho

hi

hi, there

hi ya

ho d'ye do?

hola

how are you?

how do?

how do you do?

how goes it?

how you be?

how you been?

how you doing?

howdy

howdy-do

howdy-doody

how's by you?

how's everything?

how's it going?

how's the world
treating you?

how's things?

hullo

knobanwa

konichiwa

later

later on

mañana

many happy returns

namaste

over

over and out

pax

peace

pip-pip

que pasa?

regards

roger

salaam

salud

salutations

sayonara

see ya

see you later

see you later,
alligator

see you soon

shake

shalom

take care

take it easy

ten-four

toodleoo

toodles

welcome

what it is?

what's happening?

wie gehts?

yo

289

HAIRBRUSHES

boar bristle	natural bristle	plastic	round
flat-back	nylon	quill	vent
folding	paddle	rotating	wood

HAIRCUTS AND HAIRSTYLES

Afro	big hair	buzz cut	crew cut
Apollo knot	bob	chignon	crimp
back-combed	bouffant	classic pull-back	crop
bald	braid	close-cropped	curlicue
bangs	brush cut	coif	curls
Beatle cut	bun	coiffure	D.A. or duck's arse
beaver tail	bunches	corkscrew curls	dreadlocks
beckoning curl	burr cut	cornrows	ducktail
beehive	butch	cowlick	Eton crop

feather cut
finger wave
flattop flip
forelock
French braid
French knot
French plait
French roll or French twist
fringe
frisette
frizz
fuzz cut

lappet curl
layered cut
lion's tail
marcel wave
Mohawk
moptop
mullet
pageboy
permanent wave
pigtails
pincurls
plait
pompadour

ponytail
poodle cut
porcupine
pouf
Prince Valiant
punk
Rastafarian dreadlocks
ratted
razor cut
ringlets
shag
shingle

skinhead
snood
spit curl
swirl
teased
topknot
updo
upsweep
Veronica Lake
wave
wedge
windblown bob

HAIR ORNAMENTS

barrette
bobby pin
bow
braid

comb
elastic
hairband
hair clip

hair extension
hair net
hair pin
hair stick

headband
Scrunchie
snood
tiara

HALOGENS

A halogen is defined as a reactive non-metallic element or substance which forms a salt by combining with a metal or any of the elements of group 7 of the periodic table.

astatine
bromine

chlorine
cyanogen

fluorine
iodine

HAMMERS AND MALLETS

adz-eye hammer
air hammer
ball peen hammer
beetle
blacksmith's hammer
board drop hammer
boilermaker's hammer
brick hammer
bumping hammer
bushhammer
carpenter's hammer
chipping hammer
claw hammer
cooper's hammer
cross peen hammer
deep-stroke hammer

demolition hammer
dinging hammer
double-claw hammer
drop hammer
drywall hammer
electric hammer
engineer's hammer
farrier's hammer
framing hammer
fuller
hand hammer
helve hammer
joiner's mallet
knapping hammer
long-handled hammer
machinist's hammer

mason's hammer
maul
monkey hammer
peen hammer
pile hammer
planishing hammer
pneumatic hammer
purgatory hammer
raising hammer
rip hammer
riveting hammer
rubber mallet
scutch
set hammer
shingler's hammer
shoemaker's hammer

sledgehammer
small anvil
soft-faced hammer
soft-faced mallet
spalling hammer
stamp hammer
steam hammer
stonemason's hammer
tack hammer
tilt hammer
trip-hammer
upholsterer's hammer
Warington hammer
wooden mallet

HANDLES

bail
bow
brace
brake
broomstick
crank

crop
doorknob
grip
haft
handgrip
handle bar

handstaff
helm
hilt
knob
knocker
loom

lug
panhandle
pull
rounce
rudder
sally

shaft   spindle   tote

shank   stock   trigger

snatch   tiller   withe

HANDWEAR AND GLOVES

baseball glove or   gauntlets   metal glove   shooting glove
baseball mitt
                       golf glove   mittens   sports gloves
batting glove
                       hockey gloves   mitts   suede gloves
boxing gloves
                       husking glove   motorcycle gloves   wedding gloves
driving gloves
                       kid gloves   muff   winter gloves
fingerless gloves
                       latex gloves   protective gloves   work gloves

HARDWOODS

apple   butternut   hickory   pear

ash   cherry   holly   poplar

balsa   chestnut   ironwood   rosewood

basswood   cottonwood   lime   sycamore

beech   ebony   magnolia   walnut

birch   elm   mahogany   willow

black walnut   gopherwood   maple   yellowwood

blackwood   gum   oak   zebrawood

HATS, CAPS, AND HEADWEAR

aigrette   anadem   babushka   Balmoral

Alpine   astrakhan   balaclava helmet   bandanna

bandeau

bangkok

baseball cap

basinet

bathing cap

beanie

bearskin

beaver

bellhop

beret

bicorne

biggin

billed hat

billycock

biretta

bluebonnet

boater

bobby

bonnet

boudoir cap

bowler

brass hat

Breton

brimmed hat

bubble beret

burgonet

busby

bush

calash

calotte

calpac

campaign hat

cap

capote

capuche

cartwheel

casque

castor

caul

chalet

chapeau

chaperon

chechia

cloche

cocked hat

collie hat

commode

coolie

coonskin cap

cornet

coronet

cossack

cowboy hat

coxcomb

crash helmet

crown

crush hat

crusher

Davy Crockett

deerstalker

derby

diadem

dink

Dolly Varden

dress hat

dunce cap

Dutch cap

earmuffs

eight-point cap

engineer's cap

envoy

eyeshade

fanchon

fascinator

fatigue cap

feathers

fedora

felt hat

fez

fillet

flowerpot

fool's cap

football helmet

forage cap

French beret

French sailor

fur hat

garrison cap

gas mask

gaucho

gibus

glengarry

Greek fisherman's

hair net

hairpiece

hard hat

havelock

headcloth

headdress

heaume

helmet

hennin

high hat

homburg

hood

hornburg

hunting

jester's cap

jipjapa

jockey cap

juliet cap

kaffiyeh

kamelaukion

kelly

kepi

kerchief

kossuth hat

lambrequin

lappet

leghorn

Legionnaire's

liberty cap

lid

mantilla

matador

meter

millinery

mitre

mobcap

mod

monkey cap

montero

morion

mortarboard

mountie's

mutch

newsboy

nightcap

opera hat

overseas cap

painter's cap

panache

Panama hat

pancake beret

peaked hat

pelage

penna

peruke

petasus

Phrygian cap

picture cap

picture hat

pillbox

pinner

pith helmet

pixie

planter's

plug hat

plumage

plume

poke bonnet

porkpie

postiche

postilion

pot hat

profile

pschent

puggaree

Puritan

rain hat

ramillie

rebozo

riding hood

rumal

safari hat

sailor

sallet

scarf

Scottie

scraper

service cap

shako

shovel hat

silk hat

ski mask

skimmer

skullcap

slouch hat

snap brim

snood

sombrero

sou'wester

Stetson

stingy brim

stocking cap

stovepipe hat

straw hat

sugarloaf

sunbonnet

sundown

sun hat

sun helmet

switch

taj

tam-o'-shanter

tarboosh

ten-gallon hat

terai

three-cornered hat
or tricorn

tiara

tin hat

top hat

topee

topper

toque

toupee

trilby

trooper

tuque

turban

turban veil

Tyrolean hat

veil

war bonnet

watch cap

Watteau hat

welder's helmet

wideawake

wimple

wreath

yarmulke

yashmak

Zucchetto

HAZARDOUS HOUSEHOLD CHEMICALS

acetone

air freshener

ammonia

antifreeze

asbestos

automobile wax

bleach

brake fluid

car battery

carpet shampoo

contact cement

degreaser

diesel fuel

dishwasher detergent

drain cleaner

flea powder

formaldehyde

fungicide

furniture polish

glue

insecticide

kerosene

lead

lice shampoo

mercury

metal polish

mold and mildew cleaner

mothballs

motor oil

oven cleaner

paint

paintbrush cleaner

paint stripper

paint thinner

pesticide

power-steering fluid

radon

rat and mouse poison

rust remover

sealant

stain

tar and bug remover

toilet bowl cleaner

transmission fluid

wood finish

wood preservative

HEATING SYSTEMS

baseboard heating

central heating

convection heating

electric heating

furnace heating

gas heating

gravity warm air heating

heat pump

hot-air heating

hot-water heating

hydronic heating

hypocaust

kerosene heating

oil heating

panel heating

radiant heating

solar heating

solar thermal heating

space heating

steam heating

stove heating

HEAVEN'S DESIGNATIONS

abode of the blessed

Abraham's bosom

better place

better world

Beulah

Beulah Land

Canaan

Celestial City

City of God

devaloka

Elysian Fields

eternal home

eternity

Fiddler's Green

firmament

future state

glory

God's kingdom

God's presence

happy hunting ground

happy land

heaven above

heavenly city

heavenly kingdom

high heaven

Holy City

Holy Kingdom

inheritance of the saints in light

kingdom come

kingdom of glory

kingdom of God

kingdom of heaven

Land o' the Leal or Land of the Leal

my Father's house

Nirvana

otherworld

Paradise

place up there

presence of God

Promised Land

realm of light

seventh heaven

Svarga

Throne of God

Valhalla

world above

Zion

HEINZ 57 VARIETIES

apple butter

apple jelly

baked beans in tomato sauce without meat

baked beans with pork and tomato sauce

baked beans without tomato sauce with Boston-style pork

baked red kidney beans

beefsteak sauce

blackberry preserves

black raspberry preserves

cherry preserves

chili sauce

chow chow pickles

cooked macaroni

cooked spaghetti

crab-apple jelly

cream of celery soup

cream of pea soup

cream of tomato soup

currant jelly

damson plum preserves

dill pickles

distilled white vinegar

evaporated horseradish

fig pudding

grape jelly

green pepper sauce

India relish

manzanilla olives

mayonnaise

mince meat

peach preserves

peanut butter

plum pudding

prepared mustard

preserved sweet gherkins

preserved sweet mixed pickles

pure cider vinegar

pure malt vinegar

pure olive oil

queen olives

quince jelly

red pepper sauce

red raspberry preserves

ripe olives

salad dressing

sour midget gherkins

sour mixed pickles

sour pickled onions

sour spiced gherkins

strawberry preserves

stuffed olives

sweet midget gherkins

sweet mustard pickles

tarragon vinegar

tomato ketchup

Worcestershire sauce

Hell Designations

abyss

Amenti

Arallu

Avernus

ballyhack

barathrum

below

bhumis

bottomless pit

brimstone

damnation

dark

down below

Erebus

eternal punishment

Gehenna

Hades

hamestagan

hell

hellfire

infernal regions

inferno

Jahannam

Jahannan

Jigoku

karmavacara

limbo

Naraka

Nastrond

nether region

nether world or Nifleheim

Pandemonium

perdition

pit

pit of Acheron

realm of Abaddon

realm of Cerebus

realm of Charon

realm of Minos

realm of Pluto

realm of Rhadamanthus

red region

river of Acheron

river of Cocytus

river of Lethe

river of Phlegethon

river of Styx

Sheol

Stygian

Tartarus

Tophet

tunket

underground

underworld

void

HEPTATHLON EVENTS

After 1981, the heptathlon replaced the pentathlon (five events) in women's Olympic athletics competition. The seven different track-and-field events are performed over two days.

100-meter hurdles	800-meter run	javelin throw	shot put
200-meter run	high jump	long jump	

HERBS

abscess root	basil	camomile	deadly nightshade
acacia bark	bay leaf	caraway	dill
adder's tongue	belladonna	cardamom	dropwort
African daisy	bergamot	catnip centella	echinacea
African valerian	birthwort	chamomile	fennel
alkali mallow	bitter orange	chervil	feverroot
alpine anemone	bitterroot	chicory	figwort
alpine aster	bitter rubberweed	chive	finochio
American mistletoe	blood root	cilantro	fraxinella or gas plant
angelica	blue flag	cinnamon	fumewort
anise	borage	climbing onion	garlic
anise hyssop	brookweed	clover	ginger
arrow grass	bugleweed	coltsfoot	ginkgo
arrowroot	butterbur	comfrey	ginseng
axseed	butterwort	coriander	goat's rue
balm	calendula	cow parsnip	gypsywort
baobab	California buttercup	cumin	harebell
Barbara's buttons	camas	datura	hemlock

hemp
henbane
herb of grace
horehound
horsemint
hyssop
jackfruit
joe-pye weed
kapok
lady's mantle
lady's smock
lavender
lemon balm
lemongrass
licorice
liverwort
lovage

lupin
mandrake
marijuana
marjoram
mint
monkshood
motherwort
mullein
mustard
oregano
parsley
parsnip
peppermint
periwinkle
pokeweed
primrose
rattlesnake weed

rosemary
rue
sacred lotus
safflower
sage
Saint John's wort
savory
sesame
silverweed
soapwort
sorrel
spearmint
spiderwort
star anise
star fruit
sweet basil
sweet bay

sweet cicely
sweet woodruff
tamarack
tansy
tarragon
thyme
tinker's root
tobacco
wasabi
water hemlock
wild ginger
wintergreen
woodruff
wormwood
yarrow
yellow bells

HINDUISM SECTS

Aghorapanthi
Ajivika
Arya Samaj
Brahmanism
Chaitanya Vaishnava
Dadu Panthis
Dakshincharin
Hare Krishna

Lingayata
Lokayata
Madhva
Pancharatra
Rama Krishna
Ramanandi
Saivism
Saktism

Sankar
Satnami
Shaktism
Shivaism
Sittar
Sivaism
Tantrism
Vaishnavism

Vaisnavism
Vamcharin
Vedantism
Vishnuism
Yogism

HOBBIES AND PASTIMES

acting
aerobics
airplane flying
angling
animation
antique collecting
antique refinishing
appliqueing
aquarium building
archaeology
archery
art collecting
astrology
astronomy
autograph collecting
backgammon
backpacking
baking
ballet
ballooning
ballroom dance
bark rubbing
baseball
basketball
basket collecting
basketry

batik
beachcombing
beadcraft
beekeeping
beermaking
bicycling
bingo
bird-watching
board games
boating
bonsai
bookbinding
book collecting
bottle collecting
bowling
box collecting
brass-rubbing
bridge
butterfly collecting
button collecting
calligraphy
camping
candlemaking
caning
canoeing
car repairs

car tinkering
cards
carpentry
cartooning
carving
ceramics
checkers
chemistry
chess
clay modeling
climbing
clock collecting
coin collecting
collage
collecting
comic collecting
computer games
cooking
crafts
crewel embroidery
crocheting
crossword puzzles
customizing
découpage
dog breeding
dogwalking

do-it-yourself
doll collecting
dollhouse building
dramatics
drawing
dressmaking
drying flowers
embroidery
enameling
exercising
fabric painting
fast-food meal toy collecting
fencing
fiber arts
field hockey
fishing
flower arranging
flower pressing
fly fishing
folk dancing
fossil hunting
fretwork
gambling
gaming
gardening

gem collecting

gem cutting and polishing

genealogy

geology

glass etching or glass engraving

glass painting

golf

gravestone rubbings

greenhouse gardening

guitar

gymnastics

ham radio

handicrafts

hang gliding

hiking

home decorating

home repairs

horseback riding

hunting

ice hockey

ice skating

ikebana

in-line skating

insect collecting

Internet surfing

inventing

jazz dance

jewelry making

jogging

judo

karate

key ring collecting

kite flying

kite making

knitting

lacemaking

landscaping

leathercraft

macramé

magic tricks

manege

marble collecting

marquetry

mask making

matchbook cover collecting

menu collecting

metalworking

meteorology

mime

miniature collecting

mobile making

model airplanes

model cars

modelmaking

model railroads

model trains

modern dance

mosaics

mountain climbing

mountaineering

moviemaking

museum-going

music

musical band

musical composition

musical instrument

needlecrafts

needlepoint

numismatics

orchestra

orchid growing

orienteering

origami

painting

painting miniatures

paper flower making

paperweight collecting

paperworking

papier-mâché

patchworking

pets

philately

photography

piano

Pilates

playing cards

playwriting

postcard collecting

pottery

preserving foods

pressing flowers

printing

puppetry

puzzles

quigong

quilting

racewalking

raffia work

reading

recipe collecting

recorder

refinishing furniture

riding

rock band

rock climbing

rocketry

rollerblading

roller skating

rug making

running

sailing

scouting

scrimshaw

scuba diving

sculpture

sewing

sheet music
collecting

shell carving

shell collecting

silver collecting

singing

skateboarding

skiing

skin diving

skydiving

sledding

snorkeling

soap carving

soccer

spelunking

spinning

spoon collecting

sports

sports card
collecting

square dancing

squash

stagecraft

stained glass

stamp collecting

stenciling

stitchery

stonecutting

surf fishing

surfing

swimming

tae kwon do

tai chi

tap dance

tapestry-making

tatting

taxidermy

tennis

terrarium building

tie-dyeing

tool collecting

topiary

toymaking

trainspotting

trapshooting

trapunto

traveling

tropical fish

upholstering

ventriloquism

video games

vocabulary building

volleyball

walking

water skiing

weaving

whitewater rafting

whittling

windsurfing

winemaking

wirecraft

woodworking

word games

word puzzles

writing

yachting

yoga

HOCKEY EQUIPMENT

abdominal protector

athletic supporter

blocking glove

catching glove

chest protector

deflector pad

elbow pads

face mask

face shield

gloves

goal cage

goaltender's glove

goaltender's stick

helmet

hip pads

hockey pants

knee pads

left-handed stick

leg guard

leg pads

mouth guard

neck guard

neutral stick

puck

right-handed stick

shin guards

shoulder pads

skates

stick

stick glove

waffle pad

wrist guard

HOCKEY FOULS AND PENALTIES

bench minor penalty

bench penalty

board-checking

butt-ending

charging

clipping

coincidental

cross-checking

delayed penalty

delay of game

double minor

ejection

elbowing

falling on the puck

fighting

freeze the puck

game misconduct

gross misconduct

handling the puck

high sticking

holding

hooking

icing

interference

kneeing

major penalty or five-minute penalty

match penalty

minor penalty or two-minute penalty

misconduct penalty

offsides

penalty shot

roughing

simultaneous penalty

slashing

smother the puck

spearing

third-man-in rule

too many players on the ice

tripping

HOCKEY POSITIONS

back

center

forward

goalie left defenseman

left wing

right defenseman

right wing

HORMONES

adrenalin or adrenaline

adrenocorticoid

adrenosterone

adrenotrophin

aldosterone

amniotin

androgen

androsterone

angiotensin

antidiuretic hormone

calcitonin

cholecystokinin

chondrotrophic hormone

corticoid

corticosterone

corticotrophin

cortisol or hydrocortisone

cortisone

dehydro-corticosterone

dexamethasone

dexoxycortico-sterone

enterocrinin

enterogastrone

epinephrine

erythropoietin

estradiol

estrin

estriol

estrogen

estrone

follicle-stimulating hormone or FSH

glucagon

gonadotrophin

growth hormone

hydroxycortico-sterone

hydroxydehydrocor-ticosterone

hydroxydesoxycorti-costerone

insulin

intermedin

interstitial-cell-stimulating hormone or ICSH

juvenile hormone

kinin

lactogenic hormone

lipocaic

lipotropin

luteinizing hormone or LH

mammin

melanocyte-stimulating hormone or MSH

melatonin

noradrenalin

oxytocin

parathyrin

parathyroid hormone

pitocin

pitressin

progesterone

progestin

prolactin

relaxin

secretin

somatrophin or growth hormone

somatostatin

testosterone

thyrocalcitonin

thyroglobulin

thyroid hormone

thyroid-stimulating hormone or TSH

thyrotrophin

thyroxine or thyroxin

vasopressin or antidiuretic hormone

vasotocin

HORSE AND PONY BREEDS AND VARIETIES

American quarter horse

American saddle horse

American trotter

Andalusian

Anglo-Arab

Appaloosa

Arabian

Barbary horse

Basuto pony

Belgian

Breton

Camargue

Caspian

Cleveland Bay

Clydesdale

Dartmoor pony

Exmoor pony

French coach horse

Friesian

Galloway

German coach horse

hackney pony

Hambletonian

Hanoverian

Highland pony

Holstein

Lippizaner

miniature

miniature Shetland

Missouri fox-trotting horse

Morgan

mustang

Narragansett pacer

palomino

Pinto

Plantation walking horse

polo pony

quarter horse

saddle horse

Shetland pony

shire horse

standardbred

Suffolk

Tennessee walking horse

thoroughbred

trotter

warmblood

Welsh pony

HORSE BITS

curb bit

egg butt snaffle bit

full-cheek snaffle bit

jointed mouth curb bit

jointed mouth snaffle bit

liverpool bit

rubber snaffle bit

sliding cheek bit

snaffle bit

HORSE COLORS

albino

bay

black

blue roan

buckskin

champagne

chestnut

cremello

dapple gray

dun

gray

grulla

iron gray

liver chestnut

overo

palomino

perlino

piebald

pinto

rabicano

roan

sabino

silver dapple

skewbald

sorrel

strawberry roan

tobiano

white

HORSE TRACK LOCATIONS OR CALLS

backstretch

clubhouse turn

eighth pole or eighth post

far turn

five-eighths pole or five-eighths post

half-mile pole or half-mile post

mile pole or mile post

post

quarter pole or quarter post

sixteenth pole or sixteenth post

straightaway or home stretch

winner's circle

HOSIERY

anklets

argyles

athletic socks

bikini pantyhose

bobbysocks

bodyshaper

body stocking

bodysuit

boothose

boot socks

business sheer pantyhose

crew socks

demi-toe

dress sheers or daytime sheers

evening sheers

fishnet stockings

footlets

footsock

full-fashioned stockings

garter stockings

halfhose

hose

knee-highs

knee-hose

knee-socks

knee warmers

leg warmers

leotard

lisle hose

mesh stockings

non-run stockings

no-show socks

nylons

pantyhose

queen size stockings

rayon stockings

run-resistant hosiery

sandalfoot hosiery

seamless stockings

sheer stockings or sheers

silk stockings

slouch socks

socks

Spandex sheers

stockings

stretch hosiery

support hosiery

sweat socks

thigh highs

tights

tinted hosiery

tube socks

ultra sheer stockings

varsity socks

walking sheer pantyhose

wigglers or toe socks

woolens

work socks

HUMAN BODY ELEMENTS

Chemically, the human body consists mainly of water (60%) and of organic compounds—i.e., lipids, proteins, carbohydrates, and nucleic acids. Water is found in the extracellular fluids of the body (the blood plasma, the lymph, and the interstitial fluid) and within the cells themselves.

Calcium (1.5%)

Carbon (18%)

Chlorine, Cobalt, Copper, Fluorine, Iodine, Iron, Manganese, Molybdenum, Selenium, Zinc (0.70%)

Hydrogen (10%)

Aluminum, Arsenic, Bromine, Lead, Lithium, Silicon, Strontium, Vanadium (trace amounts)

Magnesium (0.05%)

Nitrogen (3%)

Oxygen (65%)

Phosphorus (1.0%)

Potassium (0.35%)

Sodium (0.15%)

Sulfur (0.25%)

HUMAN BODY SYSTEMS

circulatory system

digestive system

endocrine system

integumentary system

lymphatic system

muscular system

nervous system and hormones

reproductive system

respiratory system

skeletal system

urinary system

HUMANS, EARLY

Much debate surrounds the evolution of humans. Most scientists now agree that modern humans, *Homo sapiens,* are the sole survivors of a number of human species that descended from the common ancestor of humans and apes some six million years ago. The evolutionary sequence from the early humans is not a straight line but a "tree" with many deadends. Scientists disagree about how many human species have existed and which were ancestors of others.

Australopithecus

Australopithecus afarensis

Australopithecus africanus

Australopithecus anamensis

Australopithecus boisei

Australopithecus garhi

Australopithecus ramidus

Australopithecus robustus

Border Cave man

Cro-Magnon man

Homo erectus

Homo ergaster

Homo habilis

Homo heidelbergensis or Heidelberg man

Homo rudolfensis

Homo sapiens neanderthalensis or Neanderthal man

Homo sapiens sapiens

Java man

Kabwe man

Ngaloba man

Nutcracker man

Paranthropus

Paranthropus aethiopicus

Paranthropus boisei

Paranthropus robustus

Peking man

Petralona man

Pithecanthropus

Steinheim man

Swanscombe man

Tautavel man

Vertesszollos man

Zinjanthropus

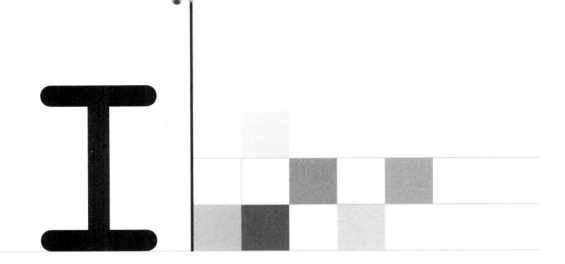

ICE SKATING MOVES

Axel	edge jump	Lutz	toe loop
camel	flip	Salchow	toe wally
closed draw	flying camel	single Axel	triple Axel
combination spin	flying sit spin	sit spin	twist
crossover	Hamill camel	spiral	waltz
death spiral	layback spin	spiral sequence	
double Axel	loop	step sequence	

IDOLATRIES

Idolatry is the religious worship of an object, person, or concept.

angelolatry	archaeolatry	Bardolatry	classicolatry
anthropolatry	astrolatry	bibliolatry	cosmolatry
arborolatry	autolatry	christolatry	curatolatry

cynolatry
demonolatry
dendrolatry
diabolatry
ecclesiolatry
epeolatry
episcopolatry
gamidolatry
gastrolatry
geniolatry
geolatry
grammatolatry
gynecolatry
gyneolatry
gyriolatry
hagiolatry

heliolatry
hierolatry
hydrolatry
hygeiolatry
ichthyolatry
iconolatry
idiolatry
idolatry
juvelolatry
litholatry
logolatry
lordolatry
martyrolatry
mechanolatry
methodolatry
mobolatry

monolatry
necrolatry
neolatry
onolatry
ophiolatry
palaeolatry
papolatry
parsonolatry
parthenolatry
patriolatry
physiolatry
phytolatry
plutolatry
pseudolatry
pyrolatry
selenolatry

self-idolatry
sociolatry
statolatry
staurolatry
symbolatry
taurolatry
thaumatolatry
theolatry
theriolatry
therolatry
topolatry
uranolatry
urbanolatry
verbolatry
zoolatry

IMAGINARY PLACES

agonic line
Annwfn
Asgard
Atlantis
Avalon
Brobdingnag
Camelot
Cloud-cuckoo-land
Cockaigne

dreamland
Earthsea
El Dorado
Emerald City
Erewhon
fantasy world
Flatland
Fortunate Isles
Fountain of Youth

Hogwarts School
Houyhnhnm
Islandia
isogonal line
Laputa
latitude
Lilliput
line of scrimmage
longitude

Looking-Glass Land
Lyonnesse
magnetic equator
meridian
Middle-Earth
Narnia
Neverland
Olympus
Oz

Pern

Ruritania

Shangri-La

Treasure Island

Utopia

Valhalla

Wonderland

Zanth

Immunizations, Childhood

DTP or DtaP or
diphtheria/tetanus/
pertussis

H. influenza type B
or hib

Hepatitis B

MMR or measles/
mumps/rubella

polio

rubella

Tetanus-diphtheria

Varicella

Insects

acarid

acarine

adobe bug

alderfly

ambush bug

ant

ant lion

aphelinid

aphid

apple leafhopper

apple maggot

arachnid

Arachnida

armyworm

ash borer

assassin bug

back swimmer

bagworm

bark beetle

bark louse

bedbug

bee

beetle

billbug

blackbeetle

black fly

black widow

bloodworm

blueberry thrips

boat bug

boll weevil

bombardier beetle

booklouse

book scorpion

bookworm

borer

bug

bumblebee

butterfly

cabbageworm

caddis fly

cankerworm

carpet beetle

caterpillar

cattle grub

cecidomyiid

centipede

chafer

chalcid fly

chestnut borer

chigger

chinch bug

cicada

citrus blackfly

click beetle

cockroach

cootie

crane fly

cricket

cutworm

daddy-longlegs

damselfly

deer fly

doodlebug

dragonfly
drone
dung beetle
earworm
emperor butterfly
false scorpion
firefly
flea
fly
froghopper
fruit fly
gadfly
glowworm
gnat
grasshopper
grub
gypsy moth
harvestman
honeybee
hornet
horse fly

housefly
Japanese bettle
June bug
katydid
ladybug
lantern fly
leafhopper
locust
long-horned beetle
looper
louse
maggot
mayfly
mealworm
mealy bug
medfly
midge
mite
mosquito
moth
nit

nymph
opilionid
phalangid
pismire
praying mantis
pseudoscorpion
pupa
queen bee
roach
scale
scorpion
screwworm
silkworm
skipper
snapping beetle
soldier ant
spider
spittlebug
stag beetle
tarantula
tent fly

termite
tick
tiger beetle
tiger moth
tumblebug
walking leaf
walking stick
wasp
water beetle
water bug
weevil
wheel bug
whitefly
wireworm
woodworm
woolly bear
worker
yellow jacket

INSTRUMENTS, BRASS WIND

alpenhorn
althorn or alto horn
or tenor horn
ballad horn
baritone horn

bass horn
bombardon
buccina
bugle

clarion
cornet
cornopean
double-bell
euphonium

E-flat horn
euphonium
F horn
flügelhorn

French horn
helicon
horn
hunting horn or corno di caccia
key trumpet
lituus
lur

mellophone
nyas taranga
oliphant
ophicleide
orchestral horn
pocket trumpet
post horn
sackbut

saxcornet
saxhorn
saxophone
saxtuba
serpent
slide trombone
sousaphone
tenor tuba

tromba
trombone
trumpet
tuba
valve trombone
valve trumpet
Wagner tuba

INSTRUMENTS, KEYBOARD

baby grand
cembalo
choralcelo
clarichord
clavichord
clavicittern
clavicymbal
clavicytherium
clavier
concert grand
console piano
cottage piano

couched harp
digital piano
dulcimer harpsichord
fortepiano
grand piano
hammer dulcimer
harmonichord
harpsichord
lyrichord
manichord
melodion
melopiano

monochord
muselar virginal
pair of virginals
parlor grand
pedal piano
pianette
pianino
piano
pianoforte
Pianola
piano-violin

player piano or mechanical piano
sostinente pianoforte
spinet
spinet virginal
square piano
street piano
upright piano
violin piano
virginal

INSTRUMENTS, PERCUSSION

afuche
anvil

bass drum
bells

block
bones

bongo drum
carillon

castanets
celesta
chimes
Chinese drum
clappers
clave
conga
cowbell
crash cymbal
cymbals
drumhead
drumskin
finger cymbals
floor tom
gamelan
glockenspiel
gong

guiro
handbells
hand drum
highhat cymbal
idiophone
kettledrum
lithophone
lyra
maraca
marimba
mbira or kalimba
membranophone
metallophone
mirliton
mridanga
musical glasses or glass harmonica
musical saw

nagara
naker
orchestral bells
rain stick
rattle
rattlebones
ride cymbal
side drum
sizzler
snappers
snare drum
spoons
steel drum
tabor
tambourine
tam-tam
temple block

tenor drum
thumb piano
timbale
timbrel
timpani
tintinnabula
tom-tom
tonitruone
triangle
troll-drum
tubular bells
tympan
vibraharp
war drum
woodblock
xylophone
xylorimba

INSTRUMENTS, PLUCKED STRINGED

acoustic guitar
angelica or angel lute
Appalachian dulcimer
archlute
Autoharp™
baglamas

balalaika
bandore
bandurria
banjo
banjolin
banjorine

banjo-ukulele
banjo-zither
bass guitar
bouzouki
centerhole guitar
charango

chitarra
chitarrone
cittern
classical guitar
colascione
concert guitar

Dobro guitar
dombra
electric bass guitar
electric guitar
F-hole guitar
gittern
guitar
gusli
harp
Hawaiian guitar

kacapi
koto
lute
lyre
mando-bass
mando-cello
mandolin
mandolute
mandore
musical bow

oud
pandora
psaltery
renaissance lute
samisen
sarod
shamisen
sitar
Spanish guitar
steel guitar

tambura
tamburitza
theorbo
tres
troubadour fiddle
'ud
ukulele veena
vihuela
vina
zither

INSTRUMENTS, SURGICAL AND MEDICAL

aspirator
audiometer
bistoury
bougie
bronchoscope
burr
cannula
cardiograph
cardioscope
CAT scanner
catheter
clinical thermometer
colposcope
curette

cytoscope
defibrillator
depressor
dermatome
dialysis machine
diaphanoscope
diathermy machine
dilator
drain
drain tube
ecraseur
electrocardiograph
electroencephalo-
graph

electromyograph
endoscope
fiberscope
fluoroscope
forceps
gastroscope
gorget
gouge
guillotine
heart-lung machine
hemostat
hypodermic needle
inhalator
inspirator

iron lung
kymograph
lancet
laparoscope
manometer
microscope
nebulizer
needle
ophthalmoscope
orthodiagraph
orthoscope
osteoclast
osteotome
otoscope

oxygen mask

percussion hammer

pneumatograph

pneumatometer

polygraph

probe

radio knife

raspatory

resectoscope

respirometer

resuscitator

retinoscope

retractor

scalpel

scarificator

scoop

sigmoidoscope

snare

speculum

sphygmograph

sphygmomanometer

sphygmometer

spirograph

spirometer

stethograph

stethometer

stethoscope

stomach pump

stomach tube

stylet

surgical needle

suture

syringe

tenaculum

trephine

trocar

X-ray machine

xyster

INSTRUMENTS, SYMPHONY ORCHESTRA

bass clarinet

bass drum

bassoons

celesta

cellos

clarinets

contrabassoon

cor anglais

cornet

cymbals

double basses

English horn

first violins

flutes

French horns

glockenspiel

gong

harp

oboes

piano

piccolo

second violins

snare drum

timpani

triangle

trombones

trumpets

tuba

tubular bells

violas

xylophone

INSTRUMENTS, VIOLA OR VIOLIN

alto viol

baritone viol

baryton

bass fiddle

bass viol

basso da camera

bull fiddle

cello

contrabass

crowd

descant viol

double bass

fiddle
gigue
gudok
gue
gusle
kit fiddle
kit violin
lira da braccio
lira da gamba
lyra viol

nun's fiddle
nyckelharpa
pardessus de viole
pocket fiddle
rebab
rebec
ribible
string bass
tenor viol
treble viol

trumpet marine
vielle
viola da braccio
viola da gamba
viola da spalla
viola di bordone
viola di fagotto
viola alta
viola bastarda
viola d'amore

viola or tenor
viola pomposa
violette
violin
violinette
violino piccolo
violoncello piccolo
violone
violotta

INSTRUMENTS, WEIGHING

alloy balance
analytical balance
assay balance
automatic indicating scale
balance
balance of precision
barrel scale
bathroom scale
beam

bullion balance
counter scale
cylinder scale
Danish balance
digital scale
doctor's scale
drum scale
fan scale
flexure plate scale
French scale

lever scale
long-arm balance
pair of scales
plate fulcrum scale
platform scale
precision scale
Roman balance
scale
short-arm balance
spiral balance

spring balance
spring scale
steelyard
torsion scale
weighbeam
weighbridge
weighing machine
weigh scale
weight voltameter

INSTRUMENTS, WOODWIND

alto flute
aulos

bagpipe
baritone oboe

baritone saxophone
baroque recorder

bassanello
bass clarinet

318

basset horn
bass oboe
bassoon
bombarde
bombardon
clarinet
contrabassoon
crumhorn
double bassoon
English horn
fife
fipple flute

flageolet
flute
heckclarina
heckelphone
hornpipe
musette
nose-flute
oaten reed
oboe da caccia
oboe d'amore
oboe ocarina
Pandean pipe

panpipe
pibgorn
piccolo
piccolo heckelphone
pipe
pommer
recorder
saxophone
shakuhachi
shawm or shalm
sonorophone
soprano recorder

soprano saxophone
syrinx or shepherd's pipe
tabor pipe
tenor saxophone
tenoroon
tin-whistle or penny-whistle
transverse flute
vertical flute
whistle

INSURANCE TYPES

accident
annuity
automobile collision
automobile liability
aviation
business liability
business property
coinsurance
college education
credit
dental
disability
endowment

export credit
fidelity bond
fire
flood
glass
group
group annuities
group health
group life
health
homeowner's
hospitalization
income

injury
inland marine
liability
life
limited-payment
long-term care
major medical
marine
merchandise credit
ocean marine
parcel post
personal liability
postal

private health
professional liability
property
property damage
public liability
rain
real estate
retirement
self-insurance
social security
split-dollar
surety bond
term

| theft | transportation | unemployment | weather risk |
| title | travel | war damage | workmen's compensation |

INTELLIGENCE TEST TYPES

Allport-Vernon	Binet or Binet-Simon	intelligence quotient or IQ	Wechsler Adult Intelligence Scale or WAIS
alpha	Cattell's Infant Intelligence Scale	Kent	
Army General Classification Test or AGCT	General Aptitude Test Battery or GATB	Minnesota Preschool Scale	Wechsler Intelligence Scale for Children or WISC
Babcock-Levy	Goldstein-Sheerer	Stanford-Binet Intelligence Scale	Wechsler-Bellevue Intelligence Test
beta			

INTERJECTIONS

adios	avast	chop-chop	eureka
ah	aw	ciao	fiddlesticks
aha	aw-shucks	crikey	fie
ahem	aye	criminy	fore
ahoy	bah	cripes	forsooth
alack	banzai	dear	gadzooks
alas	bleep	dear me	gee
alleluia	boo	ditto	gee whillikers
all hail	boy	doh	gee whiz
aloha	bravo	duh	gesundheit
amen	by jingo	eek	giddyyap
and how	cheerio	egad eh	glory
attaboy	cheers	er	golly

golly gee	hosanna	oh dear	shaddup
golly whillikers	hot dog	oh my	shalom
good golly	howdy	okay	sheesh
good gracious	hoy	okey-doke	shucks
goody	huh	okey-dokey	shush
gosh	hup	ole	skoal
gracious	hurrah	oops	tallyho
gracious me	huzzah	oopsy-daisy	ten-four
ha	jeepers	ouch	there, there
hallelujah	jeepers creepers	ow	timber
hark	jeez	oy	touch
heads up	lackaday	oyez	touche
hear ye, hear ye	lo	peekaboo	tsk
heave-ho	lo and behold	phew	tsk tsk
heavens	Lordy	phooey	tush
heavens to Betsy	mama	pish	tut-tut
heigh-ho	marry	pooh	ugh
hem	mazel tov	presto	uh-huh
hep	my gracious	prithee	uh-oh
here here	my my	prosit	uh-uh
hey	my stars	pshaw or psha	um
hi-hip	my word	rah	viva
ho	nah	rah-rah	voila
ho-hum	nay	rats	wahoo
holy cow	nerts	righto	welcome
holy mackerel	nope	roger	well
holy moly	nuts	rot	what
holy Toledo	oh	salud	whatever
hooray	oh boy	scram	whee

whew	wow	yikes	yup
whoa	wowie	yippee	zap
whoop-de-do	wowie-zowie	yo	zooks
whoopee	yahoo	yoicks	zounds
whoops	yea	yo mama	zowie
why	yeah	yoo-hoo	zut
wilco	yech	yuck	
woe is me	yep	yum-yum	

INVERTEBRATE TYPES

Acanthocephala	Chaetognatha	Entoprocta or Ectoprocta	Phoronida
Annelida	Chordata	Mesozoa	Platyhelminthes
Arthropoda	Coelenterata or Cnidaria	Mollusca	Pogonophora
Aschelminthes	Ctenophora	Nematoda	Porifera
Brachiopoda	Echinodermata	Nemertina	Protozoa
Bryozoa	Echiuroidea	Oncopoda	Sipunculoidea

ISLAMIC RELIGIOUS GROUPS

Admadiya	Bahaism	Ja'alin	Qadarite
Ahmadiya	Carmathian or Karmathian	Khawarij	Sanusi
Almohades	Druses or Druze	Malikite	Shi'ites Shiah
Almoravides	Ibadhi	Mohammedanism	Sufism Sunni
Babism	Ismailis or Isma'ilil	Mu'tazilah	Wahhabiyah or Wahhabis

Island Types

ait or eyot

archipelago

atoll

barrier island

cay

continental island

coral island

coral reef

floating island

holm

iceberg

ice floe

inch

island

island chain

island continent

island group

isle

islet

key

microcontinental island

reef

river bar

river island

skerry

volcanic island

Ivy League Colleges/ Universities

Brown University

Columbia University

Cornell University

Dartmouth College

Harvard University

Princeton University

University of Pennsylvania

Yale University

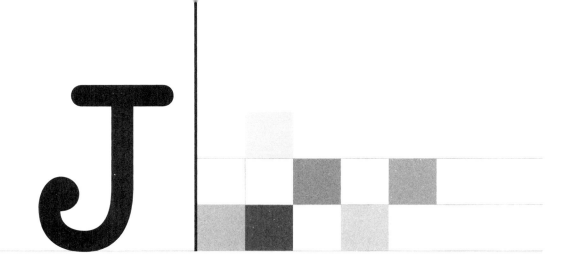

JAZZ TYPES

Afro-Cuban	free jazz	mainstream	skiffle
avant-garde	fusion	modal jazz	soul jazz
barrelhouse	Harlem	modern jazz	swing
bebop	harmolodics	neo jazz or new jazz	third stream
boogie-woogie	honky-tonk	New Orleans	traditional jazz
bop	hot jazz	progressive jazz	west coast
cool	jive	ragtime	
Dixieland	Kansas City	razzmatazz	
electric	Latin	rooty-toot	

JELLY BELLY JELLYBEAN FLAVORS

A&W cream soda	blueberry	buttered popcorn	cappuccino
A&W root beer	bubble gum	cantaloupe	champagne punch

chocolate pudding
cinnamon
coconut
cotton candy
cream soda
crushed pineapple
grape
grape jelly
green apple
Hawaiian Punch

island punch
jalapeno
juicy pear
lemon
lemon lime
licorice
margarita
orange juice
orange sherbet
peach

peanut butter
peppermint stick
piña colada
pink grapefruit
raspberry
root beer
sizzling cinnamon
strawberry cheesecake
strawberry daiquiri

tangerine
toasted marshmallow
top banana
tutti-frutti
very cherry
watermelon

JEWELRY

aigrette
anklet
armlet
band
bangle
bauble
beads
bezel
bibelot
bijou
bling-bling
bracelet
brooch
cameo
carcanet

chain
chaplet
charm
chatelaine
circlet
coronet
costume jewelry
crown
crown jewels
cuff links
diadem
diamante
earring
engagement ring
fob

gem
gemstone
gewgaw
girandole
glass
intaglio
labret
lavaliere
locket
money clip
necklace
nose ring
parure
pearl
pendant

pin
pinkie ring
post
precious stone
rhinestone
ring
riviere
rondelle
semiprecious stone
setting
signet ring
solitaire ring
stickpin
stone
stud

tiara   tiepin   trinket   wristband

tie clip   torque   wedding band   wristlet

JEWISH MOVEMENTS

Ashkenazim

Assimilationism

Boethusian

Chazar

Conservative

Ebionite

Essenes

Falasha

Hasidim

Humanistic

Kabbalah

Karaites

Messianic

Mizrachi

Nazarite

Orthodox

Pharisaism

Rabbinism

Reconstructionism

Reform or Non-Orthodox

Sadduceeism

Sephardim

Zionism

JOINT TYPES

In anatomy, a joint is a structure that separates two or more adjacent elements of the skeleton. Depending on the type of joint, such separated elements may or may not move on one another.

ball and socket joint   gliding joint or plane joint   hinge joint   saddle joint

JEWISH HOLY DAYS, FESTIVALS, FASTS, AND SEASONS

Days of Awe

Fast of Tammuz

Fast of Tevet

Hanukkah

High Holy Days

Lag B'Omer

Passover

Purim or Feast of Lots

Rosh Hashanah or New Year

Rosh Hodesh

Sabbath

Shavuoth Shemini Atzeres

Simhath Torah   Taanith Esther   Tu B'Shevat   Yom Kippur

Sukkoth   Tishah b'Av   Tzom Gedaliah

JUDGES

amicus curiae

arbiter

assessor or legal assessor

associate justice

bankruptcy judge

barmaster

bench

chancellor

chief justice

circuit judge

commissary

dayan

Dean of the Arches

district judge

faujdar

hearing officer

judex ordinarius

judge advocate general judge advocate judge delegate

judge or justice of assize

judge ordinary

judgess

judicator

jurat

justice in eyre

justice of the peace

justicer

justiciar

lay judge

lord justice

magistrate

master

military judge

ombudsman

ordinary or judge ordinary

police judge

presiding judge

probate judge

puisne judge

quaestor

recorder

side judge

tax judge

trial judge

vice-chancellor

JUDO HOLDS AND THROWS

armlock

choke hold

circular throw

harai goshi

juji-gatame

kochiki-taoshi

morote-seoi-nage

reap

seoi-nage

shoulder throw

tai-otoshi

tomoe-nage

uchi-mata

JUICES

apple juice

apricot juice

carrot juice

cherry juice

cranberry juice

fruit juice

grapefruit juice

grape juice

kiwi juice

lemon juice

lime juice

loganberry juice

mango juice

orange juice

papaya juice

peach juice

pear juice

pineapple juice

prune juice

raspberry juice

strawberry juice

tomato juice

vegetable juice

watermelon juice

JURIES

common jury

coroner's jury

elisor jury

foreign jury

grand jury

hung jury

jury of inquest

jury of matrons or jury of women

jury of the vicinage

locked jury

packed jury

petty jury

police jury

pyx jury

sheriff's jury

special jury

struck jury

trial jury

KARATE MOVES

age-uke

ashi-barai

ate

choku-zuki

chudan

chudan hasami uke

chudan shotei ate

chudan shotei uke

chudan shuto uke

chudan soto mawashi uke

chudan soto shuto uke

chudan soto uke

chudan uchi uke

chudan uke

chudan wari uke

chudan yoko uke

chudan yoko-shuto uke

chudan zuki

fukubu geri

gedan

gedan barai

gedan barai uke

gedan haito yoko uke

gedan kosa uke

gedan shotei ate

gedan shotei uke

gedan shuto uke

gedan shuto yoko barai uke

gedan uke

gedan yoko barai uke

gedan zuki

geri or keri

gyaku-zuki

haito uchi

haito uke

hangetsu barai uke

hangetsu zuki

hazushi uke

hiji ate

hiji uke

hiza ate

jodan

jodan kosa uke

jodan shotei ate

jodan uchi shuto uke

jodan uke

jodan wari uke

jodan zuki

juji-uke

kaku zuki

kansetsu geri

keage

keikoken zuki

kekomi

keri waza

kinteki geri

kizami-geri

kizami-zuki

kyobu geri

kyobu morote shuto uchi

mae geri

mae hiji ate

magetori barai uke

makite uke

mawashi geri

mawatte

mikazuki-geri

morote barai uke

morote nuki zuki

morote soe uke

morote zuki

morote-uke

nidan geri

niren geri

nukite zuki

oi zuki

oi-zuki

osae-uke

otoshi uke

sagurite uke

sanbon-zuki

sasae hiji ate

sasae uke

sayu barai uke

sayu zuki

seiken ude uke

shotei ate

shotei uke

shuto uchi

shuto uke

shuto waza

sokuto geri

soto-ude-uke

tomoe shotei ate

tomoe zuki

tsuki waza

tsumasaki geri

tzuki or tsuki

uchi

uchi-ude-uke

uke

ura ken uchi

ushiro geri

ushiro hiji ate

wari uke

wari uke zuki

yoko geri

yoko hiji ate

yoko-geri-keage

yoko-geri-kekomi

zenkutsu dachi gedan-barai-uke

KILLING AND KILLER TYPES

aborticide

amicicide

autocide

avicide

biocide

ceticide

deicide

dominicide

ecocide

elephanticide

episcopicide

felicide

femicide

filaricide

filicide

foeticide

formicicide

fratricide

fungicide

genocide

germicide

giganticide

gynecide or gynaecide

herbicide

hereticide

homicide

infanticide

insecticide

larvicide

mariticide

matricide

microbicide

ovicide

parenticide

parricide

patricide

pesticide

phytocide

prolicide

regicide

rodenticide

senicide

serpenticide

siblicide

sororicide

spermicide suicide

tauricide

tickicide

tyrannicide

ursicide

uxoricide

vaticide

vermicide

vespacide

viricide

vulpicide

KITES

airfoil kite

bowed kite

box kite

compound kite

conyne kite

delta-wing kite

eddy bow kite

eddy kite

fighter kite

flat kite

hexagonal kite

high-performance kite

Malay kite

man-lifting kite

parafoil

pennon-type kite

power kite

rotor kite or kinetic kite

sled kite

sport kite

stunt kite

tailed kite

tailless kite

weather kite

KNIGHTS OF THE ROUND TABLE

Bedivere

Bors

Galahad

Gareth

Gawain

Kay

Lamorack

Lancelot

Mordred

Perceval

Torre

Tristan

KNITTING STITCHES

cable stitch

double seed stitch

garter stitch

loop stitch

moss stitch

plain stitch

purl stitch

ribbing

seed stitch

shell stitch

slip stitch

stocking stitch

trellis stitch

KNIVES

barong

bistoury

bolo knife

boning knife

bowie knife

bread knife

butchering knife

butterfly knife

butter knife

butter spreader

carving knife

case knife

cheese knife

chef's knife

citrus knife

clam knife

clasp knife

cleaver

commando knife

cook's knife

craft knife

dessert knife

dinner knife

dough knife

drawknife

filleting knife

fish knife

flick knife

frozen-food knife

fruit knife

gorgonzola knife

grapefruit knife

gravity knife

ham knife

hunting knife

jackknife

lancent

luncheon knife

machete

mezzaluna

oyster knife

palette knife

panga

paperknife

parang

paring knife

Parmesan knife

pen knife

pocket knife

pruning knife

roast beef slicer

salami slicer

salmon slicer

sandwich spatula

scallop knife

scalpel

scimitar knife

serrated knife

sheath knife

shellfish knife

slicing knife

Stanley knife

steak knife

Swiss Army knife

switchblade

table knife

throwing knife

tomato knife

trench knife

utility knife

X-acto knife

yataghan

KNIVES, KITCHEN

boning knife

bread knife

butchering knife

butter knife

butter spreader

carving knife

cheese knife

chef's knife

citrus knife

clam knife

cleaver

cook's knife

dessert knife

dinner knife

dough knife

filleting knife

fish knife

frozen-food knife

fruit knife

gorgonzola knife

332

grapefruit knife

ham knife

luncheon knife

mezzaluna

oyster knife

paring knife

Parmesan knife

roast beef slicer

salami slicer

salmon slicer

sandwich spatula

scallop knife

scimitar knife

serrated knife

shellfish knife

slicing knife

steak knife

tomato knife

Knots

anchor knot

barrel knot

becket knot

Blackwall hitch

bow

bowknot

bowline

bowline knot

builder's knot

buntline hitch

butcher's knot

butterfly knot

carrick bend

cat's-paw

chain knot

clinch knot

clove hitch

constrictor knot

crossing knot

crown knot

cuckold's neck

diamond hitch

diamond knot

double Englishman's knot

double fisherman's knot

double hitch

Englishman's tie

eye splice

figure-eight knot

figure-of-eight bend

fisherman's bend

fisherman's knot

flat knot

Flemish knot

French shroud knot

German knot

Ghiordes knot

gordian knot

granny knot

grapevine knot

hackamore knot

half crown

half hitch

half-knot

half-Windsor knot

hangman's knot

harness hitch

hawser bend

hawser fastening

heaving-line bend

inside clinch

Japanese knot

kettle stitch

Klemheist knot

lanyard knot

lineman's loop knot

long splice

loop knot

love knot

lubber's knot

magnus hitch

manrope knot

marlinespike hitch

marling hitch

masthead knot

Matthew Walker knot

mesh knot

midshipman's hitch

monkey's fist

nail knot

netting knot

open hand knot

outside clinch

overhand knot

perfection loop knot

prolonge knot

Prusik knot

reef knot

reeving-line bend

ring hitch

ring knot

rolling hitch

rope-yarn knot

round seizing

round turn and half hitch

running bowline

running knot

sailor's breastplate

Sehna knot

sennit knot

sheepshank

Shelby knot

short splice

shoulder knot

shroud knot

simple knot

single knot

slide knot

slipknot

snitch knot

square knot

star knot

stevedore's knot

stopper's knot

studding-sail halyard bend

stunner hitch

surgeon's knot

sword knot

tack bend

thumb knot

timber hitch

Tom Fool knot

truckman's knot

truelove knot

Turkish knot

Turk's-head

turle knot

turtle knot

wall knot

water knot

waterman's knot

weaver's hitch

Windsor knot

LACE VARIETIES

Alencon

bobbinet

bobbin lace

Breton

Brussels lace

Carrickmacross

Chantilly

Dieppe

duchesse

fillet or filet

Greek olace or point guipure

gros point

guipure

illusion

lace

Limerick

Mechlin lace

mignonette

Milan point

needle lace

needlepoint lace

pillow lace

point lace

raised point

reticella

Roman lace

rose point

Shetland

tambour

tatting

Tenerife

torchon

Valenciennes

Venetian point

LACROSSE POSITIONS

1st Home

2nd Home

3rd Home

3rd man

attackman

center attack

cover point

defender

goalkeeper

left attack wing

left defense wing

midfielder

point

right attack wing

right defense wing

Ladders

aerial ladder	fruit-picking ladder	multi-purpose ladder	sea ladder
cage ladder	gangway ladder	platform ladder	ship's ladder
companion ladder	hook ladder	pool ladder	stepladder
extension ladder	jack ladder	rolling ladder	step stool
foldaway ladder	ladder scaffold	rope ladder	straight ladder

Ladles

bail	dip	punch bowl ladle	soup ladle
calabash	dipper	scoop	spade
cyathus	gourd	shovel	spatula

Lake Types

artificial lake or manmade lake	glacial lake	loch	ribbon lake
circular lake	glacial till lake	lough	rift valley lake
crater lake	inland sea	marine lake	river lake
freshwater lake	kettle lake	mountain lake	saltwater lake
glacial deposition lake	lagoon	natural lake	tarn
glacial erosion lake	landslip lake	oxbow lake	tectonic lake
	lava-dammed lake	reservoir	volcanic lake

LAKES, LARGEST FRESHWATER

Baikal

Erie

Great Bear

Great Slave

Huron

Malawi

Michigan

Superior

Tanganyika

Victoria

LAMB CUTS

arm chop

blade chop

boneless leg

boneless loin

boneless shoulder chops

boneless sirloin

breast or brisket

butterflied leg

crown roast

cushion roast

Denver ribs

double loin chop

flank

foreshank

French rib chop

French style leg

half shank

leg

loin

loin roast

medallion

neck slices

patties

rack for one

rack roast

rib chop

riblets

roast

rolled shoulder

round leg steak

Saratoga chops

shank

shish kebab cubes

shoulder blade chop

sirloin chop

sirloin roast

sirloin shank half

sirloin steak

square-cut shoulder roast

stew meat

LAMPS AND LIGHTING FIXTURES

arc lamp

battery lamp

bed lamp

book light

brake light

candle

Chinese lantern

courtesy light

Davy lamp

desk lamp

discharge lamp

electric candle

fairy lights

filament lamp

flasher

flashlight

floodlight

floor lamp

fluorescent light

fog light

footlight

gaslight

halogen light

hazard lights

headlight

hurricane lamp

incandescent light

infrared lamp

jack-o'-lantern

klieg light

lamplet

landing lights

lantern

lava lamp

limelight

magic lantern

mercury vapor lamp

miner's lamp

navigation light

neon light

night light

oil lamp

parking light

pilot light

projector lamp

quartz lamp

railroad lantern

reading light

roof light

running lights

safety lamp

searchlight

sodium vapor lamp

spotlight

stop light

storm lantern

street light

strip light

strobe light

sunlamp or sun lamp

table lamp

taillight

torch light

tungsten lamp

ultraviolet lamp

vapor lamp

LANDLOCKED COUNTRIES

Afghanistan

Andorra

Armenia

Austria

Azerbaijan

Belarus

Bhutan

Bolivia

Botswana

Burkina Faso

Burundi

Central African Republic

Chad

Czech Republic

Ethiopia

Hungary

Kazakhstan

Kyrgyzstan

Laos

Lesotho

Liechtenstein

Luxembourg

Macedonia

Malawi

Mali

Moldova

Mongolia

Nepal

Niger

Paraguay

Rwanda

San Marino

Slovakia

Swaziland

Switzerland

Tajikistan

Turkmenistan

Uganda

Uzbekistan

Vatican City

Zambia

Zimbabwe

LANGUAGE FAMILIES

Afro-Asiatic

Algonquian

Altaic

Andean-Equatorial

Australian Aboriginal

Austro-Asiatic

Autronesian

Aztec-Tanoan

Caucasian

Dravidian

Eskimo-Aleut

Ge-Pano-Carib

Hokan

Indo-European

Indo-Pacific

Japanese

Khoisan

Korean

Macro-Chibchan

Macro-Siouan

Na-Dene

Niger-Congo

Nilo-Saharan

Oto-Manguean

Palaeosiberian

Penutian

Sino-Tibetan

Tai

Uralic

LANGUAGE REFERENCE BOOKS

almanac

bilingual dictionary

biographical dictionary

children's dictionary

children's encyclopedia

collegiate dictionary

crossword puzzle dictionary

desk dictionary

dialect dictionary

encyclopedia

etymological dictionary

foreign language dictionary

geographical dictionary or gazetteer

glossary

grammar guide

idiom dictionary

learner's dictionary

lexicon

new words dictionary

phrasal verb dictionary

phrase and fable dictionary

pocket dictionary

quotations dictionary

reverse dictionary

rhyming dictionary

school dictionary

science dictionary

slang dictionary

special subject dictionary

style guide

synonym dictionary

thesaurus

unabridged dictionary

usage dictionary

usage guide

word trivia book

Language Types

Different languages are often based on the same principles. For example, English and Hebrew are based on a language called "affixing," that uses prefixes and suffixes. Listed below are the different types of languages that each culture has used to develop its own language, plus some examples of each type.

affixing language (English, Hebrew, Arabic, Swahili)

agglutinative language (Turkish)

analytic or isolating language (Chinese)

contact language or pidgin (a mix of any two or more languages)

endangered language (Lenape, Istro-Romanian)

fusional or inflectional language (Latin, German)

monosyllabic language (Chinese, Vietnamese)

polysyllabic language (Finnish, Hungarian)

polysynthetic language (Mohawk, Cherokee)

polytonic language (Cantonese)

synthetic language (Russian)

tonal language (Yoruba)

Languages of United Nations, Official

Arabic

Chinese

English

French

Russian

Spanish

Languages, Artificial

Though all language is manmade, artificial languages are created systematically for some particular purpose. They take many forms, from mere adaptations of an existing writing system (numerals), through completely new notations (sign language), to fully expressive systems of speech devised for fun (Tolkien) or secrecy (Poto and Cabenga) or learnability (Esperanto).

Antido	Interlingua	Novial	Romanal
Arulo	Latinesce	Nov-Latin	sign language
Blaia Zimondal	Latino	numerals	Sindarin
constructed language	Lincos	Occidental	Solresol
Esperantido	Lingualumina	Optez	Tolkien
Esperanto	Lingvo Kosmopolita	Pasigraphy	Volapuk
Europan	Lojban	pidgin	
Idiom Neutral	Monario	Poto and Cabenga	
Ido	Nov-Esperanto	Ro	

LANGUAGES, DEAD/ENDANGERED/ EXTINCT

Abenaki	Dacian	Lingua Franca	Oneida
Ainu	Dutch Creole	Livonian	Oscan
Alsatian	Eblaite	Luwian	Pali
Aragonese	Edomite	Lycian	Phoenician
Aramaic	Elamite	Lydian	Phrygian
Aromanian	Eyak	Manchu	Potawatomi
Basque	Gothic	Michif	Sami
Beaver	Han	Moabite	Samnite
Belarussian	Hare	Molise Slavic	Sarcee
Breton	Hittite	Mordvin	Scottish Gaelic
Canaanite	Illyrian	Nabatean	Seneca
Cayuga	Italkian	Nahuatl	Sumerian
Chukchi	Krimchak	Occitan	Taino
Coptic	Latin	Old Prussian	Thracian
Corsican	Ligurian	Onandaga	Udmurt

Umbrian
Urartian

Votian
West Flemish

Yevanic

LANGUAGES, ROMANCE

Catalan
Franco-Provencal
French

Italian
Occitan
Portuguese

Rhaetian
Romanian
Sardinian

Spanish

LAST SUPPER GUESTS

Andrew
Bartholomew
James the Elder
James the Less

Jesus Christ
John
Judas Iscariot
Matthew

Peter
Philip
Simon
Thaddeus or Jude

Thomas

LAVA TYPES

aa
acidic
basalt

high water/high silica
high water/low silica
low water/high silica

low water/low silica
mafic
pahoehoe

rhyolite

LAW TYPES

administrative
canon
civil

commercial
constitutional
contract and
business

corporation
criminal
delict or tort

family
inheritance
international

maritime

martial

military

private

property

public

salvage

LAWYER TYPES

adoption lawyer

ambulance chaser

attorney-at-law

attorney general

attorney-in-fact

bankruptcy lawyer

barrister

business lawyer

civil rights lawyer

common lawyer

contracts lawyer

corporate lawyer

counselor

criminal lawyer

defense lawyer

district attorney

divorce lawyer

employee rights lawyer

estate planning lawyer

family lawyer

general counsel

immigration lawyer

insurance lawyer

legal aid lawyer

legal representative

litigation lawyer

mediation lawyer

medical malpractice lawyer

military lawyer

patent lawyer

prosecuting attorney

prosecutor

public defender

real estate lawyer

solicitor

state's attorney

trial lawyer

workers' compensation lawyer

LAXATIVES

agar

aloe

bran

calomel

cascara

castor oil

colocynth

Culver's root

Epsom salt

fecal softener

fiber

fig

gamboge

Glauber's salt

glycerol

Gregory powder

ipecacuanha or syrup of ipecac

jalap

lactulose

licorice

liquid paraffin

magnesia

magnesium citrate

magnesium sulfate

mann

methylcellulose

milk of magnesia or magnesium hydroxide

mineral oil

phenolphthalein

prune

psyllium

rhubarb   Seidlitz powder   sodium phosphate

scammony   senna

LEAF METALS

These metals can be prepared in extremely thin sheets. Leaf is gold, silver, or other metal in the form of very thin foil.

aluminum foil	Dutch gold Florence leaf	gold leaf	silver foil
composite leaf		lead foil	silver leaf
	gold foil	sheet metal	tin foil

LEAF SHAPES AND TYPES

acerose	cordate	equitant	multifoliate
acicular	cotyledon or seed leaf	falcate	obcordate
acuminate		feather-veined	oblong
awl-shaped	crenate	geminate	obovate
bifacial	crispate	hastate	obvolute
bipinnate	cuneate	involute	odd-pinnate
bipinnatifid	decompound	isobilateral	orbiculate
biserrate	decurrent	laciniate	oval
biternate	deltoid	lanceolate	ovate
bract	dicotyledon	linear	palmate
cataphyllary	digitate	lingulate	panduriform
ciliate	dorsiventral	lobed	partite
compound	elliptical	lyrate	pectinate
conduplicate	ensiform	monocotyledon	pedate
conjugate	entire	multifid	pedatifid

peltate	quinate	sagittate	triangular
perfoliate	reniform	scutate	trifoliate
pinnate	resupinate	serrate	tripinnate
pinnatifid	reticulate	simple	trullate
pinnatipartite	revolute	spatulate	umbilicate
pinnatisect	rhombic	stipulate	undulate
plicate	rhomboid	subulate	unifoliolate
prophyll	runcinate	ternate	unijugate

LEAVENING AND FERMENTING AGENTS

air	brewer's yeast	invertase	sour milk
ammonium carbonate	buttermilk	maltase	sourdough
bacteria	carbon dioxide	pepsin	steam
baking ammonia	cream of tartar	potash	vinegar
baking powder	diastase	potassium bicarbonate	yeast
baking soda	egg	soda	zymase
barm	enzyme	sodium bicarbonate	zyme

LENS SHAPES

A lens, such as a magnifying glass, is a curved piece of transparent material that changes the direction of light rays passing through it by refraction.

biconcave	concavo-convex	double concave	plano-convex
biconvex	convex	double convex	
concave	convexo-concave	plano-concave	

Letter Types

accountant's letter

aerogram or aerogramme

air letter

airgraph

apostolic or papal brief

billet

bull

business letter

chain letter

circular letter

collection letter

comment letter

cover letter

crank letter

dead letter

Dear John

declining an offered favor

dimissory letter

drop letter

e-mail or email

encyclical letter

epistle

fan letter

follow-up letter

follow-up sales letter

form letter

fund-raising letter

investment letter

invitation

job application letter

letter credential

lettergram

letter of application

letter of appreciation

letter of condolence

letter of congratulations

letter of credence

letter of credit

letter of delegation

letter of introduction

letter of marque

letter of recommendation

letter of request

letter of resignation

letter of tribute

letter overt

letter patent

letter providing information

letter refusing credit

letter rogatory

letter testamentary

letter to employees

love letter

market letter

memorandum

missive

monitory letter

newsletter

open letter

paschal letter

pastoral letter

personal letter

pink slip

poison-pen letter

query letter for publishing

request of favor

round robin

sales letter

short letter

sympathy letter

termination letter

thank-you letter

traveler's letter of credit

Liberal Arts

arithmetic

astronomy

geometry

grammar

logic

music

rhetoric

LIBRARIES, TYPES

academic library or school library

association library

Braille library

business library or corporate library

children's library

church library

club library

college library

digital library or electronic library

distributed library

film library

free library

home library or personal library

institutional library

Internet library or cybrary

law library

medical library

municipal public library

music library

national library

non-profit library

prison library

public library

research library

school district public library

software library

special collections library

special district public library

subscription library

technical library

virtual library

LIGHT HOLDERS

bracket

candelabrum or candelabra

candle holder

candlestand

candlestick

chandelier

girandole

lamp base

lamp holder

lampstand

lantern

light fixture

light socket

sconce

tea light holder

torch

torch staff or torch holder

votive holder

wall bracket

LIGHTHOUSE TYPES

brick

caisson

cast-iron plate

crib

offshore or aquatic

onshore or terrestrial

pier or breakwater

reinforced concrete

screwpile

skeletal

stone masonry

straightpile

Texas tower

tower

waveswept

wood

Linens

antimacassar

apron

bath towel

cozy

dish towel doily

dresser scarf

glove

handkerchief

hand towel

hot pad

lace

napkin

pillow case

place mat

potholder

serviette

sheet

tablecloth

tidy

towel

wash cloth

Linguistics Branches

anthropological linguistics

applied linguistics

cognitive linguistics

comparative linguistics

computational linguistics

contrastive linguistics

corpus linguistics

descriptive linguistics or synchronic linguistics

dialect geography

dialectology

epigraphy

etymology

evolutionary linguistics

folk linguistics

general linguistics

geolinguistics

glossematics

glottochronology

grammar

grammatology

graphemics

historical linguistics or diachronic linguistics

language classification

lexicography

lexicology

lexicostatistics

linguistic geography

macrolinguistics

mathematical linguistics

metagraphemics

microlinguistics

morphology

neurolinguistics

nomenclature

onomasiology

onomastics orthoepy

paleography

philology

philosophy of language

phonemics

phonetics

phonography

phonology

pragmatics

psycholinguistics

semantics

semasiology

semiotics

social dialectology

sociolinguistics

stratification linguistics

structural linguistics

stylistics

subgraphemics

synchronic linguistics

syntactics

syntax   tagmemics   typology

systemic linguistics   theoretical linguistics

LITERARY CRITICISM APPROACHES

archetypal	Freudian	new	rhetorical
contextualist	genre	new new	sociological
deconstruction	historical	ontological	speech-act
epistemological	ideological	post-structuralist	structuralist
ethical	impressionistic	practical	textual
existential	Jungian	psychoanalytical	theoretical
feminist	Marxist	reader-response	
formalist	mythic	revisionist	

LITERARY DEVICES AND TECHNIQUES

A literary device is a form of words intended to produce a particular effect in speech or a literary work, such as a rhetorical device.

abridgment	agon	amplification	anapest
abstraction	Alexandrine	ana	anecdote
acronym	allegory	anachronism	anticlimax
acrostic	alliteration	anagogue	antigram
adumbration	allusion	analects	antiphrasis
affidavit	ambiguity	analogy	antithesis
agenda	amphigory	analysis	aphorism

appendix	climax	double rhyme	foreword
archaism	clue	effect	free verse
arsis	coda	elegiac	fustian
assonance	cognomen	elision	georgic
asterism	colloquialism	ellipsis	gloss or glossary
atmosphere	common meter	encomium	gossip
bathos	comparison	enigma	hamartia
bibliography	complaint	epilogue	hapax legomenon
bibliotics	conceit	epithet	heading
blank verse	condensation	euphemism	hendiasys
bombast	conflict	euphony	heroic couplet
bowdlerization	controlling image	euphuism	hexameter
brevity	conversation	exaggeration	hiatus
bucolic	corollary	example	homonym
bulletin	couplet	excerpt	Hudibrastic verse
cacophony	dactyl	exegesis	hyperbole
cadence	dead metaphor	explanation	iamb
caesura	declamation	explication de texte	iambic pentameter
canto	definition	exposition	illustration
caricature	denouement	eye dialect	imagery
carmen figuraturum	device	falling rhythm	implication
catachresis	diagram	fantasy	index
character sketch	diatribe	feminine rhyme	insinuation
characterization	digression	figurative language	interactive fiction
cipher	dipody	flashback	interior monologue
circumlocution	dithyramb	flash-forward	interjection
clarity	ditty	flyting	internal rhyme
clerihew	doggerel	foil	introduction
cliche	double entendre	footnote	irony

kenning

lampoon

leitmotif

lesson

letter

lipogram

litotes

locale

macaronic

metalepsis

metaphor

metathesis

meter

metonymy

metrics

mimesis

monologue

motif

narrative

news

nickname

obscurantism

octave

octet

onomatopoeia

palindrome

pandect

parable

paradox

paraenesis

parallelism

paralogism

paranomasia

paraphrase

passim

passus

pathetic fallacy

pathos

pentameter

periphrasis

personification

plagiarism

plea

plot

poeticism

poetic license

point of view

polymythy

postscript

preface

problem

proem

prolegomenon

prologue

prophecy

proverb

pun

purple prose

pyrrhic

quatrain

question

quotation

rebuttal

recension

record

refrain

reiteration

repetition

report

review

rhetorical question

rhyme

rhythm

rising action

rising rhythm

roundelay

sarcasm

satire

scansion

secret

sestina

simile

slang

slogan

solecism

soliloquy

speech

spondee

sprung rhythm

stanza

stichomythy

story line

straw man

stream of
consciousness

strophe

style

stylized

subplot

subtext

suspense

syllepsis

syllogism

symbolism

syncope

synecdoche

synopsis

taste

telestich

tetrameter

theme

tragic flaw

tralation

transposition

trimeter

triple rhyme

trochee

trope

tropology

turgescence

tushery

verisimilitude

vignette

villanelle

voice

warning

wordplay

tabulation

zeugma

LITERARY FORMS AND GENRES

abstract poetry

accentual verse

aestheticism

animal epic

antinovel

autobiography

avant-garde

ballad

ballad stanza

baroque

belles-lettres

Bildungsroman

biography

chanson

chanson de geste

chronicle

classical

classicism

comedy

comedy of intrigue

comedy of manners

comedy of morals

comic relief

concrete poetry

confession

courtly love

criticism

deconstruction

detective story

diary

dime novel

drama

elegy

epic

epic poem

epigram

epistle

epistolary novel

epithalamium

epos

erotica

essay

exemplum

fable

fabulism

fairy tale

fantasy

farce

festschrift

fiction

fin de siècle

grotesque

haiku

heroic

high comedy

historical novel

idyll

jeremiad

juvenilia

lampoon

letter

limerick

low comedy

lyric poetry

masque

melic

melodrama

memoir

minimalism

miracle play

missive

mock-heroic

modernism

monograph

mystery

mystery play

myth

naturalism

nonfiction

novel

novelette

novella

nursery rhyme

occasional verse

ode	prose	saga	tanka
parody	prosody	satire	technothriller
pasquinade	prothalamion	science fiction	textual criticism
pastel	psychobiography	serial	thriller
pastiche	psychological novel	short story	tragedy
penny dreadful	quantitative verse	sirvente	tragicomedy
picaresque novel	realism	sketch	translation
poetry	rhyme	soap opera	trilogy
polemic	roman	socialist realism	verse
polyphonic prose	roman à clef	song	western
postmodernism	roman-fleuve	sonnet	whodunit
poststructuralism	rondeau	speech	
potboiler	rondel	surrealism	

Literary Groups, Movements, and Schools

Absurdism	Dadaism	Imagism	Metaphysical poets
Acmeism	Decadence	Impressionism	Minimalism
Aesthetic Movement	Elizabethan	Irish Renaissance	Modernism
Angry Young Men	Encyclopedistes	Jacobean	Naturalism
Augustans	Enlightenment	Kailyard school	Neoclassicism
Baroque	Existentialism	Lake poets	Neorealism
Beat Generation	Expressionism	Liverpool poets	Occultism
Bloomsbury group	Futurism	Lost generation	Parnassians
Cavalier poets	Georgian poets	Magical realism	Pleiade
Classical	Graveyard school	Mannerism	Postmodernism
Classicism	Harlem Renaissance	Medievalism	Post-Structuralism

Pre-Raphaelites

Pre-Romanticism

Primitivism

Realism

Renaissance

Renaissance humanism

Romanticism

Russian formalists

Sentimentalism

Social Realism

Structuralism

Sturm and Drang

Surrealism

Symbolism

Transcendentalism

Verismo

Victorian

Vorticism

LITHOSPHERIC PLATES

The Earth's outermost rigid, rocky layer is called the lithosphere and it is made up of the crust (upper layer) and the upper mantle. The lithosphere is broken, like a slightly cracked eggshell, into about a dozen separate rigid blocks, or plates.

African plate

Antarctic plate

Arabian plate

Australian plate

Caribbean plate

Caroline microplate

Cocos plate

Eurasian plate

Indian plate

Nazca plate

North American plate

Pacific plate

Philippine plate

Somali plate

South American plate

LOANS

adjustable mortgage

amortized

assumable

automobile

balloon

bank

bill consolidation

blanket

boat

bridge

broker

building

business

callable chattel mortgage

collateral

commercial

consolidated

construction

consumer

conventional

credit

credit union

demand

development

discount

equity

estate

fiduciary

fixed-rate

gift

government

home equity

I.O.U.

industrial

installment

insurance-policy

interest-only

jumbo

life-insurance

long-term

maritime

medical

mortgage

no-cost

pawn

personal

pledge

real estate

remodeling

secured

single-payment

student

term

unsecured

vacation

variable-rate

warehousing

working-capital

wraparound

LOCK VARIETIES

barrel lock

bathroom lock

bicycle lock

brake lock

clasp lock

combination lock

crossbolt lock

cylinder lock

D lock

deadbolt lock

disk-tumbler lock

door lock

double lock

drawback lock

ignition lock

key lock

keypad lock

knob lock

lever lock

lever-tumbler lock

mortise lock

night lock

padlock lock

pin lock

pin-tumbler lock

radial pin-tumbler lock

reversible lock

rim lock

safety lock

security lock

shackle lock

snap lock

spring lock

steering lock

stock lock

time lock

twist lock

tubular lock

tumbler lock

U lock

warded lock

wheel lock

window lock

Yale lock

yoke lock

LUMINESCENCE TYPES

Luminescence is the emission of light by certain materials when they are relatively cool, which is different from light given off by incandescent bodies like burning wood or electric light bulbs. Luminescence may be seen in neon and fluorescent lamps; television screens; organic substances that make fireflies and glowworms light up; certain pigments used in outdoor advertising; and natural electrical phenomena such as lightning and the aurora borealis.

bioluminescence	electrochemilumine-scence	isoluminescence	somnoluminescence
cathodolumine-scence	electroluminescence	phosphorescence	sonoluminescence
chemiluminescence	epiluminescence	photoluminescence	thermoluminescence
chemoluminescence	fluorescence	piezoluminescence	triboluminescence
		radioluminescence	

LUNAR SEAS

A lunar sea is any flat, dark plain of lower elevation on the Moon.

Bay of Dew	Lake of Death	Sea of Cold	Sea of Rains
Bay of Heats	Lake of Dreams	Sea of Crises	Sea of Serenity
Bay of Rainbows	Marsh of Decay	Sea of Fertility	Sea of Tranquility
Border Sea	Marsh of Epidemics	Sea of Humors	Sea of Vapors
Central Bay	Marsh of Mists	Sea of Ingenuity	Sea of Waves
Eastern Sea	Marsh of Sleep	Sea of Knowledge	Smyth's Sea
Foaming Sea	Ocean of Storms	Sea of Moscow	Southern Sea
Humboldt's Sea	Sea of Clouds	Sea of Nectar	

MACHINE ELEMENTS

There are five so-called "simple machines" plus some other basic elements that make up devices we call "machines." Each machine has a unique purpose that augments or replaces human or animal effort for the accomplishment of physical tasks.

beveled gear	gear	rack and pinion	worm gear
cam	inclined plane	ratchet	
chain and belt	lever	screw	
crank and rod	pulley	wheel and axle	

MACHINE GUNS

autocannon	burp gun	Hotchkiss	Maxim gun
automatic rifle	chain gun	Lewis gun	MG30
Breda	chopper	M2	MG34
Browning	Gatling	M249	MG42

mitrailleuse

peacemaker

RPK74

Schmeisser

Spandau

Sten gun

Sturmgewehr 44

sub-machine gun

Thompson gun

tommy gun

Uzi

Vickers

Vickers-Maxim

MAGAZINE TYPES

arts and crafts magazine

automotive magazine

book and publishing magazine

bridal magazine

business and finance magazine

children's magazine

color supplement magazine

comic magazine

computer and Internet magazine

digest

educational magazine

electronics and audio magazine

entertainment magazine

family and parenting magazine

fanzine

fashion and style magazine

food and gourmet magazine

games and hobbies magazine

gay and lesbian magazine

geographic magazine

girls' magazine

health and fitness magazine

history magazine

house and garden magazine

international magazine

lifestyle and cultures magazine

literary magazine

men's interest magazine

monthly magazine

movie magazine

music magazine

news magazine

periodical magazine

pets magazine

photography magazine

political magazine

professional magazine

psychology magazine

quarterly magazine

recreation and leisure magazine

regional magazine

religion and spirituality magazine

science magazine

sports magazine

tabloid magazine

technology magazine

teenage magazine

television magazine

theatrical magazine

trade magazine

travel magazine

weekly magazine

women's interest magazine

Magic '8' Ball Messages

As I see it, yes.

Ask again later.

Better not tell you now.

Cannot predict now.

Concentrate and ask again.

Don't count on it.

It is certain.

It is decidedly so.

Most likely.

My reply is no.

My sources say no.

Outlook good.

Outlook not so good.

Reply hazy, try again.

Signs point to yes.

Very doubtful.

Without a doubt.

Yes—definitely.

Yes.

You may rely on it.

Mah-Jongg Suits

bamboos or sticks

characters or cracks

circles or dots

flowers and seasons

honors or dragons

winds

Mammals

Artiodactyla (even-toed hoofed)

Carnivora

Cetacea (whales and porpoises)

Chiroptera (bats)

Dermoptera (colugos or flying lemurs)

Edentata (toothless)

Hyracoidae (hyrax, dassie)

Insectivora

Lagomorpha (pikas, hares, rabbits)

Marsupialia

Monotremes (egg-laying mammals)

Perissodactyla (odd-toed hoofed)

Pholidata (pangolins)

Pinnipedia (seals and walruses)

Primates

Proboscidea (elephants)

Rodentia

Sirenia (dugongs and manatees)

Tubulidentata (aardvarks)

MANICURE SET

cuticle nippers

cuticle pusher

cuticle scissors

cuticle trimmer

emery board

eyebrow tweezers

nail clippers

nail file

nail scissors

nail shaper

nail whitener pencil

safety scissors

toenail scissors

MAP PROJECTIONS

Cartographers (map makers) use different projections to show the spherical surface of the Earth on a flat piece of paper. All projections involve some distortion of the globe. Cartographers must therefore choose projections that best suit the purpose of the map.

Aitoff

Albers

azimuthal

azimuthal equidistant

conformal

conic or conical

cylindrical

equal-area

Gall-Peters

gnomonic

homolographic

homolosine

Lambert conformal conic

mathematical

Mercator

Mollweide

oblique

orthographic

orthomorphic

Peters

polyconic

Robinson

Sanson-Flamsteed

sinusoidal

stereographic

zenithal

zenithal equidistant

MAP TYPES

aerial

aeronautical

antique

archaeological site

astronomical

atlas

automobile

base

bus line

celestial globe

city street

climate

contour

digital

general-purpose

geologic

image

key

land-use

military

mind

national

nautical

navigation

ocean

physical

pocket

political

population

projection

railroad

regional

relief

road

site

sketch

special-purpose

street

subway

survey

terrain

terrestrial globe

thematic

topographical

town

transportation

weather

world

zoning

MAPLE VARIETIES

ash-leaved

big-leaved

big-toothed

bird's-eye

black

broad-leaved

coliseum

curled

dwarf

field

flowering

garden

ginnala or Amur

great

hard

hedge

Japanese

mountain

Norway

Oregon

paperbark

parlor

pointed-leaf

red

rock

Rocky Mountain

scarlet

Scottish

shrubby

Siebold

silver

striped

sugar

swamp

sycamore

three-flowered

tiger

vine

white

MARBLE VARIETIES

arabescato

azul

bianco carrara

bianco statuario

birds'eye

botticino

breccia

calico

cremo

Egyptian

Elgin

Florentine

forest

moncervetto

peacock

perlato

361

rosa

rosso

statuary

travertino

verde

MARBLES

aggie

alley

bird's egg

boulder

bumblebee

bumbo

butterfly

butterfly agate

cat's eye

china

cleary

cloud

comic

corkscrew

crystal

cub scout

flame

flint

ghost

gooseberry

half-pint

Indian

lucky taw

lutz

mica

onionskin

oxblood

peanut butter and jelly

peawee

plaster

popeye

puree

rolled commy

root beer float

shooter

steely

MARKERS

art marker

brush-pen marker

calligraphy marker

changeable marker

chart marker

china marker

colorless blender marker

dry-erase marker

fabric-painter marker

fine-line marker

fragrant marker

highlighter

layout marker

opaque marker

overwriter

paint marker

permanent marker

poster marker

projection marker

washable marker

water-based marker

white marker

MARRIAGE, FORMS OF

arranged marriage

civil marriage

common-law marriage

commuter marriage

companionate marriage

endogamy

exchange marriage

exogamy

free marriage

gay marriage

group marriage

levirate marriage

monogamy

morganatic marriage

open marriage

polyandry

polygamy or polygyny

proxy marriage

royal marriage

same-sex marriage

shotgun marriage

sororate marriage

starter marriage

trial marriage

voidable marriage

white marriage

MARSUPIALS

anteater

antechinus

bandicoot

bettong

bilby

brushtail

cuscus

dasyure

dibbler

dunnart

flying phalanger

glider

honey mouse

honey possum

kangaroo

kangaroo bear

koala

kowari

kultarr

marsupial cat

marsupial mole

marsupial mouse

marsupial rat

mouse opossum

mulgara

numbat

opossum

opossum rat

pademelon

phalanger

phascogale

planigale

possum

potoroo

pouched mole

pygmy possum

quokka

quoll

rainforest bandicoot

rat kangaroo

ringtail

rock wallaby

shrew opossum

sminthopsis

Tasmanian devil

Tasmanian tiger

thylacine or Tasmanian wolf

Virginia opossum

wallaby

wallaroo

wombat

yapok

Martini Types

apple martini
Bikini
blue Hawaiian
blue lagoon
cherry martini
chocolate martini
classic dry martini

cosmopolitan
crantini
dirty martini
dry martini
extra dry martini
FDR
French martini

Gibson
gimlet
lemon martini
lime martini
Manhattan
medium martini
Montgomery

pink martini
St. Tropez
sweet martini
vesper
vodka martini

Mathematical Elements

addend
aggregate
algorithm
aliquot
antilogarithm
argument
array
auxiliary equation
base
Bessel function
binomial
characteristic
characteristic equation
characteristic function

characteristic polynomial
characteristic root
characteristic vector
coefficient
collineation
combination
common divisor
complement
congruence
constant
coordinate
cosecant
cosine
cotangent
cube

cube root
decimal
denominator
derivative
determinant
difference or remainder
differential
discriminate
dividend
division sign
divisor
domain
e
elliptical function
empty set

equal sign
equation
exponent
exponential
expression
factor
factorial
formula
fraction
function
greatest common divisor
haversine
hyperbolic
i
identity element

364

increment

index

integral

Laplace transform

least common denominator

least common multiple

logarithm or log

mantissa

matrix

minuend

minus sign

mixed decimal

modulus

monomial

multinomial

multiple

multiplicand

multiplicator

multiplier

norm

numerator

parameter

part

permutation

pi

plus sign

polynomial

power

quadratic equation

quaternion

quotient

radical

radix

reciprocal or multiplicative inverse

repeating decimal or circulating decimal

replacement set

root

secant

sequence

series

set

simultaneous equations

sine

solution

square root

submultiple

subset

subtrahend

summand

tangent

tensor

topological group

topological space

variable

vector

vector product

vector sum

versed sine or versine

vulgar fraction

MATHEMATICAL NAMED CONCEPTS, LAWS, AND THEOREMS

Abelian group

Apollonius' theorem

Archimedean axiom

Argand diagram

Banach space

Bayes's theorem

Bernoulli trial

Bessel functions

Bolzano-Weierstrass theorem

Booean algebra

Briggsian logarithms

Brouwer fixed-point theorem

Cantor set

Cardano's formula

Cartesian coordinates

Cauchy sequence

Cauchy-Schwarz inequality

Cavalieri's principle

Cayley-Hamilton theorem

Chebyshev's inequality

Chinese remainder theorem

Cramer's rule

de Moivre's formula

de Moivre-Laplace theorem

de Morgan's rules

Desargues's theorem

Diophantine equation

Dirichlet series

Euclid's axioms

Euclidean geometry

Euler's constant

Euler's formula

Fermat prime

Fermat's last theorem

Fibonacci numbers

Fourier analysis

Fourier series

French curve

Galois group

Gauss's lemma

Gauss's theorem

Gaussian distribution

Godel numbers

Goldbach conjecture

Green's theorem

Gregory's series

Hamilton's principle

Heron's formula

Hilbert space

Hilbert's problems

Julia set

Klein bottle

L'Hospital's rule

Lagrange's theorem

Laplace operator or Laplacian operator

Lebesgue measure

Legendre polynomials

Legendre symbol

Leibnitz's theorem

Lie group

Lobachevskian geometry

Maclaurin series

Mandelbrot set

Markov chain

Markovian chain

Mersenne numbers

Mersenne prime

Mobius strip

Monte Carlo method

Napierian logarithm

Newton's method

Pascal's theorem

Pascal's triangle

Peano's axioms

Pell's equation

Poisson distribution

Pythagorean theorem

Riemann hypothesis

Riemann surface

Riemannian geometry

Rolle's theorem

Russell's paradox

Schur's lemma

sieve of Eratosthenes

Simpson's rule

Stokes's theorem

Taylor series

towers of Hanoi

Venn diagram

witch of Agnesi

Zorn's lemma

MATHEMATICAL TOOLS

abacus

calculator

compass

computer

graph

graticule

histogram

multiplication table

protractor

quadrille

ruler

scale

slide rule

trammel

Venn diagram

MATHEMATICS BRANCHES AND KINDS

addition algebra

affine geometry

algebra

algebraic geometry

algebraic topology

analysis

analytic geometry

applied mathematics

arithmetic

associative algebra

binary arithmetic

Boolean algebra

calculus

calculus of differences

calculus of variations

category theory

circle geometry

combinatorial analysis

combinatorial mathematics

combinatorial topology

commutative algebra

complex algebra

complex analysis

control theory

denumerative geometry

descriptive geometry

differential calculus

differential geometry

division algebra

elementary algebra

elementary arithmetic

equivalent algebras

Euclidean geometry

field theory

financial mathematics

Fourier analysis

functional analysis

game theory

G-del's proof

general topology or point set topology

geodesic geometry

geodesy

geometry

graph theory

graphic algebra

group theory

harmonic analysis

higher algebra

higher arithmetic

homological algebra

hyperalgebra

hyperbolic geometry

infinitesimal calculus

integral calculus

intuitional geometry

invariant subalgebra

inverse geometry

Lagrangian function

Laplace's equation

linear algebra

line geometry

mathematical biology

mathematical biophysics

mathematical computing

mathematical ecology

mathematical geography

mathematical logic

mathematical physics

matrix algebra

matrix theory

measure theory

metageometry

modular arithmetic

multiple algebra

natural geometry

nilpotent algebra

noncommutative algebra

non-Euclidean geometry

non-standard analysis

n-tuple linear algebra

number theory

numerical analysis

operational calculus

operations research

P-adic analysis

plane geometry

plane trigonometry

point-set topology

political arithmetic

potential theory

probability theory

projective geometry

proper subalgebra

pure mathematics

quadratics

quaternian algebra

reducible algebra

reverse mathematics

Riemannian geometry

semisimple algebra

set theory

simple algebra

solid geometry

speculative geometry

sphere geometry

spherical trigonometry

statistics

Stochastic calculus

subalgebra

systems analysis

topology

trigonometry or trig

universal algebra

universal geometry

vector algebra

zero algebra

MATTER DESCRIPTORS

Scientists define matter as anything that occupies space and all matter is made up of atoms and molecules. The three states of matter—gas, liquid, and solid—may be described in various ways.

brittleness

color

density

ductility

elasticity

hardness

malleability

mass

shape

smell

solubility in water

texture

viscosity

MATTRESSES

air

bed

blow-up

bolster

California king

California queen

crib

daybed

double

extra-firm

extra-long

firm

foam

futon

inner-spring

king-size

Olympic queen

orthopedic

queen-size

round

spring

super king

three-quarter

twin or single

water

wire

Meals

afternoon tea

al desko or deskfast

antipasto

appetizer

banquet

barbecue

blue-plate special

breakfast

brown-bag lunch

brunch

buffet

business breakfast

business dinner

business lunch

clambake

coffee break

collation

continental breakfast

cookout

crudités

dashboard breakfast or cupholder meal

dinner

dinner party

doggie bag

drive-through meal

elevenses

entrée

evening meal

fast food meal

feast

fry-up

high tea

hors d'oeuvres

last supper

love feast

lunch

luncheon

meals-on-wheels

mess

midday meal

midnight snack

morning

nooning

nosh

nosh-up

Oslo breakfast

picnic

potluck

power breakfast

power lunch

prix fixe

refection

refreshment

repast

rere-banquet

salad bar

smorgasbord

snack

supper

takeout

table d'hôte

tapas

tea

tea party

tiffin

tuck-in or tuck-out

TV dinner

wedding breakfast

Measurement Combining Forms

A combining form is a part of a word normally used in compounds in combination with another element to form a word, e.g. nano- to make *nanosecond*. Ten is the magic metric number and each power of ten is assigned a prefix, which can be attached to nearly any metric measure.

atto- femto- micro- pico-

centi- giga- milli- tera-

deci- hecto- myria-

deka- kilo- nano-

exa- mega- peta-

MEASUREMENT TYPES

acidimetry	bolometry	electrometry	mariners' measure
actinometry	calorimetry	ergometry	metric system
aerometry	campimetry	eudiometry	microcalorimetry
alcoholometry	cephalometry	fluorometry	microdensitometry
algometry	chronometry	galvanometry	micrometry
alkalimetry	circular measure	goniometry	microphotometry
altimetry	clinometry	gravimetry	morphometry
anemometry	colorimetry	hydrometry	nephleometry
angular measure	coulometry	hygrometry	odometry
anthropometry	craniometry	hypsometry	odorimetry
apothecaries' measure	cryometry	imperial system or customary system	olfactometry
apothecaries' weight	cubic measure	interferometry	olfactronics
astrometry	cytophotometry	iodometry	ophthalmometry
atrometry	densitometry	keratometry	optometry
audiometry	diffractometry	land measure	orometry
avoirdupois weight	dilatometry	lichenometry	oscillometry
barometry	dolorimetry	linear measure	osmometry
bathymetry	dosimetry	liquid measure	osteometry
biometry	dry measure	magnetometry	pelvimetry
board measure	dynamometry	manometry	perimetry

photoclinometry

photometry

planimetry

plastometry

plezometry

pneumotachography

polariometry

porosimetry

potentiometry

profilometry

psychometry

pupillometry

pyrometry

quantitative analysis

radiometry

reflectometry

refractometry

respirometry

rheometry

saccharimetry

salinometry

seismometry

sensitometry

spectrometry

spectrophotometry

sphygmomanometry

spirometry

square measure

stereometry

stoichiometry

surveyor's measure

tachometry

tachymetry

telemetry

tensiometry

thermometry

time measure

tintometry

tonometry

troy weight

turbidimetry

U.S. units

velocimetry

viscometry

volumetry

wood measure

zoometry

MEASUREMENT AND SCIENTIFIC
UNITS NAMED FOR PEOPLE

Ampere	Farad	Maxwell	Siemens
Angstrom	Gauss	Neper	Sievert
Becquerel	Gray	Newton	Stokes
Bel	Henry	Oersted	Svedberg
Celsius	Hertz	Ohm	Tesla
Coulomb	Jansky	Pascal	Volt
Curie	Joule	Poise	Watt
Fahrenheit	Kelvin	Rontgen	Weber

MEASURES, LIGHT

British candle	flux	lamp-hour	nit
candela	foot-candle	lumen	nox
candle	footlambert	lumen-hour	phot
candle-foot	Hefner candle	lux	stilb
candle-hour	international candle	meter-candle	
decimal candle	lambert	millilambert	

MEASURES, METRIC

are	decimeter	kiloliter	micron
centiare	dekagram	kilometer	milligram
centigram	dekaliter	liter	milliliter
centiliter	gram	long ton	millimeter
centimeter	hectare	meter	nanogram
centner	hectogram	metric hundredweight	nanometer
decameter	hectoliter	microgram	picogram
decigram	hectometer	micrometer	quintal
deciliter	kilogram		ton

MEASURES, RADIOACTIVITY

becquerel	gray	microcoulomb	milligray
coulomb	half-life	microcurie	millirad
curie	megabecquerel	microsievert	millirem
dose equivalent	megacurie	millicurie	milliroentgen

multicurie   rem   sievert

rad   roentgen

MEASURES, TIME

A.D.	C.E.	minute	standard time
age	Coordinated Universal Time	month	U.S. Standard Time
a.m. or ante meridiem	day	nanosecond	Universal Time
apparent solar time	Daylight Saving Time	o'clock	week
atomic time	decade	p.m. or post meridiem	year
B.C.	hour	second	
B.C.E	mean solar time	sidereal time	

MEAT CUTS AND JOINTS

back rib	cutlet	medallion	shoulder
belly slice	escalope	middle neck	shoulder chop
blade	filet mignon	neck fillet	side
brain	fillet or tenderloin	noisette	sirloin
breast	flank	rack	skirt
brisket	fore rib	rib	spare rib
butt	hock	riblet	steak
center loin chop	joint	round	T-bone
chop	knuckle	rump	tenderloin
chuck	leg	saddle	tournedos
collar	loin	shank	undercut
cubes	loin chop	shin	

MEAT TYPES

bacon

beef

beefburger

burger

capon

chicken

chitterlings

cold cuts

corned beef

Cornish hen

deviled meat

dried meat

duck

duckling

elk

frankfurter or hotdog

frog leg

game

goat

goose

grouse

guinea fowl

ham

hamburger

hare

horsemeat

jerky

kidney

lamb

liver

moose

mutton

oxtail

partridge

pea fowl

pheasant

pork

poultry

quail

rabbit

red meat

reindeer

salt pork

sausage

smoked meat

steak

sweetbreads

tripe

turkey

turtle

veal

venison

MECHANICS BRANCHES

Mechanics was among the first of the classical sciences to be developed and it deals with motion and forces producing motion.

aerodynamics

aeromechanics

animal mechanics

applied mechanics

atomechanics

auto mechanics

biomechanics

celestial mechanics

classical mechanics

dynamics

electromechanics

energetics

fluid mechanics or fluid dynamics

gyroscopics

hydromechanics or hydrodynamics

kinematics

kinetics

magnetohydrodynamics or MHD

matrix mechanics

mechanical arts

micromechanics

Newtonian mechanics

pneumatics

practical mechanics

pure mechanics or abstract mechanics

quantum mechanics

rational mechanics

servomechanics

statics

statistical mechanics

telemechanics

theoretical mechanics or analytical mechanics

wave mechanics

zoomechanics or biomechanics

MEDICAL AND SURGICAL SPECIALTIES

adolescence medicine

aeromedicine

allergology

anatomy

anesthesiology

audiology

aviation medicine

bacteriology

bariatrics

cardiography

cardiology

chemotherapy

chiropody

critical care medicine

dental medicine

dental surgery

dentistry

dermatology

diagnostics

dolorology

embryology

emergency medicine

endocrinology

epidemiology

etiology

family practice

fetology

fluoroscopy

gastroenterology

general medicine

general practice

geomedicine

geriatrics or gerontology

gynecology

hematology

hospice care

hygiene

immunochemistry

immunology

immunopathology

internal medicine

materia medica

mental hygiene

midwifery

mycology

neonatology

nephrology

neurology

neuropsychiatry

neurosurgery

nosology

nuclear medicine

nutrition

obstetrics

odontology

oncology

ophthalmology

optometry

orthopedics

orthotics

osteopathy

otolaryngology

otology

palliative care

parasitology

pathology

pediatrics

perinatology

pharmacology

phlebology

physical medicine

physiopathology

physiotherapy

plastic surgery

podiatry

proctology

prosthetics

psychiatry

psychology

psychoneuroim-munology

psychosomatics

pulmonology

radiology

rheumatology

serology

space medicine

sports medicine

surgery

surgical anatomy

symptomatology or
semeiology

syphilology

teratology

therapeutics

thoracic medicine

tocology

toxicology

transfusion medicine

traumatology

tropical medicine

urogenital medicine

urogynecology

urology

virology

MEDICAL SUPPLIES, BASIC

acetaminophen

adhesive bandages

adhesive tape

antibacterial cream

antibiotic ointment

aspirin

baking soda

boric acid

burn ointment

butterfly closures

calamine lotion

cotton

cotton swabs

disinfectant

dropper

elastic support
bandage

emergency phone
numbers

eye-wash cup

first-aid manual

hot-water bag

hydrogen peroxide

ice pack

insect bite treatment

laxative

nail clippers

petroleum jelly

poison antidote

rubbing alcohol

scissors

soap

sterile gauze

stomach relief
medicine

sunscreen

thermometer

tongue depressors

tweezers

MEDICAL TERM
COMBINING FORMS

Medical English includes not only the official nomenclature of the basic medical sciences and clinical specialties, but also a large body of less formal expressions, a sort of trade jargon used by physicians and their professional associates.

a- or ab- or an-

acro-

adeno-

adreno-

aero-

allo-

ambi-

antero-anti-

arterio-

arthro- or arthr-

bacterio-

blephari-

brady-

broncho-

cardio-

cephalo-

cerebro-

cervico-

chole-

chondro-

chromo-

chylo-

contra-

costo-

cyst-

dacryo-

derma-

dextro-

dys-

encephalo- or encephal-

endo-

entero-

ep- or epi-

ex- or exo-

fibrino-

fibro-

galact-

gastro-

gloss-

hemi-

hepato-

hydro-

hyper-

hypo-

ileo-

ilio-

infra-

inter-

intra-

kerat-

laryngo- or laring-

leuko- or leuk-

mega-

mela-

myelo- or myel-

myo-

neo-

nephro- or nephr-

neuro- or neuri- or neur-

osteo-

peri- or pneumo-

proprio-

sacro-

sero-

tachy-

thrombo-

tracheo-

utero-

vaso-

ventro-

zymo-

MEDICAL TESTS, ROUTINE

blood cholesterol

blood pressure

breast examination

chest x-ray and lung function

colon examination

dental

electrocardiogram

fecal occult blood

glucose

hearing

mammogram

Pap smear and pelvic exam

physical examination

rectal exam

rubella screening

skin exam

testicles examination

triglycerides

tuberculin

urinalysis

vision

MEDICATION TYPES

abortifacient

alpha blocker

analeptic

analgesic

anaphrodisiac

anesthetic

anodyne

anovulant

antacid

anthelmintic

antibacterial

antibiotic

anticholinergic

anticoagulant

anticonvulsant

antidepressant

antidiarrheal

antidote

anti-emetic

anti-epileptic

antifungal

antihistamine

anti-infective

anti-inflammatory

antipruritic

antipsychotic

antipyretic

antiscorbutic

antiseptic

antispasmodic

antitussive

antiviral

anxiolytic

aperient

aphrodisiac

appetite suppressant

arsenical

balm

beta blocker

blood pressure
medication

booster

bronchodilator

calefacient

calmative

cancer treatment

carminative

cathartic

contraceptive

convulsant

counterirritant

curative

cure-all

decongestant

depressant

diaphoretic

digestive

dilator

disinfectant

diuretic

ecbolic

emetic

euphoriant

evacuant

expectorant

febrifuge

fungicide

germicide

hallucinogen

immunosuppressive

laxative

lenitive

mercurial

muscle relaxant

narcotic

nervine

neuroleptic

nootropic

painkiller

palliative

placebo

preventive

prophylactic

psychotomimetic

psychotropic

relaxant

resolvent

restorative

roborant

sedative

sleeping pill

soporific

sorbefacient

spasmolytic

steroid

stimulant

stupefacient

sudatory

sudorific

sulpha drug or
sulphonamide

suppressor

sympatholytic

tonic

tranquilizer

vasoconstrictor

vasodilator

vermifuge

MEDICATION, FORMS OF

balsam

cachet

caplet

capsule

chewable

collyrium

cream

drip

drops

enema

gargle

hypodermic

inhalant

lotion

lozenge

microcapsule

nasal spray

nebulizer

needle-free injector

ointment

pastille

pill

poultice

powder

rub

salve

sponge

suppository

tablet or tab

MEDICINE, ALTERNATIVE AND COMPLEMENTARY

acupressure

acupuncture

Alexander technique

aromatherapy

Ayurveda

Bach flower
remedies

balneotherapy

bioelectromagnetic-
based therapy

bioenergetics

biofield therapy

bodywork

chiropractic

color therapy

cranio-sacral therapy

crystal healing

dietary supplements

electro-acupuncture

energy therapy

eurhythmics

faith healing

Feldenkrais method

herbalism

homeopathic
medicine

hydropathy

iridology

magnet therapy

massage therapy

natural therapy

naturopathic
medicine

organotherapy

osteopathic medicine

psionic medicine

qi gong

radionics

reflexology

reiki

Rolfing

shiatsu

thalassotherapy

therapeutic touch

MELONS

cantaloupe

casaba

charentais

Crenshaw

galia

honeydew

macock

mango melon

muskmelon

netted melon or
nutmeg melon

ogen

Oriental pickling
melon

Persian

pomegranate melon

snake melon or
serpent melon

stinking melon

sweet melon

watermelon

winter melon

MENTAL STATES

absorption

agitation

anger

annoyance

anxiety

anxiousness

applied thought

attitude

balance

bliss

compassion

concentration

confusion

consciousness

contact

delirium

delusion

depression

desire

disturbance

enchantment

energy

engrossment

equanimity

faith

fear

feeling

fog

happiness

humor

hypnosis

ignorance

indifference

insanity

irritation

jealousy

joy

kindness

love

meditation

melancholia

mindfulness

mood

morale

nervousness

non-avarice

non-delusion

non-greed

non-hatred

non-illwill

one-pointedness

peace

perception

perturbation

preoccupation

psychotic belief

rapture

sadness

shame

sustained thought

tension

torpor

trance

tranquility

understanding   vitality   wisdom

vexation   volition

METAL FINISHES

anodized	engine-turned	matté	satin
antiqued	engraved	nickeled	scratched
baked	filled	oiled	smooth
blued	frosted	oxidized	sprayed
bronzed	galvanized	patina	stained
brush-painted	gilded	planished	stamped
buffed	glazed	plated	tinned
burnished	glossed	polished	tumbled
chromed	greased	rough	waxed
curled	ground	rusted	
enameled	hammered	sandblasted	
encrusted	lacquered	sanded	

METAL ORES

anglesite	chalcocite	ironstone	smithsonite
argentite	chalcopyrite	limonite	stibnite
arsenopyrite	chromite	litharge	tinstone
bauxite	cinnabar	lodestone	zincite
carnotite	copper pyrite	magnetite	
cassiterite	galena	pitchblende	
cerrusite	hematite	siderite	

METAL TYPES

actinide	amalgam	lanthanide	poor metal
alkali metal	base metal	noble metal	precious metal
alkaline earth metal	earth metal	non-transition metal	rare earth metal
alloy	heavy metal	platinum metal	transition metal

METALLIC ELEMENTS

actinium	europium	mercury	rhenium
aluminum	fermium	molybdenum	rhodium
americium	gadolinium	neodymium	rubidium
antimony	gallium	neptunium	ruthenium
barium	germanium	nickel	samarium
berkelium	gold	niobium	scandium
beryllium	hafnium	osmium	silver
bismuth	holmium	palladium	sodium
cadmium	indium	phosphorus	strontium
calcium	iridium	platinum	tantalum
cerium	iron	plutonium	technetium
cesium	lanthanum	polonium	terbium
chromium	lawrencium	potassium	thallium
cobalt	lead	praseodymium	thorium
copper	lithium	promethium	thulium
curium	lutetium	protactinium	tin
dysprosium	magnesium	quicksilver	titanium
erbium	manganese	radium	tungsten

uranium

vanadium

ytterbium

yttrium

zinc

zirconium

METEOR SHOWERS

Aquarids

Australids

Capricornids

Cepheids

Cygnids

Geminids

Leonids

Lyrids

Ophiuchids

Orionids

Perseids

Phoenicids

Quadrantids

Taurids

Ursids

METRICAL FEET

Metrical Feet is a group of 2 or 3 syllables forming the basic unit of poetic rhythm.

amphibrach

amphimacer

anapest

antispast

bacchius

choriambus or choriamb

cretic or amphimacer

dactyl

dispondee

dochmiac

epitrite

iamb or iambus

ionic

molossus

paeon

proceleusmatic

pyrrhic or dibrach

spondee

tribrach

trochee

MICROORGANISMS

A microorganism is a lifeform that is too small for the human eye to see unaided. This usually means that it is less than one millimeter (0.04 inches) in size.

actinomycete

aerobe

algae

amoeba

animalcule

arthrospore

bacillus

bacterium or bacteria

botulinus

bug

ciliate

coccus
diatom
dyad
entozoon
euglena
flagellate
foraminifer
fungi
germ
gonidium
mastigophoran

mastigopod
microbe
micrococcus
microphyte
microspore
microzoon
microzyme
monad
moneran
nematode
paramecium

pathogen
phage
pneumococcus
protist
protozoan rhizopod
rotifer
salmonella
saprophyte
schizomycete
spirillum
spirochete

sporozoan
staphylococcus
streptococcus
tetrade
triad
virus
yeast
zoospore

MICROSCOPES

acoustic microscope

binocular microscope

biomicroscope

blink microscope

capillaroscope

comparison microscope

compound microscope

conoscope

dark-field microscope

dissecting microscope

electron microscope

engiscope

field-emission microscope

field-ion microscope

fluorescence microscope

gravure microscope

high-powered microscope

interference microscope

laboratory microscope

light microscope

metallograph

metallurgical microscope

micrometer microscope

micropolariscope

microprojector

operating microscope

optical microscope

orthostereoscope

oxyhydrogen microscope

phase contrast microscope

photomicroscope

pinion focusing microscope

polarizing microscope

power microscope

projecting microscope

scanning electron microscope

scanning microscope

scanning tunneling microscope

simple microscope

slit lamp microscope

solar microscope

spectromicroscope

stereoscopic microscope

supermicroscope

surface microscope

telemicroscope

transmission electron microscope

traveling microscope

ultramicroscope

ultraviolet microscope

X-ray microscope

MIDDLE EASTERN PEOPLES

Abbasid

Ammonite

Amorite

Arab or Arabian

Armenian

Assyrian

Babylonian

Bahraini

Bedouin

Bengali

Cuman

Cyprian

Dravidian

Egyptian

Fulani

Gazan

Hebrew

Hittite

Hurrian

Iranian

Iraqi

Israeli

Jew

Jordanian

Kassite

Kazakh

Kurd

Kuwaiti

Lebanese

Libyan

Omani

Ottoman

Palestinian

Pashtun

Persian

Phoenician

Punjabi

Qatari

Semite

Syrian

Syro-Lebanese

Turk or Turkish

Yemeni

MILITARY DECORATIONS

Air Medal

Army Commendation Medal

Bronze Star Medal

Combat Action Ribbon

Congressional Medal of Honor

Croix de Guerre

Defense Distinguished Service Medal

Defense Superior Service Medal

Distinguished Conduct Medal

Distinguished Flying Cross

Distinguished Service Cross

Distinguished Service Medal

Distinguished Service Order

Distinguished Unit Citation

George Cross

Good Conduct Medal

Iron Cross

Legion of Merit

Médaille Militaire

Medal of Honor

Meritorious Service Cross

Meritorious Service Medal

Meritorious Unit Commendation

Military Cross

Navy Cross

Navy Unit Commendation

Presidential Unit Citation

Prisoner of War Medal

Purple Heart or Order of the Purple Heart

Service Medal

Silver Star Medal

Unit Citation

Victoria Cross

MILK VARIETIES

breast milk

buttermilk

chocolate milk

coconut milk

condensed milk

cow's milk

dried milk

evaporated milk

filtered milk

fortified milk

goat's milk

homogenized milk

ice milk

lactose-reduced milk

low-fat milk

malted milk

nonfat milk

one-percent milk

organic milk

pasteurized milk

powdered milk

raw milk

rice milk

skim milk

soy milk

sterilized milk

strawberry milk

sweetened condensed milk

two-percent milk

ultra-heat treatment milk or long-life milk

ultra-high temperature milk

untreated milk

whole milk

MINERAL AND FUEL OILS

anthracene oil

benzine

carbolic oil

coal oil

creosote

creosote oil

crude oil

diesel fuel

diesel oil

fossil fuel

fuel oil

gas oil

gasoline

heating oil

jet fuel

kerosene

lamp oil

liquid petrolatum

lubricating oil

mineral oil

mineral spirits

naphtha

naphthalene

paraffin

petrol

petrolatum

petroleum

petroleum jelly

saturating oil   shale oil   stove oil

seal oil   sperm oil

MINERALS

abukumalite	austinite	bystromite	covellite
acadialite	azurite	cahnite	cryolite
acanthite	badenite	calcite	diamond
actinolite	bararite	caledonite	diatomite
adamite	barite	carbon	dolomite
adelite	bassanite	carnelian	elaterite
afwillite	bauxite	carrollite	emery
aguilarite	beckelite	catoptrite	epidote
alabaster	benitoite	cervantite	epsomite
amarillite	berlinite	chalcedony	feldspar
amphibole	beryl	chamosite	ferrocolumbite
ancylite	beyerite	chert	flint
anhydrite	bitumen	chevkinite	fluorapatite
antimony	bixbyite	chlorite	fluorite
apatite	boothite	chromite	fluorspar
apjohnite	boron	cimolite	fool's gold
aragonite	botryogen	clarkeite	garnet
argillite	bowenite	clay	germanite
arsenic	brazilianite	coal	glauconite
arsenolite	brimstone	cobaltite	goethite
asbestos	bromine	coke	graphite
asphalt	brookite	conichalcite	gypsum
augite	brucite	corundum	holosiderite

hornblende	microlith	pumice	talc
ilmenite	mineral charcoal	pumicite	tanzanite
iolite	mineral coal	pyrite	tellurium
iron pyrites	mineral oil	pyrophyllite	thorite
jadeite	mineral salt	pyroxene	topaz
jet	mineral tallow	quartz	tourmaline
kainite	mineral tar	realgar	tripoli
kaolinite	mineral wax	red clay	turquoise
kyanite	molybdenite	rhodochrosite	umber
lazurite	monazite	rhodonite	uraninite
leucite	moonstone	rock salt	vanadinite
lignite	obsidian	rutile	vermiculite
lime	olivine	serpentine	volborthite
magnesite	orthoclase	siderite	warwickite
magnesium sulfate	ozocerite	silica	wolframite
malachite	ozokerite	silicate	wollastonite
maltha	peat	silicon	wulfenite
marcasite	peridot	sodalite	zeolite
marl	perlite	spar	zircon
massicot	phosphate rock	spinel	zoisite
meerschaum	phosphorus	strontianite	
mica	pimelite	sulfur	
microlite	pitchblende	sylvanite	

MINERALS, FOOD

calcium	chromium	copper	iodine
chlorine	cobalt	fluoride	iron

magnesium

manganese

molybdenum

phosphorus

potassium

selenium

sodium chloride

sulphur

zinc

MINING TYPES

bauxite

block caving

cut and fill

drift

glory hole

gold

hydraulic

opencast

open-pit

open stope

pan

quarrying

room and pillar

salt

shaft

shrinkage

silver

slope

sluice

slusher stopes

solution

square set

strip

stull stopes

sublevel

sublevel caving

sulphur

top slicing

undercut and fill

underground

vertical crater retreat

MOLLUSKS

abalone

aeolid

African snail

amphineuran

ark shell

auger shell

beaked cockle

bivalve

bleeding tooth

bubble shell

button shell

cephalopod

cerion

chambered nautilus

chiton

clam

club shell

conch

cone

cowry

cuttlefish

date mussel

dog cockle

dove shell

ear snail

figshell

fingernail clam

frog shell

gastropod

hammer oyster

heart shell

jingle shell

lamellibranch

lampshell

limpet

melon shell

murex

mussel

nautilus

neopilina

nucula

nudibranch

nut shell

octopod

octopus

olive shell

oyster

pearl oyster

piddock

razor clam

rock shell

scallop

scaphopod

sea lemon

shellfish

slug

snail

spider conch

squid

tusk shell

volute

zebra mussel

MONASTERY TYPES

abbey

Anglican

Antonian

Augustinian

Basilian

Benedictine

Buddhist

Carmelite

Carthusian

Celestine

Christian

Cistercian

Dominican

Episcopal

Essene

Franciscan

friary

Hindu

Jesuit

lamasery

Lutheran

Orthodox

priory

Sufi

Tibetan Buddhist

Trappist

MONOPOLY® SPACES

Atlantic Avenue

B & O Railroad

Baltic Avenue

Boardwalk

Chance (3)

Community Chest (3)

Connecticut Avenue

Electric Company

Free Parking

GO

Go to Jail

Illinois Avenue

Income Tax

Indiana Avenue

Jail

Kentucky Avenue

Luxury Tax

Marvin Gardens

Mediterranean Avenue

New York Avenue

North Carolina Avenue

Oriental Avenue

Pacific Avenue

Park Place

Pennsylvania Avenue

Pennsylvania Railroad

Reading Railroad

Short Line Railroad

St. Charles Place

St. James Place

States Avenue

Tennessee Avenue

Ventnor Avenue

Vermont Avenue

Virginia Avenue

Water Works

MONOPOLY® TOKENS

battleship	iron	Scottie dog	top hat
cannon	race car	shoe	wheelbarrow
horse and rider	sack of money	thimble	

MONSTERS

Argus	dragon	hippocerf	nixie
Baba Yaga	drake	hippogriff	ogre
basilisk	Echidna	hircocervus	ogress
Bigfoot or Sasquatch	Erebus	Hydra	opinicus
bogeyman	Fafnir	Jabberwock	Orthrus
Briareus	Frankenstein	King Kong	Pegasus
bucentur	Furies	Kraken	Pongo
bugbear	Geryon	Ladon	Python
bunyip	ghoul	Lamia	roc
Cacus	Gigantes	Leviathan	Sagittary
Caliban	gila monster	Loch Ness monster	salamander
centaur	Godzilla	manticore	satyr
Cerberus	golem	mantiger	Scylla
Ceto	Gorgon	Medusa	sea horse
Charybdis	green-eyed monster	mermaid	sea monster
chimera	Grendel	merman	sea serpent
cockatrice	griffin	Midgard serpent	simurgh
Cthulhu	Harpy	Minotaur	siren
Cyclops	hippocampus	Mylodont	Sphinx
dipsas	hippocentaur	Nemean lion	squonk

Talos	Typhoeus	werewolf	xiphopagus
Titan	Typhon	windigo	Ymir
troll	unicorn	wyvern	yowie
trow	vampire	wolfman	zombie

MORTGAGE TYPES

adjustable rate mortgage	graduated payment mortgage	renegotiable rate mortgage	shared appreciation mortgage
assumable mortgage	growing equity mortgage	rent with option to buy	shared equity mortgage
balloon mortgage			
buy-down mortgage	home equity mortgage	reverse annuity mortgage	wraparound mortgage
fifteen-year mortgage	installment contract	seller mortgage	zero interest mortgage
fixed-rate mortgage	land contract	seller take-back mortgage	

MOSQUE TYPES

| Abbasid | colonial | masjid | T-type |
| central-dome | jamaca | modern | vernacular |

MOSSES

arctic moss	flowering moss	rock moss	tree moss
beard moss	ground pine	scale moss	white moss
bog moss	Iceland moss	Spanish moss	
club moss	lycopodium	sphagnum moss	
Florida moss	peat moss	staghorn moss	

MOTOR VEHICLES

ambulance

amphibian

armored car

autobus

automobile

beach buggy

bloodmobile

bookmobile

brougham

bulldozer

bumper car

cab

cabriolet

camion

camper

caravan

car transporter

cement mixer

coach

compact car

convertible

coupé

crawler

delivery truck

double-decker bus

dragster

DUKW or duck

dump truck

dune buggy

eighteen-wheeler

electric car

estate car

farm tractor

fastback

fire engine

flatbed

float

forklift

four-by-four or 4x4

four-door car

garbage truck

go-kart

golf cart

grader

grand touring car

hardtop

hatchback

hearse

hook and ladder

horse trailer

hot rod

jalopy

Jeep

jitney

juggarnaut

limousine

lowrider

microbus

mini-bus

minicar

minivan

moon buggy

motor coach

motor home

moving van

off-road vehicle

paddy wagon

panel truck

pantechnicon

pickup truck

police car

race car

ragtop

recreational vehicle or RV

refrigerated van

rig

roadster

rocket car

runabout

scrambler

sedan

semitrailer

six-by-six

snowmobile

snow plow

sports car

squad car

station wagon

steamroller

stock car

streetcar

stretch limousine

subcompact car

swamp buggy

tanker truck

taxicab or taxi

touring car

town car

tow truck

tractor

tractor truck

trailer

tram

transporter

trolley

truck

two-door car

utility

van

wagon

MOUNTAIN TYPES

block mountain or horst

dome mountain

erosion-formed mountain

fault-block mountain

fold mountain or folded mountain or thrust-vaulted mountain

glacial mountain

reverse fault

volcanic mountain or volcano

MOUNT RUSHMORE PRESIDENTS

Abraham Lincoln

George Washington

Theodore Roosevelt

Thomas Jefferson

MUSCLES

abdominal muscle

abductor digiti minimi

abductor hallucis

abductor pollicis brevis

abductor pollicis longus

acalenus medius

adductor brevis

adductor hallucis

adductor longus

adductor magnus

adductor pollicis

anconeus

anterior tibial

articularis cubiti

articularis genu

aryepiglotticus

auricularis

biceps brachii

biceps femoris

brachialis

brachioradialis

buccinator

bulbospongiosus

constrictor of pharynx-inferior

constrictor of pharynx-middle

constrictor of pharynx-superior

coracobrachialis

corrugator supercilii

cremaster

cricothyroid

dartos

deep transverse perinei

deltoid

depressor anguli oris

depressor labii inferioris

diaphragm

digastric

erector spinae-iliocostalis

erector spinae-longissimus

erector spinae-spinalis

extensor carpi radialis brevis

extensor carpi radialis longus

extensor carpi ulnaris

extensor digiti minimi

extensor digitorum

extensor digitorum brevis

extensor digitorum longus

extensor hallucis brevis

extensor hallucis longus

extensor indicis

extensor pollicis brevis

extensor pollicis longus

external oblique abdominis

flexor carpi radialis

flexor carpi ulnaris

flexor digiti minimmi brevis

flexor digitorum brevis

flexor digitorum longus

flexor digitorum profundus

flexor digitorum superficialis

flexor hallucis brevis

flexor hallucis longus

flexor pollicis brevis

flexor pollicis longus

frontalis

gastrocnemius

gemellus inferior

gemellus superior

genioglossus

geniohyoid

gluteus maximus

gluteus medius

gluteus minimus

gracilis

hamstring

hyoglossus

iliacus

inferior oblique

infraspinatus

intercostals external

intercostals innermost

intercostals internal

interior rectus

internal oblique abdominis

interossei-dorsal of foot

interossei-dorsal of hand

interossei-palmar of hand

interossei-plantar of foot

interspinales

intertransversarii

intrinsic muscle of tongue

ishiocavernosus

lateral cricoarytenoid

lateral pterygoid

lateral rectus

latissimus dorsi

levator ani-coccygeus

levator ani-iliococcygeus

levator ani-pubococcygeus

levator ani-puborectalis

levator ani-pubovaginalis

levator labii superioris

levator labii superioris alaeque nasi

levator palpebrae superioris

levator scapulae

levator veli palatini

levatores costarum

longus capitis

longus colli

lumbricals of foot

lumbricals of hand

m. uvulae

masseter

medial pterygoid

medial rectus

mentalis

mylohyoid

nasalis

oblique arytenoid

obliquus capitis inferior

obliquus capitis superior

obturator externus

obturator internus

omohyoid

opponens digiti minimi

opponens pollicis

orbicularis oculi

orbicularis oris

palatoglossus

palatopharyngeus

palmaris brevis

palmaris longus

pectineus

pectoralis major

pectoralis minor

peroneus brevis

peroneus longus

peroneus tertius

piriformis

plantaris

platysma

popliteus

posterior cricoarytenoid

procerus

pronator quadratus

pronator teres

psoas major

psoas minor

pyramidalis

quadratus femoris

quadratus lumborum

quadratus plantae

quadriceps

rectus abdominis

rectus capitus anterior

rectus capitus lateralis

rectus capitus posterior major

rectus capitus posterior minor

rectus femoris

rhomboid major

rhomboid minor

risorius

salpingopharyngeus

sartorius

scalenus anterior

scalenus minimus

scalenus posterior

semimembranosus

semitendinosus

serratus anterior

serratus posterior inferior

serratus posterior superior

soleus

sphincter ani

sphincter urethrae

splenius capitis

splenius cervicis

stapedius

sternocleidomastoid

sternohyoid

sternothyroid

styloglossus

stylohyoid

stylopharyngeus

subclavius

subcostalis

subscapularis

superficial transverse perinei

superior oblique

superior rectus

supinator

supraspinatus

temporalis

temporoparietalis

tensor fasciae lata

tensor tympani

tensor veli palatini

teres major

teres minor

thyro-arytenoid and vocalis

thyro-epiglotticus

thyrohyoid

tibialis anterior

tibialis posterior

transverse arytenoid

transversospinalis-multifidus

transversospinalis-rotatores

transversospinalis-semispinalis

transversus abdominis

transversus thoracis

trapezius

triceps

vastus intermedius

vastus lateralis

vastus medialis

zygomaticus major

zygomaticus minor

MUSCLE TYPES

abductor	constrictor	extensor	skeletal
adductor	contractor	flexor	smooth
agonist	depressor	involuntary	sphincter
antagonist	dilator	levator	striated
articular	elevator	pronator	supinator
cardiac	erector	rotator	voluntary

MUSES

In Greek and Roman mythology, the muses were a group of sister goddesses whose cult was based on Mount Helicon in Greece.

Calliope	Euterpe	Terpsichore
Clio	Melpomene	Thalia
Erato	Polyhymnia	Urania

MUSEUM TYPES

agricultural	aviation or aeronautics	living or on-site	natural science
anthropology	children's	marine	oceanography
aquarium	city or local	military	Oriental
archaeology	commemorative	movie or film	paleontology
architecture	county	music	planetarium
art museum	ethnography	national	portrait gallery
arts and sciences	general	Native American	presidential
automobile	history	natural history	regional

science and industry   special-subject   toy   wax

science and   sports   transportation   zoo
technology
                       state   university   zoology
space

MUSHROOMS

beefsteak	destroying angel	inky cap	portobello
boletus	edible	magic or sacred	royal agaric
button	enoki	maitake	shaggymane
chanterelle	fairy-ring	matsutake	shiitake
cremini	field	meadow	snow
cultivated	fly agaric	morel	straw
deadly poisonous	forest	oyster mushroom	toadstool
death cap	green russula	poisonous	truffle
delicious lactarius	horse	porcini	white

MUSIC, MODAL

Purely melodic music was typical of the plainsong of medieval churches. These scales dominated European music for 1,100 years, approximately 400–1500 AD.

Aeolian	Hypophrygian	Lydian	Phrygian
Dorian	Ionian	Mixolydian	

MUSICAL DIRECTIONS, TEMPO, AND TIME

4/4 time

a batutta

a cappella

a deux

a tempo

a tre

accelerando

ad libitum

adagietto

adagio

adagissimo

affettuoso

affrettando

agilmente

agitato

al fine

al segno

alla breve

alla militara

allargando

allegramante

allegretto

allegro

allentando

altra volta

amoroso

ancora

andante

andantino

angstlich

animato

appassionato

arco

arioso

assai

attaca

au talon

Aufschwung

ballo

bis

bocca chiusa

bois

bouche fermee

bravura

breve

brusco

burlesco

calando

calcando

calmando

cantabile

capriccioso

cedez

chiuso

coda

col legno

commodo

common time

compound time

con alcuna licenza

con amore

con brio

con fuoco

con moto

con slancio

con sordino

coperto

courante

crescendo

crotchet

da capo

dal segno

decrescendo

delicato

delirio

demiquaver

demisemiquaver

diminuendo

dolce

dolente

doppio

doppio movimento

dotted note

dramatico

duple time

eighth note

eighth rest

eilend

elargissant

elegante

encore

espressivo

facile

fastoso

festoso

feurig

fiero

fine

forte

forte piano

399

fortissimo

frettoloso

funerale

furioso

gauche

gedampft

geheimnisvoll

Generalpause

giocoso

glissando

grave

half note

half rest

heftig

hemidemisemiquaver

in modo di

indeciso

innig

inquieto

jete

lamentoso

larghetto

largo

legato

leggiero

lento

lestissimo

maestoso

malinconico

mancando

marcato

marcia

martele

martellato

meno

meno mosso

meter

mezza voce

mezzo

mezzo forte

mezzo piano

minim

moderato

molto

morendo

mosso

moto

muta

niente

nobilmente

non troppo

obbligato

ondeggiando

ossia

parlando

parlato

pathetique

pavillons en l'air

pesante

pianissimo

piano

pique

piu

pizzicato

poco

portamento

prestissimo

presto

punta

quarter note

quarter rest

quaver

rallentando

ravvivando

rinforzando

ritardando

ritenuto

sautille

scherzando

schleppend

sciolto

scordatura

seconda volta

segno

semibreve

semiquaver

semplice

sempre

senza

sforzando

sinistra

sixteenth note

sixteenth rest

sixty-fourth note

sixty-fourth rest

smorzando

sopra

sordino

sospirando

sostenuto

sotto

sotto voce

spiccato

spiritoso

staccato

stretto

stringendo

strisciando

subito

tacet

tanto

tempo

teneramente

tenuto

thirty-second note

thirty-second rest

time	triple time	vigoroso	whole rest
time signature	troppo	vivace	zoppa
tonante	tutti	vivo	
tranquillo	una corda	volti subito	
tremolando	vide	whole note	

MUSICAL FORMS

Musical form is the structural scheme that gives shape and artistic unity to a composition. The standard forms are binary, ternary, rondo, and sonata. Each type of musical form consists of a number of musical sections or subsections.

adagio	cantabile	courante	gavotte
air	cantata	descant	glee
allemande	canticle	dirge	habanera
anthem	canzone	divertimento	humoresque
arabesque	canzonetta	duet	hymn
aria	capriccio	elegy	impromptu
arietta	carillon	entr'acte	interlude
aubade	carol	entrée	intermezzo
bagatelle	cavatina	étude	jig
ballad	chaconne	fandango	lied
ballet	chanson	fanfare	lullaby
barcarole	chant	fantasia	madrigal
binary	chorale	fantasy	march
bolero	chorus	finale	mass
boogie-woogie	concertino	folk song	mazurka
cadenza	concerto	fugue	minuet
canon	concerto grosso	galliard	monody

motet	piano quintet	rondo	song
movement	polka	round	spiritual
nocturne	polonaise	roundelay	string quartet
octet	prelude	saltarello	suite
one-step	psalm	scherzo	symphony
opera	quartet	septet	tarantella
operetta	quintet	serenade	ternary
oratorio	recitative	serenata	theme and variations
overture	reel	sextet	toccata
part-song	refrain	shanty	tone poem
passacaglia	requiem	sinfonia	trio
passion	rhapsody	solo	two-step
pastoral	romance	sonata	variation
pavane	rondino	sonatina	

MUSICAL INSTRUMENT FAMILIES

bowed string instruments	electronic and mechanical instruments	open mouthpiece wind instruments	plucked string instruments
brass winds and horns	hammered string instruments	percussion instruments and drums	reed organs
			stringed keyboards
			woodwinds

MUSICAL INSTRUMENT PERFORMERS

accordionist	bagpiper	bassist	cellist
alphornist	banjoist	bassoonist	clarinetist

cornetist

cymbalist

drummer

fiddler

flautist

guitarist

harpist

harmonicist

harpsichordist

keyboardist

lutist lyrist

mandolinist

oboist

organist

percussionist

pianist

piper

recorder player

saxophonist

sitar player

tambourinist

timpanist

trombonist

trumpeter

tubaist or tubist

vibraphonist

violinist

violist

xylophonist

MUSICAL ORGANS

American organ

barrel organ

bellows organ

chamber organ

church organ

electric organ

electronic organ

grind organ

hand organ

harmonica

harmonium

hurdy-gurdy

melodeon

mouth organ

pedal organ

piano organ

pipe organ

portative organ

positive organ

reed organ

steam organ

MUSICAL TONE PROPERTIES

duration

intensity

pitch

quality

strength

timbre

MUSICAL VARIETIES

absolute music

acid rock

acoustic rock music

Afro-beat

aleatory music

alternative rock
music

art music

art rock

atonal music

ballet music

ballroom music

baroque music

beach music

bebop

big band

bluegrass

blues

boogie

bubblegum

Cajun music

calypso

cathedral music

chamber music

choral music

Christian alternative music

church music

circus music

classical music

country-and-western music

country music

country rock

dance hall

dance music

deca-rock

Delta blues

disco

Dixieland music

doo-wop

ear candy

easy listening music

electronic music

elevator music or Muzak

ensemble music

field music

filk music

folk music

folk rock

funk

fusion

gangsta rap

ghettotech

glitter rock

gospel music

Gregorian chant

grunge

hard rock

heavy metal

heavy rock

hillbilly music

hip-hop

hip house

honky-tonk music

house music

incidental music

inspirational music

instrumental music

jazz music

jazz rock

jungle music

Latin rock

light music

loft jazz

military music

modern jazz music

new age music

operatic music

organ music

party music

piped music

plainsong

political rock

polyphonic music

pomp rock

pop music

pop-rock

post-rock music

program music

progressive jazz

progressive rock

progressive soul

protest music

psychedelic music

psychobilly

punk rock

punkabilly

raga-rock

ragtime music

rap music

rave music

reggae

religious music

rhythm and blues

rockabilly

rock 'n' roll

rococo music

romantic music

sacred music

salon music

salsa music

scat music

semiclassical music

serious music

shockabilly

ska

soft rock

soul music

spiritual music

surf music

swing music

symphony music

synthesized music

technopop

theater music

404

thirdstream music

through-composed music

twelve-tone music or serialism

vocal music

wind music

Zopf music

zydeco

MUSICAL VOICES

alto

baritenor

baritone

bass

basso profundo

castrato

coloratura

coloratura soprano

contralto

countertenor

dramatic soprano

falsetto

lyric soprano

male soprano or boy soprano

mezzo

mezzo-soprano

soprano

spinto

tenor

treble

MUSTARDS

American mustard

black mustard

Bordeaux mustard

brown mustard

Chinese mustard

chipotle mustard

Creole mustard

Dijon mustard

English mustard

European mustard

garlic mustard

German mustard

honey mustard

oriental mustard

powdered mustard

prepared mustard

table mustard

wasabi mustard

white mustard

yellow mustard

MUSTELIDS, CIVETS, AND WEASELS

The weasel family is called Mustelidae and these animals are characterized by having long, low-slung bodies, short legs, and five toes on each foot.

badger

bearcat

binturong

black-footed ferret

civet

ermine

fanaloka

ferret

ferret-badger
fisher
fitch
fossane
foumart
genet
glutton
grison
honey badger

linsang
marbled polecat
mariput
marten
meerkat
mink
mongoose
musteline
otter

palm civet
pine marten
polecat
sable
sea otter
shorttail weasel
skunk
stink badger
stoat

suricate
tayra
viverrine
weasel
wolverine
zorilla

MUTUAL FUND TYPES

aggressive growth mutual fund

asset management mutual fund

balanced mutual fund

blue chip growth mutual fund

bond mutual fund

capital appreciation mutual fund

closed-end mutual fund

corporate bond mutual fund

country specific mutual fund

dividend growth mutual fund

double tax-exempt bond mutual fund

emerging markets mutual fund

equity mutual fund

equity-income mutual fund

federal municipal bond mutual fund

federal municipal money market mutual fund

fixed-income mutual fund

focused mutual fund

global bond mutual fund

global mutual fund

government bond mutual fund

growth and income mutual fund

growth mutual fund

hedge mutual fund

income mutual fund

index mutual fund

international mutual fund

large-cap blend mutual fund

large-cap growth mutual fund

large-cap mutual fund

load mutual fund

low-priced stock mutual fund

micro-cap mutual fund

mid-cap blend mutual fund

mid-cap growth mutual fund

mid-cap mutual fund

mid-cap value mutual fund

money market mutual fund

mortgage-backed securities mutual fund

municipal bond mutual fund

mutual funds of mutual fund

no-load mutual fund

open-end mutual fund

real estate investment trust (REIT) mutual fund

sector mutual fund

small-cap blend mutual fund

small-cap growth mutual fund

small-cap mutual fund

socially responsible mutual fund

speciality fund

specialized mutual fund

state municipal bond mutual fund

state municipal money market mutual fund

state tax-exempt income mutual fund

stock mutual fund

tax efficient mutual fund

tax-exempt income mutual fund

tax-exempt money market fund

triple tax-exempt bond mutual fund

U.S. Government bond mutual fund

U.S. Government money market fund

utilities mutual fund

value mutual fund

NAIL TYPES

annular ring nail

barbed-wire box nail

barbed-wire dowel
pin

barbed-wire roofing
nail

boat nail

box nail

casing nail

clamp nail

coffin nail

common brad

common nail

common wire nail

corrugated fastener

countersunk nail

cut boat nail

cut flooring nail

diamond nail

doubling nail

duplex head nail

finishing nail

finishing wire nail

flat nail

flooring wire nail

hand-wrought nail

lath nail

machine-cut nail

machine-cut nail with
handmade head nail

modern wire nail

picture nail

ring nail

roofing nail

roofing wire nail

rosehead nail

sealing roofing nail

shank nail

sheathing nail

spiral nail

square-shank
concrete nail

staple

T head nail

tack

trunk nail

upholstery nail

wire boat nail

wire casing nail

wire fence nail

wire finishing nail

wire hinge nail

wire nail

Names, Types of

agnomen

alias

assumed name

author's name

baby name

baptismal name

binomial name

birth name

brand name

byname

Christian name

code name

cognomen

collective name

common name

cryptonym

fictitious name

family name

first name

forename

generic name

given name

hypocorism

last name

Latin name

legal name

maiden name

metronymic

microtoponym

middle name

moniker

nickname

nom de guerre

nom de plume

nom de theatre

official name

patronymic

pen name

personal name

pet name

place name

popular name

professional name

proper name

proprietary name

pseudonym

scientific name

second name

sobriquet

stage name

surname

technical name

toponym

trade name

trinomial name

Narrative Points of View

detached autobiography

diary narration

documentary

dramatic monologue

fallible observer

first-person past narrator

first-person present narrator

first-person protagonist

first-person re-teller

first-person witness

interior monologue

letter narration

memoir narration

omniscient observer

second-person narrator

stream of consciousness

subjective narration

third-person limited narrator

third-person objective narrator

third-person omniscient narrator

third-person past narrator

third-person present narrator

National Spelling Bee Winning Words

abalone
abrogate
albumen
antediluvian
antipyretic
asceticism
autochthon
cambist
canonical
catamaran
chiaroscurist
chihuahua
chlorophyll
condominium
croissant
crustaceology
deification
demarche
deteriorating
dulcimer

eczema
elegiacal
elucubrate
equipage
esquamulose (twice)
eudaemonic
euonym
fibranne
foulard
fracas
gladiolus
hydrophyte
incisor
initials
insouciant
intelligible
interlocutory
interning
kamikaze
knack

logorrhea
luge
luxuriance
lyceum
macerate
maculature
meticulosity (twice)
milieu
narcolepsy
odontalgia
pococurante
promiscuous
prospicience
psoriasis
psychiatry
Purim
ratoon
sacrilegious
sanitarium
sarcophagus

schappe (twice)
semaphore
shalloon
smaragdine
soubrette
spoliator
staphylococci
succedaneum
sycophant
syllepsis
therapy
torsion
transept
vignette
vivisepulture
vouchsafe
xanthosis

Nationalities

Abyssinian
Afghan

Albanian
Algerian

American
Andorran

Anglo-American
Anglo-Indian

Angolan

Antiguan

Arab or Arabian

Argentinean

Australian

Austrian

Azerbaijani

Bahamian

Bahraini

Bangladeshi

Barbadian

Barbudan

Belarussian

Belgian

Belizean

Beninese

Bermudian

Bhutanese

Bolivian

Bosnian

Botswanan

Brazilian

British Honduran

British

Bruneian

Bulgarian

Burkinian

Burmese

Burundian

Cambodian

Cameroonian

Canadian

Cape Verdean

Caymanese

Central Africans

Ceylonese

Chadian

Chilean

Chinese

Colombian

Comoroan

Congolese

Costa Rican

Croatian

Cuban

Cypriot

Czech or
Czechoslovakian

Dahomean

Dane

Djiboutian

Dominican

Dominican
Republican

Dutch

East German

East Timorese

Ecuadorian

Egyptian

El Salvadorian

Emiran

English

Equatorial Guinean

Eritrean

Estonian

Ethiopian

Faeroe Islander

Fijian

Filipino

Finlander

French

French Polynesian

Futunan

Gabonese

Gambian

Georgian

German

Ghanaian

Gilbertese

Greek or Grecian or
Hellene

Greenlander

Grenadian

Guatemalan

Guinea-Bissaun

Guinean

Guyanese

Haitian

Honduran

Hong Kong Islander

Hungarian

Icelandic

Indian

Indonesian

Ionian

Ionic

Iranian

Iraqi

Irish

Israeli or Israelite

Italian

Ivorian

Jamaican

Japanese

Jordanian

Kazakh

Kenyan

Kiribatian

Kittsian

Korean

Kosovar

Kuwaiti

Kirghiz

Laotian

Latvian

Lebanese

Lesothoan

Liberian

Libyan

Liechtensteiner

Lithuanian

Luxembourger

Macanese

Macedonian

Madagascan

Malawian

Malay

Malaysian

Maldivian

Malian

Maltese

Mariana Islander

Marquesan

Marshall Islander

Martinican

Mauritanian

Mauritian

Mexican

Micronesian

Moldovan

Monacan

Monegasque

Mongolian

Montenegrin

Moroccan

Mozambican

Myanmaran

Namibian

Nauruan

Nepalese

Netherlander

Netherlands Antillian

New Zealander

Nicaraguan

Nigerian

Nigerien

Nipponese

Niuean

North Korean

North Yemeni

Northern Irish

Norwegian

Omani

Pakistani

Palauan

Panamanian

Papuan

Paraguayan

Persian

Peruvian

Polish

Polynesian

Portuguese

Puerto Rican

Qatari

Rhodesian

Romanian

Russian

Rwandan

Salvadorean

Samoan

San Marinese

Sao Tomean

Saudi Arabian

Scottish

Senegalese

Serbian

Seychellois

Sierra Leonean

Sikkimese

Singaporean

Slav

Slovak

Slovenian

Solomon Islander

Somali

South African

South Korean

South Yemeni

Soviet

Spanish

Sri Lankan

St. Helenian

St. Lucian

St. Vincentian

Sudanese

Surinamese

Swazi

Swede

Swiss

Syrian

Tahitian

Taiwanese

Tajik

Tanzanian

Thai

Tibetan

Tigrean

Tobagan

Togolese

Tongan

Trinidadian

Tunisian

Turkish Tuvaluan

Ugandan

Uruguayan

Uzbek

Vanuatuan

Venezuelan

Vietnamese

Wallis and Futuna Islander

Wallisian   West Indian   Yugoslav   Zambian

Welsh   Western Samoan   Yugoslavian   Zimbabwean

West German   Yemeni   Zairian

Native and North American Tribes

Abnaki	Chippewa	Hupa	Maya
Aleut	Chitimacha	Huron	Mazahua
Algonquin	Choctaw	Illinois	Menominee
Anasazi	Chumash	Inuit	Mescalero
Apache	Comanche	Iowa	Miccosukee
Arapaho	Cora	Iroquois	Micmac
Arctic	Cree	Jicarilla	Mixtec
Arikara	Creek	Karankawa	Mohawk
Assiniboine	Crow	Karok	Mohegan
Athapascan	Dakota	Kekchi	Mohican
Aztec	Delaware	Keres	Mojave
Bannock	Dene	Kickapoo	Montagnais
Blackfoot	Dogrib	Kiowa	Muskogee
Caddo	Eskimo	Klamath	Narrangansett
Cayuga	Fox	Kutenai	Natchez
Cayuse	Goshute	Kwakiuti	Navajo
Cherokee	Haida	Lakota	Nez Percé
Cheyenne	Hidatsa	Lummi	Nootka
Chichimec	Hopi	Malecite	Ojibwa
Chickasaw	Huastec	Maliseet	Okanagan
Chinook	Huichol	Mandan	Olmec

Omaha

Oneida

Onondaga

Osage

Otomi

Ottawa

Paiute

Palouse

Papago

Passamaquoddy

Pawnee

Peigan

Penobscot

Pequot

Pima

Potawatomi

Powhatan

Pueblo

Quapaw

Quinault

Salish

Sarcee

Sauk

Seminole

Seneca

Shawnee

Shoshone

Shuswap

Sioux

Slavey

Spokane

Squamish

Tahltan

Tarascan

Tewa

Tiwa

Tlapanec

Tlaxcalan

Tlingit

Toltec

Trique

Tsimpshian

Tsimshian

Tunica

Tuscarora

Twana

Tzeltal

Tzotzil

Umatilla

Ute

Walapai

Wallawalla

Wampanoag

Washoe

Wichita

Winnebago

Wyandot

Yakima

Yana

Yaqui

Yavapai

Yucatec

Yuchi

Yuki

Yuma

Yurok

Zapotec

Zuni

NEBULAE

Coalsack

Crab Nebula

Dumbbell Nebula

Great Looped or
Loop or Tarantula
Nebula

Great Nebula in
Orion

Helix Nebula

Hind's Nebula

Horsehead Nebula

Hubble Nebula

Keyhole Nebula

Lagoon Nebula

North American
Nebula

Omega Nebula or
Swan Nebula

Ophiuchus Nebula

Owl Nebula

Ring Nebula

Rosette Nebula

Saturn Nebula

Trifid Nebula

Veil Nebula

NECKWEAR

ascot	cravat	muffler	shawl
band	dickey	neckband	stand-up collar
bandanna	dog collar	neckerchief	stiff collar
bertha collar	fichu	necktie	stock
boa	foulard	old school tie	stole
bolo tie	four-in-hand	plunging neckline	string tie
bow tie	fur	polo neck	tallith
button-down collar	Geneva bands	priest's collar	tie
chemisette	golilla	rebato	tippet
choker	guimpe	Roman collar	tucker
clerical collar	high collar	ruff	vestee
clip-on tie	jabot	scapular	Windsor tie
collar	kerchief	scarf	
comforter	lei	school tie	

NEEDLE VARIETIES

between needle	darning needle	long-eyed sharp needle	sharp needle
blue-pointed needle	double-point needle		spear-point needle
blunt	drill-eyed needle	packing needle	straw needle
carpet needle	embroidery needle	sacking needle	tacking needle
crochet hook	ground-down needle	sailmaker's needle	three-cornered needle
crochet needle	knitting needle	sewing-machine needle	tufting needle
curved needle	knitting wire	sewing needle	upholstery needle
darner			

NEEDLEWORK

appliqué
basting
binding
buttonholing
casting
chain-stitching
crewelwork
crochet
cross-stitching

drawnwork
embroidery
fagoting
gros point
hemming
knitting
knitwork
lacemaking
machine stitching

macramé
mending
needlepoint
netting
overcasting
patchwork
petit point
purling
quilting

ribbing
sewing
smocking
tacking
tatting
textile art
whipstitching

NEUTRONS

cold neutron
cold nonpolarized neutron
cold polarized neutron
continuum region neutron

delayed neutron
epithermal neutron
fast neutron
low energy region neutron
monoenergetic neutron

nonpolarized neutron
photoneutron
polarized neutron
resonance region neutron
slow neutron

tetraneutron
thermal neutron
ultra-cold neutron
very cold neutron

NEW ENGLAND STATES

Connecticut
Maine

Massachusetts
New Hampshire

Rhode Island
Vermont

New Testament Prophets

Agabus	Jesus	Judas	Silas
Anna	John	Paul	Zechariah
James	John the Baptist	Peter	

New York City Boroughs

Bronx	Manhattan	Staten Island
Brooklyn	Queens	

New Zealand Islands

North Island	South Island	Stewart Island

Newspaper Types

broadsheet	gazette	local newspaper	school newspaper
daily newspaper	hard news newspaper	national newspaper	soft news newspaper
electronic newspaper	independent newspaper	popular press	tabloid
free newspaper		quality press	weekly newspaper

Nixon's Enemies List

Anderson, Jack	Clark, Ramsey	Dane, Maxwell	Dellums, Ronald
Barkan, Alexander E.	Conyers, John	Davidoff, Sidney	Dogole, S. Harrison

Dyson, Charles

Feld, Bernard T.

Fonda, Jane

Gibbons, Harold J.

Gregory, Dick

Guthman, Edwin O.

Halperin, Morton

Lambert, Samuel M.

Lowenstein, Allard

McGrory, Mary

McQueen, Steve

Mott, Steward R.

Munro Jr., S. Sterling

Namath, Joe

National Welfare Rights Organization

Newman, Paul

Picker, Arnold M.

Schorr, Daniel

Socialist Workers' Party

St. Louis Post-Dispatch

Stein, Howard

Streisand, Barbra

Talbot, George H.

Taylor, Arthur R.

The New York Times

The Washington Post

Watson Jr., Thomas J.

Woodcock, Leonard

NOVEL TYPES

adventure novel

antinovel

autobiographical novel

Bildungsroman

bodice ripper

cliffhanger

cloak-and-sword novel

collage novel

comic novel

detective novel

dime novel

dystopia

entertainment

epic novel

epistolary novel

erotic novel

experimental novel

fantasy novel

fictional biography

Gothic novel

graphic novel

historical novel

historical whodunnit

Kunstlerroman

lyrical novel

mystery novel

naturalistic novel

nonfiction novel

nouveau roman

novel of character

novel of ideas

novel of incident

novel of manners

novel of sensibility or sentimental novel

novel of the soil

novelette

novella or nouvelle

penny dreadful

picaresque novel

political novel

pornographic novel

problem novel

proletarian novel

propaganda novel

psychological novel

psychological thriller

realistic novel

regional novel

roman à clef

romance novel

roman-fleuve or river novel

satirical novel

science-fiction novel

semi-autobiographical novel

shilling shocker

social melodrama

sociological novel

stream-of-consciousness novel

surrealistic novel

swashbuckler novel

techno-thriller

thesis novel

tie-in novel

utopian novel

whodunit novel

yellowback

NUCLEAR REACTOR TYPES

advanced gas-cooled reactor

atomic reactor

boiling-water reactor

breeder reactor

chain reactor

converter reactor

fast breeder reactor

fission reactor

fusion reactor

gas-cooled reactor

heavy-water reactor

light-water reactor

liquid metal reactor

magnox reactor

nonpower reactor

plasma reactor

plasma-arc reactor

pool reactor

power reactor

pressurized-water reactor

supercritical reactor

thermal reactor

thermonuclear reactor

water-cooled reactor

NUMBER TYPES

All ancient cultures devised their own number systems for the purposes of counting.

abbreviated number

abundant number

accession number

algebraic number

almost perfect number or slightly defective number

antenumber

Archimedes number

Avogadro number

cardinal number or cardinal

complex integer or Gaussian integer

complex number

composite number or rectangular number

compound number

deficient number

definable number

directed number

even number or pair

Fermat number

Fibonacci number

figurate number

finite number

fixed-point number

floating-point number

fraction

hyperperfect number or k-hyperperfect number

imaginary number

infinity

integer or whole number

irrational number

large number

Mersenne number

mixed number

multiply perfect number or multiperfect number or pluperfect number

natural number

negative number

419

nonnegative number

normal number

odd number or impair

ordinal number

perfect number

polygonal number

positive number

prime number

primeval number

pure imaginary number

pyramidal number

quasiperfect number

random number

rational number

real number or real

round number

serial number

Sherwood number

Sierpinski number

signed number

surd quantity.

transcendental number

transfinite number

weird number

whole number

Woodall number

NURSE TYPES

auxiliary nurse

charge nurse

community health nurse

dental nurse

general duty nurse

geriatric nurse

head nurse

home health nurse

hospital nurse

intensive care nurse

licensed practical nurse or LPN

midwife or nurse midwife

night nurse

nurse practitioner

occupational health nurse

oncology nurse

pediatric nurse

practical nurse

private duty nurse

private nurse

psychiatric nurse

public health nurse

registered nurse or RN

school nurse

scrub nurse

special nurse

staff nurse

student nurse

NUTS

acorn

almond

areca nut

beechnut

ben nut

betel nut

bitternut

black walnut

bonduc nut

Brazil nut

breadnut

butternut

candlenut

cashew

chestnut

chinquapin

cika

cobnut

coconut

coffee nut

cohune nut

conker

coquilla nut

corozo

cumara nut	hazelnut	monkey nut	pistachio
dika nut	hickory nut	palm nut	quandong
earthnut	hognut	peanut	quinoa
English walnut	horse chestnut	pecan	sal nut
filbert	ivory nut	physic nut	sassafras nut
groundnut	kola nut	pignola	souari nut
grugru	litchi nut	pine nut	walnut
gum nut	macadamia nut	pinon	water chestnut

Oak Varieties

black oak	cork oak	live oak	valley oak
blue oak	duck oak	mountain oak	white oak
brown oak	dwarf oak	pin oak	willow oak
burr oak	English oak	red oak	yellow oak
chestnut oak	gray oak	scrub oak	
cinnamon oak	iron oak	shingle oak	
common oak	laurel oak	swamp oak	

Ocean Currents

Ocean currents constitute the horizontal and vertical circulation system produced by gravity, wind friction, and water density variation in different parts of the ocean. The Coriolis forces (forces exerted by the rotating Earth on all moving objects at or near the Earth's surface) cause ocean currents to move clockwise in the Northern Hemisphere and counterclockwise in the Southern Hemisphere.

Agulhas Current

Alaska Current

Aleutian Current

Anadyr Current

Antarctic Current

Antilles Current

Atlantic North and South Equatorial Current

Benguela Current

Bering Current

Brazil Current

California Current

Canaries Current

Cape Horn Current

Caribbean Current

East Australian Current

East Greenland Current

El Niño

Equatorial Counter Current

Falkland Current

Florida-Yucatan Current

Guinea Current

Gulf Stream Current

Gulf Stream-North Atlantic-Norway Current

Indian South Equatorial Current

Japan Current

Kuroshio Current

Kuroshio-North Pacific Current

Labrador Current

Monsoon Current

Mozambique Current

North Atlantic Drift Current

North Equatorial Current

North Pacific Drift Current

Norwegian Current or Norway Current

Oya Current or Oyashio Current

Pacific North and South Equatorial Current

Peru Current or Humboldt Current

South Atlantic Current

South Equatorial Current

West Australian Current

West Greenland Current

West Spitsbergen Current

OCEANS

Antarctic Ocean

Arctic Ocean

Atlantic Ocean

Indian Ocean

Pacific Ocean

OIL TYPES

animal

drying

engine or motor

essential

fixed or non-volatile

fuel

glyceride

mineral

non-drying

specialty

sulfonated

vegetable

volatile

423

OLD TESTAMENT PROPHETS

Amos

Balaam

Daniel

Elijah

Ezekiel

Habakkuk

Haggai

Hosea

Isaiah

Jeremiah

Joel

Jonah

Lamentations

Malachi

Micah

Moses

Nahum

Nathan

Obadiah

Samuel

Zechariah

Zephaniah

OLYMPIAN GODS AND GODDESSES

Aphrodite or Venus

Apollo or Phoebus

Ares or Mars

Artemis or Diana

Athena or Minerva

Hades or Pluto

Hephaestus or Vulcan

Hera or Juno

Hermes or Mercury

Hestia or Vesta

Poseidon or Neptune

Zeus or Jupiter

OPERATION™ GAME PLAYING PIECES

apple or Adam's apple

bread slice or bread basket

broken heart

butterfly or butterflies in stomach

funny bone

horse or Charlie horse

pail or water on the knee

pencil or writer's cramp

rubber band or anklebone

spare rib

wishbone

wrench or wrenched ankle

ORANGE COLOR VARIETIES

acid orange

apricot

aurora

brass-colored

burnt ocher

burnt orange

burnt Roman ocher

burnt sienna

cadmium orange

carnelian

carotene

carrot

chrome orange

copper

copper red

dark orange

Dutch orange

Florida gold

helianthin

hyacinth

madder orange

mandarin

marigold

Mars orange

melon

methyl orange

mikado

neon orange

ocher

ocher orange

old gold

orange chrome yellow

orange lead

orange madder

orange mineral

orange ocher

orange-red

orange vermilion

orange-yellow

orpiment

pale orange

peach

pumpkin

raw sienna

realgar orange

red-orange

Rubens' madder

saffron

Spanish ocher

sunset orange

tan

tangerine

Tangier ocher

terra cotta

titian or Titian

yellow carmine

yellow-orange

zinc orange

Paint Types

acrylic paint	gouache	mildew-resistant paint	stain
alkyd paint	greasepaint	non-toxic paint	synthetic paint
Chinese lacquer	house paint	oil-base paint	undercoat
color wash	japan	oil paint or oils	varnish
distemper	lacquer	poster paint	washable paint
emulsion paint	latex paint	primer	water-base paint
enamel	lead-base paint	rubber-base paint	watercolor paint
finger paint flat paint	luminous paint	rustproof paint	waterproofing paint
gilt or gilding	masonry paint	shellac	whitewash
glaze	matt paint	sizing	
glossy paint	metal paint		

PAINTER TYPES

colorist

finger painter

genre painter

historical painter

landscapist

luminist

marine painter

miniaturist

monochromist

mural painter

oil painter

pavement artist

polychromist

portrait painter

scenographer

still-life painter

watercolorist

PAINTING METHODS AND TECHNIQUES

abstract

acetate color

acrylic painting

action painting

advancing color

aerial perspective

alla prima

appliqué

aquarelle

aquatint

brushwork

cartoon

cerography

chalk

charcoal

chiaroscuro

chih-hua

chinoiserie

chromolithography

collage

coloration

color-field painting

contrast

craquelure

crayon

crosshatching

decoupage

emulsion

enamel

encaustic

figurative

finger paint

foreshortening

fresco

fugitive color

genre painting

gesso

gilding

glazing

gouache

graphic art

grisaille

grotesque

highlight

iconography

illumination

impasto

imprimatura

japan

lacquer

landscape painting

linear perspective

long paint

madder

malerisch

mandala

miniature painting

monochromy

mural painting

nude painting

oil painting

opalesce

panorama painting

pastel

pastiche

pentimento

perspective

polychromy

portrait painting

poster paint

proportion

religious painting

restoration

rock painting

sand painting

saturation

scumbling

seascape painting

secco

sfumato

sgraffito

shellac

short paint

sign painting

sizing

spray painting

still life painting

sumi-e

tempera

tenebrism

texture

touch-up painting

tracing

trompe l'oeil

underpainting

wall painting

wash

water-base paint

watercolor

wax painting

Yamato-e

PAINTING SCHOOLS AND STYLES

abstract art

abstract expressionism

academic art

action painting

aestheticism

altarpiece

analytical cubism

anastasis

antiart

archaism

art brut

art deco

art nouveau

Ashcan school

avant-garde

Barbizon School

baroque

Bauhaus

Blaue Reiter

body painting

Brucke

Byzantine

cabinet picture

calathus

capriccio

cave art

ceiling painting

cherub

cityscape

classical

cloissonism

colorfield

computer painting

conceptual art

concrete art

constructivism

contrapposto

cubism

Dada

de Stijl

decadent art

deiesis

diablerie

diptych

distressed art

divisionism

dreamscape

drip painting

earthwork

easel painting

ecce homo

expressionism

ex-voto

fantastic realism

Fauvism

fin de siècle

folk art

Fontainebleau School

funk art

fusuma

futurism

genre

Gothic

Grand Manner

grotesque

hard-edge

Hellenic hieratic

historical painting

Hudson River School

hyperrealism

icon

illuminated manuscript

Impressionism

international style

intisme

Italianate

Jugendstil

kakemono

kalathos

Kamakura

kinetic art

kwacho

landscape

life drawing

light art

lyrical abstraction

maesta

makemono

mandala

Mannerism

marz

memento mori

metaphysical painting

Ming

miniature

minimal art

modernism

Mogul school

mosaic

mural

Nabis

namban

naturalism

nature morte

neoclassicism

neo-expressionism

neo-impressionism

neoplasticism

neue wilde

new objectivity

new secession

new wave

New York school

nocturne

nonobjective

nouveau realisme

nude

op art

Orphism

panel painting

pantocrator

pastoral

performance art

photorealism

pittura metafisica

plein-air

pointillism

polyptych

pop art

portrait

Post-Impressionism

postmodernism

postpainterly abstraction

pre-Columbian

prehistoric

pre-Raphaelite

primitivism

proletarian art

psalter

putto

Quattrocento

realism

Renaissance

representational

rococo

Romanticism

rotulus

seascape

seicento

self-portrait

silhouette

social realism

stick figure

still life

sumi-e

suprematism

surrealism

Symbolism

synchromism

synthetic cubism

synthetism

tachism

T'ang

tanka

Tantra art

tenebrism

tondo

triptych

triskelion

uchiwa-ye

ukiyo-e

vanitas

verism

video art

vignette

vorticism

wall painting

wen-jen-hua

Yamato-e

Palette for Oil Painting

Arylamide yellow 10G

Arylamide yellow GX

Arylide yellow RN

Azo condensation red

Azo condensation yellow 128

Burnt sienna

Burnt umber

Cadmium red

Cadmium yellow

Cerulean blue

Cobalt blue

Cobalt green

Cremnitz white

Diarylide yellow

Dioxazine violet

Flake white

Indanthrone blue

Indian red

Isoindolinone yellow

Ivory black

Lamp black

Lemon yellow

Light red

Mars brown

Mars violet

Mars yellow

Naphthol red

Naples yellow

Nickel titanate yellow

Oxide of chromium

Permanent red FGR

Phthalocyanine blue

Phthalocyanine green

Quinacridone or Permanent rose

Raw sienna

Raw umber

Terre verte

Titanium white

Transparent gold ocher

Ultramarine blue or French ultramarine

Venetian red

Viridian

Yellow ocher

Zinc white

Paneling and Lumber

beaverboard

buttonboard

ceiling tile

Celotex

chipboard

Coltwood

Compoboard

composite board

compreg

corkboard

diffuser

drywall

fiberboard

firred plywood

Formica

gyp board

gypsum board

hardboard

homosote

impreg

insulation board

laminate

laminated board

Masonite

panelboard

paperboard

particle board

pasteboard

pegboard

perfboard

pinboard

plasterboard

plastic laminated wood

plastic plywood

plyboard

plywood

Pregboard

Pregwood

Pressboard

pressed hardboard

Scagliola

Sheetrock

Upson board

wallboard

weatherboard

Weldwood

PAPER TYPES

albumen paper

album paper

art paper

baryta paper

block paper

blotting paper

blueprint paper

body paper

bond paper

book paper

butcher paper

butter paper

cameo paper

carbon paper

cardboard

cartridge paper

catalog paper

chalky paper

check paper

cigarette paper

computer paper

construction paper

copying paper

corrugated paper

crepe paper

double paper

drawing paper

fiberboard

filter paper

foolscap

glossy paper

graph paper

India paper

laminated paper

linen paper

litmus paper

manila paper

music paper

newsprint

notepaper

oilpaper

onionskin

paper towel

posterboard

rag paper

rice paper

rolling paper

score paper

stationery

tissue paper

toilet paper

tracing paper

typing paper

wallpaper

watermarked paper

wax paper

wove paper

wrapping paper

writing paper

PARASITE TYPES

animal parasite

bacterium

ectoparasite

endoparasite

facultative parasite

fluke

hookworm

intracellular parasite

leech	parasitic plant	roundworm	virus
louse	pinworm	tapeworm	
obligatory parasite	plant parasite	temporary parasite	
parasitic insect	protozoa	useful parasite	

PARLIAMENT COUNTRIES

The Parliament countries are those countries whose system of government is based on a democratic system modeled after that of the United Kingdom.

Austria	Germany	Ireland	Norway
Bulgaria	Great Britain	Israel	Spain
Denmark	Greenland	Japan	Sweden
Ethiopia	Iceland	Mongolia	Switzerland
Finland	India	Nepal	
France	Iran	Netherlands	

PARTICLES, SUBATOMIC AND FUNDAMENTAL

Subatomic and fundamental particles refer to those particles that are smaller than an atom.

alpha particle	antineutron	B meson or B particle	cascade particle
antibaryon	antiparticle	b or bottom quark	D meson or D particle
antielectron	antiproton	baryon	deuteron
antilepton	antiquark	beta particle	electron
antimeson	axion	boson	energy particle
antineutrino			

eta meson

fermion

flavor

gauge boson

gluino

gravitino

graviton

hadron

Higgs boson or Higgs particle

hyperon

intermediate-vector boson

J/psi or J or psi particle

kaon or K meson or K particle or kappa-meson

lambda particle or lambda

lepton

magnetic monopole

matter particle

meson or mesotron

muon or mu-meson

neuclean

neutrino

neutron

omega or omega-zero or omega nought particle

pentaquark

phi-meson

photino

photon

pion or pi-meson

positron or positive electron

proton

quark

quark color

quark flavor

quarkonium

rho particle

s or strange quark

sigma particle or sigma

slepton

squark

strange particle

subnuclear particle

superstring

t or top quark

tachyon

tardyon

tau meson

tau neutrino or tauonic neutrino

tau or tauon or tau lepton

technifermion

triton

u or up quark

upsilon

virtual particle

W particle

weakon

WIMP or weakly interactive massive particle

xi-particle

Z particle

zino

Z-zero particle

PARTIES

aloha party

at-home

baby shower

bachelor dinner

bachelor party

ball

banquet

birthday party

block party

bottle party

candy pull

Christmas party

cocktail party

coffee klatsch

dinner party

donation party

fête champêtre

garden party

graduation party

Halloween party

hen party

hoedown

holiday party

house party

housewarming

ladies' night out or men's night out

lawn party

433

masked ball	pajama party	smoker	tea party
masquerade party	rave	social	thé dansante
mixer	shindig	soiree	wedding reception
New Year's party	shower	stag party	wedding shower
open house	slumber party	surprise party	wingding

PASSOVER MEAL OR SEDER

affikomen	egg	lamb shank bone	salt water
betza	gefilte fish	maror	wine
bitter herbs	haroseth karpas	matzo	zeroah
chicken soup	kishke	parsley	

PASTA SHAPES AND TYPES

agnellotti	chifferoni	farfalline	knodel
amori	chitarra	fettucce	kreplach
angel hair	chow mein noodles	fettuccine	lasagne
annellini	conchiglie	fettucelle	lasagnette
bavette	conchigliette	fidelini	linguine
bigoli	cravattine	filini	lo mein noodles
bucatini	ditali	fusilli	lumache
campanelle	ditalini	fusilli col bucco	macaroni
cannelloni	ditaloni	gelatin noodles	maccheroncini
capelli	dumpling	genovesini	mafalde
capellini	egg noodles	glass noodles	manicotti
cappelletti	eliche	gnocchi	maruzze
casareccia	farfalle	gramigna	mezza

mezzani

mostaccioli

nidi

noodles

orecchiette

orzo

paglia e fieno

pappardelle

pasta

penne

penne rigate

pipe

pipette

quentelle

radiatore

ravioli

rice

rigatoni

risoni

rotelle

rotini

ruoti

sedani

sedanini

soba

spaetzle

spaghetti

spaghettini

spaghettone

stelline

tagliatelle

tagliolini

taglioni

tempesta

tortelli

tortellini

tortelloni

tortiglioni

trenette

tuffoli

tuffoloni

vermicelli

vermicellini

won ton

ziti

PASTRY TYPES

baked pastry

cake

choux paste

croissant

cruller

crumpet

Danish pastry

éclair

fine-layered pastry

hot-water crust pastry

layered flaky pastry

phyllo pastry

pie

puff pastry

scone

shortcrust pastry

strudel

suet pastry

sweet roll

tart

turnover

PATTERNS, TYPES OF

argyle

cable-stitch

check

clock

criss-cross

dogtooth

herringbone

honeycomb

houndstooth

latticed

marbled

microcheck

millefleurs

mosaic

mottled

ombre

paisley   print   tartan   willow

plaid   quilted   tattersall

polka dot   striped   waffle

PEACH VARIETIES

Autumn Red peach

Cardinal and Earlired peach

Charles-Roux peach

Dixired peach

Elberta peach

Flameprince peach

Flavorcrest peach

Greensboro peach

Heath peach

Late Crawford peach

Loring peach

Lovell peach

Melocotoon peach

Merrill Gemfree peach

Michelini peach

Mountain Rose peach

Muir peach

nectarine

Pavie peach

Phillips peach

Red Haven peach

Redwing peach

Ribet peach

Robin peach

Springtime peach

Suncrest peach

Susquehanna peach

Triumph peach

white peach

yellow peach

PEAR VARIETIES

Anjou pear

Bartlett pear

beurre Hardy

Bosc pear

Chinese pear

choke pear

Clapp Favorite pear

Comice pear

conference pear

cooking pear

dessert pear

Docteur Jules Guyot

doyenne du Comice

General Leclerc

Japanese sand pear

Kieffer pear

Le Conte pear

Louise Bonne of Jersey

native pear

passe Crassane

sand pear

Seckel pear

Sheldon pear

snow pear

sugar pear

Wilder Early pear

Williams' Bon Chretien

winter nellis pear

winter pear

436

PELLETS

BB shot

bead

bird shot

buckshot

bullet

globule

grapeshot

hailstone

ink pellet

lozenge

marble

musket ball

pea

pearl

pearl tapioca

pebble

pill

shot

snow pellet

styrofoam pellet

tablet

PENCILS

bowling pencil

carbon pencil

carpenter's pencil

charcoal pencil

china marker

colored pencil

compass pencil

drafting pencil

drawing pencil

educational pencil

erasable pencil

foil pencil

golf pencil

graphite pencil

grease pencil

hard pencil

hexagon pencil

indelible pencil

jumbo pencil

layout pencil

lead pencil

litho pencil

mechanical pencil

oil-based pencil

pastel pencil

personalized pencil

sketching pencil

slate pencil

soft pencil

stylographic pencil

transfer pencil

underglaze pencil

watercolor pencil

water-soluble pencil

wax-based pencil

woodless drawing pencil

writing pencil

Philosophical Doctrines, Movements, Schools, and Theories

absurdism

Academicism

aestheticism

agnosticism

Alexandrian

altruism

animism

Aristotelianism

atheism

Atomism

Augustinianism

Averroism

axiology

Baconism

behaviorism

Benthamism

Bergsonism

Berkeleianism

Bonaventurism

Bradleianism

Brahmanism

Buddhism

Cartesianism

Catholicism

centrism

commonsense realism

communism

Comtism

Confucianism

consequentialism

contextualism

cosmotheism

creationism

criticism or critical philosophy

Cynicism

Cyrenaicism

deconstructionism

deism

deontology

determinism

dialectical materialism

dogmatism

Donatism

dualism

dynamism

eclecticism

egoism

egoistic hedonism

Eleaticism

empiricism

Epicureanism

epiphenomenalism

Eretrian school

eristic school

essentialism

ethicism

ethics

eudemonism

existentialism

Fabianism

fatalism

Fichteanism

functionalism

Gnosticism

hedonism

Hegelianism

Heideggerianism

Heracliteanism

Herbartianism

Hinduism

Hobbism

holism

humanism

Humism

hylomorphism

hylotheism

hylozoism

idealism

immaterialism

individualism

instrumentalism

intuitionism

Ionian school

Jainism

Judaism

Kantianism

Leibnizianism

linguistic and analytic philosophy

logical empiricism

Manichaeanism

Marxism

materialism

mechanism

Megarianism

mentalism

Mimamsa

Mithraism

Modernism

monasticism

monism

mysticism

naturalism

neocriticism

Neo-Hegelianism

Neoplatonism

Neo-Pythagoreanism

Neo-Scholasticism

new ethical
movement

nihilism

nominalism

noumenalism

Nyaya

objectivism

occasionalism

ontologism

ontology

optimism

ordinary language
philosophy

organicism

organic mechanism

pacifism

panlogism

panpneumatism

panpsychism

pantheism

panthelism

Parmenidean school

patristic philosophy

patristicism

Peripateticism

pessimism

phenomenalism

phenomenology

philosophy of
organism

philosophy of signs

philosophy of the
ante-Nicene Fathers

philosophy of the
post-Nicene Fathers

physicalism

physicism

Platonism

pluralism

positivism

pragmatism

probabilism

Protestantism

psychism

psychological
hedonism

Puritanism

Purva Mimamsa

Pyrrhonism

Pythagoreanism

rationalism

realism

relativism

Sankhya

Sartrianism

Satyagraha

Schellingism

Scholasticism

Schopenhauerism

Scotism

secular humanism

semiotics

sensationalism

sensism

Shintoism

Sikhism

skepticism

socialism

Socratic philosophy

solipsism

Sophistry

Spencerianism

Spinozism

Stoicism

substantialism

syncretism

Taoism

theism

Thomism

transcendentalism

universalistic
hedonism

utilitarianism

Uttara Mimamsa

Valsheshika

veganism

vitalism

voluntarism

yoga

zetetic philosophy

PHILOSOPHIES, EASTERN

Eastern philosophy refers very broadly to the various philosophies of India, Iran, China, Japan, and to an extent, the Middle East.

Buddhism	Jainism	Sikhism	Zen Buddhism
Confucianism	Maoism	Sufism	
Hinduism	Shinto	Taoism	

PHILOSOPHIES, WESTERN

Western philosophy is a line of philosophical thinking, beginning in ancient Greece, that continues to this day. Western philosophy has had a tremendous influence on, and has been greatly influenced by, Western religion, science, and politics.

aestheticism	existentialism	materialism	pragmatism
analytic philosophy	formal logic	metaethics	Pythagoreanism
animalism	Hegelianism	metaphysics	rationalism
Aristotelianism	Heideggerianism	monotheism	Scholasticism
Augustinianism	Heracliteanism	moral philosophy	semiotics
Cartesianism	humanism	mysticism	Socratism
collectivism	idealism	naturalism	Sophism
conceptualism	Kantianism	Neoplatonism	Spinozism
cosmology	Leibnizianism	New Age	stoicism
deism	liberalism	ontology	Stoicism
dialectics	linguistic philosophy	Peripateticism	teleology
Epicureanism	local empiricism	pessimism	theism
epistemology	logic	phenomenology	transcendentalism
Eretrian school	Machiavellianism	Platonism	utilitarianism
ethics	Marxism	positivism	vitalism

PHILOSOPHY BRANCHES

aesthetics

analytic philosophy

axiology

casuistry

commonsense

cosmology

deontology

epistemology

ethics

logic

metaphysics

ontology

phenomenology

philosophy of biology

philosophy of education

philosophy of history

philosophy of law

philosophy of logic

philosophy of nature

philosophy of physics

philosophy of religion

philosophy of science

political philosophy

semantics

semiotics

sentential calculus

teleology

theology

PHONETIC ALPHABET

Alpha

Bravo

Charlie

Delta

Echo

Foxtrot

Golf

Hotel

India

Juliet

Kilo

Lima

Mike

November

Oscar

Papa

Quebec

Romeo

Sierra

Tango

Uniform

Victor

Whiskey

X-ray

Yankee

Zulu

PHOTOGRAPHS

acetate photograph

aerial photograph

air-brushed photograph

baby photograph

black-and-white photograph

blow-up photograph

candid photograph

color photograph

composite photograph

daguerrotype

digital photograph

double exposure photograph

dye-transfer photograph

enlargement

fabric finish photograph

fish-eye photograph

glass negative photograph

glossy

headshot

holograph

infrared photograph

macrophotograph

microfilm

micrograph

microphotograph

microscopic photograph

miniature photograph

model photograph

monochrome photograph

motion picture photograph

mug shot

mural photograph

negative photograph

news photograph

panoramic photograph

passport photograph

photocopy

photomicrograph

photomural

photostatic

pinpoint photograph

Polaroid

portrait photograph

radiophotograph

retouched photograph

rotograph

school class photograph

senior photograph

sepia photograph

slide projection photograph

snapshot

stereoscopic photograph

stroboscopic photograph

telephotograph

time-exposure photograph

time-lapse photograph

tintype

transparency

vertical photograph

wedding photograph

wirephoto

X-ray

PHOTOGRAPHY TYPES

acoustical holography

aerial photography
animation photography

architectural photography

astrophotography

available-light photography

candid photography

chronophotography

cinematography or motion-picture photography

cinephotomicro-graphy

color photography

digital photography

documentary photography

electrophotography

fashion photography

flash photography

glamour photography

heliophotography

holography

infrared photography

integral photography

kite aerial photography

landscape photography

laser photography

macrophotography

microfilming

microphotography

miniature photography

panoramic photography

phonophotography

photoheliography

photojournalism

photomacrography

photomicrography

photoreproduction

phototopography

portraiture

pyrophotography

radiation-field
photography or
Kirlian photography

radiography

reprography

rollout photography

schlieren
photography

skiagraphy

spark photography

spectroheliography

spectrophotography

sports photography

stereophotography

still-life photography

stroboscopic
photography

studio photography

subminiature
photography

telephotography

thermography

three-color
photography

time-lapse
photography

underwater
photography

uranophotography

wildlife photography

xerography

X-ray photography

PHYSICAL SCIENCES

acoustical
engineering or
acoustics

aerodynamics

aerostatics

applied geoscience

applied physics

architectural
engineering

astronomy

astrophysics

atomic physics

biophysics

chemical physics

chemistry

civil engineering

coal technology

condensed-matter
physics

cosmic physics

cryogenics

dynamics

earth sciences

economic geology

electromagnetism

electronic
engineering

electronics or solid
state physics

engineering geology

environmental
geology

geochemistry

geodesy

geodynamics

geognosy

geology

geomagnetology

geomorphology

geophysics

geoscience

glaciology

health physics

high-temperature
research

historical geology

hydrodynamics

hydrogeology

hydrology

hydrostatics

isostasy

kinematics

mechanics

metallurgical
engineering

meteorology

mineralogy

mining geology

molecular physics

nuclear physics

oceanography

optics

paleontology

particle physics

pedology

petrography

petroleum geology

petrology

physics

public health engineering

quantum mechanics

research Physics

seismology

statics

statistical mechanics

stratigraphy

structural geology

thermal physics

thermodynamics

tribology

ultrasonics

volcanology

PHYSICS BRANCHES

acoustics

aerodynamics

aerophysics

applied physics

astrophysics

atomic physics

basic conductor physics

biophysics

chaos theory

chemical physics

classical physics

computational physics

condensed-matter physics

cryogenics

crystallography

cytophysics

dynamics

electricity

electrodynamics

electrokinetics

electromagnetism

electronics

electron optics

electrophysics

electrostatics

experimental physics

fluid dynamics

fluid mechanics

geometric optics

geophysics

health physics

high-energy physics

hydrostatics

hygrology

hyperphysics

hypophysics

iatrophysics

kinematics

macrophysics

magnetism

magnetohydrody-namics

magnetostatics

materials physics

mathematical physics

mechanics

medical physics

medicophysics

microphysics

modern physics

molecular physics

morphophysics

myophysics

naive physics

Newtonian physics

nuclear physics

optics

organismic physics

particle physics

photoelectricity

photonics

physical chemistry

physical optics

physicomathematics

plasma physics

psychophysics

quantum physics

radiation physics

radionics

solar physics

solid-state physics

statics

statistical physics

stereophysics

theoretical physics

thermionics

thermodynamics

tribophysics

X-ray crystallography

zoophysics

PICKLES AND RELISHES

aspic

beet relish

brandied fruit

bread-and-butter pickle

caponata

chili sauce

chow-chow

chutney

conserve

corn relish

cranberry relish

dill pickle

fruit relish

gherkin

hamburger relish

horseradish relish

hot dog relish

Indian relish

jam

jelly

ketchup or catsup

kosher pickle

marmalade

mustard pickle

pepper relish

picalilli

pickle relish

pickled onion

pickled vegetable

preserves

salsa

spiced apples

sweet and sour puree

sweet pickle

tomato pickle

vegetable relish

watermelon pickle

PIES

apple pie

banana cream pie

banoffi pie

blackberry pie

blueberry pie

Boston cream pie

butterscotch pie

cherry pie

chicken pot pie

chiffon pie

chocolate cream pie

cream pie

custard pie

deep-dish pie

fish pie

fruit pie

game pie

huckleberry pie

Key lime pie

lattice-top pie

lemon meringue pie

meat pie

mince pie

Mississippi mud pie

open-faced pie

pecan pie

peach pie

pot pie

prune pie

pudding pie

pumpkin pie

raspberry pie

rhubarb pie

shepherd's pie

shoofly pie

sour cream raisin pie

squash pie

steak and kidney pie

strawberry pie

strawberry rhubarb pie

vegetable pie

Pines, Firs, Conifers, and Evergreens

alpine fir

arbor vitae

bald cypress

balsam fir

big-cone pine

black pine

black spruce

bristlecone pine

broad-leaved evergreen

Canadian balsam

cedar

Chinese evergreen

Christmas tree

cypress

Douglas fir

Eastern hemlock

Eastern white pine

fir

Frankincense pine

giant fir

hard pine

hemlock

hickory pine

jack pine

juniper

knobcone pine

larch

loblolly pine

lodgepole pine

mountain pine

myrtle

needle-leaved evergreen

Northern white cedar

Norway spruce

Oregon fir

pine

pinon pine

pitch pine

red pine or red fir

red spruce

redwood

Scotch pine

sequoia

short-leaf pine

silver fir

silver pine

soft pine

southern pine

spruce

spruce pine

stone pine

sugar pine

tamarack

true pine

white fir

white pine

white spruce

yellow pine or yellow fir

yew

Pink Color Varieties

amaranth pink

annatto

begonia

blush

burnt rose

cameo pink

carnation

casino pink

chrome primrose

coral pink

deep pink

fiesta

flamingo

flesh pink

geranium pink

hot pink

incarnadine

livid pink

mallow pink

neon pink

nymph

ombre

opera pink

orange-pink

orchid pink

orchid rose

pale pink

peachblossom pink

peach red

petal pink

primrose

purplish pink

red-pink

rose

rose pink

rose quartz

royal pink

salmon

scarlet madder

shell pink

shocking pink

tea rose

watermelon

PIZZA TOPPINGS

anchovy

asparagus

bacon

barbecue

basil

black olive

broccoli

Buffalo chicken

Canadian bacon

cheese

chicken

clam

dried tomato

eggplant

European bacon

feta cheese

four-cheese

garlic

Gorgonzola cheese

green pepper

ham

hamburger

Hawaiian or ham and pineapple

jalapeno

meatball

mozzarella cheese

mushroom

onion

Parmesan cheese

pastrami

pepperoncini

pepperoni

pineapple

plum tomato

prosciutto

provolone cheese

ricotta cheese

Romano cheese

salad

salami

sausage

shrimp

spinach

taco

Thai chicken

thyme

vegetable white

PLANETS, INNER

The inner planets are the four planets found closest to the sun.

Earth (with Moon)

Mars (with Deimos, Phobos)

Mercury

Venus

PLANETS, MINOR

These are minor bodies in the solar system that orbit the sun. They are larger than meteoroids but smaller than the major planets.

Achilles	Aten	Euphrosyne	Icarus
Adonis	Ceres	Hebe	Iris
Amor	Chiron	Hermes	Juno
Apollo	Eros	Hidalgo	Pallas
Astraea	Eunomia	Hygeia	Vesta

PLANETS, OUTER

The outer planets are the five planets found farthest from the sun.

Jupiter	Pluto	Uranus
Neptune	Saturn	

PLANT DIVISIONS

club mosses or Lycopodophyta or Lycophyta

conifers or Coniferophyta

cycads or Cycadophyta

ferns or Pteridophyta or Filicophyta

flowering plants or angiosperms or Angiospermophyta or Magnoliophyta

ginkgos or Ginkgophyta

gnetophytes or Gnetophyta

gymnosperms or Gymnospermophyta

horsetails or Sphenophyta

mosses and liverworts or Bryophyta

whisk ferns or Psilophyta

PLANTS DANGEROUS TO CHILDREN

aconite or monkshood

azalea

belladonna

bird of paradise

bittersweet

black locust

bleeding heart

Boston fern

boxwood

burning bush

buttercup

caladium

castor bean

chinaberry

chrysanthemum

columbine

crocus

cyclamen

daffodil

daphne

death camas

delphinium

dieffenbachia

elderberry

elephant ear

English ivy

English Jew

four o'clock

foxglove

geranium

holly

horse chestnut

hyacinth

hydrangea

iris

jack-in-the-pulpit

jequirity bean or rosary pea

Jerusalem cherry

jimson weed

jonquil

lantana

larkspur

lily of the valley

marigold

mistletoe

mock orange

morning glory

mother-in-law

mountain laurel

mushrooms and toadstools

narcissus

nightshade

oak

oleander

philodendron

pinks

poinsettia

poison hemlock

poison ivy

poison oak

potato sprouts and eyes

rhododendron

rhubarb leaves

rosary pea (jequirity bean)

Scotch broom

skunk cabbage

spider lily

sumac

sweet pea

water hemlock

yew

PLASTICS

acetate

acetate nitrate

acrylic

albolite

alkyd

amino plastic

Bakelite

casein plastic

449

cellophane

celluloid

cellulose acetate

cellulose ether

cellulose nitrate

cellulosic

coumarone-indene

epoxy

expanded plastic

fluorocarbon plastic

foamed plastic

Formica

furane

laminate

lignin

Lucite

melamine

multiresin

Mylar

neoprene

nitrate

nylon

phenolic

phenolic plastic

plastic cement

Plexiglas

polyester

polyethylene

polymeric amide

polypropylene

polystyrene

polyurethane

polyvinyl chloride

polyvinyl-formaldehyde

resinoid

rubber

silicone resin

Styrofoam™

Teflon™

terpene

tetrafluoroethylene

thermoplastic

thermosetting plastic

urea

urea formaldehyde

vinyl

Vinylite

PLAYS AND DRAMAS, TYPES OF

antimasque

bedroom farce

burlesque

closet play

comedy

commedia dell'arte

docudrama

duologue

fabula

farce

Grand Guignol

Greek drama

harlequinade

history

improvisation

kabuki

kitchen-sink drama

masque

melodrama

mime

miracle play

monodrama

monologue

morality play

mystery play

Noh

pantomime

sociodrama

teleplay

tragedy

tragicomedy

two-hander

PLEATS

Pleats refer to a design style where a pattern of creases is applied to a fabric. Several pleat designs are listed here.

accordion pleat

bellows pleat

box pleat

cartridge pleat

crystal pleat

French pleat

inverted pleat

kick pleat

kilt pleat

knife pleat

pinch pleat

sunburst pleat

sunray pleat

umbrella pleat

Watteau pleat

PLOW VARIETIES

buggy plow

chisel plow or ripper

cultivating plow

disk plow

ditching plow

double-moldboard plow

drill plow

electric plow

grading plow

hand plow

harrow plow

ice plow

leveling plow

moldboard plow

pulverizing plow

ridging plow

rotary plow

snow plow

subsoil plow

tractor-drawn plow

trench

turning plow

two-way plow

walking plow

wheel plow

PLUM VARIETIES

Allegheny plum

American red plum

August plum

beach plum

Bonne de Bry plum

Brignole plum

brown plum

Canada plum

cherry plum

common plum

Czar plum

damask plum

Damson plum

date plum

dried plum

goose plum

green plum

greengage plum

ground plum

hog plum

Japanese plum

Kirke Blue plum

marmalade plum

myrobalan plum

Pacific plum

Pershore plum

purple plum

red plum

Sierra plum

Victoria plum

violet plum

wild plum

yellow plum

Plumbing Fittings

45-degree elbow

cap

elbow

flush bushing

hexagon bushing

nipple

offset

pipe coupling

reducing coupling

square-head plug

tee

threaded cap

trap

U-bend

Y-branch

Pockets

bellows pocket

breast pocket

broad-welt side pocket

cargo pocket

envelope pocket

flap pocket

gusset pocket

half pocket

hand-warmer pouch

hip pocket

inset pocket

patch pocket

pouch pocket

seam pocket

slash pocket

slide-fastener pocket

slit pocket

stand pocket

vest pocket

watch pocket

welt pocket

Poem or Verse Forms and Types

alba

aubade

ballad

ballade

bucolic or pastoral

cento or pastiche

chanson

choric ode

cinquain

clerihew

complaint

conversation poem

dirge

dithyramb

ditty

double dactyl

dramatic monologue

dramatic poem

eclogue

elegiac poem

elegy

encomium

epic poem

epigram

epithalamion

epode

epyllion

free verse

georgic

haiku

hymn

idyll

jingle

lay

limerick

lyric poem

macaronic

madrigal

monody

narrative poem

nursery rhyme

ode

palinode

prothalamion

psalm

quatorzain

renga

reverdie

rondeau

rondel

roundelay

saga

sapphics

satire

sestina

song

sonnet

sonnet sequence

tanka

threnody

triolet

troubadour poem

verse epistle

villanelle

virelay

POINTS OF SAILING

beam reach

broad reach

close hauled

close reach

dead run

downwind

full and by

headwind

on the wind

trailing run

wind abeam

POISONOUS GASES
AND SUBSTANCES

aconitine

afterdamp

Agent Orange

aldrin

alkaloid

allyl alcohol

ammonia

antifreeze

antimony

arsenic

arsine

atropine

beryllium

bleach

blister gas

bromine

cacodylic acid

cadmium

carbolic acid

carbon disulphide

carbon monoxide

carbon tetrachloride

chlordane

chlorine

coniine

cuastic soda

curare

cyanic acid

cyanide

cyanide gas

cyanogen

DDD

DDT

diazomethane

diborane

dichloroethyl sulfide

453

digitalin

digoxin

dioxane

endrin

ethylene oxide

fluorine

formaldehyde

hydrocyanic acid

hydrocyanide

hydrogen cyanide

hydrogen fluoride

hydrogen sulfide

hyoscyamine

iodine

lead

lead arsenate

lead tetraethyl

lewisite

lindane

Malathion

mephitis

mercuric chloride

mercury

methanol or wood
spirit methyl alcohol

methyl bromide

miasma

muscarine

mustard gas

nerve agent

nerve gas

nicotine

nitric acid

nitric oxide

nitrogen dioxide

osmium tetroxide

ouabain

oxalic acid

paraquat

parathion

Paris green

perchloric acid

perchloroethylene

phenol

phosgene

poison gas

potassium cyanide

prussic acid

pyrethrum

quinine

radiation

rat poison

ricin

rotenone

santonin

sarin

selenium

solanine

strophanthin

strychnine

sulfur dioxide

sulfur mustard

tartar emetic

tetraethyl lead

tetrodotoxin

toxin

turpentine

venom

veratrine

warfarin

white spirit

zinc chromate

POISONOUS MUSHROOMS

amanita

big laughing
mushroom

deadly galerina

death cap or death
cup or destroying
angel or death
angelemetic
mushroom

false morel

fly agaric

fly fungus

gyromitra

jack-o-lantern

lawn funnel cap

magic mushroom

Satan's mushroom

yellow stainer

POISONOUS PLANTS

aconite
angel's trumpet
baneberry
banewort
bearded darnel
belladonna
bittersweet
black henbane
black nightshade
bleeding heart
castor-oil plant
chinaberry
climbing lily
copperweed
corn cockle
cowbane
darling pea
datura
deadly nightshade

death camas
deathin
devil's trumpet
elderberry
ergot
fiddleneck
fool's parsley
foxglove
gastrolobium
hairy vetch
hellebore
hemlock
henbane
herb Christopher
horsetail
jack-in-the-pulpit
jimsonweed
killer plant
laburnum

larkspur
lobster plant
locoweed
marijuana
mayapple
mescal bean
modecca flower
monkshood
nightshade
nux vomica
opium poppy
poinsettia
poison bean
poisonberry
poison bush
poison hemlock
poison ivy
poison oak
poison rye grass

poison sumac
poison tobacco
poison vetch
poisonweed
pokeweed
rauwolfia
rose bay
sheep laurel
thornapple
toadstool
tobacco
upas
water fennel
water hemlock
white snakeroot
wild tobacco
wisteria
wolfsbane

POISONOUS PLANTS FOR PETS

aconite
amaryllis
azalea
black locust

black walnut
bleeding heart
Boston fern
buckeye

bulbs
buttercup
catnip
cherries

Christmas rose
chrysanthemum
daffodil
dieffenbachia

Easter lily	Jerusalem cherry	moonseed	rhododendron
elderberry	jimson weed	morning glory	rhubarb
English ivy	larkspur	mushrooms	rosary pea
fescue	laurel	mustards	St. John's wort
foxglove	lily of the valley	narcissus	star of Bethlehem
geranium	lupine	nightshades	sweet clover
holly	marigold	oak	sweet pea
honeysuckle	marijuana	oleander	tobacco
horse chestnut	mayapple	philodendron	water hemlock
hyacinth	milkweed	poinsettia	wisteria
iris	mistletoe	poison hemlock	yew
jack-in-the-pulpit	monkshood	red maple	

POKER HANDS

flush	high card	straight	two pair
four of a kind	one pair	straight flush	
full house	royal flush	three of a kind	

POLITICAL PHILOSOPHIES AND SYSTEMS

absolutism	collectivism	evolutionary socialism	Fourierism
anarchism	communism	extremism	guild socialism
anarcho-syndicalism	conservatism	Fabianism	imperialism
authoritarianism	democracy	fascism	individualism
Bolshevism	egalitarianism	federalism	laissez-faire
capitalism	environmentalism		leftism

Leninism

liberalism

libertarianism

Maoism

Marxism

meritocracy

monarchism

nationalism

national socialism

Nazism

Neofascism

neo-Marxism

patriotism

pluralism

plutocracy

populism

radicalism

republicanism

rightism

situationism

social democracy

socialism

Stalinism

state capitalism

state socialism

statism

syndicalism

technocracy

theocracy

timocracy

totalitarianism

utilitarianism

utopianism

utopian socialism

POLLINATION TYPES

bird pollination

cross-pollination

insect pollination

mammal pollination

self-pollination

water pollination

wind pollination

POLYMERS

Polymers are composed of very large molecules that are multiples of simpler chemical units called monomers. Polymers make up many of the materials in living organisms, including, for example, proteins.

acrylic

addition polymer

atactic polymer

autopolymer

biopolymer

bouncing putty

chain polymer

chloroprene rubber

condensation polymer

copolymer

cross-linked polymer

epoxide resin

hexamer

homopolymer

hydrol

isoprene rubber

isotactic polymer

lactoprene

lignin

macromolecule

monomer

natural polymer

nylon

octamer

paracyanogen

pentamer

plasticizer

Plexiglas

polyacrylate

polybutene

polybutylene

polycarbonate

polyester

polyether

polyethylene

polyisoprene

polymeric amide

polymethyl methacrylate or plexiglass

polypropene

polypropylene

polystyrene

polyterpene

polytetrafluoro-ethene or PTFE

polythene or polyethylene

polyurethane

polyvinyl acetate

polyvinyl chloride or PVC

polyvinylpyrrolidone

resin

sporopollenin

stereoregular polymer

syndiotactic polymer

synthetic polymer

Teflon

terpolymer

thermosetting plastic

vinyl

vulcanite

PORK CUTS

arm shoulder

bacon

back

belly

blade shoulder

boneless chop

Boston butt

chop

clear plate

crown roast

Cumberland

English style

fat back

foot

ham

hock

jowl

knuckle

leg

loin

picnic ham

pigs' feet

riblet

rib roast

roast

side

spare rib

tenderloin

POTATO VARIETIES AND DISHES

au gratin potato

baked potato

Baking potato

blue potato

boiled potato

common potato

duchess potatoes

French-fried potato

German-fried potato

hash browns

home fries

Idaho potato

Irish potato

Julienne potato

long white potato

lyonnaise potato

mashed potato

new potato

O'Brien potato

potato chip

potato pancake

potato salad

potato skin

potato sticks

potato straw nest

red potato

riced potato

russet potato

458

| scalloped potato | soufflé potato | white potato |
| shoestring potato | twice-baked potato | white round potato |

POTS AND PANS

baking pan	Crockpot	pie tin	springform pan
bean pot	double boiler	pipkin	steamer
biggin	Dutch oven	pizza pan	stew pan
boiler	frying pan	poacher	stewpot
brazier	griddle	pressure cooker	stockpot
bread pan	jelly-roll pan	quiche pan	tandoor
broiler	kettle	roaster or roasting pan	tart tin
Bundt pan	loaf pan		teakettle
cake pan	muffin pan	saucepan	teapot
caldron	muffin tin	sauté pan	turn urn
coffeepot	omelet pan	skillet	tube pan
coffee urn	paella pan	slow cooker	wok
cookie sheet	percolator	smoker	
corn popper	pie pan	soufflé dish	

PRAYERS

Adhan	Apostles' Creed	blessings	Dies Irae
afternoon prayer	Ave Maria	canonical hours	Divine Office
Agnus Dei	bedtime prayer	collect	doxology
Alenu	benedicite	compline	du a
Amidah	benison	Confiteor	epiclesis
Angelus	bidding prayer	dawn prayer	evening prayer

Evensong

Fatiha

Gayatri Mantra

Gloria in Excelsis

Gloria Patri

grace

Hail Mary

Hare Krishna Mantra

Hesychasm

Hosanna

intercession

intercessory prayer

Introit

invocation

Japji

Kaddish

Kol Nidre

Kyrie Eleison

litany

Lord's Prayer

Lord's Supper or
Last Supper

Magnificat

matins

meal prayer

Miserere

morning prayer

Mourner's Kaddish

Namaz

Nicene Creed

nighttime prayer or
bedtime prayer

noon prayer

Nunc Dimittis

obsecration

orison

Our Father

Paternoster

petitionary prayer

Prayer for the dead

prayer of quiet

Prayer of Thanks

Prayer of
thanksgiving

prime

Requiescat

rogation

Salat

Sanctus

sext

Shema

Sign of the Cross

special prayer

sunset prayer

Sursum Corda

Te Deum

terce

vespers

Precipitation Types

acid precipitation

acid rain

acid snow

blizzard

downpour

drizzle

fog-drip

freezing drizzle

freezing rain

graupel

hail

ice crystals

ice pellet shower

ice pellets

ice storm

rain

rain shower

sleet

snow

snow flakes

snow flurries

snow pellets

snow shower

snow storm

squall

thunderstorm

Prehistoric Animals

allosaurus

ammonite

anatosaurus

ankylosaurus

apatosaurus

archaeohippus

archaeopteryx

archaeornis

archaeotherium

archelon

archosaur

arsinoitherium

arthrodiran

atlantosaurus

aurochs

baryonyx Walker

basilosaurus

bothriolepis

brachiosaurus

brontops

brontosaurus

brontothere

brontotherium

camarasaurus

cantius trigonodus

ceratopsid

ceratosaurus

cetiosaurus

coccostean

coelacanth

coelodonta

compsognathus

coryphodon

cotylosaur

creodont

crossopterygian

cynodictis

cynodont

deinonychus

denversaurus

diacodexis

diatryma

dimetrodon

dinichthyid

dinosaur

dinothere

diplodocus

dipnoan

diprotodon

dire wolf

dodo

duck-billed dinosaur

edaphosaurid

elasmosaurus

enteledon

eohippus

eryopsid

eurypterid

eurypterus remipes

gallimimus

giant sloth

glyptodont

gorgosaurus

hadrosaurus

hesperornis

hoplophoneus

hyaenodon

hyracodont

hyracothere

icaronycteris

ichthyornis

ichthyosaurus

iguanodon

imperial mammoth
or imperial elephant

indricotherium

kentrosaurus

kuehneotherium

labyrinthodont

machairodont

maiasaurus

mamenchisaurus

mammoth

mammuthus

mastodon

megaloceros

megalosaurus

megathere

megatherium

merodus

merychippus

merycoidodon

merycopotamus

mesohippus

mesosaur

miacis

mosasaurus

mussaurus

nummulite

ornithomimid

ornithopod

ostracoderm

pachycephalosaurus

pakicetus

palaeodictyopteron

palaeomastodon
palaeoniscid
palaeophis
palaeosaur
palaeospondylus
parasaurolophus
pelycosaur
phytosaur
pinchosaurus
plateosaurus
plesiosaurus
pliosaur
polacanthus
proailurus
prokaryote

procoptodon
propalaeotherium
protoceratops
protohippus
protylopus
pteranodon
pteraspid
pterichthys
pterodactyl
pterosaur
purgatorius
quetzalcoatlus northropii
raptor
rhamphorhynchus

saber-toothed tiger
saltasaurus
sauropod
scelidosaurus
seismosaurus
shantungosaurus
smilodon
stegocephalian
stegodon
stegosaurus
struthiomimus
supersaurus
teleoceras
therapsid
theriodont

theropod
thoatherium
thrinaxodon liorhinus
thylacoleo
thylacosmilus
titanosaurus
titanothere
torosaurus
trachodon
triceratops
trilobite
tyrannosaurus rex
uintathere
urus
woolly mammoth

PREHISTORIC MAN AND MANLIKE PRIMATES

angwantibo
anthropoid ape
ape
ape-man
Aurignacian man
Australanthropus
Australopithecine
Australopithecus

Australopithecus afarensis
Australopithecus africanus
Australopithecus boisei
Australopithecus robustus
aye-aye
baboon

Barbary ape
Bengal monkey
bonnet monkey
Bronze Age man
Brünn race
bush baby
capuchin
caveman
chacma

chimpanzee
colobus
Cro-Magnon man
drill
entellus
eolithic man
Florisbad man
Furfooz man or Grenelle man

galago

Galley Hill man

gibbon

Gigantopithecus

gorilla

great ape

Grimaldi man

grivet

guenon

guereza

hanuman

Heidelberg man

hominid

Homo erectus

Homo habilis

Homo rhodesiensis

Homo soloensis

howling monkey

Iron Age man

Java man

Kennewick man

king monkey

langur

lemur

lion-tailed monkey

loris

Lucy

macaque

man

mandrill

marmoset

Meganthropus

monkey

mountain gorilla

Neanderthal man

neolithic man

orangutan or orang

Oreopithecus

Ötzi the iceman

owl monkey

paleolithic man

Paranthropus

patas monkey

Peking man

Pithecanthropus

Plesianthropus

pongid

pottos

proboscis monkey

protohuman

pygmy marmoset

ramapithecine

rhesus

Rhodesian man

saki

siamang

Sinanthropus

sloth monkey

spider monkey

squirrel monkey

Stone Age man

Swanscombe man

tamarin

tarsier

vervet

Zinjanthropus

PREHISTORIC THINGS
ALIVE TODAY

Australian lungfish

bristlecone pine

coelacanth

crocodile

dawn redwood

duckbill platypus

ginkgo

horseshoe crab

lingula

okapi

peripatus

Stephens Island frog

tuatara

turtle

welwitschia

Prepositions

a
a la
abaft
aboard
about
above
according to
across
adown
afore
after
again
against
aloft
along
alongside
amid
amidst
among
amongst
an
anent
apart from
après
apropos
around

as
as of
as per
as regards
as to
as well as
aside
aside from
aslant
astraddle
astride
at
athwart
atop
bar
barring
batting
because
because of
bedside
before
behind
below
ben
beneath
beside

besides
between
betwixt
beyond
but
but for
by
chez
circa
concerning
considering
contra
contrary to
cross
cum
despite
down
due to
during
ere
ex
except
except for
excepting
excluding
exclusive of

failing
following
for
forby
fore
forth
foul of
frae
fro
from
given
hear
in
in between
including
inclusive of
in memoriam
in re
inside
inside of
instead of
into
irrespective of
less
like
malgre

maugre	outside of	round	under
mid	outwith	sans	underneath
midst	over	save	unless
minus	over against	saving	unlike
modulo	over and above	since	until
near	owing to	subsequent to	unto
neath	pace	syne	up
next	past	than	up and down
next to	pending	thanks to	upon
nigh	per	the	upside
notwithstanding	plus	thorough	up to
o'	preparatory to	thro	versus
o'er	previous to	throughout	via
of	prior to	thru	vice
off	pro	thwart	vis-a-vis
off of	pursuant to	till	wanting
on	qua	times	while
onto	rather than	to	with
opposite	re	together with	withal
or	regarding	touching	within
out	regardless of	toward	without
out of	relative to	tween	worth
outside	respecting	twixt	

PRINTING PROCESSES

carbon process	collotype printing	electrotype	foil stamping
cerotype	contact printing	engraving	gravure

ink jet printing
intaglio printing
laser printing
letterpress
Linotype
lithography

lithotype
logotype
monotype
offset printing
photochromography
photoengraving

photogelatin process
photolithography
phototypography
photozincography
planographic printing
process printing

relief printing
rotogravure
thermography
xerography

PROJECTILES AND PROJECTILE WEAPONS

arbalest
arrow
assegai
ball
ballista
bazooka
blowgun
blowpipe
bolas
bolt

boomerang
bow
bullet
catapult
crossbow
dart
flare
flechette
gun
harpoon

harpoon gun
howitzer
javelin
longbow
mortar
mortar shell
peashooter
pellet
rifle
shell

shot
shrapnel
sling
spear
torpedo
trebuchet
woomera

PRONOUNS

all
another
any
anybody
anyone

anything
both
each
each other
either

few
he
her
hers
herself

him
himself
his
how
I

it	nothing	their	which
its	one	theirs	whichever
itself	one another	them	who
many	other	themselves	whoever
me	our	these	whom
mine	ours	they	whomever
most	ourselves	this	whose
much	several	those	why
my	she	us	you
myself	some	we	your
neither	somebody	what	yours
nobody	someone	whatever	yourself
none	something	when	
no one	that	where	

PROSIMIANS

Prosimians are a suborder of primates that include the primates listed below.

adapid	bush baby	indri	sifaka
angwantibo	colugo	lemur	tarsier
avahi	flying lemur	loris	tree shrew
aye-aye	galago	potto	

PSYCHOLOGICAL AND MENTAL TESTS

achievement test

alpha test

apperception test

aptitude test

Arlin Test of Formal Reasoning

association test

Babcock-Levy test

Beck Depression Inventory

Bender-Gestalt test

Bernreuter personality inventory

beta test

Binet-Simon test

Brown personality inventory

California Q-set Personality Test

Cattell's infant intelligence scale

CAVD test

Children's Apperception Test or CAT

Columbia Mental Maturity Scale or CMMS

controlled association test

cross-out test

Culture-Fair IQ test

direction test

draw-a-person test

free association test

frustration test

Gesell's development schedule

Goldstein-Sheerer test

House-Tree-Person Projective Technique or H-T-P

inkblot test

intelligence quotient test

intelligence test

interest inventory

Kaufman Brief Intelligence Test or K-BIT

Kent mental test

Make a Picture Story or MAPS

Mini-Mental State Examination

Minnesota Multiphasic Personality Inventory or MMPI

Minnesota Preschool Scale

Oseretsky test

performance test

personality test

Pictorial Test of Intelligence or PTI

power test

projective test

psychometric test

Rogers's process scale

Rorschach test

Rotter incomplete sentences blank

sentence-completion test

speed test

Stanford-Binet test

Stanford revision

Stanford scientific aptitude test

Szondi test

Test of Nonverbal Intelligence or TONI

Thematic Apperception Test or TAT

Wechsler Adult Intelligence Scale

Wechsler-Bellevue intelligence scale

Wechsler Intelligence Scale for Children

Woodcock-Johnson Psycho-Educational Battery

word association test

Zung Self-Rating Depression Scale

PSYCHOLOGICAL BRANCHES, SCHOOLS, AND THEORIES

abnormal psychology

academic psychology

act psychology

analytic psychology or introspective psychology

animal psychology

applied psychology

association psychology

behavioral psychology

biological psychology

biopsychology

child psychology

clinical psychology

cognitive psychology

collective psychology

community psychology

comparative psychology

constitutional psychology

consulting psychology

consumer psychology

counseling

criminal psychology

critical psychology

depth psychology

developmental psychology

differential psychology

dynamic psychology or functional psychology

eclectic psychology

ecological psychology

educational psychology

ego psychology

empirical psychology

engineering psychology

environmental psychology

ethnopsychology

existential psychology

experimental psychology

faculty psychology

folk psychology or ethnic psychology

genetic psychology

Gestalt psychology

group psychology

haptics

hedonics

holistic psychology

hormic psychology

humanistic psychology

individual differences psychology

individual psychology

industrial psychology

introspection psychology

Jungian psychology

mass psychology

medical psychology

military psychology

morbid psychology

neoanalytic psychology

neuropsychology

objective psychology

ontogenetic psychology

parapsychology

personalistic psychology

personnel psychology

phenomenological psychology

phylogenetic psychology

physiologic psychology

polygenetic psychology

popular psychology

positive psychology

psychoacoustics

psychoasthenics

psychobiochemistry

psychobiology

psychochemistry

psychodiagnostics

psychodynamics

psychoendocrinology

psychogenetics

psychogeriatrics

psychographics

psychohistory

psycholinguistics

psychological medicine

psychological warfare

psychomathematics

psychometrics

psychonomy

psychopathology

psychopharmacology

psychophysics

psychophysiology

psychosociology

psychosomatics

psychotechnology

psychotherapy or psychotherapeutics

race psychology or racial psychology

rational psychology

reactology

reflexology

school psychology

self psychology

social psychology

structural psychology

theoretical psychology

topological psychology

transpersonal psychology

vector psychology

voluntaristic psychology

PSYCHOTHERAPY TYPES

art therapy

assertiveness training

behavior modification

behavior therapy

client-centered therapy

cognitive-behavioral therapy

couples therapy

crisis intervention

dance therapy

family therapy

Gestalt

group therapy

hynotherapy

interpersonal therapy

movement therapy

music therapy

nondirective psychotherapy

phototherapy

play therapy

primal scream therapy

role-playing

talk therapy

transactional analysis

transpersonal psychotherapy

PUNCTUATION MARKS

ampersand

angle bracket

apostrophe

asterisk or star

at sign

brace

bracket

bullet

colon

comma

dagger or obelisk

double dagger or diesis

double hyphen

ellipsis

em dash

en dash

exclamation point

guillemets

hyphen

interrobang

paragraph mark

parenthesis

470

| period | quotation mark | semicolon | swung dash |
| question mark | section mark | single quotation mark | virgule or slash mark |

PURPLE COLOR VARIETIES

amaranth	dark purple	madder violet	purple-red
amaranthine	deep purple	magenta	raisin
amethyst	eggplant	maroon	raspberry
amethystine	fuchsia	Mars violet	reddish purple
aniline purple	grape	mauve	red-violet
Argyle purple	gridelin	monsignor	royal purple
aubergine	heliotrope	mulberry	rubine
blue-violet	hyacinth	orchid	solferino
bluish purple	imperial purple	pale purple	tulip
bokhara	indigo	pansy violet	Tyrian purple
Burgundy violet	king's purple	periwinkle	violaceous
campanula	lavender	phlox	violet
cerise	light purple	plum	violetta
clematis	lilac	prune	wine purple
dahila	livid purple	puce	wisteria
damson	livid violet	purple-blue	

PURSES

animal skin handbag	beaded handbag	canvas bag	clutch
backpack	box handbag	carpet bag	cosmetic bag
baguette	bucket bag	cloth handbag	designer handbag

drawstring bag

duffle bag

embroidered handbag

evening bag

fanny pack

hobo bag

knapsack

knitted handbag

mesh handbag

messenger bag

pochette

pouch bag

rucksack

satchel

shopping bag

shoulder bag

tote bag

wallet

wristlet

PUZZLE TYPES

acrostic

anagram

Chinese puzzle

crossword puzzle

cryptogram

jigsaw puzzle

logical puzzle

magic square puzzle

mathematical puzzle

maze

number puzzle

palindrome

rebus

riddle

tangram

word puzzle

word square

Quadrilaterals, Types of

complete quadrilateral	parallelogram	rhomboid	tetragon
four-sided polygon	quadrangle	rhombus	trapezium
	rectangle	square	trapezoid

Rabbits and Hares

angora rabbit

Arctic hare

Belgian hare

brown hare

chinchilla

cottontail rabbit

Easter rabbit

European rabbit

jackrabbit

mountain hare

Old World rabbit

pika

snowshoe hare

swamp rabbit

wood rabbit

Racing Car Types

championship car

compact sprint car

dirt car

dragster

experimental car

Formula A

formula car

Formula F

Formula One

Formula SCCA

Formula Super Vee

Formula Three

Formula Two

Formula Vee

fuel dragster or slingshot or rail job

fueler

funny car

gas dragster

grand touring car or GT

hobby car

Indy car

kart

late-model sportsman

midget car

modified stock car

production car

prototype race car

quarter-midget car

rally race car

sport race car   sportsman   stock car   turbine car

sports car   sprint car   touring car

RADIATION TYPES

The rays emitted by decaying nuclei are called radiation. There are three main types of radiation: alpha, beta, and gamma rays. Gamma rays may accompany the emission of alpha or beta rays and are sometimes given out on their own.

alpha radiation

background radiation

backscatter

beta radiation

black-body radiation

coherent radiation

cosmic radiation

diffuse radiation

direct radiation

electromagnetic radiation

electron radiation

gamma radiation

gravitational radiation

infrared radiation

insolation

ionizing radiation

long-wave radiation

microwave radiation

neutron radiation

nuclear radiation

radio wave radiation

short-wave radiation

solar radiation

terrestrial radiation

ultraviolet radiation or UV radiation

visible radiation

X-ray radiation

RADIO FREQUENCY WAVES

A radio wave is an electromagnetic wave propagated by an antenna. Radio waves have different frequencies, and by tuning a radio receiver to a specific frequency you can pick up a specific signal.

extremely high frequency or EHF

extremely low frequency or ELF

high frequency or HF

low frequency or LF

medium frequency or MF

superhigh frequency or SHF

ultrahigh frequency or UHF

very high frequency or VHF

very low frequency or VF

Radio Receivers

all-wave receiver

AM receiver

AM tuner

AM-FM receiver

AM-FM tuner

antenna

aviation radio

battery radio

boom box

car radio

citizens band or CB radio

clock radio

communications receiver

crystal radio receiver

direction finder

electronic scanner

facsimile receiver or fax

FM receiver

FM tuner

ghetto blaster

Global Positioning System or GPS

headband receiver

heterodyne receiver

loudspeaker

mobile radio

multiplex receiver

pager or beeper

pocket radio

portable radio

push-button radio

radar receiver

radio direction finder or RDF

radio-gramophone

radiophone

radio-phonograph

radio-record player

railroad radio

receiver

rechargeable-battery radio

regenerative receiver

relay receiver

scanner

ship-to-shore radio

shortwave receiver

single-signal receiver

six-band receiver

stereo receiver

superheterodyne

telephone receiver

three-way receiver

transceiver

transistor radio

transmit-receiver

transponder

tuner

two-way radio

universal receiver

VHF-FM receiver

walkie-talkie

Walkman

weather radio

wireless

Radio Transmitters

AM transmitter

amateur transmitter or ham transmitter or rig

arc transmitter or spark transmitter

Collins radio

continuous-wave transmitter or CW transmitter

covert listening device

Dictograph

facsimile transmitter or fax

FM transmitter

link transmitter

microphone

picture transmitter

portable transmitter

pulse transmitter

radio beacon

radio collar

radio marker

radiometeorograph

radio range beacon

radiosonde

radiotelephone transmitter

relay transmitter

RT transmitter

shortwave transmitter

spark transmitter

standby transmitter

tape transmitter

teleprinter

television transmitter

Telex

transceiver

transmitter receiver or transceiver

vacuum-tube transmitter

VHF-FM transmitter

walkie-talkie

RADIOACTIVE ELEMENTS

Some atoms, called radioisotopes, have unstable nuclei that are liable to decay or break up. If they do, they give out high-energy rays in a process known as radioactivity.

actinium

americium

astatine

berkelium

bohrium

californium

curium

dubnium

einsteinium

fermium

francium

hahnium

hassium

lawrencium

meitnerium

mendelevium

neptunium

nobelium

plutonium

polonium

promethium

protactinium

radium

radon or radium emanation

rutherfordium

seaborgium

technetium

thorium

uranium

RAILROAD CARS

air car

baggage car

bar car

bogie truck

booster

boxcar

buffet car

bunk car

cable car

caboose

chair car

club car

coach

coal car

commuter car

container car

dandy cart

day coach or day car

dining car

drawing room car

electric car

elephant car

express car

flatcar

fly coach

freight car

gondola

handcar

hopper car

log car

lounge car

mail car

milk car

non-smoking car

observation car

officers' car

outfit car

palace car

parlor car

passenger car

piggyback car

platform car

postal car

private car

produce car

Pullman car

rack car

railcar

rail detector car

refrigerator car

restaurant car

saloon car

skeleton car

sleeping car

smoking car

stock car

streetcar

subway car

tank car

tender car

tram

trolley

trolley car

truck car

wagon-lit

yard engine

RAILWAYS

bullet train

cable railway

cog railway

commuter railway

electric railway

elevated railway or el or L

freight train

funicular railway

gravity-operated railway

heritage railway

inclined railroad

light-rail rapid-transit system

local railway

mainline

métro

model railway

monorail

mountain railway

overhead railway

passenger train

private railway

rack railway or rack-and-pinion railway

scenic railway

ship railway

streetcar

subway

surface railway

tram or tramway

trolley or streetcar line

trunk or trunk line

underground railway or tube

RAIN

acid rain

continuous rain

convectional rain

deluge

drizzle

downpour

freezing rain

frontal rain

heavy rain	moderate rain	sleet	virga
ice rain	orographic rain	sprinkle	winter rain
light rain	shower	tropical rain	

RAINBOW COLORS

blue	indigo	red	yellow
green	orange	violet	

RAYS

A ray in this list is a straight line in which light or other electromagnetic radiation travels to a given point or a specified form of non-luminous radiation.

actinic ray	cosmic ray	heat ray	nuclear radiation
alpha ray	crepuscular ray	infrared ray	ordinary ray
anode ray	delta ray	infraroentgen ray	positive ray
Becquerel ray	electromagnetic ray	ionizing ray	Roentgen ray
beta ray	extraordinary ray	Leonard ray	ultraviolet ray
canal ray	gamma ray	light ray	X-ray
cathode ray	Grenz ray	matter ray	

REACTORS

A reactor is a device or vessel within which chemical processes are carried out for experimental or manufacturing purposes.

advanced gas-cooled reactor	atomic reactor	breeder reactor	CANDU or Canada deuterium oxide-uranium reactor
	boiling water reactor		

chain reactor

converter reactor

fast-breeder reactor

fission reactor

fusion reactor

gas-cooled reactor

heterogeneous reactor

homogeneous reactor

liquid metal reactor

nuclear reactor

plutonium reactor

power reactor

power-breeder reactor

pressurized-water reactor

stellarator

thermal reactor

thermonuclear reactor

uranium reactor

water-cooled reactor

RECEPTACLES

ashcan

ashtray

autoclave

barrel

bucket

caddy

can

canister

cannikin

cask

catchall

cistern

container

crock

crucible

dish

drum

firkin

garbage can

hogshead

hopper

keg

magazine

mess kit

milk pail

oilcan

pail

palette

pitcher

salver

saucer

slop pail

tank

tin can

trash can

tray

trencher

tub

vat

wastepaper basket

RECYCLABLE MATERIALS

aluminum foil

aluminum trays

catalogs

corrugated cardboard

egg cartons

glass bottles

glass jars

junk mail

magazines

metal cans

newspaper

paper

paperback books

paper bags

plastic bottles

plastic jugs

smooth cardboard

telephone books

wrapping paper

480

RED COLOR VARIETIES

alizarin crimson

alpenglow

annatto

beet red

blood red

bois de rose

bougainvillea

Bourdeaux

brick red

bright red

bright rose

brownish red

Burgundy

burnt carmine

burnt ocher

cadmium red

cardinal

carioca

carmine

carnation

carnelian

Castillian red

cerise

cherry

Chinese red

chrome red

cinnabar

claret

cochineal

coral pink

cordovan

cranberry

crimson

damask

dark red

deep red

English red

faded rose

fire red

fire-engine red

flame red

fuchsia

garnet

geranium

grenadine

gules

hellebore red

Indian red

iron red

jockey

lake

light red

lobster

madder

magenta

maroon

Mars red

murrey

old red

old rose

orange-red

oxblood

palladium red

paprika

peach

Persian red

pinkish red

ponceau

poppy

Prussian red

puce

purple-red

red ocher

rhodamine

rose madder

royal red

rubious

ruby

ruddle

rust

scarlet

solferino

stammel

strawberry

terra rosa

tile red

Turkey red

Venetian red

vermeil

vermilion

wild cherry

wine

REDDISH-BROWN COLOR VARIETIES

auburn	cinnamon	liver	rust
baize	cocoa	madder brown	sand
bay	Columbian red	mahogany	sedge
brick	coptic	nutmeg	sepia
burgundy	cordovan	ocher	sienna
burnt ocher	ferruginous	oxblood	sorrel
burnt sienna	fulvous	piccolopasso red	terra cotta
caramel	ginger	red robin	titian
Castilian brown	henna	roan	Venetian red
chestnut	India red	rubiginous	vermilion
chocolate	light red-brown	russet	

REED ORGANS

In the 1800s, the reed organ was once an important domestic instrument, offering a cheap alternative to the ever-popular family piano. Today, reed organs are found only with collectors and in museums.

American organ	cottage organ	organ	seraphine
cabinet organ	harmonium	orguinette	street organ
chord organ	melodeon	physharmonica	string organ
chorus reed	orchestrelle	regal	

482

REFERENCE BOOK TYPES

almanac

annual

atlas

bilingual dictionary

biographical dictionary

casebook

children's dictionary

chronology

college dictionary

concordance

cyclopedia

desk dictionary

dialect dictionary

dictionary

dictionary of quotations

directory

enchiridion

encyclopedia

etymological dictionary or etymologicon

foreign-language dictionary

gazetteer

geographical dictionary or gazetteer

glossary

guidebook

handbook

how-to book

idiom dictionary

index

lexicon

manual

phrasebook

popular reference book

reverse dictionary

rhyming dictionary

Roget's Thesaurus

school dictionary

slang dictionary

special-subject dictionary

spelling dictionary

synonym dictionary

telephone directory

thesaurus

travel guide

unabridged dictionary

usage dictionary

vade mecum

wordbook

yearbook

REFERENCE OR EDITING MARKS

asterisk or star

asterism

bullet

caret

dagger or obelisk

ditto mark

double dagger or diesis

double prime

index or fist or hand

leaders

obelus

paragraph mark

parallels

prime

section mark

swung dash

REGIONS OF THE WORLD

Africa

Antarctic

Arab World

Arctic

Asia

Asia Minor

Australasia

Australia

Baltic States

Basque Country

British Isles

Caribbean

Central Africa

Central America

Central Asia

Central Europe

East Africa

East Asia

Eastern Europe

East Indies

Eurasia

Europe

Far East

Holy Land

Indian Subcontinent

Indochina

Indonesia

Latin America

Mediterranean

Melanesia

Meso-America

Micronesia

Middle East

New World

North Africa

North America

Northern Europe

Occident

Oceania

Old World

Orient

Polynesia

South America

Southeast Asia

Southern Africa

Southern Asia

Southern Europe

South Pacific

Sub-Saharan Africa

West Africa

Western Europe

West Indies

RELIGION TYPES

African religion

ancient mythology

animism

Baha'i

biblical religion

Buddhism

candomble

cargo cult

Celtic religion

Christianity

Confucianism

cosmic religion

culture religion

demonology or Satanism

Druidism

Eastern religion

Egyptian religion

Eleusinian mysteries

ethical religion

exorcism

fetishism

folk religion

Germanic religion

graphology

Greek religion

Hinduism

historical religion

idolatry

Islam

Jainism

Judaism

Middle East religion

Mithraism

modern religion

monotheism

mystery religion

Native American religion

natural religion

484

Neopaganism
New Age
nomistic religion
nontheistic religion
Norse religion
occult
Orthodox religion

Paganism
phrenology
polytheism
primitive myth or primitive religion
prophetic religion
Roman religion

Scientology
Shamanism
Shinto
Sikhism
Taoism
Teutonic religion
theosophy

totemism
universalistic religion
voodoo
Western religion
Zoroastrianism

RELIGIONS, ANCIENT

Adonism
Aegean
Ainu
Ammonite
Amorite
ancestor worship
Anglo-Saxon
animism
Assyrian
Aztec

Babylonian
Canaanite
Carthaginian
Celtic
Chaldean
Druidism
Etruscan
Germanic
Greek mythology
Heathenry

I Ching
Incan
Khond
Mammonism
Mayan
Mithraism
Norse
Nubian
Orphism
Paganism

Phoenician
Roman mythology
Sankhya
Shamanism
Shintoism
Slavonic
Tao
Totemism
Vedic

RELIGIONS, SECTS, AND BELIEFS

There are six major organized world religions—Christianity, Islam, Hinduism, Buddhism, Judaism, and Sikhism—and many more religions, some named here.

anthroposophy

Babism

Baha'i

Brahmanism

Brahmoism

Buddhism

Ch'an Buddhism

Chen Yen Buddhism

Ching-t'u Buddhism

Christianity

Confucianism

Conservative Judaism

Dakshincharin Hinduism

Eleusinianism

Ethical Culture

Gnosticism

gymnosophy

Hare Krishna

Hasidism

Hinayana Buddhism

Hinduism

Islam

Jainism

Jodo Buddhism

Judaism

Lamaism

Lingayat Hinduism

Magianism

Mahayana Buddhism

Mandaeism

Mithraism

Nichiren Buddhism

Orphism

Orthodox Judaism

Parsiism

Rastafarianism

Reconstructionism

Reform Judaism

reincarnationism

Rosicrucianism

Sabaeanism

Saivism

Shaivite Hinduism

Shamanism

Shiite Muslimism

Shin Buddhism

Shingon Buddhism

Shintoism

Sikhism

Soka Gakkai Buddhism

Sufism

Sunni Muslimism

Taoism

Tendai Buddhism

Theosophy

Theravada Buddhism

T'ien-t'ai Buddhism

Unitarianism

Vaishnavite Hinduism

Vajrayana Buddhism

Vamacharin Hinduism

Vedanta

Wahabiism

Yoga or Yogism

Zen Buddhism

Zoroastrianism

RELIGIOUS DOCUMENTS, SACRED TEXTS, AND SCRIPTURES

Abhidhamma Pitaka

Acts and Sayings of Christ

Adigranth

American Standard Version

Analects of Confucius

Angas

Apocrypha

Atharva-Veda

Avesta

Bhagavad-Gita

Bible

Book of Books

Book of Common Prayer

Book of Concord

Book of Mahavera

Book of Mormon

Book of the Dead

Brahmana and Upanishads

cabala

canon

Dead Sea Scrolls

Dhammapada

486

Didache

Doctrines and Covenants

Epistle

Five Classics

Genesis

Ginza

Good Book

Gospels

Guru Granth Sahib

Hagiographa

Hebrew Bible

Holy Bible

Holy Scriptures

Holy Wirt

hymnal

I Ching

Jataka

Kama Sutra

Kanjur and Tanjur

Ketuvim

King James Bible

Koran or Qur'an

Li Chi

Mahabharata

Megillah

Menorah

Mezuzah

Midrash

Missal

Nevi-im

New Testament

Old Testament

Oral Law

Pali Canon

Pearl of Great Price

Pentateuch

Pitaka

Popol Vuh

prayer book

Prophets

Proverbs

Psalter

pseudepigrapha

Ramayana

Revelation

Rig-Veda

Sama-Veda

Scripture

Septuagint

Shih Ching

Shu Ching

sutra

Sutta Pitaka

Synoptic Gospels

Talmud

Tantras

Tao Te Ching

Targum

Tipitaka

Torah

Upanishads

Veda

Vinaya Pitaka

Vulgate

Word

Yajur-Veda

Zend-Avesta

Zohar

RELIGIOUS FACILITIES AND BUILDINGS

barrow

cenotaph

chapel

church

colossus

dolmen

heaven

hell

hospice

mastaba

mausoleum

mecca

mission

monastery

monolith

mosque

mythical place

obelisk

pantheon

pilgrimmage

purgatory

pyramid

rune stone

sanctuary

shrine	synagogue	tower of silence
stela	temple	tumulus
stupa	tholos	ziggurat

RELIGIOUS OFFICES

archbishopric or archiepiscopate or archiepiscopacy	cardinalate	inquisition	presbytery
	chaplaincy	ministry	primacy
archdeaconry	curacy	papacy	rabbinate
benefice	deaconship	pastorate	rectorate
bishopric	deanship	prebendaryship	sinecure
canonry	episcopate	prelateship	vicarship

RELIGIOUS OFFICIALS, PARTICIPANTS, AND HONORED BEINGS

abbess	apostle	believer	canoness
abbot	archangel	bhikshu	cantor
acolyte	archbishop	bishop	cardinal
agnostic	archdeacon	Bodhisattva	celebrant
altar boy	archimandrite	bonze	cenobite
altar girl	archpriest	Brahman	chaplain
anchoress	Arhat	brother	chela
anchorite	atheist	Buddha	cherub
angel	avatar	caliph	chief rabbi
apostate	ayatollah	canon	choir

488

church

clergy

clergyman

clergywoman

cleric

college

colporteur

communicant

congregation

convert

convocation

council

crucifer

crusader

curate

cure

Dalai Lama

dastur

deacon

deaconess

dean

dervish

devil

devil's advocate

devotee

dewal

disciple

ecclesiastic

elder

elect

Eminence

eparch

eremite

evangelist

exarch

faithful

fakir

father

father confessor

Freak

freethinker

friar

gentile

giaour

glebe

guru

hajji

hazzan

heathen

heavenly host

heretic

hermit

hierarch

hierophant

high priest

Holy Roller

hugumen

illuminati

imam

infidel

Jesus

kaffir

kohen or cohen

laity

lama

latitudinarian

lay brother

lay sister

Levite

magi

magus

mahant

maharishi

mahatma

man of the cloth

manciple

martyr

master

mendicant

Messiah

metropolitan

minister

missionary

mohel

monk

monophysite

monsignor

mother superior

muezzin

mufti

mullah

neophyte

novice

nullifidian

nun

opoe

padre

pagan

palmer

Panchen Lama

panda

pandit

pariah

parishioner

parson

pastor

patriarch

penitent

pilgrim

pillar saint

pongyi

pontiff

preacher

precentor

precisian

predicant

prelate	rabbinate	seer	theologian
presbyter	rebbe	seminarian	true believer
preterite	rebbetzin	sensei	tulku
priest	recreant	seraph	twice-born
priestess	rector	sexton	verger
primate	reprobate	shaman	vicar
prior	reverend	sheikh	votary
prioress	rishi	shepherd	wali
prophet	sadhu	sister	wise man
proselyte	sage	starets	witch
provost	saint	subdeacon	witch doctor
pujari	sannyasi	swami	yogi
pundit	santero	talapoin	zahid
quadi	sayyid	televangelist	zealot
rabbi	seeker	tertiary	

RELIGIOUS ORDERS

Ambrosian Monks

Anglican Franciscan Order

Augustinian Friars or Austin Friars

Augustinian Hermit

Augustinian Monks

Barnabite

Benedictine Monks or Black Monks

Benedictine Nuns

Bernardine

Bonhomme

Brigittine Nuns

Brothers of the Christian Schools

Camaldulian Monks

Capuchin Friars

Carmelite Friars or White Friars

Carmelite Nuns

Carthusian Monks

Celestine Monks

Christian Brothers

Cistercian Monks

Cluniac Monks

Columban Fathers

Community of the Resurrection

Conventual

Crosier

Crutched Friars or Crossed Friars

Discalced Carmelite

Divine World of Missionaries

Dominican Friars or Black Friars

English Order of Saint Benedict

Franciscan Friars or Gray Friars

Friars Minor

Friars Preacher

Gilbertine

Hieronoymite Friars

Holy Cross

Hospitaler

Jesuit or Loyolite

Little Sisters of the Poor

Lorettine

Marist Brothers

Maryknoll

Maturine

mendicant order

Minim Brothers

Minorite

Missionaries of Charity

Nuns of the Community of St. Mary

Oblates

Observant

Olivetan Monks

Oratorian

Pallottine Fathers and Brothers

Passionist Nuns

Passionists

Poor Clares of Reparation

Preaching Friars or Preaching Brothers

Premonstratensian

Priests of the Sacred Heart

Recollect or Recollet

Redemptorist Nuns

Redemptorists

Resurrectionist

Salesian

Servite Monks

Servite Nuns

Sisterhood of St. John the Divine

Sisters of Mercy

Sisters of Our Lady of Charity of the Good Shepherd

Society of Jesus

Society of St. John the Evangelist

Society of the Holy Trinity

Society of the Sacred Heart of Jesus

Society of the Sacred Mission

Templar

Teutonic

Theatine Brothers

Theatine Nuns

Trappist Monks

Ursuline Nuns

Vallombrosan Monks

RELIGIOUS RITES AND SACRAMENTS

ablution

absolution

anointing of the sick

aspersion or asperges

baptism

blood sacrifice

celebration

circumcision

cleansing or purification

confession

confirmation

feet washing

greater litany

high celebration

holy communion or communion

Holy Unction

imposition or laying on of hands

invocation

invocation of saints

last rites

lectisternium

lesser litany

litany

love feast or agape

lustration

marriage

offertory

pax or kiss of peace

penitence

processional

reciting the rosary or telling one's beads

sign of the cross
sprinkling

Stations of the Cross

thurification or
censing

viaticum

RELIGIOUS SCHOOL TYPES

Bible institute

Bible school

Catholic school

church school

convent school

denominational
school

divinity school

Hebrew school or
heder

madrasah

mesivta

parish school

parochial school

religious school

Sabbath school

schola cantorum

scholasticate

seminary

Sunday school

Talmud Torah

theological seminary
or school

vacation church
school

yeshiva

REPTILES AND AMPHIBIANS

acolotl

agama

alligator

anaconda

anuran

apodan

asp

auratus

basilisk

beaded lizard

black caiman

blindworm

boa

bog turtle

box turtle

bufo toad

bullfrog

caecilian

caiman

chameleon

chelonid

chicken turtle

Chinese water
dragon

clawed frog

cobra

congo snake

constrictor

cricket frog

crocodile

dinosaur

eft

flying dragon

frog

galliwasp

gecko

Gila monster

glass snake

green frog

hellbender

horned toad

iguana

Komodo dragon

leatherback turtle

lizard

loggerhead turtle

mamba

marine toad

monitor

mudpuppy

newt

New Zealand frog

pig frog

python

rainbow snake

rattlesnake

red-eyed tree frog

salamander

sand lizard

serpent

sirenidae

skink

slowworm

snake

snapping turtle

soft-shelled turtle

spotted salamander

spring peeper

stinkpot

tadpole

terrapin

toad

tortoise

tree frog

tuatara

turtle

viper

waterdog

worm

REPUBLICS OF FORMER SOVIET UNION

Before the Soviet Union was dissolved in 1991, it was comprised of the countries listed below.

Armenia

Azerbaijan

Belarus

Estonia

Georgia

Kazakhstan

Kyrgyzstan

Latvia

Lithuania

Moldova

Russia

Tajikistan

Turkmenistan

Ukraine

Uzbekistan

RESPIRATORY SYSTEM COMPONENTS

airways

alveolar ducts

alveolus or air sac

brain

bronchioles

bronchus

diaphragm

epiglottis

esophagus

larynx

lungs

mouth

muscles of breathing

nasal cavity

nostrils

pharynx

pleural membranes

rib cage

spinal cord

thoracic cage

trachea

RESTAURANT TYPES

a la carte restaurant
alternate
barbecue
beanery
bistro
brasserie
brewpub
café
cafeteria
canteen
carvery
chophouse
coffeehouse

commissary
creperie
dairy bar
diner
drive-in
drive-through
fast casual restaurant
fast food restaurant
greasy spoon
grillroom
luncheonette
lunchroom
milk bar

mobile canteen
noshery
oyster bar
pizzeria
prix fixe restaurant
ristorante
road house
rotisserie
sit-down restaurant
snack bar
specialty
steakhouse
supper club

sushi bar
taqueria
taverna
tearoom or teahouse
theme restaurant
trattoria
truck stop
white-tablecloth restaurant
wine bar

RHETORICAL DEVICES

Rhetorical devices are employed for more effective or persuasive speaking and writing.

alliteration
allusion
amplification
anacoluthon
anadiplosis
analogy
anaphora
anastrophe

antanagoge
antimetabole
antiphrasis
antistrophe
antithesis
apophasis
aporia
aposiopesis

apostrophe
appositive
assonance
asyndeton
catachresis
chiasmus
climax
diacope

enallage
epanalepsis
epanorthosis
epiphora
epistrophe
epithet
epizeuxis
eponym

exemplum	litotes	parallelism	prosopopoeia
expletive	metabasis	parataxis	rhetorical question
hendiadys	metanoia	parenthesis	simile
hypallage	metaphor	periphrasis	symploce
hyperbaton	metonymy	personification	synecdoche
hyperbole	onomatopoeia	pleonasm	trope
hypophora	oxymoron	polyproton	understatement
hypotaxis	palindrome	polysyndeton	zeugma
hysteron proteron	paradox	procatalepsis	
isocolon	paralipsis	prolepsis	

RIGGING, RIGS, AND ROPES

Rigging or rigs are sometimes the sails, masts, booms, yards, stays, and lines of a sailing vessel—but the term may refer to cordage only. Rope is any assemblage of fibers, filaments, or wires compacted by twisting or braiding (plaiting) into a long, flexible line.

arm	brigantine	crowfoot	garland
backstay	bull's-eye	downhaul	gasket
bibb	buntline	eye	gooseneck
bitt	burton	fall	gripe
bobstay	cable	foot rope	guest rope
bolt rope	catenary	foremast	guide rope
boom	clamp	foresheet	guy
bowline	clinch	forestay	halyard
brace	club	fore-topmast	hank
brails	club foot	fox	hawser
breeching	crosshead	gaff	hobble
brig	crossjack	gantline	horse

hound
inhaul
jack
jackstay
jib sheet
jigger
ketch
lanyard
lariat
lasso
lazy jack
lead
leader or fairlead
leg rope
mainstay
manrope
Marconi

marline
mast
messenger
mizzenmast
moorings
mousing
noose
outhaul
painter
pennant
pole
preventer
ratline
rawhide
rode
runner
running rope

sail
schooner
service
sheet
shroud
sling
slip rope
snub
span
spider
spring
stay
stick
stirrup
stop
sugan
tabernacle

tack
tackle fall
tether
thimble
topmast
topping lift
top rope
tow rope
traveler
truck
truss
vang
warp
whale boat rigging
whelp
yolk

RIVER TYPES

braided river
canal
ephemeral river
flowing river

freshet
lazy river
meandering river
navigable river

perennial river
polluted river
racing river
rivulet

seasonal river
underground river or subterranean river
watercourse
waterway

ROAD INTERCHANGES

cloverleaf interchange

diamond interchange

spaghetti junction

traffic circle

trumpet interchange

ROADS AND HIGHWAYS

access road

arterial highway

artery

Autobahn

autoroute

autostrada

avenue

beltway

big road

bridgeway

broadway

busway

byroad

byway

camino real

causeway

corduroy road

country road

county road

dirt road

divided highway

dugway

expressway

feeder road

freeway

frontage road

highroad

interstate highway

king's highway or queen's highway

limited access highway

main road

motorway

parkway

pavé

pent road

pike

plank road

post road

primary road

private road

public highway

secondary road

service road

shunpike

side road

speedway

street

superhighway

switchback

throughway

toll road town way

trunk road

turnpike

twitch road

ROCK TYPES

erratic

extrusive rock

igneous rock

intrusive rock

metamorphic rock

outcrop

plutonic rock

sedimentary rock

Rockets and Missiles

AA target rocket

AAM or air-to-air missile

ABM or antiballistic missile

aerial torpedo

airborne rocket

anchor rocket

antiaircraft rocket

antimine rocket

antimissile missile

antiradar rocket

antisubmarine rocket

antitank rocket

ASM or air-to-surface missile

ATA missile or air-to-air

ATG rocket or air-to-ground

ATGM or anti-tank guided missile

atom rocket

ATS or air-to-ship

AUM or air-to-underwater missile

ballistic missile

barrage rocket

bat bomb

bazooka rocket

beam-rider

bombardment rocket

booster

buzz bomb

chemical rocket

combat high-explosive rocket

Congreve rocket

countermissile

cruise missile

demolition rocket

fin-stabilized rocket

fireworks rocket

flare rocket

GAPA or ground-to-air pilotless aircraft

glide bomb

GTA rocket or ground-to-air

GTG rocket or ground-to-ground

guided missile

harpoon rocket

high-altitude rocket

homing rocket

HVAR or high velocity aircraft rocket

hydrobomb

ICBM or intercontinental ballistic missile

incendiary antiaircraft rocket

incendiary rocket

ion rocket

IRBM or intermediate range ballistic missile

launch vehicle or launcher

line-throwing rocket

liquid-fuel rocket

long-range rocket

MIM-104 Patriot

Minuteman missile

MIRV or multiple independently targetable re-entry vehicle

MRV or multiple re-entry vehicle

multistage rocket

nuclear rocket

ram rocket

retro-float light

retrorocket

rocket bomb

rockoon

SAM or surface-to-air missile

scud

signal rocket

skyrocket

smart rocket

smoke rocket

smokeless powder rocket

snake or antimine

solid-fuel rocket

solid rocket booster or SRB

sounding rocket

space rocket

spinner

spin-stabilized rocket

SSM or surface-to-surface missile

step rocket

STS rocket or ship-to-shore

submarine killer

submarine-launched missile

supersonic rocket

target missile

Tomahawk cruise missile

torpedo rocket

TOW

training rocket or missile

trajectory missile

transoceanic rocket

ullage rocket

V-2 rocket

vernier rocket

window rocket or antiradar

winged rocket

XAAM or experimental air-to-air missile

XASM or experimental air-to-surface missile

XAUM or experimental air-to-underwater missile

XSAM or experimental surface-to-air missile

XSSM or experimental surface-to-surface missile

ROCKS, IGNEOUS

Igneous rocks are formed when molten rock (magma) or lava cools to form a solid substance.

andesite

anorthosite

aplite

appinite

basalt

breccia

diorite

dolerite

felsite

gabbro

granite

greenstone

lava

monzonite

obsidian

pegmatite

peridotite

porphyrite

porphyry

pumice

rhyolite

serpentine

syenite

trachyte

tuff

ROCKS, METAMORPHIC

Metamorphic rocks are sedimentary or igneous rocks that have been altered by heat and/or pressure.

amphibolite

blueschist

epidiorite

epidosite

gneiss

granulite

hornblende

hornfels

lapis lazuli   mylorite   quartzite

marble   phyllite   schist

mica schist   pyroxenite   slate

ROCKS, SEDIMENTARY

Sedimentary rocks are formed from pressure as particles of sediment are deposited out of air, ice, or water carrying the particles. As sediment builds up, the pressure squeezes the sediment into layered solids, which form rocks.

argillite	coal	ironstone	phosphorite
breccia	conglomerate	limestone	sandstone
chalk	diatomite	marl	shale
chert	dolomite	mudstone	siltstone
clay	flint	oil shale	tillite
claystone	gypsum	oolite	

RODENTS

agouti	common rat	guinea pig	mara
aye-aye	coypu	gundi	marmot
bandicoot rat	deer mouse	hamster	meadow vole
bank vole	desert rat	harvest mouse	mole rat
beaver	dormouse	house mouse	mountain beaver
black rat	field mouse	jerboa	mouse
brown rat	field vole	jumping mouse	muskrat
capybara	gerbil	kangaroo mouse	paca
cavy	gopher	kangaroo rat	pacarana
chinchilla	grasshopper mouse	lemming	pocket mouse

porcupine

pouched rat

rat

scaly-tailed squirrel

spiny mouse

spring hare

squirrel

swamp rat

vole

water rat

white mouse

wood mouse

woodrat

RODEO CONTESTS

bareback bronc riding

bull riding

calf roping

saddle bronc riding

single-steer roping

steer roping

steer wrestling or bulldogging

team roping

ROOF SHAPES

All roofs are designed to provide protection from the weather. The design and covering used reflects the local climate. For instance, in a rainy or snowy area, a sloping (pitched) roof will let the water run off or snow melt off easily. In a dry climate, roofs are often flat. Apart from being practical, roofs can also be ingenious and beautiful, such as those of an ornate castle.

barrack roof

bell roof

bulkhead

butterfly roof

conical broach roof

cupola

curb roof

dome roof

flat roof

French roof

gable end roof

gable roof

gambrel roof

geodesic dome

helm roof

hip-and-valley roof

hipped end roof

hip roof

imperial roof

jerkinhead roof

lean-to hipped roof

lean-to roof

M roof

mansard and gables roof

mansard hipped roof

mansard roof

monopitch roof

monitor roof

ogee roof

pantile roof

pavilion roof

penthouse roof

pitched roof

pyramid roof

rainbow roof

rotunda roof

sawtooth roof

shed roof

shingle roof

skirt roof

slate roof

sloped turret roof

thatched roof

tile roof

ROOM TYPES

antechamber

anteroom

assembly room

atelier

atrium

attic

ballroom

banquet room

basement

bathroom

bedchamber

bedroom

boardroom

boiler room

boudoir

breakfast room

buttery

calefactory

catacomb

cave

cavern

cell

cellar

chamber

chancellery

changing room

chapel

checkroom

classroom

cloakroom

coatroom

cockloft

common room

conservatory

consulting room

cubiculum

cyclone cellar

den

dining room

drawing room

dressing room

entertainment center

family room

fitting room

Florida room

foyer

front room

greenhouse

green room

guardroom

guest room

hall

hidden chamber

keep

kitchen

kitchenette

landing

larder

laundry

lavatory

library

living room

lobby

locker room

loft

loo

lounge

master bedroom

morning room

multipurpose room

nursery

office

pantry

parlor

pavilion

playroom

porch

powder room

reception room

recreation room

refectory

repository

rest room

rumpus room

sacristy

sala

salon

scullery

sickroom

sitting room

solarium

spare room

stateroom

stockroom

stoop

storeroom

storm cellar

studio

study

sunroom

tack room

taproom

throne room

toilet

tomb

TV room

utility room

veranda

vestibule

waiting room

ward

wine cellar

workroom

workshop

ROWING RACES

Racing boats carry one, two, four, or eight rowers, all on sliding seats, plus sometimes a coxswain to steer. Rowers operate a single oar each and row as two, four, or eight; scullers use two oars each and race as singles, doubles, or quadruples.

coxed pairs

coxless fours

coxless pairs

double sculls

eights

single sculls

RUGBY POSITIONS

flank forward

forward

fullback or full back

halfback

hooker

left center

left wing

lock forward

loose flanker

number eight or number eight forward

prop forward

right center

right wing

scrum half

stand-off half

three-quarters

tight flanker

RULER TITLES

adonai

aga

ameer

baal

baron

baroness

begum

bey

bishop

brahma

bwana

caesar

caliph

caudillo

chairman

chief

chief of state

commissar

count

countess

czar

dey

dictator

doge

duce

duchess

duke

emir

emperor

empress

Führer

generalissimo

governor general

grand duchess

grand mufti

infanta

kaiser

khan

khedive

king

maestro

maharajah

maharani

mahatma

marquess

marquis

marquise

mikado

mithra

mogul

nawab

negus

nizam

paraclete

pharaoh

pope

premier

president

prime minister

prince

princess

queen

rajah

rani

regent

rex

sachem

satrap

shah

sharif

sheikh

shogun

sirdar

siva

sultan

tenno

thoth

tycoon

viceroy

viscount

viscountess

SADDLES

aparejo	English cavalry saddle	pack saddle	stock saddle
bridal saddle	English riding saddle	pillion	Western Saddle
camel saddle	English saddle	racing saddle	
cavalry saddle	howdah	riding saddle	
cowboy saddle	jockey saddle	sidesaddle	

SAGES OF GREECE, SEVEN

The seven sages below were chosen from among the outstanding politicians and philosophers to be the wisest of ancient Greece.

Bias of Priene	Cleobulus of Lindus (or Lindian)	Pittacus of Mytilene (or Mitylene)	Thales of Miletus
Chilon of Sparta (or Chilo of Lacedaemonia)	Periander of Corinth	Solon of Athens	

Sailing Ships and Boats

auxiliary sailboat

bark

barkentine

barketta

bastard schooner

Bermuda rig

bomb ketch

brig

brigantine

bugeye

bully

caique

caravel

carrack

cat

catamaran

catboat

Chesapeake canoe

class boat

clipper ship

convoy ship

corsair

corvette

cutter

dandy

daysailor

dhoney

dhow

dragon boat

dromond

escort ship

felucca

fire ship

fishing schooner

fishing smack

flattie

Flying Dutchman

folkboat

fore-and-aft

four-masted brig

frigate

full-rigged ship

gabert

gaff cutter

galiot

galleon

galley

galliot

hermaphrodite brig

hooker

hoy

Hudson River sloop

iceboat

ice yacht

inland scow

in-rigger

jolly boat

junk

keelboat

ketch

knockabout

lateen

longboat

longship

lugger

man-of-war

merchantman

merchant ship

monohull

motorsailer

multihull

nuggar

ocean racer

outrigger

pilot boat

pink

pinnace

piragua

pirate ship

pirogue

polacre

pram

privateer

proa

pucan

racing yacht

razee

rigger

sabot

sailboard

sailboat

sailing canoe

sailing dinghy

sailing trawler

sandbagger

schooner

scow

shallop

skiff

skipjack

sloop

sloop of war

smack

snow

soling

square-rigger

star

tall ship

tartan

tea clipper

tempest

topsail schooner

tornado

trimaran

windglider

windjammer

xebec

yacht

yawl

SAILS

Bermuda rig

canvas

course

fore-and-aft sail

fore-course

fore-royal

foresail

forestaysail

foretop

fore-topgallant

fore-topsail

gaff foresail

gaff topsail

Genoa jib

gunter

headsail

jenny

jib

jigger

kite

lateen sail

lugsail

main course

mainsail

maintopsail

mizzen

moonraker

rig

royal

skysail

spanker

spinnaker

spritsail

square sail

staysail

storm sail

studdingsail

topgallant

topsalt

trysail

SALAD DRESSINGS

aioli

anchovy dressing

balsamic vinaigrette

blue cheese dressing

Caesar salad dressing

chipotle dressing

coleslaw dressing

creamy dill dressing

creamy garlic dressing

creamy Italian dressing

creamy Parmesan dressing

French dressing

Gorgonzola dressing

green goddess dressing

herb dressing

honey Dijon dressing

honey mustard dressing

Italian dressing

mayonnaise

oil and vinegar

orange ginger dressing

potato salad dressing

ranch dressing

raspberry vinaigrette

remoulade

Roquefort dressing

Russian dressing

salad cream   Thousand Island   vinaigrette   yogurt dressing
                     dressing

SALADS

artichoke salad   combination salad   green salad   salad Nicoise
arugula salad   congealed salad   hot salad   seafood salad
avocado salad   corn salad   house salad   spinach salad
bean salad   crabmeat salad   iceberg lettuce salad tabbouleh
beet salad   cucumber salad   insalata verde   taco salad
cabbage salad   dinner salad   lobster salad   tossed salad
Caesar salad   egg salad   macaroni salad   tuna fish salad
chef's salad   fruit salad   meat salad   vegetable salad
chicken salad   garden salad   mesclun salad   Waldorf salad
chopped salad   German potato salad   molded salad
Cobb salad   Greek salad   pasta salad
coleslaw   green goddess salad   potato salad

SALESPERSONS

baker   cosmetician   florist   part-time
butcher   couturier   foreign   representative
cheesemonger   cutler   representative   perfumer
chocolatier   divisional sales   furrier   pitchperson
clerk   manager   grocer   salaried salesperson
clothier   druggist   hatter   salary-and-
commission   field sales manager   home-based   commission
salesperson   field salesperson   salesperson   salesperson
confectioner   fishmonger   jeweler   salesclerk
                                              milliner   sales demonstrator

sales representative   shop clerk   stationer   traveling salesperson

shopboy   shopgirl   telemarketer

SAND DUNE TYPES

coastal sand dune

complex sand dune

compound sand dune

crescentic sand dune or barchan

dome sand dune

linear sand dune

longitudinal sand dune

parabolic sand dune

shifting sand dune

simple sand dune

star sand dune

transverse sand dune

SANTA'S REINDEER

Blitzen

Comet

Cupid

Dancer

Dasher

Donner

Prancer

Rudolph

Vixen

SAUCES AND DIPS

A-1 sauce

aioli

allemande

applesauce

baba ghanouj

barbecue sauce

Béarnaise

Béchamel

Bercy

bolognese sauce

Bordelaise

Bourguignonne

brown gravy

brown sauce

Burgundy sauce

caper sauce

carbonara sauce

chasseur sauce

chaud-froid

cheese sauce

chili sauce

chip dip

clam dip

cocktail sauce

cranberry sauce

cream sauce

Cumberland

curry sauce

demi-glace

diable

dill sauce

duck sauce

enchilada sauce

espagnole

giblet gravy

gravy

guacamole

harissa

hoisin sauce

hollandaise sauce

horseradish sauce

hot sauce

hummus

ketchup

Louis
Marie-Rose
marinara
matelote
mayonnaise
milanese sauce
mint sauce
molé
Mornay sauce
mousseline sauce
mushroom sauce
mustard sauce
Nantua

onion dip
onion sauce
oyster sauce
pan gravy
pepper sauce
pesto
pistou
pizzaiola sauce
ragu
ravigote
red-eye gravy
remoulade
roux

salsa
salsa verde
sambal
satay sauce
shallot sauce
soubise
soy sauce
spaghetti sauce
steak sauce
supreme sauce
sweet and sour sauce
Tabasco

taco sauce
tahini
tamari
tartar sauce
tartare sauce
teriyaki sauce
tomato sauce
velouté
vinaigrette
white sauce
wine sauce
Worcestershire sauce

Sausages

air-dried sausage
andouille banger
beef sausage
black pudding
blood pudding
blood sausage
bockwurst
bologna
boudin blanc
boudin noir
Bratwurst
Braunschweiger
cervalet

chicken liver pâté
chipolata
chorizo
Cumberland sausage
cured sausage
duck sausage
fish sausage
foie gras
forcemeat
frankfurter
fresh raw sausage
galantine
Genoa salami

German sausage
head cheese
hot dog
hot link
Italian sausage
kielbasa
knockwurst
kosher salami
linguica
liver pâté
liver sausage
liverwurst
merguez

mortadella
mulliatelle
pâté
pâté de campagne
pâté de foie gras
pâté en croute
pepperoni
Polish sausage
pork sausage
precooked sausage
salami
saucisse
saucisson

scrapple

Slim Jim

smoked sausage

summer sausage

terrine

Vienna sausage

weenie

white pudding

wiener

wurst

zampone

SCHOOL TYPES

academe

academy

adult-education school

alternative school

bible school

boarding school

business school

catholic school

charity school

charm school

charter school

church school

common school

community college

comprehensive school

conservatory

consolidated school

continuation school

correspondence school

country day school

cow college

dame school

day school

distance learning institution

elementary school

evening school

extension program

finishing school

grade school

graduate school

grammar school

gymnasium

high school

institute

intermediate school

junior college

junior high school

laboratory school

law school

library school

lyceum or lycée

medical school

middle school

military school

model school

music school

night school

nursery school

open-classroom school

polytechnic school

preparatory school

preschool

primary school

private school

public school

reformatory school

religious school

school of continuing education

secondary school

secretarial school

senior high school

separate school

special needs school

state school

summer school

Sunday school

technical school

trade school

training school

university extension

vocational school

women's college

Scientific Objects That Have Never Been Seen

antimatter

Barnard's Star

black hole

brown dwarf

cosmic ray

dark matter

Earth's core

electromagnetic spectrum

francium

graviton

quark

Scrabble Words, Acceptable Two-Letter

AA	BI	HE	MO
AB	BO	HI	MU
AD	BY	HM	MY
AE	DE	HO	NA
AG	DO	ID	NE
AH	ED	IF	NO
AI	EF	IN	NU
AL	EH	IS	OD
AM	EL	IT	OE
AN	EM	JO	OF
AR	EN	KA	OH
AS	ER	LA	OM
AT	ES	LI	ON
AW	ET	LO	OP
AX	EX	MA	OR
AY	FA	ME	OS
BA	GO	MI	OW
BE	HA	MM	OX

OY	SI	UN	XU
PA	SO	UP	YA
PE	TA	US	YE
PI	TI	UT	YO
QI	TO	WE	
RE	UH	WO	
SH	UM	XI	

Scrabble Words, Highest-Scoring

bezique	musquash	quizzed	zinkify
cazique	muzjik	rorquals	zymurgy
highjack	oxazepam	squeezy	zythums
jazzily	popquiz	whizbang	zyxomma
mezquit	quartzy	zephyrs	
mezquite	quetzal	zincify	

Screw Heads

cross head	milled head	round head	Torx
dowel screw	one-way head	slotted head	
flat head	oval head	socket head	
hexagonal head	Phillips head	square head	

Screwdrivers

auger screwdriver	auto-return screwdriver	cabinet-pattern screwdriver	clutch-head tip screwdriver

513

cordless screwdriver

cranked screwdriver

crosshead screwdriver

electric screwdriver

flat-head screwdriver

flat tip screwdriver

high-torque spiral ratchet screwdriver

impact driver

in-and-out screwdriver

insulated screwdriver

machinist's screwdriver

magnetic screwdriver

mechanical screwdriver

mechanic's screwdriver

offset screwdriver

Phillips head screwdriver ratchet screwdriver

return spiral ratchet screwdriver

screw gun

screw-holding screwdriver

slotted screwdriver

spiral ratchet screwdriver

standard screwdriver

star screwdriver

straight-slot screwdriver

stubby screwdriver

torque screwdriver

Torx screwdriver

Yankee screwdriver

SCULPTURE TECHNIQUES AND TYPES

akrolith

alto-relievo

anaglyph

annealing

anodizing

assemblage

bardiglio capella

bas-relief

benou jaune

boucharde

brazing

bronze sculpture

bronzing

burnishing

bust

campan griotte

carving

casing

casting

casting plaster

cavo-relievo

chryselephantine

cire perdue

clay modeling

clay sculpture

coil method

collage

colossal

compage melange vert

damascene

dead stone

discobolus

drilling

embossing

escalette

free-standing sculpture

French grand antique

galvanizing

ganosis

giallo antico

grounding

hammering

heroic

high relief

ice sculpture

installation

junk sculpture

Languedoc

lathe work

loredo chiaro

lost-wax process

low relief

lumachelle

maquette

marble sculpture

mezzo-relievo

mobile

modeling

molding

moulage

niello

origami

papier-mâché

pavonazza

plaster of Paris

pointing

quenching

relief

repoussé

Roman breche

rosso magnaboschi

roughing out

royal Jersey green

saccharoidal marble

Saint-Beat

Sainte-Anne marble

Sainte-Baume marble

sandblasting

sand molding

sand sculpture

sculptural relief

sculpture in the round

slush casting

soapstone

soft sculpture

stabile

statuary

statue

statuette

stone carving

totem

turning

video sculpture

wax sculpture

welding

wood carving

wood sculpture

SEAFOOD DISHES AND ENTRÉES

baked fish

barracuda

bass

bonito

broiled fish

calamari

carp

catfish

caviar

chowder

clam

cod

crab

crab cakes

crayfish

cuttlefish

eel

fish fillet

fish kabob

fish salad

fish stew

flounder

grilled fish

haddock

lobster

mackerel

mahimahi

marlin

mussel

octopus

oyster

perch

porpoise

prawn

puffer

rockfish

salmon

scallop

seafood casserole

seafood salad

seafood stir-fry

shad

shark

shellfish

shrimp

skate

snapper

sole

squid

steamed fish

surf-and-turf

swordfish

tilapia

trout

tuna

whale

whitefish

SEALS, SEA COWS, AND SEA LIONS

Alaska fur seal

Arctic seal

Australian sea lion

Baikal seal

bearded seal

California sea lion

common seal

crab-eating seal

dugong

eared seal

earless seal

elephant seal

fur seal

gray seal

harbor seal

harp seal

hooded seal

Japanese sea lion

leopard seal

manatee

monk seal

ringed seal

Ross seal

sea cow

sea elephant

seal

sea lion

South American sea lion

stellerine

Steller's sea cow

Steller's sea lion

true seal

walrus

water cow

Weddell seal

SEAS

Adriatic Sea

Aegean Sea

Amundsen Sea

Andaman Sea

Arabian Sea

Arafura Sea

Aral Sea

Baffin Bay

Bali Sea

Baltic Sea

Banda Sea

Barents Sea

Bay of Bengal

Beaufort Sea

Bellingshausen Sea

Bering Sea

Bismarck Sea

Black Sea or Euxine Sea

Bohol Sea or Mindanao Sea

Caribbean Sea

Caspian Sea

Celebes Sea

Ceram Sea

China Sea

Chukchi Sea

Coral Sea

Dead Sea

East China Sea

East Siberian Sea

Flores Sea

Greenland Sea

Gulf of California or Sea of Cortez

Gulf of Guinea

Gulf of Mexico

Gulf of Saint Lawrence

Hudson Bay

Inland Sea

Ionian Sea

Irish Sea

Kara Sea

Laptev Sea

Ligurian Sea

Mediterranean Sea

Molukka Sea

North Sea

Norwegian Sea

Persian Gulf

Philippine Sea

Red Sea

Ross Sea

Sargasso Sea   Sea of Galilee   South China Sea   Tyrrhenian Sea

Savu Sea   Sea of Japan   Sulu Sea   Weddell Sea

Sea of Azov   Sea of Marmara   Tasman Sea   White Sea

Sea of Crete   Sea of Okhotsk   Timor Sea   Yellow Sea

SEASHELL TYPES

abalone shell	clam shell	moon shell	staircase shell
ark shell	cockle shell	murex shell	sunset shell
basket shell	conch shell	mussel shell	top shell
bivalve shell	cowrie shell	nautilus shell	tower shell
bubble shell	cup shell	necklace shell	trough shell
button shell	dove shell	pearl oyster shell	trumpet shell
cameo shell	ear shell	periwinkle shell	tulip shell
canoe shell	fig shell	pyramid shell	turret shell
carpet shell	file shell	razor shell	umbrella shell
carrier shell	fingered shell	rock shell	univalve shell
cask shell	frog shell	scallop shell	vase shell
chambered nautilus shell	furrow shell	snail shell	wedge shell
	hoof shell	spindle shell	whelk shell
chiton shell	horn shell	spire shell	worm shell

SEATS AND SEATING

Adirondack chair	banana seat	basket chair	bench
armchair	banquette	batwing chair	bench seat
armless chair	bar stool	beach chair	bicycle seat
baby seat	barber chair	beanbag chair	birthing chair
back seat	barrel chair	bed chair	Boston rocket

boudoir chair
bowback chair
bucket seat
camp chair
camp stool
campaign chair
captain's chair
car seat
chaise longue
channel-back chair
club chair
comb-back chair
contour chair
cricket chair
deck chair
dentist's chair
desk chair
dining chair
director's chair

driver's seat
Eames chair
easy chair
ejector seat
fan-back chair
folding chair
folding stool
front seat
garden chair
grandstand seat
hassock
high chair
high seat
Hitchcock chair
jump seat
kitchen chair
ladderback chair
lawn chair
lifeguard chair

living room chair
lounge chair
love seat
milking stool
Morris chair
occasional chair
ottoman
overstuffed chair
passenger seat
pew
platform rocket
potty chair
potty seat
recliner
ringside seat
rocking chair
rumble seat
saddle seat
safety seat

sedan chair
settle
side chair
sling chair
split-bench seat
steamer chair
step stool
stool
straight chair
swing chair
swivel chair
taboret
throne
toilet seat
tub chair
window seat
Windsor chair
wing chair
writing chair

SECURITIES, TYPES OF

Securities are a general name for stocks and bonds issued by a company and traded on a Stock Exchange.

active securities

agency securities

American Depository Receipts or ADRs

asset-backed securities

banker's acceptance

bond

book-entry securities

cabinet securities

callable securities

certificate of accrual on treasury securities or CATS

certificate of deposit or CD

convertible securities

corporation securities

debenture or certificate of indebtedness

derivative securities

digested securities

distressed securities

droplock securities

equity securities

exchangeable securities

exempt securities

fixed-income securities

floating securities

foreign securities

futures contract

gilt-edged securities

government securities

inflation-indexed securities

international securities

junior securities

legal securities

liquid yield option notes or LYONs

listed securities

margined securities

marketable securities

money-market certificate

mortgage-backed securities

mortgage pass-through securities

municipal securities

negotiable securities

noncallable securities

note

obsolete securities

outside securities

outstanding securities

over-the-counter securities

pass-throughs or participation certificate

payment-in-kind securities

program trading

registered securities

restricted securities

senior securities

separate trading of registered interest and principal securities or STRIPS

short-term note

speculative securities or cats and dogs

stamped securities

stock

treasure inflation-protected securities or TIPS

treasury bill

treasury bond

treasury certificate

treasury investment growth receipts or TIGRs

treasury note

trustee securities

trust-preferred securities

undigested securities

unlisted securities

unregistered securities

warrant

zero-coupon securities

SEVEN DEADLY SINS

anger

envy

gluttony

greed

lust

pride

sloth

SEVEN DWARFS

Bashful

Doc

Dopey

Grumpy

Happy

Sleepy

Sneezy

Seven Hills of Rome

The seven hills featured below were prominently represented in Roman mythology, religion, and politics. They later became grouped as the city of Rome.

Aventine

Caelian

Capitoline

Esquiline

Palatine

Quirinal

Viminal

Seven Sisters (formally Seven Colleges Conference)

Barnard

Bryn Mawr

Mount Holyoke

Radcliffe

Smith

Vassar

Wellesley

Seven Wonders of the Ancient World

Colossus of Rhodes

Great Pyramids of Egypt at Giza

Hanging Gardens of Babylon

Lighthouse (Pharos) of Alexandria

Mausoleum of King Mausolus at Halicarnassus

Statue of Zeus at Olympia

Temple of Artemis (Diana) at Ephesus

Seven Wonders of the Natural World

Grand Canyon

Great Barrier Reef

Harbor of Rio de Janeiro

Mount Everest

Northern Lights

Paricutín Volcano

Victoria Falls

SEWING STITCHES AND TECHNIQUES

alteration basting
appliqué
arrowhead tack
backstitch bar tack
bargello
basting
binding
blackwork
blanket stitch
blind stitch
buttonhole stitch
cable stitch
carpet stitch
chain stitch
combination stitch
continental stitch
coral stitch
cording stitch
couching stitch
cross-stitch
crow's-foot tack
cutwork
damask stitch
darning
dart

decoration stitch
double stitch
drawn work
dressmaker basting
embroidery
even basting
facing
faggoting
feather stitch
fine drawing
French knot
French tack
fulling
garter stitch
gathering
glover's stitch
gros point
guide basting
half-cross stitch
half stitch
hemstitch
herringbone stitch
lace stitch
ladder stitch
laid work

lazy daisy stitch
lock stitch
loop stitch
machine stitch
needlepoint
outline stitch
over-and-over stitch
overcasting
overhand stitch
overlocking
oversewing
overstitch
padding stitch
patchwork
petit point
picot
pleating
quilting
rib stitch
rose stitch
ruching
ruffling
running basting
running hemming
running stitch

saddleback stitch
saddle stitch
satin stitch
scalloping
shadow stitch
shell stitch
shirring
side stitch
side thread stitch
single stitch
slant hemming
slant stitch
slip stitch
slip stitch hemming
smocking
stay stitch
stem stitch
straight stitch
Swiss darning
tacking
tailor basting
tapestry
tent stitch
topstitch
treble

tucking

tufting

twist stitch

vertical hemming

whipstitch

whitework

zig-zag stitch

SHAKESPEARE'S PLAYS

A Midsummer Night's Dream

All's Well That Ends Well

Antony and Cleopatra

As You Like It

Coriolanus

Cymbeline

Hamlet

Henry IV, part I

Henry IV, part II

Henry V

Henry VI, part I

Henry VI, part II

Henry VI, part III

Henry VIII

Julius Caesar

King John

King Lear

Love's Labours Lost

Macbeth

Measure for Measure

Much Ado About Nothing

Othello

Pericles

Richard II

Richard III

Romeo and Juliet

The Comedy of Errors

The Merchant of Venice

The Merry Wives of Windsor

The Taming of the Shrew

The Tempest

The Two Gentlemen of Verona

The Two Noble Kinsmen

The Winter's Tale

Timon of Athens

Titus Andronicus

Troilus and Cressida

Twelfth Night

SHAPES AND FORMS

acicular

acuminate

acute

amygdaloid

anchor

angular

annual

apical

arc

arch

arcuate

asymmetrical

attenuated

awry

baciliary

ball

bell

biconcave

biconvex

bifurcate

bilateral

biradial

block

bolus

botryoidal

bowl

box

branching

brick

bulbous

bump

bursiform

campanulate

capitate

cardiod

catenary

catenulate

chevron

cicullate

circinate

circle

clavate

claviform

clothoid

cloverleaf

club

coil

columnar

compass

concave

concavo-convex

cone

conoid

contour

convex

convexo-concave

convoluted

cordate

cordiform

cosahedron

crenate

crenulate

crescent

crook

cross

cruciform

cube

cuneal

cuneat

curlicue

curvature

curve

cusp

cuspidate

cycle

cylinder

decagon

dechedron

decurved

decussate

deltohedron

deltoid

dendriform

dendroid

dentiform

diamond

discoid

disk

dodecagon

dodecahedron

dogleg

dome

donut

double helix

doughnut

egg-shape

elbow

ellipse

elliptic

elongate

ensiform

falcate

falciform

fastigiated

foliate

frustrum

fungiform

fungoid

funnel

globe

globose

gurge

heart-shape

helical

helicoids

helix

hemihedral

hemisphere

heptagon

hestate

hexagon

hexagram

hexahedron

horn

hump

hyperbola

icosahedron

infundibuliform

involute

key

kidney-shape

knot

lanceolate

ligulate

linear

lobate

loop

lozenge

lump

lunette

meniscus

moline

moniliform

napiform

nodular

nodule

nonagon

notched

obcordate

oberse

oblate

oblique

oblong

obovate

obovoid

obtuse

octagon

octahedron

ogee

ogival

ogive

orb

oval

ovate

palmate

parabola

parallelepiped

parallelogram

parted

peaked

pear-shape

peltate

pentacle

pentagon

pentagram

pentahedron

pentangle

pinnate

plane

plano-concave

plano-convex

polygon

polyhedron

pophidiform

pretzel

prism

prismatoid

prismoid

prolate

pyramid

pyriform

quadrangle

quadrilateral

rectangle

rectilinear

reniform

retroflex

retuse

rhomboid

rhombus

right angle

right triangle

ring

rondure

round

sagittate

scalloped

scroll

scutate

semicircle

serrate

shape

shell

shield

sickle

sigmois

solid

spade

spatulate

sphere

spicate

spiral

square

star

stellate

straight line

styliform

switchback

tapering

tear-shape

terete

ternate

tetrahedron

toothed

toroid

toroidal

torus

trapezium

trapezoid

triangle

trifoliate

trifurcate

trihedral

trilateral

trochoid

truncated cone

truncated pyramid

tube

turnip-shape

turtleback

unciform

uncinate

vermiculate

villiform

virgate

volute

wheel

whorl

winding

worm

zigzag

SHEEP BREEDS

Abyssinian

Africander

American merino

American Rambouillet

American Tunis

Ancon

argali

arui

Berber

bighorn

black sheep

Black-faced Highland

Blackhead Persian

broadtail

Cheviot

Cimarron

Columbia

Corriedale

Corsican

Cotswold

Dall's sheep

Darwin's sheep

Delaine Merino

Dorset Down

Exmoor

fat-rumped sheep

fat-tailed sheep

Hampshire

Karakul

Kerry Hill

Leicester

Lincoln

Marco Polo sheep

Merino

Mongolian

Mouflon

mountain sheep

otter sheep

Oxford

Panama

Rambouillet

Rocky Mountain

Romanov

Romeldale

Romney

Romney Marsh

Ryeland

Scottish Blackface

Shetland

Shropshire

Southdown

Suffolk

Tajik

Targhee

Tibetan

Welsh Mountain

Wensleydale

white sheep

SHELLFISH

abalone

American lobster

clam

conch

crab

crawdad

crawfish

crayfish

crustacean

Dungeness crab

echinoderm

hard-shell clam

king crab

langouste

limpet

mollusk

mussel

Norway lobster

octopus

oyster

prawn

rock lobster

scallop

sea cucumber

sea urchin

shrimp

soft-shell clam

South African rock lobster

spiny lobster

squid

whelk

SHIP AND BOAT OCCUPATIONS

able seaman
admiral
Argonaut
bilge rat
boatswain
bo's'n
bowman
buccaneer
cabin boy
captain
chief petty officer
commander
commodore
coxswain
crewman
crew member
deck hand
dockhand

ensign
ferryman
first mate
fisherman
Flying Dutchman
gondolier
grinder
gunner
helmsman
jack
longshoreman
marine
mariner
mate
merchant seaman
middy
midshipman
navigator

oarsman
pilot
pipes
pirate
provateer
purser
quartermaster
radio operator
rapparee
sailmaker
sailor
salt
Seabee
sea dog
seafarer
seaman
sea rover
shipbuilder

ship chandler
shipfitter
shipmaster
shipmate
shipwright
skipper
steersman
stevedore
steward
swabby
tar
Viking
warrant officer
watch
whaler
windjammer
yachtsman
yeoman

SHIPS AND BOATS

airboat
aircraft carrier
amphibious landing craft
argosy
ark

auxiliary
banana boat
barge
bark
barkentine

bateau
battle cruiser
battleship
bilander
bireme

brig
brigantine
bucentaur
bulk carrier
bullboat

bumboat

cabin cruiser

caique

canal boat

canoe

caravel

cargo liner

cargo ship

carrack

catamaran

catboat

clipper ship

coble

cockboat

cockleshell

collier

container ship

coracle

corsair

corvette

crabber

cruiser

cruise ship

currach

cutter

dahabeah

dandy

destroyer

dhow

dinghy

diving boat

dory

dragon boat

dreadnought

dredger

drift boat

dromond

dugout

escort vessel

faltboat

felucca

ferry

fishing boat

flagship

flatboat

foldboat

fore-and-after

freighter

frigate

galiot

galleass

galleon

galley

galliot

gig

gondola

gunboat

hermaphrodite brig

hospital ship

houseboat

hovercraft

hoy

hydrofoil or hydroplane

iceboat

icebreaker

inboard

Indiaman

inflatable

ironclad

jackass rig

jangada

jet boat

jolly boat

junk

kayak

keelboat

ketch

knockabout

lateen

launch

lifeboat

life raft

lighter

liner

longboat

longship

lugger

luxury liner

mailboat

man-of-war

medical ship

merchant ship

minelayer

minesweeper

monitor

motorboat

motorized fishing vessel or MFV

nuclear-powered submarine

nuggar

ocean liner

oiler

oil tanker

outboard

outrigger

packet

paddleboat

paddle streamer

paddle wheeler

passenger steamer

patrol boat

pink

pinnace

piragua pirate ship

polacre
pontoon
powerboat
pram
prison ship
privateer
proa
PT or patrol torpedo boat
punt
Q-ship
quinquereme
racing boat
raft
randan
refrigeration ship
research vessel
riverboat
rowboat

runabout
sailboard
sailboat
sailer
sailing dinghy
sailing vessel
sampan
schooner
scow
scull
shallop
shell
sidewheeler
skiff
sloop
smack
speedboat
square-rigger
steamboat

steamer
steamship
stern-wheeler
submarine
submarine chaser
supertanker
swamp boat
tall ship
tanker
tartan
tender
torpedo boat
towboat
tramp steamer
trawler
trimaran
trireme
troopship
tug

tugboat
U-boat
umiak
underwater craft
vaporetto
vedette
warship
weather ship
whaleback
whaleboat
whaler
wherry
windjammer
workboat
xebec
yacht
yawl

Shirts

aloha shirt or Hawaiian shirt
barong tagalog
basque
benjamin
blouse
blouson

body shirt
boiled shirt
bush shirt
bustier
button down shirt
camise
camp shirt

chambray shirt
coat shirt
crop top
denim shirt
dickey
doublet
dress shirt

evening shirt
flannel shirt
garibaldi shirt
gipon
habit shirt
hair shirt
halter or halter top

hickory shirt

hunting shirt

jersey

long-sleeved shirt

middy blouse

nightshirt

olive-drab shirt or
OD shirt

overshirt

Oxford shirt

palaka

plaid shirt

polo shirt

pourpoint

pullover

Rough Rider shirt

rugby shirt

sark

shell

shirt-jacket

shirtwaist

short-sleeved shirt

silk shirt

sleeveless shirt

sport shirt

sweatshirt

tank top

T-shirt or tee shirt

top

tube top

turtleneck

undershirt

workshirt

SHRUBS

acacia

alder

azalea

barberry

bayberry

blackberry

blackthorn

blueberry

bougainvillea

boxwood

broom

burning bush

caper

chokeberry

cinchona

coffee

cranberry bush

currant

daphne

elder

flowering quince

forsythia

frangipani

fuchsia

furze

gardenia

gooseberry

gorse

haw

hawthorn

hazel

heather

henna

hibiscus

holly

hydrangea

inkberry

ivy

jasmine

Juneberry

juniper

laurel

lavender

lilac

magnolia

mesquite

mimosa

mock orange

myrtle

oleander

olive

poinsettia

privet

pussy willow

quince

rhododendron

rockspray

rose acacia

rosemary

sage sarsaparilla

snowberry

spiraea

tamarisk

winterberry

wintergreen

witch hazel

yew

zinnia

529

SIGNERS OF THE DECLARATION OF INDEPENDENCE

Adams, John

Adams, Samuel

Bartlett, Josiah

Braxton, Carter

Carroll, Charles

Chase, Samuel

Clark, Abraham

Clymer, George

Ellery, William

Floyd, William

Franklin, Benjamin

Gerry, Elbridge

Gwinnett, Button

Hall, Lyman

Hancock, John

Harrison, Benjamin

Hart, John

Hewes, Joseph

Heyward, Jr., Thomas

Hooper, William

Hopkins, Stephen

Hopkinson, Francis

Huntington, Samuel

Jefferson, Thomas

Lee, Francis Lightfoot

Lee, Richard Henry

Lewis, Francis

Livingston, Philip

Lynch, Jr., Thomas

McKean, Thomas

Middleton, Arthur

Morris, Lewis

Morris, Robert

Morton, John

Nelson, Jr., Thomas

Paca, William

Penn, John

Read, George

Rodney, Caesar

Ross, George

Rush, Benjamin

Rutledge, Edward

Sherman, Roger

Smith, James

Stockton, Richard

Stone, Thomas

Taylor, George

Thornton, Matthew

Treat Paine, Robert

Walton, George

Whipple, William

Williams, William

Wilson, James

Witherspoon, John

Wolcott, Oliver

Wythe, George

SIKHISM TYPES

Sikhism is a monotheistic religion based on the teachings of ten Gurus who lived in northern India during the 16th and 17th centuries. It is one of the world's major religions with over 20 million followers. It is broken down into the sects below.

Akali

Khalsa

Namdharis

Nirankaris

Nirmalin

Ram Raiyas

Udasin or Udasis

SILK VARIETIES

brocade

charmeuse

chiffon silk

China silk

corn silk

crepe de Chine

damask

floss silk

glove silk

kapok

moire

noil

organza

pongee

raw silk

samite

sewing silk

shantung

sleave silk

spider silk

spun silk

surah

taffeta

thrown silk

tussah silk

vegetable silk

washable silk

watered silk

wild silk

SIX FLAGS OVER TEXAS

Confederate States
of America

France

Mexico

Republic of Texas

Spain

United States

SKIING DISCIPLINES AND EVENTS

Alpine combined

Alpine downhill race

Alpine giant slalom

Alpine slalom

Alpine supergiant
slalom

biathlon

cross-country
combined

cross-country relay
race

cross-country skiing

freestyle acro or
freestyle ballet

freestyle aerials

freestyle moguls

freestyle ski ballet

freestyle skiing

Nordic cross-
country race

Nordic jumping

ski jumping

slalom

SKIING EQUIPMENT

Alpine boots

aluminum alloy pole

Arlberg or safety strap

basket or snow basket

bent pole

binding

cross-country binding

cross-country pole

cross-country ski

double boot

downhill pole

downhill ski

expert ski

fiberglass pole

freestyle ski

giant slalom ski

jumping ski

laminated wood ski

metal ski

molded boot

plastic ski

pole

powder ski

racing ski

racing ski pole

release binding

short ski

ski boots

ski goggles

ski helmet

ski jump

ski pole

ski wax

slalom ski

snowboard

snowboard binding

snowboard boot

step-in binding

Telemark ski

toe clamp

SKIING MANEUVERS AND TURNS

carved turn

check

Christiania or christie

climb

diagonal stride

double-pole stride

double-poling

downhill turn

edging

Gelandesprung

herringbone

hockey stop or safety stop

jet turn

jump turn

kick turn

lifted stem turn

parallel christie

parallel swing

parallel turn

pole drag

pole plant

quersprung

rotation turn

schuss

short swing

sideslip

sidestep

ski-pole glissade

snap

snowplow

snowplow turn

stem christie or stem christiania

stem turn

step acceleration

step turn

Telemark

tempo turn

traverse

tuck

unweighting

uphill christie

wedeln

SLEEPWEAR

baby doll pajamas	housecoat	nightcap	robe
bathrobe	intimate apparel	nightdress	robe de chambre
bed gown	jammies	nightgown	romper
bed jacket	kimono	nightie	sleeper
dishabille	lingerie	night-robe	sleeping suit
dressing gown	morning dress	nightshirt	smoking jacket
dressing jacket	negligee	pajamas peignor	

SLEEVES

angel sleeve	dolman sleeve	long sleeve	shirt sleeve
bag sleeve	elbow sleeve	mandarin sleeve	short sleeve
balloon sleeve	epaulet sleeve	pagoda sleeve	shoulder puff sleeve
batwing sleeve	funnel sleeve	peasant sleeve	tailored sleeve
bell sleeve	goddess sleeve	puff sleeve	three-quarter sleeve
bishop sleeve	kimono sleeve	push-up sleeve	virago sleeve
cap sleeve	lantern sleeve	raglan sleeve	
cornet sleeve	leg-of-mutton sleeve	set-in sleeve	

SMITHS

A smith is one who works in iron or other metals—but the term may be extended to one who has a special skill or work described by the first element of the combination, e.g. *wordsmith*.

anchorsmith	blacksmith	bronzesmith	chainsmith
arrowsmith	bladesmith	bucklesmith	clocksmith

coppersmith

farrier

forger

goldsmith

gunsmith

hammerman

hammersmith

housesmith

ironsmith

keysmith

knifesmith

locksmith

silversmith

songsmith

stonesmith

tinsmith

toolsmith

tunesmith

weaponsmith

Websmith

whitesmith

wiresmith

wordsmith

SNAKES

adder

anaconda

asp

black-banded

black snake

boa

boa constrictor

brown snake

bull snake

carpet snake

cobra

constrictor

copperhead

coral snake

corn

cottonmouth

diamondback

fer de lance

gaboon viper

garter snake

grass snake

gray-banded king

ground

hognose snake

king snake

long-nosed

mamba

milk snake

moccasin

monocled cobra

non-poisonous snake

ophidian

pine snake

pit viper

poisonous snake

puff adder

python

rat snake

rattlesnake

red-tailed racer

ringed snail-eating

rock python

rock snake

sea snake

serpent

smooth green

viper

water snake

western long-nosed

worm snake

SNOOPY'S SIBLINGS

Andy

Belle

Marbles

Molly

Olaf

Rover

Spike

Snow Conditions and Types

acid snow

blizzard

blowing snow

champagne powder

corn snow

crust or crusted snow

drifting snow

firn

frost snow

graupel

lake-effect snow

low driving snow

névé

onion snow

powder red snow

slush

snow flurries

snow-ice

snow showers

snowstorm

spring snow

thunder snow

whiteout

wind pack

windslab

yellow snow

Soaps

antibacterial soap

baby soap

bar soap

bath soap

castile soap

cosmetic soap

cream soap

deodorant soap

detergent

dish detergent

exfoliating soap

face soap

floating soap

glycerin soap

granulated soap

hand-milled soap

industrial soap

laundry soap or laundry detergent

liquid soap

medicated soap

milled soap

perfumed soap

pumice soap

saddle soap

shampoo

shaving soap

soap flakes

soft soap

toilet soap

Soccer Fouls

carrying the ball

charging dangerously

charging from behind

charging into an opponent

charging the goalkeeper

continual breaking of rules

dangerous play

dissenting from referee's decision

foul or abusive language

handling the ball

holding an opponent

impeding the progress of an opponent

jumping at an opponent

kicking an opponent

making contact with an opponent before touching the ball when tackling an opponent

obstruction

offside

personal foul

preventing the goalkeeper from releasing the ball

professional foul

pushing an opponent

sandwiching

spitting at an opponent

striking an opponent

tactical foul

tripping an opponent

ungentlemanly conduct

unsportsmanlike conduct

SOCCER KICKS

banana kick

bicycle kick

chip

corner kick

direct free kick

direct kick

drop kick

flick kick

free kick

goal kick

half-volley

indirect free kick

indirect kick

instep

inswinger

lofted kick

long corner

long pass

low drive

outswinger

overhead volley

penalty kick

punt

scissors kick

short corner

spot kick

toe kick

volley

SOCCER POSITIONS

center

center forward

center midfielder

center striker

goalie

left defense

left forward

left fullback

left inside forward

left midfielder

left wing right defense

right forward

right fullback

right inside forward

right midfielder

right wing

striker

sweeper

SOCIAL SCIENCES

anthropology

anthropometry

applied psychology

archaeology

cartography

cultural anthropology

domestic science

economics

ethnography

ethnology

experimental psychology

genetics and growth studies

geography

history

human evolution

human geography

linguistic anthropology

linguistics

paleoanthropology

physical anthropology

physical geography

political science

primatology

psychology

social anthropology

social geography

social psychology

social statistics

sociology

SOFTBALL POSITIONS

catcher

designated hitter

extra hitter

first base

left center

left field

pitcher

right center

right field

second base

third base

SOFTWOODS

A softwood is a conifer such as pine, fir, or spruce as distinguished from broadleaved or hardwood trees. Softwood is comprised of fibers and tracheids (no vessels) and the wood is relatively soft or easily cut. These are common and representative examples.

balsam

basswood

box elder

bristlecone fir

cedar

cypress

Douglas fir

hemlock

Japanese cedar

northern white pine

ponderosa pine

poplar

redwood

spruce

sugar pine

tulipwood

tupelo

white fir

white pine

yellow longleaf pine

SOIL TYPES

A horizon

acidic soil

adobe soil

alkaline soil

alluvial soil

alluvium

arable soil

argil

B horizon
backfill soil
bedrock
bog soil
bole
boulder clay
C horizon
chalk
china clay
clay
clunch
D horizon
decalcified soil

deflocculated soil
desertic soil
diatomaceous earth
dispersed soil
eluvium
fertile soil
friable soil
fuller's earth
horizon
humus
indurated clay
kaolin
kaolinite

laterite
leaf mold
lithosol
loam
loess
marl
mold
mulch
peat
plow soil
porcelain clay
potter's clay
red clay

regosol
residual clay
sand
sedimentary clay
silt
spodosol
subsoil
till
topsoil
tundra soil

SOLDIER TYPES

askari
bashi-bazouk
cadet
carabineer
cavalryman
centurion
chasseur
commando
commissioned officer
condottiere
conscript
cuirassier
doughboy

dragoon
foot soldier
fusilier
ghazi
GI
grenadier
guardsman
guerrilla
gunner
halberdier
hoplite
hussar
infantryman

janissary
kern
landsknecht
lascar
legionary or legionnaire
man-at-arms
marine
mercenary
minuteman
non-commissioned officer
officer

orderly
paratrooper
peltast
poilu
private
ranger
rapparee
recruit
regular
rifleman
scout
sentry
sepoy

sowar

spahi

standard-bearer

trooper

trumpeter

vexillary

SOUPS

alphabet soup

asparagus soup

avgolemono

beef broth

beef stew

bird's-nest soup

bisque

borscht

bouillabaisse

boullion

broccoli soup

broth

burgoo

cheddar soup

chicken broth

chicken noodle soup

chicken soup

chowder

clam chowder

cock-a-leekie

congee

consommé

corn soup

cream soup

egg drop soup

fish soup

French onion soup

fruit soup

gazpacho

gumbo

hot and sour soup

lentil soup

lobster bisque

madrilene

matzo ball soup

minestrone

miso soup

mock turtle soup

mulligatawny

mushroom soup

onion soup

oxtail soup

pea soup

pistou

potage

potato and leek soup

potato soup

pot-au-feu

Scotch broth

split-pea soup

stock

tomato soup

turtle soup

vegetable soup

vichyssoise

wonton soup

SOUTH AMERICAN INDIAN PEOPLES

Araucanian

Arawak

Aymara

Aztec

Carib

Cashinahua

Chibcha

Chimu

Ge

Guarani

Inca

Makuna

Maraco

Maya

Mixtec

Quechua

Toltec

Tupi

Zapotec

SPACECRAFT TYPES

capsule
fly-by probe
flying saucer
lander
launch vehicle

missile
module
orbiter
planetary lander
probe

retro-rocket
rocket
satellite
spaceship
space shuttle

space station
space vehicle
starship
subsatellite

SPECTROSCOPES AND SPECTROMETERS

analytical spectrometer

crystal spectrometer

diffraction spectroscope

direct-reading spectrometer

direct-reading spectroscope

direct-vision spectroscope

mass spectrograph

mass spectrometer

mass spectroscope

microspectrophotometer

microspectroscope

microwave spectroscope

monochromator

ocular spectroscope

prism spectroscope

reversion spectroscope

spectrobolometer

spectrograph

spectrometer

spectrophotometer

spectroradiometer

star spectroscope

telespectroscope

X-ray spectrometer

SPICES

allspice
anise
basil
bay leaves
beau monde
black pepper

bouquet garni
Cajun spice
caraway
cardamom
cayenne
celery seed

chervil
chili powder
chipotle powder
chives
cilantro
cinnamon

cloves
coriander
cumin
curry powder
dill
fennel

540

fines herbes
five spices
garlic powder
garlic salt
ginger
kosher salt
mace
marjoram
mustard seed

nutmeg
onion powder
onion salt
oregano
paprika
parsley
pepper
peppermint
pickling spice

poppy seed
red pepper
rosemary
saffron
sage
salt
savory
sea salt
sesame seed

sugar
summer savory
tarragon
thyme
turmeric
vanilla
white pepper

SPOONS

after-dinner coffee spoon
bouillon spoon
chocolate spoon
citrus spoon

coffee spoon
demitasse spoon
dessert spoon
five o'clock spoon

ice cream spoon
iced beverage spoon
place spoon
salt spoon

soup spoon
sundae spoon
tablespoon
teaspoon

SPORTING ACTIVITIES

air sport or aerial sport
angling sport
animal sport
athletic sport or athletics
auto sport or motor sport
ball and stick sport
blood sport

combat sport
contact sport
court sport
cycle sport
equestrian sport
gymnastic sport
hunting sport
indoor sport

martial art or combat sport
non-contact sport
Olympic sport
outdoor sport
participator sport
racket sport
Special Olympics sport

spectator sport
target sport
team sport
throwing sport
track and field sport
water sport
wheel sport
winter sport

SPORTS, AIR

aerial skiing

aerobatics

aeromodeling

aerotow

air racing

ballooning

bungee jumping

flying

freefalling

gliding

hang gliding

helicopter flying

hydroplane racing

kiting

microlighting

parachuting

paragliding

parasailing

parascending

pylon racing

sky-diving

soaring

sports parachuting

SPORTS, ANGLING

big-game fishing

coarse fishing

fly-fishing

game fishing

match fishing

sea fishing

SPORTS, ANIMAL

barrel racing

bronc riding and bronco busting

bullfighting

bull riding

calf roping

camel racing

carriage driving

cockfighting

cross-country riding

deer hunting

dog racing

dogsled racing

dressage

driving

endurance riding

equestrian sport

falconry

fishing

fox hunting

greyhound racing

gymkhana

harness racing

horseback riding

horsemanship

horse racing

hunting

ice fishing

pack riding

pato

pigeon racing

point-to-point

polo

rodeo

show jumping

steeplechase

steer roping

steer wrestling

team penning

team roping

three-day event

trail riding

trotting

vaulting

Western riding

SPORTS, AUTO AND MOTOR

autocross

automobile racing

demolition derby

dirt car racing

drag racing

Formula One racing

go-carting

Grand Prix

GT or grand touring

hot-rod racing

Indy car racing

midget racing

motocross or scrambling

motorcycle racing

motor racing

off-track racing

rally cross

rallying and cross-country racing

sidecar racing

sports car racing

sprint car racing

stock-car racing

track-racing

vintage car racing

SPORTS, BALL AND BALL-AND-STICK

bandy

baseball

basketball

beach volleyball

billiards

bocce

boules

bowls

cricket

croquet

curling

field hockey

fivepin bowling

football

golf

handball

hurling

ice hockey

jai alai

korfball

lacrosse

lawn tennis

netball

ninepins

paddleball

paddle tennis

pelota

pétanque

polo

pool

rackets

raquetball

roller hockey

rounders

rugby

shinty

skittles

snooker

soccer

softball

speedball

squash

stickball

table tennis

tennis

tenpin bowling

touch football

volleyball

water polo

Sports, Combat and Martial Arts

aikido

archery

arm and wrist wrestling or Indian wrestling

arnis

bando

bersilat

bojutsu

boxing

capoeira

choi kwang-do

Cornish wrestling

daito ryu

dumog

escrima

fencing

freestyle wrestling

genbukan

glimae

go-ti

Greco-Roman wrestling

Greek boxing

haphido

himizu ryu

Hsing yi

hwarang-do

laijutsu

Icelandic wrestling

jeet kune do

jobajutsu

jogo do pau

jojutsu

jousting

judo

jujitsu

jukendo

kalari payat

karate

kendo

kenipo

kenjutsu

kenpo

kiaijutsu

kickboxing

kobu-jutsu

kung fu

kyujutsu

laido

lua

main tindju

mud wrestling

naginata-jutsu

ninjutsu

pankration

pentjak-silat

pukulan

sambo wrestling

savate

self-defence

shorinji kempo

spearmanship

stick fighting

sumo wrestling

swordsmanship

tae kwon do

t'ai chi taijutsu

tang soo do

tegumi

Thai kick boxing

wing tsun

wrestling

wu shu

zipota

Zulu stick fighting

Sports, Court

badminton

basketball

court tennis

deck tennis

handball

jai alai or pelota

lawn tennis

paddleball

paddle tennis

pallone

platform tennis

racquetball

544

roller hockey

rugby fives

shuffleboard

squash

table tennis or
Ping-Pong

tennis

volleyball

SPORTS, CYCLE

bicycling

BMX racing

cycle racing

cyclocross

in-line skating

mountain biking

road cycle racing

roller blading

roller derby

roller hockey

roller skating

roller skiing

skateboarding

track cycle racing

SPORTS, EQUESTRIAN

cross-country
jumping

cross-country riding

dressage

endurance riding

eventing

grand prix

gymkhana

harness racing

horse racing

hunting

jumping

marathon driving

modern pentathlon

one-day event

point-to-point

polo

puissance

riding

rodeo

roping

showing

showjumping

stadium jumping

steeplechasing

steer wrestling

three-day event

track racing

trail riding

trotting

SPORTS, GYMNASTIC

acrobatics or sports
acrobatics

asymmetric bars

balance beam

floor exercises

high bar

horizontal bar

individual all-around

long horse

mini-trampolining

parallel bars

pommel horse

rhythmic gymnastics

rings

side horse

trampolining

tumbling

uneven parallel bars

vault

SPORTS, HUNTING

beagling
blood sport
bullfighting
chase
cockfighting
coursing

deerstalking
falconry
ferreting
fishing
fox hunting
grouse shooting

mink hunting
otter hunting
pheasant shooting
pigeon shooting
pigsticking
shoot

still-hunt
turkey hunting
waterfowl hunting
wildfowling

SPORTS, OLYMPIC

aquatics (diving, swimming, synchronized swimming, water polo)
archery
badminton
baseball
basketball
biathlon
bobsled
boxing
canoe-kayak

curling
cycling
diving
equestrian
fencing
field hockey
figure skating
freestyle skiing
gymnastics
handball
ice hockey
judo

luge
modern pentathlon
Nordic skiing
rowing
sailing
shooting
skiing or alpine skiing
snowboarding
soccer or football
softball
speedskating
swimming

synchronized swimming
table tennis
taekwondo
tennis
track and field
triathlon
volleyball
water polo
weightlifting
wrestling

SPORTS, OUTDOOR

backpacking
camping

croquet
cross-country skiing

downhill skiing
fishing

Frisbee
geocaching

golf

hiking

hunting

ice climbing

kayaking

mountain biking

mountaineering

orienteering

rock climbing

sailing

speleology or spelunking

superalpinism or Alpine climbing

surfing

trapshooting

wilderness survival

windsurfing

SPORTS, SPECIAL OLYMPICS

alpine skiing

aquatics

athletics

badminton

basketball

bocce

bowling

cycling

equestrian

figure skating

floor hockey

golf

gymnastics

ice hockey

judo

kayaking

pitch & putt

powerlifting

roller skating

sailing

soccer softball

speed skating

table tennis

team handball

tennis

volleyball

SPORTS, TARGET

archery

billiards

boccie or bocci

bowling

Canadian 5-pin bowling

candlepin bowling

carom billiards

clay pigeon shooting

croquet

crossbow archery

curling

darts

duckpin bowling

Frisbee golf

golf

green bowling

horseshoe pitching

laser clay shooting

lawn bowling

pistol shooting

pool

rifle shooting

sharpshooting

shuffleboard

skeet shooting

skittles

snooker

ten-pin bowling

trapshooting

Sports, Team

Australian rules football

bandy

baseball

basketball

beach volleyball

beeball

cabinet ball

Canadian football

cornerball

crew

cricket

curling

dodge ball

doubles tennis

field hockey

flag football

football

Gaelic football

hurling

ice hockey

jai alai

kickball

korfball

lacrosse

netball

paintball

polo

polocrosse

relay race

roller hockey

rounders

rugby

six-man football

soccer

softball

speedball

stickball

team bobsledding

team handball

touch football

ultimate Frisbee

volleyball

water polo

Sports, Throwing

Aunt Sally

boomeranging

darts

discus throw

dwarf throwing

Frisbee

Frisbee golf

hammer throw

horseshoe pitching

javelin throw

shot put

ultimate Frisbee

Sports, Track and Field or Athletics

1,500 meter run

10 km walk

10,000 meter run

100 meter dash

100 meter run

100 meter hurdles

110 meter hurdles

20 km walk

200 meter run

3,000 meter steeplechase

400 meter run

400 meter hurdles

4×100 meter relay

4×400 meter relay

5,000 meter run

548

50 km walk

800 meter run

cross-country running

decathlon

discus throw

fitness walking

hammer throw

heptathlon

high jump

hurdles

javelin throw

long-distance running

long jump

marathon

middle-distance running

modern pentathlon

pole vault

race walking

relay racing

shot put

sprinting

steeplechasing

triathlon

triple jump

wheelchair racing

SPORTS, WATER

birling

boating

body surfing

canoe polo

canoe sailing

canoe slalom racing

canoeing

distance swimming

diving

dragon boat racing

fin swimming

fishing

foldboating

free diving

inner tube water polo

jet skiing

kayaking

laser sailing

lifesaving

motorboat racing

offshore yacht racing

powerboat racing

rafting

rowing

sailing

sailplaning

scuba diving

sculling

skin diving

snorkeling

surfing

surf lifesaving

swimming

synchronized swimming

underwaterball

underwater diving

underwater hockey

underwater rugby

wakeboarding

wakeskating

water aerobics

water gymnastics

water polo

water skiing

water ski jump

whitewater canoeing

whitewater rafting

windsurfing

yachting

SPORTS, WINTER

Alpine combined event

Alpine skiing

bandy

biathlon

bobsledding

broomball

cross-country skiing

549

curling

dogsled racing

downhill skiing

figure skating

freestyle skiing

giant slalom

heli-skiing

ice blocking

ice boating

ice dancing

ice hockey

ice sailing

ice skating

luge

mogul skiing

Nordic combined event

Nordic skiing

off-piste skiing

short-track speed skating

skating

skibob racing

skiing

skijoring

ski jumping

ski mountaineering

slalom

sledding

snowboarding

snowmobiling

snowshoeing

snow tubing

speed skating

speed skiing

super giant slalom

synchronized skating

telemark skiing

tobogganing

winter pentathlon

SPREADS AND FILLINGS

anchovy paste

apple butter

butter

cheese spread

chicken salad

chicken spread

conserves

cream cheese

egg salad

fruit butter

goose liver

ham salad

ham spread

honey

hummus

jam

jelly

low-fat spread

margarine

marmalade

marshmallow fluff

mayonnaise

oleo

peanut butter

preserves

sandwich spread

soft margarine

tofu

tuna salad

turkey spread

vegetable spread

STARS, BRIGHTEST

Achernar

Acrux

Adhara

Aldebaran

Alpha Centauri

Altair

Antares

Arcturus

Becrux

Betelgeuse

Canopus

Capella

Castor

Deneb

Fomalhaut

Gacrux

Hadar or Agena   Regulus   Sirius

Pollux   Rigel   Spica

Procyon   Shaula   Vega

STARS, MAIN SEQUENCE

blue star   brown dwarf   white star

blue/white star   red dwarf   yellow star

STARS, NEAREST

Alpha Centauri A   Lutten 726–8 or L   Proxima Centauri or   Ross 248

Alpha Centauri B   726–8   Alpha Centauri C   Sirius A

Barnard's Star   Luyten 726–8 B or   Rigil Kentaurus or   Sirius B

Lalande 21185   UV Ceti   Rigil Kent   Wolf 359

Ross 154

STAR TYPES

A star   blue-white giant   dark star   fixed star

astral body   brown dwarf   double star   flare star

B star   C star or carbon star   dwarf star   G star

binary star   cataclysmic variable   early-type star   giant star

black dwarf star   star   eclipsing binary star   gravity star

blaze star   Cepheid   eclipsing variable star   Greenwich star

blue giant star   circumpolar star   eruptive variable star   hydrogen star

blue star   close binary star   evening star   intrinsic variable star

blue supergiant star   comparison star   F star   irregular star

K star

late-type star

long-period variable star

M star

main sequence star

morning star

multiple star

N star

nautical star

nebulous star

neutron star

nova

O star

orange star

O-type star

R star

radio star

red dwarf star

red giant star

red star

red supergiant star

RR Lyrae star

runaway star

S star

semiregular variable star

silicon star

solar star

spectroscopic binary star

standard star

sun star

supergiant star

supermassive star

supernova

variable star

visible binary star

white dwarf star

white star

X-ray binary star

X-ray star

yellow dwarf star

yellow giant star

zenith star

STATES, CONFEDERATE

Alabama

Arkansas

Florida

Georgia

Louisiana

Mississippi

North Carolina

South Carolina

Tennessee

Texas

Virginia

STATES, ORIGINAL U.S.

Connecticut

Delaware

Georgia

Maryland

Massachusetts

New Hampshire

New Jersey

New York

North Carolina

Pennsylvania

Rhode Island

South Carolina

Virginia

STATICS BRANCHES

Statics is the branch of mechanics concerned with the maintenance of equilibrium in bodies by the interaction of forces upon them. The principles of statics are widely applied in the design and construction of buildings and machinery.

aerostatics	gnathostatics	hydrostatics	social statics
biostatics	graphostatics	hygrostatics	stereostatics
electrostatics	gyrostatics	magnetostatics	thermostatics
geostatics	hematostatics	rheostatics	

STEEL VARIETIES

alloy steel	crucible steel	high-strength steel	soft steel
bearing steel	electrical steel	medium-carbon steel	stainless steel
Bessemer steel	electric-arc steel	mild steel	tool steel
blister steel	flat-rolled steel	open-hearth steel	wear-resistant steel
carbon steel	hard steel	oxygen steel	
cold-rolled steel	high-carbon steel	rolled steel	

STEWS

beef bourguignon	cassoulet	fish stew	lobscouse
beef stew	chicken purloo	fricassee	lobster stew
bouillabaisse	chicken stew	goulash	mulligan stew
Brunswick stew	chili	grillade	olio
burgoo	chili con carne	hotpot	olla podrida
carbonade	chowder	Irish stew	osso bucco
casserole	coq au vin	jambalaya	oyster stew

pepper pot	pottage	salmagundi	turkey stew
pot-au-feu	ragout	slumgullion	
potpie	ratatouille	tsimmes	

STOCK TYPES

active stock

air pocket stock

alphabet stock

assessable stock

authorized capital stock

bank stock

bargain stock

blue chip stock

borrowed stock

capital stock

cheap stock

classified stock

common stock

contramarket stock

control stock

convertible adjusted preferred stock

convertible exchangeable preferred stock

convertible preferred stock

corporate stock

countercyclical stock

cumulative convertible preferred stock

cumulative preferred stock

cyclical stock

deal stock

debenture stock

defensive stock

deferred stock

dummy stock

Dutch auction preferred stock

eighth stock

first preferred stock

floating stock

glamor stock

growth stock

guaranteed stock

half-stock

high-grade stock

high-tech stock

hot stock

hypothecated stock

inactive stock

income stock

initial public offering

interest-sensitive stock

issued capital stock

legend stock

letter stock

leveraged stock

listed stock

loaned stock

long stock

margin stock

micro-cap stock

new issue

no-load stock

nonassessable stock

noncumulative preferred stock

nonvoting stock

no-par stock

no-par-value stock

one-decision stock

ordinary shares

orphan stock

out-of-favor stock

over-the-counter stock

pale blue chip

participating preferred stock

penny stock

performance stock

preference stock

preferred stock

protective stock

quality stock

quarter stock

reacquired stock

restricted stock

seasoned stock

secondary stock

short stock

small cap stock

special situation stock

specialty stock

speculative stock

standard stock

ten-share unit stock

tracking stock

treasury stock

unissued capital stock

unlisted stock

value stock

vetoing stock

voting-right certificate

voting stock

watered stock

whisper stock

widow-and-orphan stock

yo-yo stock

STONE AGE CULTURES

The Stone Age is a broad prehistoric time period that began about 2 million years ago, when humans widely used stone for toolmaking. The period encompasses the first widespread use of technology in human evolution.

Acheulean

Aurignacian

Azilian

Capsian

Chellean

Combe-Capelle

Cro-Magnon

Dabban

Eolithic

Epipaleolithic

Goodwin

Magdalenian

Mesolithic

Middle Awash

Mousterian

Neolithic

Oldowan

Olduvai

Paleolithic

Pre-Chellean

STONES

agalmatolite

anthraconite

aplite

basalt

beetlestone

bloodstone

bluestone

boulder

brimstone

brownstone

burstone

cairngorm

calcarenite

chalk

claystone

clinkstone

cobblestone

dendrite

diabase

diorite

dolerite

dolmen

dolomite

dolostone

dripstone

eaglestone

emery

fieldstone

flagstone

flint

floatstone

freestone

geode
gneiss
goldstone
granite
granulite
graywacke
greenstone
grit
hairstone
hoarstone
hone slate
ironstone
lava
limestone

lithic sandstone
lodestone
marble
megalith
menhir
milkstone
monolith
moorstone
mudstone
obsidian
omphalos
pitchstone
porphyry
pumice

quarrystone
quartz
quartz arenite
quartzite
rance
rottenstone
sandstone
serpentine
shale
slab
slate
smokestone
snakestone
soapstone

stalactite
stalagmite
starstone
steatite
stinkstone
thunderstone
tilestone
tinstone
touchstone
trap tufa
wacke
whitestone

Stores

apothecary
auto parts store
baby store
bakery
big-box store
bodega
bookstore
boutique
butcher
candy store
card store
chain store

chandlery
charcuterie
charity shop
cheese shop
china shop
clothing store
computer store
confectioner
consignment store
convenience store
corner store
dairy

delicatessen
department store
dime store
discount store
dollar store
dress shop
drugstore
electronics store
factory store
fishmonger
five-and-dime

florist or flower store
furniture store
general store
gift shop or gift store
grocery store
haberdashery
hardware store
hat shop
hobby store
housewares store
Internet e-tailer

jeweler

junk shop

kitchen store

lawn and garden
store

liquor store

marine store

men's store

music store

novelty shop

one-stop shop

outlet store

package store

patisserie

pawn shop

perfumery

pet shop

pharmacy

pro shop

retail store

secondhand store

shoe store

soda fountain

specialty store

sporting goods store

stationer

supermarket

superstore

ten-cent store

thrift shop

tobacconist

toy store

variety store

video store

warehouse store

women's store

STORM TYPES

anticyclone

blizzard

cloudburst

cyclone

deluge

downpour

dust storm

electrical storm

gale

graupel

haboob

hailstorm

hurricane

ice storm

isolated storm

line squall

maelstrom

monsoon

multicell cluster
storm

multicell line storm

neutercane

nor'easter or
northeaster

perfect storm

rainsquall

rain storm

rainstorm

sandstorm

single-cell storm

sirocco

sleet

southeaster

southwester

squall

subtropical storm

supercell storm

tempest

thundershower

thunderstorm

tornado

torrential rain

tropical cyclone

tropical storm

twister

typhoon

violent storm

wind storm

winter storm

STORY TYPES

adventure story

allegory

apologue

autobiography

beast epic

beast fable

bedtime story

biography

chiller

chivalric romance

classical detective story

conte

crime story

detective story

dime novel or penny dreadful

drama

epic or epos

exemplum or didactic tale or moral tale

fable

fabliau

fairy tale fantasy

fish story

folktale or folk story

gest or geste

ghost story

hard-boiled detective story

hero tale

horror story

lai

legend

long-short story

love story

Märchen

Milesian tale

mystery

myth

narrative

novel

nursery tale

parable

penny dreadful

romance

romantic adventure

running story

saga

saint's legend

science fiction story

short short story

short story

sketch

solar myth

spy story

supernatural tale

suspense story

thriller vignette

Western

whodunit

S T O V E S   A N D   F U R N A C E S

arc furnace

assay furnace

Bessemer furnace

blast furnace

boiler

box stove

butane stove

calefactor

camp stove

cast-iron stove

coal furnace

coal stove

coke oven

cook stove

crucible furnace

Dutch stove

electric-arc furnace

electric furnace

electric stove

fireplace

fireplace stove

forced-air furnace

Franklin stove

freestanding stove

fuel-cell furnace

gas furnace

gas stove

grill

hibachi

induction furnace

kerosene stove

kitchen stove

melting furnace

Norwegian stove

oil furnace

oil stove

open-front furnace

open-hearth furnace

oven

portable stove

potbellied stove

radiant stove

range

reducing furnace

resistance furnace

reverberatory furnace

shaft furnace

slag furnace

smelter

solar furnace

wall furnace

STREETS AND ALLEYS

alleyway	bystreet	drive	stop street
artery	close	lane	thoroughfare
avenue	court	mews	through street
back street	crescent	one-way street	two-way street
blind alley	cross street	place	vennel
boulevard	cul-de-sac	row	wynd
by-alley	dead-end street	side street	

SUFFIXES

ability	an	ate	chroous
able	ana	athon	cide
ably	ance	ation	clase
acea	ancy	ative	clasis
aceae	andry	biosis	cle
aceous	ane	blast	coccus
acious	anmdrous	carp	coele
acity	anthous	carpic	colous
acy	arama	carpous	cracy
adelphous	arch	cele	crat
agogue	archy	cene	cule
aholic	arian	ceno	cyst
al	aroo	cephalic	cyte
ales	arooni	cephalous	dactyl
algia	asis	chrome	dactylous
amine	ast	chronic	dendron

derm	fication	ial	ing
drome	fid	ian	ious
ectomy	florous	iasis	isation
efy	fug	iatrics	ise
elle	gamy	iatry	ish
emia	gen	ibility	ism
ence	genesis	ible	ist
ensis	genetic	ibly	istic
eous	genic	ic	istical
er	genous	ical	istics
erce	geny	ician	itis
ergic	glot	ics	ite
ern	gnathous	id	itious
eroo	gnomy	ide	itive
ers	gnosis	idea	ity
ery	gnostic	idine	ium
escence	gon	idion	ization
escent	gony	idium	ize
ese	grade	ie	kinesis
esis	gram	iensis	latry
esque	graph	ier	lepsy
ess	graphy	iform	less
est	gynous	iformes	like
eur	gyny	ify	lilia
euse	hedral	il	ling
ey	hedron	ile	lith
fest	hile	ility	lithic
fex	holic	illion	logue
fic	ia	ine	logy

ly	ola	phagia	pode
lysis	oma	phagous	podium
lyte	onym	phagy	poiesis
lyze	oon	phany	poietic
machy	opia	phasia	poodous
mancy	opic	phil	pterous
mania	opsia	philia	rel
megalia	opsis	philiac	rhiza
megaly	opsy	philic	rrhagia
ment	opy	philism	rrhaphy
mer	or	philous	rrhea
merous	orama	phily	rrhexis
metric	orial	phobia	rrhiza
metry	ory	phony	rrhoea
morph	ose	phore	sauer
morphic	osis	phorous	saurus
morphism	ota	phrenia	scope
morphous	ote	phrone	sepalous
mycete	otic	phyllou	ski
mycetes	our	plasia	sky
ness	ous	plasm	some
nomy	pagus	plast	sophy
oate	parous	plasty	sperm
ock	pathic	plasy	spermal
odont	pathy	plegia	sphyte
odus	ped	ploid	sporous
odynia	pede	pnea	stichous
oid	penia	pod	stome
oidea	phage	poda	stomous

stomy	tomous	trophy	vorous
taxis	tomy	tropic	ward
taxy	ton	tropism	wards
teen	tonia	tropous	xion
therm	tonic	tropy	yer
thermy	trix	tudety	zoa
tion	trope	type	zoon
tious	troph	urgy	
tome	trophic	vore	

SUGAR VARIETIES

barley malt syrup	crystallized sugar	light brown sugar	raw sugar
beet sugar	dark brown sugar	liquid sugar	refined sugar
brown sugar	decorative sugar	loaf sugar	refined sugar syrup
burnt sugar	demerara sugar	lump sugar	sanding sugar
cane sugar	fondant sugar	maple sugar	simple sugar
caramelized sugar	fruit sugar	maple syrup	sorghum
castor sugar	golden syrup	milk sugar	superfine sugar
cinnamon sugar	golden yellow sugar	molasses	syrup
coarse sugar	granulated sugar	muscovado sugar	table sugar
compound sugar	grape sugar	pearl sugar	treacle
confectioner's sugar or powdered sugar	honey	plantation sugar	turbinado sugar
corn sugar	icing sugar	raisin syrup	white sugar

Sugars and Sweeteners, Artificial

acesulfame potassium

alitame

aspartame

cyclamate

hydrogenated glucose syrup

saccharin

sorbitol

stevia

sucralose

xylitol

Sugars, Biological

arabinose

deoxyribose

dextrose

fructose

fucose

galactose

glucose

lactose

lactulose

levulose

maltose

mannose

pentose

raffinose

rhamnose

ribose

ribulose

saccharose

sorbose

sucrose

tetrose

trehalose

triose

xylose

Suits

anti-G suit

bathing suit

bodysuit

boiler suit

business suit

camouflage suit

casual suit

cat suit

coordinates

coveralls

diving suit

double-breasted suit

dress suit

dry suit

exposure suit

flight suit

G suit

gray flannel suit

jogging suit or track suit

jumpsuit

leisure suit

lounge suit

mod suit

monkey suit

one-piece suit

pantsuit

pinstripe suit

playsuit

pressure suit

rain suit

riding habit

romper suit

sack suit

seersucker suit

separates

single-breasted suit

ski suit

slack suit

snowsuit

space suit

sports suit

summer suit

sun suit

sweat suit

swimsuit

tailored suit

tank suit

three-piece suit

town-and-country
suit

tropical suit

trouser suit

tunic suit

tuxedo

two-piece suit

wet suit

zoot suit

SULFA DRUGS

Clear up bacterial infections by interfering with the metabolism of the bacteria. Sulfa drugs have been largely replaced by antibiotics.

para-
aminobenzene-
sulfonamide

phthalylsulfathiazole

prontosil

succinylsufathiazole

sulfacetamide

sulfadiazine

sulfadimethoxine

sulfaguanidine

sulfamerazine

sulfamethazine

sulfamethizole

sulfamethoxazole

sulfamezathine

sulfanilamide

sulfapyradine

sulfapyrazine

sulfasalazine

sulfathiazole

sulfisoxazole

sulfonamide

SURGERIES

abdominoplasty

acetabuloplasty

allograft or
homograft

apicectomy

appendectomy

arterioplasty

arthroplasty

autograft

blepharoplasty

cesarean section

cheiloplasty

chiroplasty

cholecystectomy

cholelithotomy

closed-heart surgery

colostomy

cordotomy

craniotomy

cryosurgery

cystectomy

D & C or dilatation
and curettage

debridement

episiotomy

face lift

fenestration

gastrectomy

goniopuncture

hepatectomy

hysterectomy

ileostomy

iridectomy

keratoplasty

labioplasty

laparotomy

laryngectomy

lithonephrotomy or
nephrolithotomy

lobotomy

mammaplasty

mastectomy

meloplasty

necrotomy

nephrectomy

neurosurgery

neurotomy

nose job

oophorectomy or ovariectomy

open-heart surgery

orchiectomy or testectomy

ostectomy

osteoplasty

otoplasty

phlebotomy or venesection

pneumonectomy

prefrontal lobotomy

rectoplasty

rhinoplasty

rhizotomy

salpingectomy

splenectomy

strabotomy

thoracotomy

tonsillectomy

tracheostomy or tracheotomy

tummy tuck

ulnar collateral ligament reconstruction or Tommy John surgery

vasectomy

SUSHI

akagai

amaebi

anago

aoyagi

bara sushi

Boston roll

California roll

chirashi-sushi

datemaki

ebi

fugu

futomaki

gari

gomoku sushi iso-don

gunkan

hamachi

hashi

hirame

holiday roll

hosomaki

hotate

ika

ikura

inari sushi

kaibashira

kani

kappa

kappa ma

kobashira

maguro

maki sushi

masago

masu

maze-sushi

mirugai

New York roll

nigiri sushi

nori

ocha

okonomi sushi

onigri

oshizushi

pesto roll

Philadelphia roll

saba

sake

sashimi

shimesaba

shoyu

shrimp roll

smoked salmon roll

spider roll

summer melon roll

sushi

tako

tai

tamago

tekka maki

temaki

Texas roll

toro

tuna salad roll

unagi

uni

uramaki

wasabi

SWEATERS

boatneck sweater

bolero

boucle

bulky

cable-knit sweater

cardigan

cashmere sweater

coat sweater

crewneck sweater

envelope-neck sweater

evening sweater

Fair Isle sweater

fisherman's sweater

hand-knit sweater

jersey

mohair sweater

polo sweater

poor boy sweater

pull-on sweater

pullover sweater

rollneck sweater

ski sweater

slip-on

slipover sweater

sloppy Joe

sweater vest

sweatshirt sweater

turtleneck sweater

twin sweater set

V-neck sweater

woolly

SWIMMING STROKES AND KICKS

American crawl

Australian crawl

back crawl

back kick

backstroke

breaststroke

butterfly

crawl

dog paddle

dolphin kick

fishtail kick

flutter kick

freestyle

frog kick

front crawl

overarm stroke

recovery stroke

scissors kick

sidestroke

trudgeon

wedge kick

whip kick

SWIMWEAR

bathing suit

beach hat

beach pants

bikini

bikini skirt

board shorts

board skirt

coverup

flip-flops

flippers

goggles

halter top

hipster shorts

jams

maillot

monokini

one-piece bathing suit

pareo

sarong

sheath

shorts

string bikini

sundress

surf shorts

swimdress

swimming trunks

swimsuit

tankini

tank suit or tank

tank top

thong

trunks

T-shirt

tunic

two-piece bathing suit

wetsuit

SWINE BREEDS

American Landrace

babirusa

Berkshire

boar

bush pig

Cheshire

Chester White

domestic pig

Dorset

Duroc

Duroc Jersey

Essex Saddleback

Gloucester Old Spots

Hampshire

Hereford

Landrace

Large Black

Large White

Mangalitsa

Middle White

Minnesota Number One

Minnesota Number Two

National Long White Lop-eared

Ohio Improved Chester White or OIC

pig

Poland China

suid

Vietnamese Pot-bellied

warthog

Wessex Saddleback

wild boar

wild pig

Yorkshire

SWISS ARMY KNIFE TOOLS

awl

ballpoint pen

belt clip

bottle opener

can opener

cap lifter

combination tool

compass

corkscrew

cut and picker blade

cuticle pusher

divot fixer

electrician blade

emergency blade

fine screwdriver

fish scaler

flashlight

gutting blade

hoof cleaner

key ring

lanyard hole

large blade

large screwdriver

large serrated blade

magnifying glass

metal file

metal saw

mini screwdriver

multi-purpose hook

nail cleaner

nail file

orange peeler

Phillips screwdriver

pliers

reamer with punch

ruler

scissors

shackle key

small blade

small screwdriver

567

spirit level

straight pin

thermometer

toothpick

tweezers

wire stripper

wood chisel

wood saw

Swords

backsword

baldric

bilbo

broadsword

claymore

cutlass

ensiform

épée

Excalibur

falchion

false edge

foil

gladiate

hand-and-a-half

hanger

hilt

knuckle-bow

one-hand sword

pommel

quillons

rapier

saber

scabbard

scimitar

shamshir

sidearm

smallsword

spear point

Toledo

two-handed sword

yalaghan

TABLES AND DESKS

ambo	coffee table	drop-leaf table	lampstand
banquet table	computer table	drum table	lamp table
bar	conference table	duchesse	lap desk
basin stand	console table	end table	lectern
bedside table	counter	envelope table	library table
bed table	credence table	escritoire	nesting tables
billiard table	credenza	extension table	nightstand
buffet	davenport	folding table	night table
bureau	dinette table	gaming table	occasional table
butterfly table	dining table	gate-leg table	operating table
capstan table	dissecting table	head table	Parsons table
captain's table	door desk	high table	partners' table
card table	drawing table	kitchen table	pedestal table
carrel	dresser	kneehole desk	Pembroke table
cocktail table	dressing table	laboratory table	piecrust table

pier table

pool table

pouch table

reading desk

refectory table

rent table

roll-top desk

round table

salon table

secretaire

secretary

sideboard

side table

steam table

step table

taboret

tambour

teapoy

tea table

tea wagon

tray table

trestle table

tripod

trivet table

trolley

TV table

typewriter table

vanity table

vargueno

workbench

work table

writing desk

writing table

TAE KWON DO MOVES

ahp cha-gi

ahre maggi

cha-gi

chi-gi

dolryo cha-gi

dung-joomock chi-gi

dwi-cha-gi

guligi cha-gi

guligi chi-gi

gyoroogi

hecho maggi

hosinsool

kyong-ye

maggi

me-joomok chi-gi

momtong maggi

palkoop chi-gi

pyon-joomock chi-gi

sob-nal chi-gi

son-nal dung chi-gi

son-nal maggi

twi o-cha-gi

wee maggi

yeot pero maggi

yop cha-gi

TAPES

adhesive tape

black photographic tape

cellulose tape

colored tape

double-sided tape

drafting tape

duct tape

friction tape

gummed tape

handlebar tape

hinging tape

insulating tape

lead tape

masking tape

paper tape

Scotch tape

transparent tape

Velcro

570

Tarot Cards

Ace

Batons

Chariot

Coins

Cups or Hearts

Death

Devil

Disks

eight

Emperor

Empress

five

Fool

four

Hanged Man

Hermit

Hierophant

High Priestess

Judgment

Juggler or Magician

Justice

King

Knave or Jack

Knight

Last Judgment

Lightning-struck Tower or Tower

Lovers

Magician

Moon

nine

Page

Papess or Female Pope

Pentacles

Pope

Queen

Rods

seven

six

Star

Strength or Fortitude

Sun

Swords or Spades

Temperance

ten

three

Tower

two

Universe

Wands

Wheel of Fortune

World

Tastes

acerbic

acidic

acrid

aftertaste

appetizing

astringent

biting

bitter

brackish

briny

caustic

delectable

delicious

dry

dulcet

dulcify

flavorful

flavoring

fruity

full-bodied

gamy

gout

honey

hot

juicy

mouth-watering

palatable

peppery

pickled

piquant

pungent

rancid

rank

saccharine

saline

salt

salty	spicy	syrupy	treacly
saporific	strong	tang	yummy
savory	succulent	tart	zesty
scrumptious	sugary	tasteless	
sharp	sweet	tasty	
sour	sweet-and-sour	toothsome	

Taxes

abusive tax	excess-profits tax	maximum tax	severance tax
ad valorem tax	excise tax	minimum tax	sin tax
airport tax	federal tax	municipal tax	single tax
alcohol tax	franchise tax	personal property tax	Social Security tax
alternative minimum tax	gasoline tax	poll tax	stamp duty
amusement tax	gift tax	progressive tax	state tax
capital gains tax	graduated tax	property tax	surtax
capital transfer tax	hidden tax	proportional tax	tariff
capitation tax	income tax	purchase tax	tithe
corporation tax	indirect tax	real estate tax	toll
customs	inheritance tax	regressive tax	unemployment tax
death tax	insurance tax	revenue tax	value-added tax or VAT
direct tax	land tax	sales tax	windfall profits tax
estate tax	license tax	school tax	window tax
estimated tax	local tax	self-employment tax	withholding tax
	luxury tax		

TEA VARIETIES

Assam tea

black currant tea

black pearl tea

black tea

bohea

bush tea

cambric tea

camomile tea

Ceylon tea

chai

China tea

cinnamon tea

congou

cream tea

Darjeeling tea

Earl Grey tea

English breakfast tea

fruit tea

green tea

herbal tea

hyson

iced tea

jasmine tea

Labrador tea

lemon tea

mint tea

oolong tea

orange pekoe tea

pekoe tea

peppermint tea

pouchong

rosehip tea

sassafras tea

souchong

sun tea

tilleul

tisane

TECTONIC PLATES

There are nine major tectonic plates and a number of smaller ones. They fit together like the pieces of a jigsaw puzzle, covering the whole of the Earth's surface. The continents are carried by continental plates, such as the Eurasian. Oceanic plates, such as the Pacific plate, form most of the seafloor; the rest is made up of the fringes of the continental plates, which lie underwater.

African

Antarctic

Arabian

Australian

Caribbean

Caroline

Cocos

Eurasian

Indian

Juan de Fuca

Nazca

North American

Pacific

Philippine

Scotia

South American

TEETH TYPES

baby tooth or primary tooth or temporary tooth

bicuspid

canine

cuspid

eye tooth

incisor

milk tooth

molar

permanent tooth

premolar

tricuspid

wisdom tooth

TELEPHONES

car telephone

cellular telephone

closed circuit telephone

cordless telephone

desk telephone

dial telephone

extension telephone

field telephone

flip telephone

French telephone

Internet videophone

magnetotelephone

microtelephone

mobile telephone

pay telephone

picture telephone

polarized telephone

push-button telephone

radiotelephone

smartphone

text telephone

thermophone

touch-tone telephone

trimline telephone

videophone

wall telephone

wireless telephone

wristphone

TELESCOPE TYPES

astrograph

astronomical telescope or Kepler telescope

autocollimator

binoculars

Cassegrain telescope

celestial telescope

collimator

comet seeker or comet finder

coudé telescope

Dobsonian telescope

double-image telescope

elbow telescope

electron telescope

equatorial telescope

finder telescope

Galilean telescope

Gregorian telescope

guiding telescope

Hale telescope

heliometer

Herschelian telescope

Hubble Space Telescope

inverting telescope

Keck telescope

Maksutov telescope

mercurial telescope

metascope

Mills cross

Multiple Mirror Telescope or MMT

Newtonian telescope

off-axis reflector

optical telescope

panoramic telescope

phototelescope

polar telescope

prismatic telescope

radio telescope

reflecting telescope

refracting telescope

Schmidt telescope

solar telescope

spotting scope

telescopic sight

telestereoscope

terrestrial telescope

tower telescope

twin telescope

vernier telescope

water telescope

zenith tube

TELEVISION PROGRAM TYPES

action/adventure show

adult entertainment program

agricultural show

animal show

anthology show

audience participation show

awards ceremony

beauty pageant

biographical show

book review

candid camera show

cartoon or animation program

chat show

children's program

comedy series

concert or theatrical show

cooking show

crime series

dating game show

daytime drama

decorating show

discussion panel

docudrama

documentary

dramatic series

dramedy

early-morning show

educational show

exercise show

fashion and style show

foreign-language show

game show

gimmick show

give-away show

health and fitness show

historical show

home shopping program

horror show

infomercial

infotainment

international newscast

interview show

late-night talk show

local newscast

magazine show

medical show

miniseries

musical program

music video

national newscast

nature and wildlife show

newscast

newsmagazine show

pay-per-view movie

pay television movie

pilot

political announcement

political convention broadcast

promotional program

public television show

quiz show

reality show

religious show

repeat

rerun

science and technology show

science fiction program

season finale

serial

shoot-'em-up

shopping program

sitcom or situation comedy

soap opera

space opera

special

spectacular program

spin-off show

sports anthology program

sportscast or sports event

sports commentary program

sports news program

studio program

subscription television show

summer repeat

syndicated show

talk show

teleplay

telethon

televangelist show

travelogue

variety show

weather report

western

whodunit

TENNIS COMPETITIONS

Australian Open

Davis Cup or International Law

Tennis Challenge Trophy

Federation Cup

French Open

Olympic Games

United States Open

Wightman Cup

Wimbledon or British Open

TENNIS STROKES AND SHOTS

American twist

approach shot

backhand drive

backhand shot or backhand stroke

chip or chip shot

chop

cross-court shot

daisy cutter

defensive lob

defensive volley

down-the-line shot

drag volley

drive

drop shot

forcing shot

forehand drive

forehand shot or forehand stroke

ground drive

groundstroke

half volley

jump smash

kick serve

lob

lob volley

offensive lob

offensive volley

overhead

passing shot

passing stroke

pickup shot

punch volley

reverse twist

service or serve

service return

slice

smash or overhead smash

snap volley

stop volley

topspin

twist service

two-handed
backhand

undercut

underhand stroke

volley

TENTS

backpacking tent

barrel-vaulted tent

bell tent

black tent

box tent

canvas tent

circus tent or big top

conical tent

cottage tent

dome tent

explorer tent

field tent

fly tent

frame tent

kibitka

lean-to tent

marquee

mountain tent

pack tent

pavilion

pop tent

pup tent

pyramidal tent

ridge tent

shelter tent

Sibley tent

tepee

touring tent

trailer tent

tunnel tent

tupik

two-person tent

umbrella tent

wall tent

wigwam

yurt

TESTS

academic test

achievement test

aptitude test

attitude test

beta test

blood test

citizenship test

college admission
test

diagnostic test

employment test

essay test

field test

final examination

fitness test

flight test

inkblot test

intelligence test

interest inventory
test

litmus test

medical test

midterm
examination

multiple-choice test

open-book test

patch test

personality test

pop quiz

pregnancy test

projective test

psychological test

quiz

road test

Rorschach test

scholastic aptitude
test

scientific test

scratch test

skin test

soil test spot test stress test true-false test

spelling test Stanford-Binet test take-home test word-association test

THEATRICAL FORMS AND VENUES

avant-garde

ballet

benefit

black comedy

Broadway

bunraku

burlesque

cabaret

Chinese opera

chronicle play

circus

classical Greek drama

classical theater

closet drama

comedy

comedy of manners

commedia dell' arte

community theater

dinner theater

documentary drama

drama

drama festival

epic theater

experimental theater

expressionism

farce

floor show

fringe theater

guerrilla theater

high comedy

improvisation

Kabuki

legitimate stage

little theater

low comedy

masque

medieval drama

melodrama

minstrel show

miracle play

morality play

music hall

musical

musical comedy

mystery play

national theater

naturalism

neighborhood playhouse

No theater odeum

off Broadway

off off Broadway

one-act play

open-air theater

opera

operetta

pageant

pantomime

passion play

performance art

playlet

puppet theater realism

repertory company

revue

ritual drama

road show

send-up

shadow play

sketch

skit

slapstick

stand-up

street theater

Sturm and Drang

summer stock

symbolism

theater-in-the-round

theater of cruelty

theater of fact

theater of silence

theater of the absurd

tragedy

tragicomedy

variety show

vaudeville

THEOLOGY BRANCHES

Theology is any systematic study of God or gods. It can be the investigation or expression of the beliefs and precepts of a religion or can be philosophical and historical studies that strive to achieve an understanding of various beliefs.

Alexandrianism

angelology

apologetics

Apophatic theology

ascetical theology

Barthianism

Biblical theology

Buddhist theology

canonics

catechetics

Christian theology

Christology

covenant theology

crisis theology

Dalit theology

demonology

doctrinal theology

dogmatics

eschatology

existential theology

federal theology

feminist theology

fideism

hagiology

hierology

homiletics

Hopkinsianism

Islamic theology

Judaism theology

liberation theology

Mercersburg theology

moral theology

natural theology

negative theology

neoorthodoxy

nonformalogical theology

patristics

phenomenological theology

philosophical theology

physicotheology

positive theology

practical theology

rationalism

rational theology

revealed theology

sacerdotalism

sacred theology

scholastic theology

secularism

sophiology

soteriology

speculative theology

symbolic theology

systematics

theological hermeneutics

THERAPY TYPES

acupressure or shiatsu

acupuncture

Alexander technique

allopathy

aromatherapy

art therapy

autogenic therapy

aversion therapy

Ayurveda

balneotherapy

behavioral therapy

bibliotherapy

bioenergetics

biofeedback

breathing therapy

chemotherapy

chiropractic

cognitive-behavioral therapy

579

cognitive therapy

color therapy

combination therapy

confrontation therapy

contact therapy

counter-conditioning

couples therapy

craniosacral therapy

cryotherapy

crystal therapy

dance therapy

detoxification

drama therapy

drug therapy

electroconvulsive therapy

electroshock therapy

electrotherapy

faith healing

family therapy

gene therapy

Gestalt therapy

group therapy

heat treatment

heliotherapy

herbalism

homeopathy

hormone replacement therapy

humanistic therapy

hydrotherapy

hypnotherapy

immunotherapy

insulin shock therapy

magnetic therapy

massage therapy

mechanotherapy

meditation

megavitamin therapy

milieu therapy

moxibustion

music therapy

narcotherapy

naturotherapy

neurolinguistic programming

occupational therapy

organotherapy

osteopathy

pharmacotherapy

phototherapy

physical therapy

physiotherapy

play therapy

primal therapy

psychoanalysis

psychotherapy

radiation therapy

rational-emotive therapy

rebirthing

recreational therapy

reflexology

regression therapy

reiki

relaxation therapy

release therapy

Rolfing

sandwich therapy

self therapy

sex therapy

shock therapy

sleep therapy

sound therapy

speech therapy

spiritual healing

supportive therapy

thalassotherapy

touch therapy

will therapy

yoga therapy

THREADS

basting thread

buttonhole twist thread

carpet thread

cotton thread

cotton-wrapped polyester thread

crochet thread

darning thread

embroidery thread

fine thread

floss thread

general-purpose thread

heavy-duty thread

nylon thread

polyester thread

silk thread

THREE FATES

In Greek and Roman mythology, these three goddesses determined human destinies, in particular the span of a person's life and their degree of misery and suffering.

Atropos   Clotho   Lachesis

THREE FURIES

In Greek and Roman mythology, these three goddesses provided vengeance. They were either personified curses or ghosts of murdered people.

Alecto   Megaera   Tisiphone

THREE MAGI

In Christian tradition, these three noble pilgrims "from the East" followed a miraculous guiding star to Bethlehem, where they paid homage to the infant Jesus as king of the Jews.

Balthazar   Caspar   Melchior

TIMEPIECES, CLOCKS, TIMERS, AND WATCHES

alarm clock	astronomical clock	box chronometer	cesium clock
alarm watch	atomic clock	bracket clock	chronograph
ammonia clock	battery-operated clock	calendar clock	chronometer
analog clock		calendar watch	chronoscope
analog watch	bell clock	carriage clock	

clepsydra or water clock

clock radio

clock watch

cuckoo clock

dial clock

digital clock

digital watch

egg timer

elapsed-time clock

electric clock

electronic clock

fob watch

gnomon

grandfather clock

grandmother clock

gravity clock

half-hour glass

half-hunter watch

half-minute glass

hourglass

hunting watch or hunter

impulse clock

isochronon

journeyman watch

kitchen timer

long-case clock or tall-case clock

marine chronometer

metronome

musical clock

nuclear clock

oven timer

parking meter timer

pendule

pendulum clock

pneumatic clock

pocket chronometer

pocket watch

program clock

quartz-crystal clock

quartz watch

repeater

sandglass

self-winding watch

ship's watch or ship's bell

sidereal clock

steeple clock

stemwinder watch

stopwatch

striking clock

sundial

synchronous clock

tabernacle clock

telechron clock

three-minute glass

time clock

time lock

time recorder

time stamp

time switch

transistor clock

travel clock

turret clock

wall clock

watchman's clock

water clock

wind-up clock

wristwatch

TIRE TYPES

all-terrain tire

all-weather tire

automobile tire

balloon tire

belted-bias tire

belted-radial tire

belted tire

bias-belted tire

bias-ply tire

bicycle tire

black wall tire

collapsible spare tire

cross-ply tire

double tire

dual-bead tire

flexible rubber tire

hard rubber tire

industrial tire

metal cable tire

metal-stud tire

metal tire

mud-and-snow tire

nylon cord tire

off-road tire

ply tire

pneumatic tire

polygas tire

racing tire

radial-ply tire

radial tire

rayon cord tire

recapped tire

rubber tire

run-flat tire

snow tire

spare tire

steel-belted tire

steel cord tire

synthetic rubber tire

tubeless tire

tube tire

whitewall tire

winter tire

TOOL BOX

adjustable crescent wrenches

anchors

assorted fasteners

ax

bolts

carpenter's level

C-clamp

channel pliers

chisel

chisel set

claw hammer

combination square

crosscut saw

drill bits

electrical tape

electric drill

extension cords

file

flashlight

flat screwdrivers

fuses

glues

goggles

hack saw

hammer

hex key wrenches

ladder

nails

needle-nose pliers

nuts

pencil

Phillips screwdrivers

pipe wrench

plane

pliers

plumber's snake

plunger

putty knife

rotary hand drill

rubber-headed hammer

sanding block

screws

slip-jointed pliers

staple gun

staples

steel tape

steel wool

stud finder

tape measure

toolbox

twist ties

utility knife

vise

washers

wire

wire-cutting pliers

work gloves

yardstick

TOOL TYPES

agricultural tool

blacksmithing tool

carving tool

cutting tool

digging tool

drilling tool

edge tool

fastening tool

gardening tool

gripping tool

hammering tool

marking tool

measuring tool

pointed tool

power tool

sawing tool

scraping tool

shaping tool

sharpening tool

shaving tool

shoveling tool

smoothing tool

soldering tool

tightening tool

welding tool

Tools, Agricultural and Gardening

ax

baler

billhook

binder

blower

brush cutter

cant hook

chisel plow

claw

colter

combine

crop duster

cultivator

dibble

digging bar

draw hoe

edger

flail

flower pruner

garden spade

grass shear

grub hoe

half moon edger

harvester

hayfork

hay rake

hedge clipper

hoe

hose

lawn cart

lawn mower

leaf blower

loy

manure fork

mattock

maul

mulcher

pick

pickax

pitchfork

plow

pole tree trimmer

poly grain scoop

post hole digger

pruner

pruning saw

rake

reaper

roller

roto edger

rototiller

scuffle hoe

scythe

shears

shovel

shredder

sickle

sledge hammer

spade

spading fork

sprinkler

thatch rake

tiller

tractor

weed cutter

weed trimmer

wheelbarrow

wood splitter

Tools, Blacksmithing

anvil
ball peen hammer
battering-ram
bellow
blower
brush
chisel
clinch cutter
clincher
clipping hammer
cold chisel
creaser
cross peen hammer

dipper
drift
drill
fileflatter
flatter
floor mandrel
forge or furnace
fuller
hammer
hardie
hoof gauger
hoof tester
hot chisel

ladel
mallet
mandrel
nipper
post drill
post vise
power hammer
pritchel
puncher
rasp
set hammer
slack tub
sledge hammer

stithy
straight peen hammer
swage
swage block
swedge
swedge block
tongs
treadle hammer
tue-irons
vise

Tools, Carving, Cutting, Edged, and Pointed

adz
awl
ax
bezel
bill
billhook
blade
bodkin
bolster chisel

bolt cutter
box-cutter knife or utility knife
burin
butcher knife
carving knife
chisel
circular saw
cleaver

clipper
cold chisel
cornering tool
drove or boaster
edge tool
firmer chisel
glass cutter
gouge
graver

hand ax
hardy
hatchet
hob
hook
jackknife
knife
machete
masonry chisel

585

paring chisel
pick
pinking shears
pipe cutter
plane
power saw

punch
race knife
razor
reamer
router
saw

scissors
scorper
scraper
scythe
shears
sickle

square-end chisel
stylus
tile cutter
wire cutter

TOOLS, DIGGING AND SHOVELING

air shovel
bail
bar spade
bull tongue
coal shovel
cultivator
digging fork
ditch spade
draw hoe
duckbill
electric shovel

fire shovel
fork
garden spade
grubbing mattock
grub hoe
hand fork
hand shovel
hoe
irrigating shovel
loy
mattock

muckstick
peat spade
pitchfork
plow
posthole digger
power shovel
rake
salt shovel
sampling shovel
scoop
scooper

spade
Spanish spoon
spatula
split shovel
spud
steam shovel
trenching spade
twisted shovel

TOOLS, DRILLING

air drill
auger
automatic drill
bench drill

bore
bottoming drill
bow drill or fiddle drill

brace
breast drill
broach
carpenter's brace

center drill
chaser
cordless drill
core drill

corkscrew

countersink

diamond drill

drill press

eggbeater drill

electric drill

gimlet

hand drill

oilhole drill

piston drill

portable drill

power drill

pump drill

push drill

reamer

rock drill

rose reamer

seed drill

sensitive drill

shell drill

sinker drill

star drill

tap drill

traverse drill or cotter drill

twist drill

wimble

woodborer

TOOLS, FASTENING, GRIPPING, AND TIGHTENING

adjustable bar clamp

band clamp

bar clamp

bench dog

bench vise

bent-nose pliers

brace

C-clamp

channel-type pliers

chuck

clamp

clamp-on vise

claw

clip

corner clamp

cutting pliers

diagonal-cutting pliers

edging clamp

electric riveter

forceps

glue gun

grip

hand vise

holddown clamp

joint fastener

lineman's pliers

locking pliers

long-nose pliers

miter clamp

nail gun

nail puller

needlenose pliers

pincers

pipe clamp

plate joiner

pliers

power nailer

pucellas

puller

riveter

screw clamp

slip-joint pliers

snap ring pliers

spring clamp

staple gun

stapler

toggle clamp

tongs

tweezers

vise

vise grip

web clamp

welding clamp

Z-clip

TOOLS, MARKING AND MEASURING

angle square	electronic level	miter box	slide caliper
bevel	feeler gauge	miter square	square
bevel square	folding rule	mortise gage	steel rule
butt gauge	framing square	pencil	straight edge
caliper	gauge	plumb rule	studfinder
carpenter's level	grease pencil	plummet	surveyor's level
carpenter's pencil	level	protractor	T square
carpenter's square	line level	rafter square	tapeline
center punch	machinist's rule	rule	tape measure
chalk liner	marking gauge	ruler	t-bevel
combination square	mason's level	scale	torpedo level
compass	measuring rod	scratch awl	try square
depth gauge	measuring stick	screed	turning caliper
dividers	micrometer gauge	scriber	wing divider

TOOLS, SAWING, SHAPING, AND SMOOTHING

adz	belt sander	buffer	carpenter's saw
anvil	bench plane	bullnose plane	chain saw
backsaw	bench saw	burnisher	chamfering plane
band saw	block plane	butcher's saw	circular file
band tool	bow saw	buzz saw	circular saw
beading plane	bucksaw	carpenter's plane	compass saw

coping saw
crosscut saw
crown saw
cutoff saw
diamond saw
die
disk sander
double cut file
dovetail saw
dragsaw
drum sander
dry-wall saw
electric sander
electric saw
emery wheel
file
finishing sander
flat file
flatter
float
flooring saw
flush cut saw
folding saw
fore plane
frame saw
fretsaw
gangsaw

grinder
grinding wheel
grindstone
grooving plane
hacksaw
half-round file
hand sander
hand saw
hone
howel
jack plane
jeweler's saw
jigsaw
keyhole saw
lathe
log saw
lumberman's saw
machine tool
meat saw
metal saw
millstone
multiplane
musical saw
oilstone
one-man crosscut saw
pad saw
panel saw

pit saw
plane
planer
plasterer's float
plumber's saw
polisher
portable saw
power sander
power saw
pruning saw
putty knife
radial arm saw
rasp
reciprocating saw
rift saw
ripsaw
round file
router
router plane
saber saw
sander
sandpaper
scraper
scroll saw
scurfer
shaper
sharpener

shavehook
single cut file
slipstone
smoother
smoothing plane
spokeshave
spoon tool
stationary circular saw
stone
swage
swage block
table saw
tamper
thickness planer
tournasin
tree saw
trimming plane
trying plane
two-handed saw
two-man crosscut saw
utility saw
vertical saw
waterstone
whetstone
whipsaw
woodworking plane

Tools, Sharpening

bench grinder

drill bit sharpener

edge

emery

emery wheel

file

grindstone

hand grinder

hand stone

hone

oilstone

scythe stone

slipstone

steel

strop or strap

whetstone

whittle

Tools, Welding and Soldering

AC welder

acetylene welder

arc welder

atomic-hydrogen welding

blowtorch

DC welder

electric welder

electronic welder

flame heater

flash welder

gas welder

induction heater

oxyacetylene welder

pipe welder

soldering gun

soldering iron

spot welder

tack welder

torch

welding blowtorch

wire welder

Torpedoes

acoustic torpedo

aerial torpedo

anti-torpedo torpedo

bangalore torpedo

fish torpedo

heavy torpedo

homing torpedo

rocket torpedo

spar torpedo

submarine torpedo

whitehead torpedo

TORTILLA DISHES

burrito

chalupa

chilaquile

chimichanga

enchilada

fajita

nacho

papatzul

quesadilla

sopa seca

sopes

taco

tortilla chips

tortilla de harina

tortilla de mais

tortilla de patatas

tortilla wrap

tostada

TOWER TYPES

barbican

bastion

belfrey

bell tower

belvedere

broch

campanile

church tower

clock tower

column

control tower

cooling tower

demi-bastion

donjon

fire tower

gate tower

high-rise

hill fort

ivory tower

keep

lighthouse

lookout tower

martello tower

mast

minaret

mirador

mooring tower

nuragh

observation tower

oil-drilling tower

pagoda

pele tower

power tower

shot tower

siege tower

signal tower

silo

skyscraper

solar tower

spire

stair tower

steeple

supporting tower

telephone tower

tower block

turret

utility tower

watchtower

water tower

ziggurat

TOY TYPES

action figure

arts and crafts toy

baby toy

ball

blocks

board game

building set

computer game

construction toy

die-cast vehicle

doll

electronic toy

game

handheld game

learning toy

mechanical toy

military toy

model

moving toy

musical toy

novelty

outdoor toy

playing cards

playset

preschool toy

pull toy

puzzle

riding toy

science toy

sports toy

stuffed animal

trading cards

vehicle

video game

windup toy

TRACTORS

amphibious tractor

bulldozer

calfdozer

Caterpillar

continuous-track
tractor

crawler tractor

creeper tractor

dozer

duck

farm tractor

grader

halftrack

lawn tractor

scraper

semi tractor

single-axle tractor

tank

tracklayer

truck tractor

walking tractor

wheeled tractor

yard tractor

TRAIL TYPES

bikeway

bridle path

cattle trail

cross-country trail

deer trail

forest trail

heritage trail

hiking trail

horse trail

logging trail

mountain trail

nature trail

recreation trail

running trail

ski trail

track

walking trail

Transparent and Translucent Things

alabaster
amber
aquamarine
beryl
carnelian
cellophane
celluloid
chalcedony
chiffon
chrysolite
citrine
clear plastic
crystal
diamond
emerald
gauze
gelatin
glass
gossamer
hyaline
hyalite
lens
Lucite
mica
milk glass
moonstone
onionskin
opal
peridot
plastic wrap
quartz
rose quartz
ruby
sapphire
tissue paper
transparency
voile
water
wax paper
window

Trees

aalii
abele
abura
acacia
acajou
African blackwood
African cypress
ailanthus or tree of heaven
akeake
alder
alder buckthorn
Aleppo pine
Algerian fir
alligator juniper
allspice
almond
alpine ash
alpine fir
American aspen
American beech
American elm
apple
apricot
argan tree
ash
aspen
avocado or alligator pear
bald cypress
balsa
balsam
balsam fir
banyan
baobab
basswood
bay
bayberry
bay cedar
bean
beech
beefwood
bendy tree
betel palm
birch
black hickory

593

black pine

bonsai

bo tree

boxwood

Brazil nut

breadfruit

buckeye

buckthorn

butternut

buttonwood

cabbage tree

cacao

camphor tree

carnauba

carob

cashew

cassia

catalpa

cedar

cherimoya

cherry

chestnut

chinaberry tree or China tree

chinquapin

chokecherry

Christmas tree

cinnamon

citron

clove

coconut or coco

cork oak

cork tree

cottonwood

crab apple

cypress

date palm

devilwood

dogwood

Douglas fir

dwarf

ebony

elder

elephant tree

elm

eucalyptus

evergreen

ficus

fig

filbert

fir

flame tree

fruit

ginkgo

ginkgo biloba

grapefruit

guava

gum

hardwood

hawthorn

hazel

hemlock

henna

hickory

holly

hoptree

hornbeam

horse chestnut

horseradish tree

inkwood

ironwood tree

Judas tree

jujube

jumbie bead

juniper

king orange

kingwood

kola

kumquat

laburnum

lancewood

larch

laurel

laurel oak

laurelwood

lemon

lignum vitae

lime

linden

litchi or litchi nut

locust

logwood

loquat or Japanese plum

love tree

macadamia

madrone

magnolia

mahogany

mandarin orange

mango

mangrove

maple

marblewood

medlar

mesquite

mimosa

monkey puzzle

mountain ash

mountain ebony

mountain pine

mulberry

nakedwood

nutmeg

nux vomica

oak

olive	princewood	Spanish elm	wayfaring tree
orange	pussy willow	spruce	weeping willow
osier	quince	sugar maple	western hemlock
pagoda tree	raffia palm	sycamore	whitebeam
palm	rain tree	tamarillo	white birch
papaw	red beech	tamarind	white cedar
papaya	red pine	tamarugo	white oak
paradise tree	redwood	tangerine	white pine
peach	rice-paper tree	teak	white poplar
pear	rosewood	thorn tree	white spruce
pecan	rubber tree	thuja	whitethorn
pepper tree	sandalwood	tolu tree	wicopy
persimmon	sapodilla	torchwood	willow
pine	sassafras	tulip tree	witch hazel
pistachio	satinwood	tupelo	woollybutt
pitch pine	senna	turkey oak	wychelm
plane tree	sequoia	umbrella tree	yellow birch
plum	serviceberry	upas	yellow poplar
poison sumac	shade tree	varnish tree	yellowwood or gopher wood
pomegranate	shagbark	walnut	
pomelo	shortleaf pine	wandoo	yew
poplar	silkwood	water elm	ylang-ylang
prickly ash	silver maple	wax palm	zebrawood
Pride-of-India	sorrel tree	wax tree	

TREES, DECIDUOUS

Deciduous trees are broad-leaved trees that shed all their leaves during one season.

apple tree	chestnut	larch	serviceberry
bayberry	cottonwood	linden	silverberry
beech	crab apple	lotus tree	sugar maple
birch	elm	maple	tupelo
black locust	ginkgo	mountain ash tree	walnut tree
buckeye	gum tree	oak	willow
butternut	hickory	pear tree	winterberry
cherry tree	horse chestnut	poplar	yellowwood

TRIANGLES

acute-angle triangle	equilateral triangle	right-angle triangle
circular triangle	isosceles triangle	scalene triangle
congruent triangles	obtuse-angle triangle	spherical triangle

TRIGONOMETRIC FUNCTIONS

There are six functions of an angle commonly used in trigonometry.

cosecant or csc	cotangent or cot	sine or sin
cosine or cos	secant or sec	tangent or tan

TROUSERS AND PANTS

baggies	blue jeans	buckskins	chinos
bell-bottoms	bombachas	calzoneras	churidars
Bermuda shorts	braies	Capri pants	clamdiggers
bloomers	breeches	chaps	corduroys or cords

cutoffs

drainpipe trousers

ducks

dungarees

gaiters

galligaskins

harem pants

high-waters

hiphuggers

hot pants

jeans

jodhpurs

knee breeches

knickers

lederhosen

Levi's

loincloth

loose trousers

matador pants or
toreador pants

moleskins

nankeens

overalls

Oxford bags

palazzo pants

pantaloons

parachute pants

pedal pushers

pegleg trousers

peg top trousers

petticoat trousers

plus fours

riding breeches

salopettes

shorts

short shorts

ski pants

slacks

stirrup pants

stretch pants

sweat pants

tin pants

trunk hose

waders

zouave pants

TROWELS

In gardening, a trowel is a tool with a pointed, scoop-shaped metal blade and a handle. It is used for breaking up earth and for digging small holes, especially for planting and weeding.

angle trowel

brick trowel

buttering trowel

cement trowel

circle trowel

concrete trowel

corner trowel

cove trowel

edging trowel

flat trowel

flooring trowel

garden trowel

gauging trowel

guttering trowel

London trowel

margin trowel

Marshalltown trowel

mason's trowel

midget trowel

notched trowel

plastering trowel

pointing trowel

radius trowel

slick

TRUCK TYPES

armored car

articulated vehicle

autotruck

bobtail

box truck

camionette

car transporter

cement mixer

crash truck

delivery van

dromedary

duck or DUKW

dump truck

express truck

fire engine

fork or forklift truck

four-by-four or 4x4

garbage truck

lift truck

lorry

motortruck

panel truck

peddler truck

pick-up truck or pickup

recreational vehicle or RV

semitrailer six-by-six

sound truck

stake truck

tank truck

tipper truck

tow truck

tractor-trailer or 18-wheeler

van

TUSKED ANIMALS

boar

elephant

walrus

wart hog

wild boar

TWELVE TRIBES OF ISRAEL

According to the Old Testament, Jacob fathered twelve sons. They are the ancestors of the tribes of Israel, and the ones for whom the tribes are named.

Asher

Benjamin

Dan

Gad

Issachar

Joseph

Judah

Manasseh and Ephraim

Naphtali

Reuben

Simeon or Levi

Zebulun

TYPE STYLES AND TYPEFACES

antique

Arial

Avant Garde

Balmoral

Baskerville

Bembo

blackface

black letter

Bodoni

boldface

Bookman

Boston

Bulmer

Caledonia

Calisto

capitals

Caslon

Centaur

Century

Century Gothic

Century Schoolbook

Chicago

Clarendon

Cloister

Colonna

condensed

Courier

cursive

Delphian

dingbat

Doric

Egyptian

Electra

elite

expanded

extended

Fournier

Fraktur

Franklin

Franklin Gothic

Futura

Galliard

Garamond

Gothic

Goudy

Grotesque

Helvetica

Hobo

Ionic

italics

lightface

lowercase

Lucida Bright

minuscule

modern

Monotype

Multigraph

Old English

old style

Optima

Palatino

Plantin

Renaissance

Rockwell

roman

sans serif

script

serif

small capitals

Spartan

Tahoma

Times New Roman

Times Roman

Typewriter

Univers

uppercase

Vivaldi

Windsor

UNDERGARMENTS

all-in-one

athletic supporter or jockstrap

Balmoral

bandeau

bikini

bloomers

bodice

body stocking

body suit

boxer shorts

brassiere or bra

breechcloth or loin-cloth

briefs

bustle

BVD's

camiknickers

camisole

chemise

chemisette

corselet

corset

crinoline

diapers

drawers

foundation garment

full slip

garter

garter belt

girdle

G-string

half-slip

hosiery

Jockey shorts

knickers

leggings

leotard

liberty bodice

lingerie

long underwear or long johns

merry widow

padded bra

pannier

panties

panty girdle

pantyhose

peek-a-boo

petticoat

push-up bra

red flannels

scanties

shift

shorts

singlet

skivvies

slip

smock

snuggies

soakers

sport bra or sports bra

step-ins

string vest

support garment

tap pants

teddy

thermal underwear

thong

tournure

T-shirt

underbodice

underclothes

underdrawers

underpants

undershirt

undershorts

underskirt

underthings

undervest

underwear

underwire bra

undies

union suit

unitard

unmentionables

woolens

UNIFORMS

battle dress

blues

boat cloak

continentals

dress blues

dress uniform

dress whites

fatigues

full-dress uniform

jump suit

khakis

livery

military uniform

monkey suit

nauticals

olive-drab uniform

regimentals

sailor suit

school uniform

service uniform

soldier suit

stripes

student uniform

undress uniform

whites

UNITED NATIONS AGENCIES

The United Nations, besides its goals of maintaining peace and security, has set up agencies with other important objectives. These include developing friendly relations among countries based on respect for equal rights and self-determination of people; achieving worldwide cooperation to solve international economic, social, cultural, and humanitarian problems; and promoting human rights.

Food and Agricultural Organization or FAO

General Agreement on Tariffs and Trade or GATT

Internation Fund for Agricultural Development or IFAD

International Atomic Energy Agency or IAEA

International Bank for Reconstruction and Development or World Bank or IBRD

International Civil Aviation Organization or ICAO

International Development Association or IDA

International Finance Corporation or IFC

International Labor Organization or ILO

International Maritime Organization or IMO

International Monetary Fund or the Fund or IMF

International Telecommunication Union or ITU

United Nations Children's Fund or UNICEF

United Nations Educational, Scientific and Cultural Organization or UNESCO

United Nations High Commissioner for Refugees or UNHCR

United Nations Industrial Development Organization or UNIDO

United Nations Office for Drug Control and Crime Prevention or DCCP

United Nations Relief and Works Agency or UNRWA

Universal Postal Union or UPU

World Health Organization or WHO

World Intellectual Property Organization or WIPO

World Meteorological Organization or WMO

World Tourism Organization or WTO

U.S. AIR FORCE BRANCHES AND CORPS

Air Combat Command

Air Education and Training Command

Air Force Materiel Command

Air Force Reserve Command

Air Force Space Command

Air Force Special Operations Command

Air Mobility Command

Pacific Air Forces

United States Air Forces, Europe

U.S. Army Branches and Corps

101st Airborne Division or Screaming Eagles

10th Mountain Division

13th Corps Support Command

19th Theater Army Area Command

1st Armored Division or Old Ironsides

1st Cavalry Division

1st Corps Support Command

1st Personnel Command

21st Theater Army Area Command

25th Infantry Division or U.S. Army Hawaii

28th Infantry Division or Keystone

29th Infantry Division or Blue and Grey

2nd Infantry Division or Indianhead

34th Infantry Division

35th Infantry Division or Sante Fe

38th Infantry Division or Cyclone

3rd Corps Support Command

3rd Infantry Division/ Rock of the Marine

40th Infantry Division or Sunshine

42nd Infantry Division or Rainbow

49th Armored Division or Lone Star

4th Infantry Division or The Ivy Division

82nd Airborne Division or All American

8th Army

Army Intelligence and Security Command

Army Materiel Command

Army Special Operations Command

Army Training and Doctrine Command

Central Command/Third U.S. Army

Corps of Engineers

Criminal Investigation Command

Fifth U.S. Army

First U.S. Army

Forces Command

I Corps

III Corps Artillery

III Corps or Phantom Corps

Information Systems Command

Medical Command

Military Police Command

National Training Center

Seventh Army Training Command

U.S. Army Alaska

U.S. Army Europe

U.S. Army Japan or 9th Theater Army Area Command

U.S. Army Pacific

U.S. Army South

V Coprs

XVIII Airborne Corps

XVIII Airborne Corps Artillery

603

U.S. COAST GUARD BRANCHES AND CORPS

1st District	8th District	14th District	Coast Guard Headquarters
5th District	9th District	17th District	Pacific Area
7th District	13th District	Atlantic Area	

U.S. MARINES BRANCHES AND CORPS

Atlantic Fleet Marine Force	II Marine Expeditionary Force	Marine Corps Air Ground Combat Center	Development Command
Pacific Fleet Marine Force	III Marine Expeditionary Force	Marine Corps Combat	Marine Corps Systems Command
I Marine Expeditionary Force			Marine Reserve Forces

U.S. NAVY BRANCHES AND CORPS

Atlantic Fleet	Naval Forces Central Command	Naval Special Warfare Command	Seventh Fleet
Fifth Fleet	Naval Forces Southern Command	Operational and Test Evaluation Force	Sixth Fleet
Military Sealift Command	Naval Reserve Force	Pacific Fleet	Third Fleet
Mine Warfare Command		Second Fleet	US Naval Forces Europe

604

U.S. Territories and Dependent Outlying Areas

American Samoa

Antarctica (reserved right for future claim)

Baker, Howland, and Jarvis Islands

Guam

Guantanamo Bay

Johnston Atoll

Kingman Reef

Midway Islands

Navassa Island

Northern Mariana Islands

Palmyra Atoll

Puerto Rico

Trust Territory of the Pacific Islands

U.S. Virgin Islands

Wake Island

Utensils, Baking

baking knife

baking sheet

baking spatula

biscuit cutter

cookie cutters

cookie sheet

cooling rack

croissant cutter

doughnut cutter

dredger

egg beater

English muffin rings

flour wand

icing syringe

jelly roll pan

loaf pan

mixing bowl

muffin tin

pastry bag and nozzles

pastry blender

pastry board

pastry brush

pastry cutter

pie tin

pizza peal

pizza stone

quiche plate

removable-bottomed pan

roasting pan

rolling pin

round cake pans

scraper

sifter

square cake pan

tart pan

tube pan

whisk

Utensils, Grinding and Grating

citrus juicer

citrus press

citrus reamer

coffee grinder

egg slicer

food mill

food processor

garlic press

grain mill

grater

juice extractor

mandolin

masher

meat grinder

meat pounder and tenderizer

mincer

mortar and pestle

nutcracker

pasta maker

peeler

pepper mill

potato masher

potato ricer

pounder

rasp

reamer

rolling pin

salt mill

scraper

spice grinder

squeezer

stoner

zester

UTENSILS, MEASURING

balance

balance scale

candy thermometer or jelly thermometer

deep-fat thermometer

digital scale

dough thermometer

dry measures

egg timer

hydrometer

kitchen scale

kitchen timer

liquid measures

measuring cups

measuring spoons

meat thermometer

oven thermometer

ruler

salometer

spring scale

UTENSILS, STRAINING AND DRAINING

cheesecloth

chinois

colander

draining spoon

egg separator

fat separator

filter

food strainer

funnel

gravy separator

salad spinner

screen

sieve

sifter

skimmer

skimming ladle

tea ball

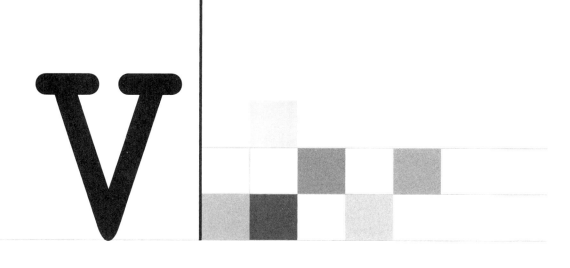

VACUUM ATTACHMENTS

baseboard attachment

ceiling fan attachment

crevice tool

dusting brush

floor brush

mini blind attachment

refrigerator vacuum brush

rug rake

telescopic wand

upholstery nozzle

vacuum extension

vacuum hose

vertical blind attachment

window screen attachment

VAULT TYPES

barrel vault

cloister vault

closegmented dome vault

corbel vault

coved vault

cross-barrel vault

cylindrical vault

domical vault

fan vault

groin vault or cross vault

lierne vault

longitudinal barrel vault

oblong vault

quadrant vault

rib vault or ribbed vault

sexpartite vault

squinch arch vault

tunnel vault

underpitch vault or Welsh vault

wagon vault

Vegetable Oils

almond oil

aniseed oil

avocado oil

Brazil nut oil

canola oil

clove oil

cocoa oil

coconut oil

coffee seed oil

copra oil

coriander oil

corn oil

cottonseed oil

flaxseed oil

grain oil

grape seed oil

groundnut oil

gum spirit

hazelnut oil

hempseed oil

lemon oil

macadamia nut oil

maize oil

mustard seed oil

nut oil

oat oil

olive oil

palm kernel oil

palm oil

peanut oil

pecan oil

peppermint oil

pine oil

poppyseed oil

pumpkin seed oil

rapeseed oil

rice bran oil

safflower oil

sesame oil

soybean oil

spearmint oil

sunflower oil

sweet oil

walnut oil

wintergreen oil

Vegetables

alfalfa sprout

artichoke

arugula

asparagus

aubergine

bamboo shoot

bean

bean sprout

beet

bell pepper

black-eyed pea

Boston lettuce

broad bean

broccoli

Brussels sprout

butter bean

cabbage

cardoon

carrot

cassava

cauliflower

celery

celery cabbage

celery root

chard

chayote

chickpea

chicory

Chinese cabbage

chive

collard greens

corn

courgette

cress

cucumber

dandelion

earthnut

eggplant

endive

English pea

escarole

fennel

garbanzo bean

garlic

glasswort

globe artichoke

gourd

green bean

green corn

green pepper

iceberg lettuce

jalapeno pepper

Jerusalem artichoke

kale

kidney bean

kohlrabi

leek

lentil

lettuce

lima bean

marrow squash

mung bean

mushroom

muskmelon

mustard

navy bean

New Zealand spinach

okra

olive

onion

parsley

parsnip

pea

pepper

petsai

pinto bean

plantain

pokeweed

potato

pumpkin

radiccio

radish

rampion

red bean

red cabbage

red pepper

rhubarb

rice

romaine

rutabaga

sauerkraut

scallion

sea kale

seaweed

shallot

snap bean

snow pea

sorrel

soybean

spinach

squash

string bean

succotash

sugar pea

summer squash

sunchoke

sweet cassava

sweet corn

sweet potato

taro root

tomato

truffle

turnip

water chestnut

watercress

wax bean

white bean

white potato

wild spinach

yam

yellow pepper

yellow squash

zucchini

Vegetables with Highest Sugar Content

acorn squash

artichoke

baked beans

beets

Brussels sprout

butternut squash

carrot

corn

leek

parsnip

peas

potato

rutabaga   taro   yam

sweet corn   white rice

Vegetables, Bulb and Stalk

asparagus   chicory   leek   rutabaga

broccoli   chive   onion   scallion

Brussels sprouts fennel   palm hearts   sea kale

cardoon   garlic   radish   shallot

celery   globe artichoke   rhubarb   Swiss chard

Vegetables, Leaf

Brussels sprouts corn salad   kale   spinach

cabbage   cress   lettuce   spinach beet

celery   dandelion   mustard   Swiss chard

chard   endive   rhubarb   watercress

chicory   grape leaf   Romaine lettuce   white cabbage

Chinese cabbage   green cabbage   sorrel

Vegetables, Root and Tuber

beet   ginger   kohlrabi   rutabaga

burdock   ginseng   lobok   salsify

carrot   gobo   parsley   skirret

celeriac   horseradish   parsnip   sweet potato

chervil   Jerusalem artichoke potato   taro

Chinese artichoke jicama   radish   turmeric turnip

wasabi

water chestnut

yam

yuca

VEGETABLES, SEED

baby corn	flageolet	Navy bean	split green pea
bean	French bean	pea	split yellow pea
bean sprouts	green bean	peanut	sugar snap pea
black bean	green pea	pink bean	sweet corn
broad bean	kidney bean	pinto bean	sweet pea
chick pea	legume	red bean	wax bean
corn	lentil	runner bean	yellow snap bean
English pea	lima bean	snow pea	
fava bean	mung bean	soybean	

VEGETARIAN TYPES

fruitarian	macrobiotic eater	raw foodist or living foodist	vegan
lacto-ovo-vegetarian or ovo-lacto-vegetarian	ovo-vegetarian		vegetarian
	pescetarian or pesco-vegetarian	semi-vegetarian or demi-vegetarian or part-vegetarian	
lacto-vegetarian			

VEINS AND ARTERIES

aorta	axillary vein	brachial artery	cephalic vein
auricular artery	azygos vein	carotid artery	coeliac artery
axillary artery	basilic vein	cephalic artery	coronary artery

crural artery

crural vein

cubital vein

deep vein

digital artery

digital vein

diploic vein

dorsal metatarsal
artery

dorsal venous arch

facial artery

femoral artery

femoral vein

gastric artery

gastroepiploic vein

hepatic artery

hepatic portal vein

hypogastric artery

iliac artery

iliac vein

inferior vena cava

innominate artery

innominate vein

jugular vein

labial artery

laryngeal artery

lingual artery

maxillary artery

meningeal artery

mesenteric artery

mesenteric vein

ophthalmic vein

ovarian artery

ovarian vein

palatine artery

palmar arch

palmar network

peroneal artery

plantar artery

popliteal artery

popliteal vein

portal vein

pulmonary artery

pulmonary vein

radial artery

renal artery

renal vein

splenic artery

subclavian artery

subclavian vein

sublingual artery

submental artery

superficial vein

superior vena cava

suprarenal vein

systemic vein

temporal artery

testicular artery

testicular vein

thoracic artery

thyroid artery

tibial artery

tympanic artery

ulnar artery

ulnar vein

vena cava

vertebral artery

VERSE FORMS

Verse is a metrical composition (writing arranged with a metrical rhythm, typically having a rhyme) or the poetic technique of a particular poem.

alcaic verse

alexandrine verse

alliterative verse

ballad

ballade

blank verse

cento

clerihew

dactylic verse

dirge

dithyramb

doggerel

dramatic monologue

echo verse

elegy

English sonnet

epic

epigram

epode

epopee

epos

fixed form

free verse

ghazel

haiku

heroic verse

Horatian ode or Sapphic ode

iambic verse

Italian sonnet

Leonines

limerick

lyric

macaronic verse

madrigal

monody

narrative poem

nursery

ode

palinode

Petrarchan sonnet

Pindaric ode

quatorzain

rhyme

ritornello

rondeau

rondel

roundel

roundelay

satire

secondary epic

sestina

Shakespearean sonnet

sloka

song

sonnet

sonnet sequence

tail rhyme

tanka

terza rima

threnody

triolet

triplet

trochaic verse

villanelle

virelay

Vertebrates

amphibian

bird

bony fish

cartilaginous fish

chordate

jawless fish

mammal

reptile

Vines and Climbers

actinidia

air potato

Algerian ivy

American milk pea

appleberry

Arabian jasmine

balloon vine

balsam apple

balsam pear

baybean

bittersweet

black bryony

bleeding heart vine

blue creeper

Boston ivy

bower plant

boxthorn

branch-climber

bryony

butterfly pea

cantaloupe

cassabanana

catclaw vine

Chile-bells

chocolate vine

cinnamon vine

cissus

clematis

common ivy

coral greenbrier

coral vine

creeping cucumber

cross vine

cucumber

cypress vine

elephant creeper

English ivy

Enslen's vine

false buckwheat

flame vine

gloryvine

goa bean

golden vine

grape ivy

grapevine

greenbrier

honeysuckle

honeyvine

hop

horsebrier

indigo plant

ivy

Jackson vine

jade vine

jasmine

kangaroo vine

liana

Madeira vine

manettia vine

marine ivy

matrimony vine

melon

monkshood vine

morning glory

mosquito plant or mosquito trap

paradise flower

pink vine

poison ivy

potato vine

primrose jasmine

pumpkin

railroad vine

rosary vine

rubber vine

sandpaper vine

silk vine

silver lace vine

silvervine

star cucumber

star jasmine

sweet potato

sword bean

thunder god vine

traveler's-joy

trumpet creeper

trumpet flower

trumpet honeysuckle

trumpet vine

velvet bean

Virginia creeper

virgins-bower

winter jasmine

wire vine

wisteria

woodbine

VIRUSES

actinophage

adenovirus

AIDS virus

alfalfa mosaic virus

alphavirus

animal virus

arbovirus

arenavirus

bacteriophage

baculovirus

bromovirus

bunyavirus

carlavirus

caulimovirus

closterovirus

comovirus

computer virus

coronavirus

corticovirus

Coxsackie virus

cuccmovirus

cystovirus

cytomegalovirus

DNA virus

Ebola virus

echovirus

enterovirus

Epstein-Barr virus

filovirus

filterable virus

hantavirus

herpes simplex virus

herpesvirus

herpes zoster virus

hordevirus

human immunodeficiency virus or HIV

human papilloma virus or HPV

human virus

614

ilavirus

influenza virus

inidovirus

inovirus

Lassa virus

lentivirus

leukovirus

levivirus

luteovirus

Marburg virus

mengovirus

microvirus

morbillivirus

myovirus

myxovirus

nepovirus

oncornavirus

orbivirus

orthomyxovirus

otbravirus

papillomavirus

papovavirus

parainfluenza virus

paramyxovirus

parvovirus

pedovirus

picornavirus

piliovirus

plant virus

plasmavirus

pogtyvirus

poliovirus

polyoma virus

polyomavirus

potexvirus

poxvirus

reovirus

retrovirus

rhabdovirus

rhinovirus

RNA virus

rotavirus

Rous sarcoma virus

slow virus

stylovirus

tectivirus

tobacco mosaic virus

tobacco necrosis virus

tobamovirus

togavirus

tomato spotted wilt virus

tombusvirus

tumor virus

tymovirus

ultravirus

varicella virus

West Nile virus

VISUAL ARTS

advertising art

animation

architecture

basketry

body decoration

bookbinding

calligraphy

caricature

clothing design

communicative art

currency design

decorative arts and crafts

drawing

enamelwork

fine art

floral decoration

functional design

furnishings

glass design

graphic arts

illustration

industrial design

intaglio

interior design

jewelry design

lacquerwork

landscape design

landscape drawing

lithography

metalwork

mixed media

mosaic

painting

photography

plastic art

portraiture

pottery

printmaking

relief or engraving

rug and carpet

screen-printing   serigraphy   tapestry   woodcut

sculpture   stained glass   typography

VITAMINS

biotin or vitamin H

carotene

cholecalciferol or vitamin D3

choline

cryptoxanthin

ergocalciferol

folic acid

inositol

menadione

niacin

vitamin A

vitamin A1

vitamin A2

vitamin B

vitamin B complex

vitamin B1 or thiamine

vitamin B12 or pantothenic acid

vitamin B13 or orotic acid

vitamin B15 or pangamic acid

vitamin B17 or laetrile

vitamin B2 or vitamin G or riboflavin

vitamin B6 or pyridoxine or adermin

vitamin BC

vitamin C or ascorbic acid

vitamin D

vitamin D2 or calciferol

vitamin E or tocopherol

vitamin K or phylloquinone

vitamin K1

vitamin K3

vitamin M

vitamin P or bioflavinoid

vitamin PP

VOLCANO TYPES

active volcano

ash and cinder cone volcano

cinder cone volcano

composite cone volcano

dormant volcano

extinct volcano

ice volcano

lava cone volcano

mud volcano

plug dome volcano

sand volcano

shield volcano

stratovolcano

VOLLEYBALL POSITIONS

center back

center forward

left back

left forward

right back

right forward

server

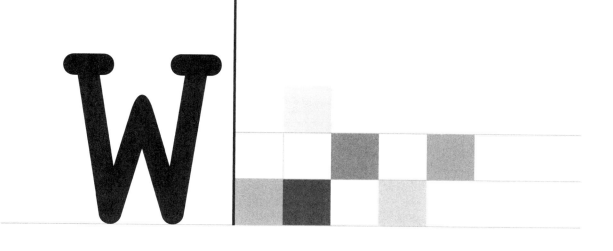

WAISTBANDS AND BELTS

baldric

band

bandolier

bellyband

belt

breechcloth or loincloth

cartridge belt

ceinture

cestus

cinch

cincture

cummerbund

fascia

garter belt

girdle

girt

girth

hamaki

money belt

obi

rope belt

safety belt

safety harness

sash

surcingle

suspender belt

suspenders

waistband

waist belt

waistcloth

WALKING AIDS

cane

crutch

English cane

folding cane

forearm crutch

hiking staff

ortho-cane

quad cane

rollator

staff

stilt

underarm crutch

walker

walking stick

Zimmer frame

WATERFALL TYPES

block waterfall

cascading waterfall

cataract

combination waterfall

fan waterfall

horsetail waterfall

ledge waterfall

multi-cascading waterfall

overhanging ledge waterfall

parallel waterfalls

plunge waterfall

punch bowl waterfall

river waterfall

segment waterfall

slide waterfall

staircase waterfall

stream waterfall

tier waterfall

WAVE TYPES

In physics, a wave is a disturbance traveling through a medium by which energy is transferred from one particle of the medium to another without causing any permanent displacement of the medium itself. Different mediums create different kinds of waves.

electromagnetic wave

gamma ray

high frequency long wave

high frequency medium wave

high frequency short wave

infrared radiation

light wave

longitudinal wave

low frequency long wave

low frequency medium wave

low frequency short wave

mechanical wave

ocean wave

radar wave

radio wave

sound wave

standing wave

stationary wave

transverse wave

traveling wave

ultraviolet radiation

visible radiation

water wave

X-ray

WAXES

ambergris

animal wax

beeswax

candle wax

car wax

carnauba wax

casting wax

cerate

ceresin

ear wax or cerumen

floor wax

fossil wax

hot wax plant wax ski wax

mineral wax scale wax vegetable wax

paraffin wax sealing wax wood wax

WEAPONS NAMED AFTER PEOPLE

Armstrong breech-loading gun

Big Bertha

Bowie knife

Browning automatic rifle

Colt revolver

Derringer

Garand M1 rifle

Gatling gun

guillotine

Mauser rifle

Maxim gun

Molotov cocktail

Shrapnel shell

Thompson submachine gun

Uzi submachine gun

Winchester rifle

WEATHER ELEMENTS AND PHENOMENA

breeze

clouds

cold front

depression

dew

drizzle

El Niño

fog

front

frontal system

frost

gulf stream

hail

haze

high pressure

humidity

ice

La Niña

lightning

low pressure

mist

occlusion

ocean currents

pressure system

rain

rainbow

sleet

smog

snow

sprinkles

storm

thermal

thunder

trough

turbulence

warm front

wind

WEAVES

basket weave

broken twill weave

dobby weave

flat-woven

hatching

interlocking weave

jacquard

knot

lace

open weave

plain weave

satin weave

slit weave

taffeta weave

tapestry

twill weave

waffle weave

WEDDING ANNIVERSARIES

1st: paper (plastic), cotton/clocks

2nd: cotton (calico), paper/china

3rd: leather/crystal, glass

4th: linen (silk, synthetics), iron/ appliances, fruit/ flowers

5th: wood/silverware

6th: iron, sugar/ wood

7th: wool (copper, brass)/desk sets

8th: bronze (electrical appliances)/linens, lace

9th: pottery (china), copper/leather

10th: tin (aluminum)/ diamond

11th: steel/fashion jewelry

12th: silk (fine linen)/ pearl, colored gems

13th: lace/textiles, furs

14th: ivory/gold jewelry

15th: crystal (glass)/ watches

20th: china/platinum

25th: silver/sterling silver

30th: pearl/diamond

35th: coral (jade)/ jade

40th: ruby (garnets)/ ruby

45th: sapphire (tourmalines)/ sapphire

50th: gold/gold

55th: emerald (turquoise)/emerald

60th: diamond (gold)/gold

70th: platinum

WEDDING PARTICIPANTS

attendant

best man

bride

bridesmaid

cake attendant

clergyman

flower girl

groom

groomsman

guest

guest book attendant

head usher

maid of honor

matron of honor

parents of bride

parents of groom

ringbearer

usher

Weeds

agueweed

American thistle

barren strawberry

bedstraw

beggar-ticks

Bermuda grass

bindweed

bird's-eye pearlwort

bitter nightshade

black bindweed

black-eyed Susan

bluegrass

blueweed

bracken

brake

broad-leaved dock

buckthorn

buckthorn plantain

bugleweed

bull thistle

bur

burdock

butterweed

cactus

Canada thistle

Carolina horse nettle

carpetweed

cat's-ear

cattail

charlock

chickweed

chicory

cinquefoil

clover

cocklebur

corn spurry

cottonweed

couch grass

cowweed

crab grass

crane's-bill

crazy weed

creeping buttercup

creeping cinquefoil

creeping speedwell

creeping veronica

curled dock

daisy

dandelion

devil's paintbrush

dewberry

dock

duckweed

English lawn daisy

Eurasian water milfoil

field bindweed

field chickweed

field horsetail

field sorrel

figwort

fireweed

foxtail

galinsoga

goldenrod

goose grass

goutweed

ground ivy

groundsel

hawkweed

heal-all

hedge bindweed

hemlock

hemp nettle

henbit

hogweed

horehound

horseradish

horsetail

horseweed

hydrilla

ice plant

Japanese fleeceflower

Japanese knotweed

jimson weed

Johnson grass

knawel

knotweed

lace grass

lady's-thumb

lamb's-quarters

liverwort

locoweed

madder

mallow

mayweed

milfoil

milkweed

motherwort

mouse-ear chickweed

mouse-ear hawkweed

mustard

nettle

nut sedge

Oldfield cinquefoil

oxalis

oxeye daisy

pearlwort

peppergrass

pepperweed

pigweed

pilewort

pineapple weed

plantain

poison ivy

poke or pokeweed

pokeberry

prickly lettuce

prostrate knotweed

purslane

quack grass

Queen Anne's lace

quitch

ragweed

redroot pigweed

red sorrel

Russian thistle

sanbur

scarlet pimpernel

Scotch broom

self-heal

sheep's sorrel

shepherd's purse

skunk cabbage

smartweed

sorrel

sow thistle

spatterdock

speedwell

spotted lady's-thumb

spotted spurge

spurge

spurry

St.-John's-wort

statice

stinging nettle

stinkweed

strawflower

sulfur cinquefoil

swallowwort

tail buttercup

tansy

tarweed

tassel flower

thistle

thorn apple

toadflax

tumbleweed

velvetleaf

Virginia pepperwood

water chestnut

water hyacinth

western sage

wheatgrass

white clover

wild aster

wild carrot

wild garlic

wild lettuce

wild mustard

wild oat

wild onion

wild parsnip

wild radish

wild vetch

witch grass

witchweed

yarrow

yellow foxtail

yellow nut sedge

yellow weed

yellow wood sorrel

WHEAT VARIETIES

buckwheat

bulgur wheat

club wheat

common wheat

cracked wheat

durum wheat

einkorn wheat

emmer wheat

germinated wheat

hard wheat

macaroni wheat

soft wheat

spelt

spring wheat

starch wheat

summer wheat

whole wheat

wild wheat

winter wheat

WHEELS

automobile wheel

axle wheel

balance wheel

bicycle wheel

buffing wheel

cam wheel

caster

cogwheel

color wheel

crown wheel

cycle wheel

daisy wheel

drive wheel

escape wheel

Ferris wheel

flywheel

furniture wheel

gearwheel

gyrowheel

idler wheel

mill wheel

paddle wheel

pinwheel

potter's wheel

prayer wheel

ratchet wheel

spinning wheel

spoked wheel

sprocket wheel

steering wheel

tracing wheel

vortex wheel

wagon wheel

waterwheel

worm wheel

WHISKIES

barley whiskey

blended whiskey

bonded whiskey

bourbon

Canadian whiskey

corn whiskey

grain whiskey

Irish whiskey

malt whiskey or malt

moonshine

rye

Scotch whiskey

single malt whiskey

sour mash whiskey

Tennessee whiskey

vatted malt whiskey

wheat whiskey

whisky

WHITE COLOR VARIETIES

alabaster

antimony white

argent

bismuth white

blond

bone white

chalk

Chinese white

columbine
dove
Dutch white
eggshell
flake white
gauze
ivory

lily white
marble
milk-white
nacre
off-white
oyster white
Paris white

pearl
pearl white
platinum
pure white
putty
silver
snow white

strontium white
swan white
titanium white
white lead
zinc white

WILLS, TYPES OF

formal will

holographic will or handwritten will

individual will

joint will or mutual will

legate will

living will

mutual will

oral will or noncupative will

probate will

recorded will

simple will

unwitnessed will

witnessed will

WINDMILLS AND WATER MILLS

overshot-wheel water mill

post mill

smock mill

tower mill

undershot-wheel water mill

waterwheel

working windmill

WINDOWS

bay window

bow window

bulkhead

bull's-eye window or oeil-de-boeuf

casement window

Catherine wheel

clerestory window

compass window

deadlight

Diocletian window

dormer window or lucarne

double-glazed window

double-hung window

embrasure

fanlight

fenestella

French window

gable window

624

garret window

glazed window

grisaille

guichet

horizontal pivoting window

horizontal sliding window

lancet window

lattice window

leaded light

louvered window

lucarne

lunette

mullion window

oculus

opera window

oriel window

oval window

Palladian window

picture window

porthole

quarter-light

ribbon window

roof light

rose window

roundel

sash window

sidelight

skylight

sliding folding window

sliding window

squint

stained-glass window

storm window

top light

transom window

triple-glazed window

vertical pivoting window

viewport

wheel window

windshield

WINDS

anabatic wind

arctic wind

austral wind

austru

backing wind

berg wind

bise

bora

boreal wind

breeze

brickfielder

buran

Cape doctor

chinook

doldrums

dust devil

el Niño

Etesian

favonian wind

foehn or fohn

fresh breeze

fresh gale

gale

gentle breeze

ghibli or gibli

gregale or Euroclydon

gust

haboob

harmattan

headwind

howling wind

katabatic wind

khamsin

land breeze

levanter

libeccio

light breeze

local wind

maestrale

meltemi

mistral

moderate breeze

moderate gale

monsoon

mountain wind

nor'easter

norther

northerly

nor'wester

ocean breeze

offshore wind

onshore wind

pampero

papagayo

prevailing wind

Santa Ana

sea breeze

shamal

simoom or
samielsirocco

solano

southeaster

southerly

southerly buster

southwester

squall

strong breeze

strong gale

strong wind

tailwind

Tehuantepec

trade wind

tramontana

tramontane

updraft

upwind

veering wind

vortex

waft

westerlies

wet chinook

whirlwind

whole gale

williwaw

willy-willy

windshear

windstorm

zephyr

zonda

WINE AND GRAPE VARIETIES

Alsace

altar wine

American wine

amontillado

amoroso

appetizer wine

apple wine

Asti spumante

Australian wine

Aveleda

Barbera

Bardolino

Barolo

Beaujolais

Bergerac

blanc de noir

blush wine

Bordeaux

Bordeaux Blanc

Burgundy

Cabernet Sauvignon

cabinet wine

California wine

Canary wine

Cape wine

carbonated wine

Chablis

Champagne

Chardonnay

Chateauneuf-du-
Pape

Chenin blanc

Chianti

Christi

claret wine

cold duck

Condrieu

Cote Rotie

Cotes de Nuit

Cotes du Rhone

dandelion wine

Dao

dessert wine

DolcettoFrascati

Douro

dry wine

Empire wine

Entre-deux-Mers

fortified wine

Frascati

fruit wine

Fume Blanc

German wine

Gewurztraminer

Graves

Grenache

Hermitage

hock

Johannesburg
Riesling

jug wine

Lacrima

Lambrusco

Liebfraumilch

light wine

Macon

Madeira

Malaga

Marsala

Mateus Rosé

Medoc

Merlot

Mosel

Moselle

mulled wine

Muscadet

Muscat

Muscatel

Napa Valley wine

natural wine

Navarra

Nierstein

noble wine

old wine

Oporto

orange wine

Orvieto

Pauillac

pink wine

Pinot Blanc

Pinot Grigio

Pinot Gris

Pinot Noir

plum wine

Pomerol

Pommard

port

Pouilly-Fuisse

Pouilly-Fume

red Bordeaux

red wine

retsina

Rhine

Rhone wine

Riesling

Rioja

rosé wine

ruby port

sacramental wine

sake

Sancerre

Sangiovese

Sauternes

Sauvignon Blanc

Sekt

sherry

Shiraz

Soave

sparkling wine

St. Estephe

St. Julien

strawberry wine

straw wine

sweet wine

Sylvaner

Syrah

table wine

tapestry red

tawny port

Tokay-Pinot Gris

Valdepenas

Valpolicella

vermouth

vinho verde

vintage wine

Vouvray

white cabernet

white wine

white zinfandel

zinfandel

WINES, SHERRY AND DESSERT

amontillado sherry

amoroso

auslese

Bual

canary wine

Commandaria

cream sherry

dry sherry

fino sherry

fortified wine

Grenache

ice wine

jerepigo

late harvest riesling

Madeira

malmsey

manzanilla

Marsala

medium sherry

Monbazillac

moscato

muscat

muscatel

oloroso

palo cortado

port

Sauternes

Sercial

sherry

straw wine

sweet sherry

Verdelho

vermouth

vin de paille

vino de pastu

WINTER VEHICLES

blade

bobsled

dogsled

drag

kibitka

luge

pung

skibob

skiddoo

skimobile

sled

sledge

sleigh

snowcat

snowmobile

snowplow

toboggan

troika

weasel

WIRE VARIETIES

aluminum wire

annealed wire

brass wire

bronze wire

cable wire

carbon wire

coated wire

copper wire

drawn wire

electrical wire

electronic wire

extruded wire

fencing wire

flat wire

florist wire

galvanized wire

gold wire

hexagonal wire

high wire

ignition wire

insulated wire

iron wire

magnetized wire

nickel wire

piano wire

picture frame wire

plated wire

platinum wire

resistance wire

round wire

silicone wire

silver wire

spool wire

spring wire

square wire

steel wire

telephone wire

tempered wire

tight wire

weatherproof wire

zinc wire

WOLVES AND WILD DOGS

African hunting dog
African wild dog
Arctic wolf
black wolf
blue heeler
brush wolf
bush dog
Cape hunting dog

coyote
cuon
dhole
dingo
golden jackal
gray wolf
guara
hyena dog

Indian dhole
jackal
lobo
maikong
maned wolf
pariah dog
prairie wolf
pye-dog

raccoon dog
red dog
red wolf
tanate
Tasmanian wolf
timber wolf
warrigal
white wolf

WOOD TREATMENTS

air-dried wood
blockboard
clapboard
close-grained wood
edge-glued wood
edge-matched wood
end-matched wood

flat-grained wood
hardboard
kiln-dried wood
knotty wood
laminboard
mixed-grain wood
multi-ply plywood

open-grained wood
particle board
peeled veneer
perforated
hardboard
plastic-laminated
particle board

pressure-treated
wood
rabbeted wood
seasoned wood
veneer
waferboard
weatherized wood

WOOD TYPES

acacia
acuyari wood
alder
aleppo pine
almondwood

applewood
ash
aspen
Australian oak
balsa

balsam
banyan
basket oak
bass bay cedar
beech

beefwood
Bermuda cedar
betel palm
billetwood
birch

birchwood

black ironwood

black mahogany

black maple

blackwood

bog pine

bogwood

bowwood

boxwood

Brazilian boxwood

brazilwood

brierwood

brushwood

budwood

burl

buttonwood

buttwood

cacao

calico wood

camwood

carrotwood

cedar

cherry

chestnut

citrus

coconut

cork

cottonwood

cypress

dogwood

driftwood

ebony

elder

elm

eucalyptus

fig

fir

fruitwood

gum

hardwood

hawthorn

hazel

heartwood

hemlock

hickory

ironwood

juniper

knotty pine

lancewood

larch

laurel

lightwood

lignum vitae

linden

loblolly pine

locust

logwood

magnolia

mahogany

maple

matchwood

mesquite

monkeypod

myrtle

oak

olive

palm

pear

pecan

pine

poplar

redwood

rosewood

rubber

sandalwood

satinwood

sequoia

sisal

softwood

sour gum

spruce

sugar maple

sumac

sycamore

teak

tulipwood

tupelo

walnut

whitewood

willow

yellow pine

yellowwood

yew

zebrawood

Wool Varieties

angora wool	combing wool	lamb's wool	raw wool
boiled wool	cotton wool	Persian wool	Shetland wool
carpet wool	fleece wool	pulled wool	virgin wool

Words in Written English, Most Commonly Used

a	down	into	on
about	each	is	one
all	find	it	or
an	first	its	other
and	for	like	out
are	from	long	part
as	get	look	people
at	go	made	said
be	had	make	see
been	has	many	she
but	have	may	so
by	he	more	some
call	her	my	than
can	him	no	that
come	his	not	the
could	how	now	their
day	I	number	them
did	if	of	then
do	in	oil	there

these	up	were	with
they	use	what	word
this	was	when	would
time	water	which	write
to	way	who	you
two	we	will	your

WORMS

acorn worm	clam worm	giant kidney worm	marine worm
angleworm	composting worm	gizzard worm	mawworm
annelid	cottonworm	glowworm	measuringworm
apple pomice worm	crop worm	grey worm	medina worm
armyworm	cutworm	ground worm	muckworm
arrowworm	deathworm	gullet worm	mud-blister worm
bamboo worm	dew worm	hairworm	mudworm
barber's pole worm	dragon worm	heartworm	nematode
bearded worm	dung worm	heligrammite	nightcrawler
black scour worm	earthworm	hookworm	nightwalker
bladder worm	earwom	hornworm	nodular worm
bloodsucker	eelworm	horsehair worm	palisade worm
bloodworm	eye worm	inchworm	palolo worm
bollworm	fecal worm	kidney worm	parasitic worm
bookworm	fireworm	leech	parchment worm
bowel worm	fishworm	lobworm	peanut worm
bristle worm	flatworm	looper	pinworm
cankerworm	fluke	lugworm	platyhelminth
cecal worm	gapeworm	manure worm	polychaete

red hybrid

red wiggler

red worm

ribbon worm

rotifer

roundworm

sandworm

sea mouse

sea worm

segmented worm

shipworm

silkworm

sludgeworm

spoonworm

stink worm

striped worm

taintworm

tapeworm

threadworm

tiger worm

tobacco hornworm

tomato hornworm

tubeworm

vinegar eel

vinegar worm

webworm

wheatworm

whipworm

wireworm

woodworm

WRENCHES

adjustable box wrench

adjustable wrench

Allen wrench

alligator wrench

automobile wrench

back rack wrench

basin wrench

bedkey

bicycle wrench

box-end wrench

box or open-end wrench

box wrench

brace wrench

bulldog wrench

capstan wheel nut wrench

carriage wrench

center screw wrench

chain wrench

combination wrench

construction wrench

crescent wrench

crocodile wrench

crowfoot wrench

dog wrench

double-ended wrench

flare-nut wrench

footprint wrench

front rack wrench

front screw wrench

gooseneck wrench

grabber wrench

hexagonal wrench

hook wrench or hook spanner

impact wrench

lug wrench

monkey wrench

multiple box wrench or multi-purpose wrench

obstruction wrench

offset wrench

open end wrench

pin wrench or pin spanner

pipe wrench

pipe-gripping wrench

ratcheting box-end wrench

S wrench

screw wrench or screw spanner

setscrew wrench

slip wrench

socket wrench

spanner

spark plug wrench

split box wrench

spoke wrench

Stilson wrench

strap wrench

T wrench

tap wrench

tappet wrench

torque wrench

tube wrench

valve wrench

WRITING INSTRUMENTS

ballpoint pen

cane pen

cartridge pen

chalk

crayon

felt-tip pen

fountain pen

gel pen

highlighter

lead pencil

lettering pen

marker

marker pen

mechanical pencil

pen

pencil

permanent marker

plastic tip pen

quill

reed pen

rollerball pen

stylus

washable marker

WRITING SYSTEMS

Akkadian

Anatolian

Arabic

Aramaic

Armenian

Assyrian

Avestan

Babylonian

Bengali

Berber

Brahmi

Burmese

Carolingian

Chalcidian

Cherokee

Chinese writing

Coptic

Cree

Cretan

Cypriot

Cypro-Minoan

Cyrillic

demotic

Devanagari

Egyptian demotic

Egyptian hieratic

Egyptian hieroglyphic

Elamite

Ethiopic

Etruscan

Georgian

Gothic

Greek

Gujarati

Gurmukhi

Hebrew

hieratic

hieroglyphic

Hiragana

Hittite

Humanist

Hurrian

Iberian

Indus Valley

International Phonetic Alphabet

Ionian

Irish

Japanese writing

Jewish

Kana

Kanji

Kannada

Katakana

Kharoshthi

Khmer

Korean

Lao

Latin

Libyan

Linear A

Linear B

Lycian

Lydian

Malayalam

Manchu

Mayan

Meroitic

Mesoamerican

Minoan

Mongolian

Nubian

Ogham

Oriya

Oscan

Permian

Persian

Phoenician

Phrygian

Romaji

Roman

Rongorongo

Runic

Sanskrit

Scandinavian

Semitic

Sinaitic

Sinhala

Siniform

Slavic

Sumerian

Tamil

Telugu

Thai

Tibetan

Tuareg

Turkish runic

Uighur

Umbrian

Uncial

Urartian

Vietnamese

Yi

X - Rays

bone X-ray	diagnostic X-ray	industrial X-ray	panoramic X-ray
chest X-ray	fluoroscopic X-ray	lateral X-ray	soft X-ray
dental X-ray	hard X-ray	medical X-ray	superficial X-ray

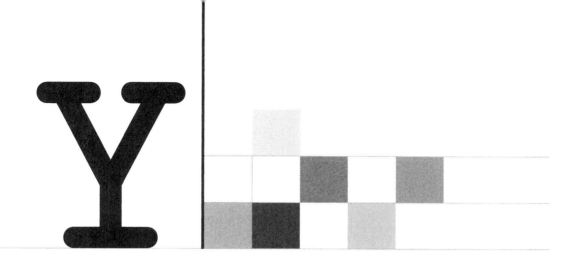

YELLOW COLOR VARIETIES

acid yellow	butter	dandelion	luteous
amber	cadmium yellow	ecru	madder yellow
apricot yellow	calendula	flax	maize
arsenic yellow	canary	gamboge	marigold yellow
auramine	Cassel yellow	gilded	mikado yellow
aureate	chalcedony	gilt	mustard
aureolin	chamois	gold	Naples yellow
azo yellow	champagne	golden	ocher or ochre
barium yellow	chartreuse yellow	goldenrod	oil yellow
blond	chrome lemon	golden yellow	old gold
brass	chrome yellow	green-yellow	orange-yellow
brazen	citron	honey	orpiment
brazilin	corn	jonquil	pale yellow
brownish-yellow	cream	lemon	palomino
buff	crocus	linen	Paris yellow

peach yellow

pear

phosphine

primrose

purree

quince yellow

reed

saffron

safranine

sallow

sand

snapdragon

straw

sulfur

sunflower

sunshine yellow

topaz yellow

wheaten

xanthic

xanthous

yellow madder

yellow ocher

yellowstone

yolk yellow

zinc yellow

YOGA TYPES

ananda yoga

anusara yoga

ashtanga yoga

bhakti yoga

bikram yoga

chakra yoga

classical yoga or
traditional yoga

gentle yoga

hatha yoga

healing yoga

integral yoga

Iyengar yoga

jivamukti yoga

jnana yoga

karma yoga

Kripalu yoga

kriya yoga

kundalini yoga

meditative yoga

power yoga

prana yoga

raja yoga

restorative yoga

sivananda yoga

tantric yoga

Tibetan yoga

white lotus yoga

ZODIAC SIGNS

Aquarius	Capricorn	Libra	Scorpio
Aries	Gemini	Pisces	Taurus
Cancer	Leo	Sagittarius	Virgo

ZOO TYPES

aquarium	invertebrate house	petting zoo	vertebrate house
aviary	menagerie	reptile house	wildlife park
birdhouse	national zoo	safari park	zoological garden
drive-through zoological park	open-range zoo	urban zoo	zoological park

ZOOLOGY BRANCHES

acarology

amphibiology

animal behavior

animal chemistry or zoochemistry

animal pathology or zoopathology

animal physiology or zoonomy

animal psychology

applied zoology

arachnology

araneology

ascidiology

bugology

carcinology

cenozoology

cetology

coccidology

coleopterology

conchology

crustaceology

cytogenetics

cytology

echinology

ecology

embryology

endocrinology

entomology

ethology

evolution

genetics

helminthology

herpetology

ichthyology

invertebrate zoology

malacology

mammalogy

marine biology

morphology

nematology

oligochaetology

ophiology

ornithology

paleontology

parasitology

pathology

physiology

primatology

protozoology

research zoology

systematic zoology or taxonomy

vermeology

vertebrate zoology

zoogeography

zoography

ZOROASTRIANISM TYPES

Zoroastrianism is the ancient, pre-Islamic religion of Persia (modern Iran). It contains both monotheistic and dualistic features. Its concepts of one God, judgment, heaven, and hell are similar to the major Western religions of Judaism, Christianity, and Islam.

Mazdaism

Parsiism or Parsee or Parsi

Yezidi